Columbia University Press   New York

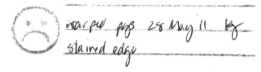
12-22-10
$35.00
B&T

AS
14day

1/11

D0046247

THE WORST-KEPT SECRET

THE
WORST-KEPT
SECRET

AVNER COHEN

ISRAEL'S
BARGAIN WITH
THE BOMB

COLUMBIA UNIVERSITY PRESS
Publishers Since 1893
NEW YORK   CHICHESTER, WEST SUSSEX

LIBRARY OF CONGRESS CATALOGING-IN-PUBLICATION DATA
Cohen, Avner, 1951–
    Worst-kept secret : Israel's bargain with the bomb / Avner Cohen.
    p. cm.
    Includes bibliographical references and index.
    ISBN 978-0-231-13698-3 (cloth : alk. paper) — ISBN 978-0-231-51026-4 (ebook)
    1. Nuclear weapons—Government policy—Israel.   2. Israel—Defenses.   3. Israel—
    Military policy.   4. Ambiguity—Political aspects—Israel.   5. Israel—Politics and government—
    1993–   6. Israel—Foreign relations.   7. Middle East—Politics and government—1945–
    8. Middle East—Foreign relations—1979–   I. Title.

    U264.5.I75C65 2010
    355.02'17095694—dc22

                                                          2010003950

COLUMBIA UNIVERSITY PRESS BOOKS ARE PRINTED ON
PERMANENT AND DURABLE ACID-FREE PAPER.
THIS BOOK IS PRINTED ON PAPER WITH RECYCLED CONTENT.
PRINTED IN THE UNITED STATES OF AMERICA
C 10 9 8 7 6 5 4 3 2 1

This book is dedicated to
Shalheveth Freier, who inspired it;
Yatza, whose legal ordeal was the impetus for it;
And two special women—my mother, Adina, and my wife, Karen.

Our interest is in preventing Israel's possession of nuclear weapons. But since we cannot—and may not want to try [to]—control the state of Israel's nuclear program and since Israel may already have nuclear weapons, the one objective we might achieve is to persuade them to keep what they have secret. This would meet our objective because the international implications of an Israeli program are not triggered until it becomes public knowledge.

—National Security Adviser Henry Kissinger, memo to President Richard Nixon, July 1969

Israel—along with her well-known friend the United States—suffers from what looks to other countries in the region like hypocritical pretense, but the Israelis face great difficulties in the open recognition of reality. They have an elaborate pretense that they are reluctant to abandon. Many of them argue that a secret program gives less pain to their neighbors, and probably also do not wish to trouble any friend (especially in the United States) for whom a declared Israeli bomb would be embarrassing. Their pretense grows thinner as public debate about their nuclear capability becomes more candid. The number of those outside Israel who are comforted by the pretense shrinks, and the number who find it absurd and even offensive grow. The pretense [of amimut] prevents any public defense of the Israeli program by the Israeli government and any effective argument that no state or group need fear an Israeli bomb unless it attempts the destruction of Israel.

—National Security Adviser McGeorge Bundy, chairman of the Joint Chiefs of Staff William J. Crowe, Jr., and Sidney D. Drell, *Reducing the Nuclear Danger*

Contents

Preface

I have written this book to encourage reflection and policy discussion on a subject rife with domestic, regional, and global implications, a subject that has been largely untouchable for decades: Israel's bargain with the bomb (the meaning of this phrase is discussed in the introduction). In Israel, such a discussion is constrained by a societal taboolike prohibition enforced by strict state censorship encompassing all factual aspects of the subject. In Washington, however, the prohibition is more subtle and less absolute. Nevertheless, the American public does not know that American policymakers also adhere to their own code of silence on the subject. The Israeli bargain thus is also an American bargain.

A study of the Israeli bargain with the bomb is long overdue. My purpose in this book is threefold. First, I decode the politics, sociology, and psychology that set apart Israel's bargain with the bomb from all other nuclear-armed states.[1] We cannot appreciate the prohibition that sustains this bargain without understanding its underlying cultural and psychological layers. Second, I assess both the strategic achievements and the democratic shortcomings of the bargain. Third, I describe a new bargain framed primarily, but not exclusively, in domestic terms, and offer new thoughts about how Israel, with the help of other countries, especially the United States, can rewrite its bargain to better confront relevant domestic, regional, and global challenges.

This study views Israel's nuclear history as closely related to deeper issues of national identity. The country's nuclear arrangement is intertwined with—

indeed, it is the result of—deeper identity issues. Israel's nuclear uniqueness thus can be understood only by addressing identity issues.

There is a parallel between the Israeli bargain with the bomb and the larger Israeli-Zionist national project. The bargain could even be seen as a condensed version of that project. If the Israeli-Zionist national narrative is the path from *Shoah* (in Hebrew, Holocaust) to *Tkumah* (in Hebrew, national revival), the bomb is the result of the narrative's most existential aspects—the grounding, anchoring, and ensuring—of that path.

The Israeli essayist Ari Shavit alluded to this when comparing the Israeli nuclear project and its product—the bomb—to a greenhouse that seals and shields Israel against external existential threats. Only when shielded by this glasslike greenhouse can the Zionist enterprise thrive in an hostile external environment.[2] What Shavit meant is that the bomb is the embodiment of the vow "Never Again"; that is, the purpose of the bomb is to make sure that another Holocaust will not happen again to the Jewish people.

The analogy between Israel's bargain with the bomb and the nation's general condition goes deeper, as it also is a condensed version of the Zionist dialectics of exceptionalism and normalcy. The purpose of the Zionist project was to heal and normalize the Jewish condition by creating a Jewish nation-state, and the bomb is an anchor of that endeavor. But the Zionist project has not yet been fully realized, as Israel has yet to be accepted by its neighbors or to determine its own identity (e.g., by adopting a constitution). Likewise, Israel's bargain with the bomb has not been granted legitimacy, either at home or abroad.

My book *Israel and the Bomb* (Columbia University Press, 1998) told the early political history (1948 to 1970) of the Israeli nuclear project from a historical and descriptive perspective. In it, I recounted the origins of the policy that guided Israel's pursuit of nuclear ambitions during its formative days, a policy commonly referred to today as "nuclear opacity" or "nuclear ambiguity" (in Hebrew, the phrase is *amimut*). This policy has allowed Israel to build formidable nuclear capabilities while minimizing tension with the rest of the world, especially with the United States, and also minimizing the incentive for others in the region to follow Israel in acquiring nuclear weapons.

Israel and the Bomb ended with the secret nuclear deal between President Richard Nixon and Prime Minister Golda Meir in September 1969, when the two leaders arrived at an unwritten understanding concerning Israel and its possession of nuclear weapons. This understanding opened the door for nuclear opacity, or *amimut*, as a code of conduct for the two countries on the nuclear issue.

Since then, amimut has become Israel's original contribution to the nuclear age, a commitment that has been widely appreciated.[3] Most nations view amimut as a helpful fiction that serves international security and stability. At home, amimut has extended beyond a governmental policy to become a sociocultural prohibition that is at the core of Israel's national attitude toward the bomb.

The ending point of *Israel and the Bomb* is the starting point of this book. My central questions here are different: What enables the Israeli bargain with the bomb to endure, both domestically and internationally? Is Israel's nuclear bargain compatible with its commitment to democracy? Has the nuclear bargain outlived its usefulness? Could Israel find a better way to meet the challenges of the early twenty-first century?

The prohibitions against discussing nuclear matters in Israel have eroded somewhat over the years, but amimut still serves a powerful sociopolitical function. Israel refuses to acknowledge its possession of nuclear weapons; Israeli publications are forbidden to refer directly to the nation's nuclear weapons (publications may refer to them only by quoting "foreign sources"); and state organizations are officially committed to guarding and enforcing nuclear opacity.

Tensions between the requirements of nuclear weapons and the norms of liberal democracy are not unique to Israel. But Israel's insistence on a commitment to *absolute* nonacknowledgment makes its bargain and the resulting tensions most incompatible with democratic values at home and with norms of transparency in the international arena. Domestically, the entire national nuclear enterprise resides in a legal twilight. Because Israel has no explicit laws governing nuclear matters, it is the legal status of the government itself that grants legality to Israel's secret nuclear decision making. Internationally, opacity has enabled Israel to maintain what one scholar calls "nuclear exceptionalism," in which Israel is effectively outside the global nuclear order.[4]

The world now faces a number of challenges concerning both nuclear weapons and nuclear energy that are relevant to Israel's nuclear bargain. The most urgent is dealing with the rise of a nuclear-armed Iran. Although this is a problem for the international system, it is of special concern to Israel, whose leaders and citizens view a nuclear-armed Iran as an existential threat.

Although amimut has served Israel well in many respects, not acknowledging its possession of nuclear weapons may now limit its ability to address the Iranian problem in a straightforward, internationally supported way.

This book is divided into ten chapters. The introduction lays out the *problématique* for the entire study. It describes the links between Israel's predicament and the nuclear issue, using amimut as the key to Israel's exceptionalism in the nuclear field, on which the notion of Israel's bargain with the bomb is based. Chapter 1 recounts the birth of amimut as a bilateral American-Israeli nuclear understanding. Using newly declassified American documents, I reconstruct the events and circumstances that led to the secret deal, culminating in the Nixon and Meir meeting in September 1969. Chapters 2 and 3 present the political and strategic case favoring amimut. Chapter 2 introduces amimut as a compromise between resolve and caution, allowing technological resolve to coexist with political caution. Chapter 3 traces Israel's nuclear historiography, describing the big decisions as a recapitulation of the same basic clash between resolve and caution. Sometimes resolve won (e.g., the initiation decision, the Nuclear Non-Proliferation Treaty), but at other times caution and self-restraint won (e.g., the declaratory stance, keeping the nuclear separate from the nation's conventional national security doctrine, no tactical nuclear weapons).

Chapters 4 and 5 describe the domestic infrastructure of the bargain. Chapter 4 details the three-layered institutional framework that shields the nuclear secret: the Israel Atomic Energy Commission (IAEC), the defense department's Bureau of Security of the Defense (MALMAB), and the office of the military censor (known in Israel as the Censora). Chapter 5 focuses on amimut's social and cultural aspects using three case studies of individuals involved with Israel's nuclear issue. Chapters 6 and 7 constitute the bulk of the democratic and moral criticism of the bargain. Chapter 6 explores this conflict between amimut and democracy in the context of the democratic public, and chapter 7 moves the conflict to the governance process, including oversight and accountability. Finally, chapters 8, 9, and 10 address the future of the bargain, in reference to both its domestic and international aspects. Chapter 8 addresses the issue at home and proposes ideas for reforms. Chapter 9 focuses on Iran's nuclear quest and its impact on the Israeli bargain and on the proposal for a fissile materials cutoff treaty (FMCT). Chapter 10 reflects on the international aspects of modifying the bargain. The book ends with a brief epilogue reiterating the book's central theme.

I cannot claim to be a neutral, objective observer of these matters. On the contrary, it was my own battle for a decade and a half (1989 to 2004) over the research, writing, and publication of *Israel and the Bomb*, a battle against the establishment guarding Israel's nuclear secrets, that revealed to me the importance of the culture of opacity, amimut. Given my long personal involvement with the subject, I am acutely aware of my obligations as a scholar to be as detached and objective as possible. Nevertheless, my readers should know that this book reflects a personal as well as a scholarly engagement with the issue.

This study has an agenda, but it is not an ordinary political agenda, that is, an agenda associated with any particular political or ideological stance or organized movement. Rather, it is a commitment to deeply held civic norms that are fundamental to both Israel's democracy and a liberal vision of a community of nations mutually accountable under the rule of law. I argue that the old Israeli bargain with the bomb has outlived its usefulness, that it has become increasingly incompatible with contemporary democratic values at home and with the growth of the international norms of transparency, and that it is time for Israel and others to consider a new bargain.

My conclusions about amimut are not criticism of Israel's possession of nuclear weapons, especially given the prospect of a nuclear-armed Iran. Rather, they are an effort to persuade people on all sides that the time has come for Israel (and others) to revisit and openly discuss Israel's bargain with the bomb in its domestic, regional, and global contexts. By itself, Israel cannot move away from its policy and culture of amimut; from the start, the bargain was a bilateral arrangement with the United States. Indeed, according to the old secret agreement between Israel and the United States, Israel cannot make unilateral changes in the bargain.

Any significant change of Israel's bargain with the bomb would require the involvement of other countries, principally the United States. Given the current international climate, particularly the advance of a nuclear-armed Iran, overturning the policy and the culture of amimut will not be easy and may be impossible in the short run.

Israelis commonly praise the bargain for its wisdom, as Ze'ev Schiff and many others did (and with good reason). They hardly ever criticize the bargain. The difficulty of proposing intellectual, social, and psychological reforms derives from amimut itself. The Israeli public believes that opening the nuclear bargain to serious discussion would likely undermine it and hence harm national security and ultimately deprive the nation of its nuclear capacity. It is striking that Israelis often identify the policy of opacity with the country's nuclear capability itself, assuming that the fate of Israel's weapons depends on the fate of this particular policy.

The knowledge claims made in this book are constrained by the very phenomenon the book seeks to study. The code and practice of amimut are not easily accessible to outsiders who seek to understand and study it. By its nature, amimut aims to conceal, obscure, blur, and mask hidden realities. It systematically and purposefully withholds access to its own inner workings. At times, to compensate for the lack of factual knowledge, I have had to use educated guesses. I have tried to keep readers informed as to when I am venturing a conjecture and when I am presenting established facts, but this is not always easy to do.

It is also difficult to assess the political and social effects of amimut on Israeli society or on the conduct of international nuclear diplomacy generally. It is hard to evaluate the impact of Israel's and the United States' policy of nuclear opacity on the Middle East: To what extent has amimut helped to make the Middle East more stable—or less so? To what extent has it played a role in bringing an end to the era of the big Arab-Israeli conventional wars? To what extent has it inspired the move toward a resolution of the Arab-Israeli conflict? To what extent has it worked to advance the cause of peace?

Finally, I should call attention to one linguistic matter. I have decided to use the Hebrew word *amimut* throughout the book rather than its English equivalent, *opacity*. There are a number of reasons for this decision. First, only by using the Hebrew term could I highlight the variety of layers of culturally related meanings and contexts involved in this Israeli concept. Second, I refer to amimut as an Israeli concept rather than simply a Hebrew word. None of the term's English translations, including "nuclear opacity," captures and conveys the rich and layered meaning and signification attached to the Hebrew term. I believe that amimut encapsulates a distinctly Israeli attitude or disposition—the particular "Israeliness" of a code of conduct. Only the Hebrew *amimut* conveys the three characteristics indispensable to it: the native approach of the Sabra, a flavor of the Jewish element of *chutzpa*, and a Talmudic love of *pilpul*—a fascination with linguistic and legalistic argumentation and exactitude.

Acknowledgments

The origins of this book may be found in the conversations I had in the early 1990s with the late Shalheveth Freier, one of the few individuals who was involved in Israel's nuclear program from its start until his death in 1994. In those conversations he often noted that the tension between governing the atom and democracy was universal and inevitable. "This is an important and worthwhile subject to study," he often said to me, but he also advised me not to touch the Israeli case as long as Israel sticks to its amimut policy (a policy of which he was one of the prime architects). I respected Freier greatly; I took his observations seriously but did not follow his advice. This book, in a sense, was inspired by his insight.

But it was the affair associated with retired general Yitzhak Yaakov (known as "Yatza") that persuaded me to write this book. This affair, which involved the secret arrest and trial of Yatza in 2001 for revealing "state secrets," convinced me that the larger issue on which the affair touched must be openly discussed. The Yatza affair was about amimut and how far the state can go to protect amimut. The Yatza affair is as relevant today as it was ten years ago. A new documentary film that was just made on the affair—*The Secrecy Kingdom*—was banned in December 2009 by the Israeli military censor.

It took me nearly a decade to bring this project to conclusion. It has been a long and difficult road. I could not have done it without a great deal of material and intellectual help and encouragement from institutions and individuals. It is a pleasure now to thank all those who helped.

The John D. and Catherine T. MacArthur Foundation provided a generous research and writing grant in 2004 that supported the early phase of this project. I was a senior fellow in 2007–8 at the Jennings Fellowship Program of the United States Institute of Peace (USIP), which allowed me to continue my research. Steven Heydemann and Chantal de Jonge Oudraat, who ran the program, were attentive to my needs. I finished the book as a Public Policy Scholar at the Woodrow Wilson Center for International Scholars (WWCIS) in 2009–10. Lucy Jilka, Robert Litwak, and Michael Van Dusen helped make it possible. The Ploughshares Fund, and in particular Paul Carroll and Haleh Hatami, also helped with critical travel grants.

Over the last eight years I have had conversations with countless colleagues and friends on issues relating to this project. I cannot express my gratitude to each of them individually for all their patience and goodwill. Here is a partial list of those who read and commented on draft chapters or provided substantial insight: James Acton, Steve Aftergood, David Albright, the late Arnan Azaryahu (Sini), Uri Bar Joseph, Aluf Benn, Ronen Bergman, Kai Bird, Hans Born, Shlomo Brom, Joe Cirincione, Merav Datan, Alan Dowty, Harold A. Feiveson, Mark Fitzpatrick, Victor Gilinsky, Hugh Gusterson, Mark Hibbs, David Holloway, Rebecca Johnson, Catherine Kelleher, Joseph Klaits, Michael Krepon, Steven Lee, the late Paul Leventhal, Sverre Lodgaard, Ze'ev Maoz, Zia Mian, Marvin Miller, Reuven Pedatzur, George Perkovich, Joseph Pilat, Sasha Polekov, Joshua Pollack, Judith Reppy, Maria Rost Rublee, Larry Schienman, Ze'ev Segal, Leonard Spector, Nina Tannenwald, Frank von Hippel, William Walker, and Leonard Weiss. In addition, there were others who made significant contributions but who asked that they remain anonymous. I respect their wishes. They know who they are, and they also know how much I am grateful to them.

I also thank a few special friends who many years ago shared with me their memories, reflections—even doubts—on this sensitive topic. Only years later have I come to realize how critical their insights were in shaping this book. Since Azaryahu Arnan (Sini), Avraham Hermony, Yuval Ne'eman, Ze'ev Schiff, Paul Warnke, and Ezer Weizman are no longer with us, I feel an obligation to thank them posthumously.

Finally, I extend special thanks to Marvin Miller, my good friend and collaborator for more than two decades. The fruits of our collaboration fill almost every page in this book. Chapter 9 is based on a joint paper that Marvin and I co-authored in 2008 under commission from the International Panel on Fissile Material.

Ideas in this book were tested over the last few years before various audiences in many conferences, lectures, and seminars, including most particularly: The College of Netanya (2005); the East-West Institute in workshops held in Washington, D.C., and Singapore (2006); the Managing the Atom seminar at Harvard (2007); the Program on Science and Global Security at Princeton (2007); Georgia Institute of Technology (2007); the International Panel on Fissile Material (IPFM) in London (2007); Pacific Northwest Lab in Seattle (2008); CNS Strategy Group in Milan (2008); INSS seminar in Tel Aviv (2008); USIP (2007–8); ISODARCO in Italy (2009); and the DCAF workshops in Geneva (2005 and 2009). I am thankful to all who engaged me in these discussions.

Then there are those who provided me direct assistance in researching and preparing this manuscript. Christopher Neu was a most caring research assistant for most of my time at USIP. Russ Burns at USIP and Matt Irvine at WWICS were by my side at later stages and prepared the manuscript for its final delivery. Finally, I am most grateful to Ben Frankel, my friend of more than thirty years and probably the best editor I have ever known. As a labor of love, Ben devoted dozens of precious hours not only to improving the writing and style of this manuscript but also to sharpening the argument. This book owes a great deal to Ben's knowledge and wisdom.

It is a pleasure to continue to work with a professional and caring team at Columbia University Press. Peter Dimock was the acquiring editor of this project, and he was there from the beginning. He had complete faith in my work until his last day with the Press. Others—in particular, Anne Routon, Jennifer Crewe, Anne McCoy, and President Jim Jordan—provided me with encouragement and support. Finally, my fantastic agent, Mary Cunnane, was always with me—caring, fighting, and cheering me on. Every author should have an agent like Mary.

My last words of gratitude go to my wife, Karen. She was not always in love with this project, but she supported my commitment to it.

Introduction

Amimut as a National Nuclear Bargain

In an article published in 2006 in the *Ha'aretz Weekly Magazine* on the eve of Israel's independence day, Israeli journalist Yossi Klein reflected on the nation's coming of age:

> [Israel] has an age, but it does not have the characteristics of aging. Our attributes as a nation defy age; they persist, regardless of time. We will always be a tiny country surrounded by enemies vowing to destroy it. Likewise, we will never mention, never, that in a push of a button we can destroy them and, along with them, the entire Middle East. This is our own self-image when we look at ourselves in the mirror, from a particular angle and in the right light. (trans. Avner Cohen)[1]

These lines capture the paradox of the Israeli nuclear condition.

The Israeli Predicament

More than sixty years after its birth as an independent state, Israel is in many ways an extraordinary success story. Its tale is one of national redemption, a transition from *Shoah* (Holocaust) to *Tkumah* (Revival). Since its birth in 1948, it has become the region's most formidable military power; it has turned a small, backward, service economy into one of the world's great centers of technological innovation; it has absorbed waves of Jewish emigrants who made Israel their home and consequently has become the demographic center of the Jewish people; and it has replaced eastern Europe and is now eclipsing the United States as the center of Jewish culture and learning. In sum, Zionism appears to have been one of the most successful national liberation movements of the twentieth century.

Despite all these achievements, however, the Israeli mind is tortured with questions about the country's very survival. On the surface, there is civic normalcy, but below the surface there is a certain anxiety that Israel's condition in the world is far from "normal."[2] This insecurity regarding the long-term survival of the Zionist project is revealed in the way that Israelis (and non-Israeli Jews) discuss ad nauseam questions like "Will Israel survive?" and "Is Israel finished?"[3]

Underlying this uncertainty is the old image of Israel as a tiny enclave of Hebraic civilization in the Middle East surrounded by a larger, much more populous, and hostile Muslim world. David Grossman recently described this Israeli condition as an "inner feeling of absolute fragility."[4] Another prominent Israeli writer, Amos Oz, compared the Israeli condition from its birth to living "on the slopes of the volcano."[5] This is not merely a writer's literary metaphor. Since childhood, I have heard Israelis describe their national predicament as like that of a small colony living in the shadow of a large volcano that could erupt at any moment. In the summer of 2006, when thousands of Hezbollah rockets rained for a month on villages and towns all over northern Israel, many Israelis experienced once again that sense of living near a volcano. In addition, as of this writing, many Israelis fear that a military confrontation with Iran—most likely a clash over the latter's nuclear program—could again engulf the region in war without warning.

The founders of modern Zionism, most prominently Theodor Herzl, believed that if Jews could have a state of their own, if they were taken out of the Diaspora, their national predicament would be normalized. If they could live inside well-defined and internationally recognized territorial borders, enjoying all the rights of a sovereign nation-state, then the "Jewish problem" would disappear.[6] Zionism was about "normalizing" and "healing" the Jewish condition by creating a Jewish state that would be like all other nation-states in the world.

But six decades of sovereign independence have not created a Jewish state with a sense of normalcy. Contrary to the hopes of Zionism's founders, Israel does not yet have internationally recognized borders or a peaceful relationship with its neighbors. Despite formal peace agreements with Egypt and Jordan, Israel has still not been recognized as a legitimate state by most of its neighbors, including the Palestinians. Although Hamas still insists that

Zionist Israel is an illegitimate entity, Israel still strives for a sense of normalcy and legitimacy.

The Bomb and Israel's Predicament

Nuclear weapons embody a paradoxical duality: they are at once the most nebulous and the most tangible representation of total annihilation. Distinguished by the scientific predictability of their effects, nuclear weapons are the most demonic weapons ever devised. They make possible the obliteration of entire communities, states, and, in some scenarios, even civilizations. At the same time, contemplating such catastrophes in human terms is limited; thinking about nuclear weapons is "thinking about the unthinkable," as Herman Kahn put it.[7]

For these and other reasons, the bomb in its enemies' hands has become Israel's ultimate nightmare. Given Israel's geographical size and population density, one or two bombs may well mean the end of the Zionist enterprise,[8] and Israelis are keenly aware of this existential predicament.[9] Consequently, most Israelis view with great anxiety the emergence of a nuclear balance of terror between Israel and its enemies.[10] To prevent this, Israel has traditionally been committed to taking unorthodox actions, such as hunting down German scientists who worked on unconventional weapons in Egypt in the early 1960s, bombing the Osiraq reactor in Iraq in 1981, and bombing a suspected reactor in Syria in September 2007.[11]

A long time ago, Israelis realized that existential deterrence under what cold-war warriors called "mutual assured destruction" (MAD) would not bring nuclear parity in the Middle East. Indeed, the possession of such weapons by Israel's enemies would cripple Israel both politically and psychologically. More than a decade ago, Iran's president, Ali Akbar Rafsanjani, noted that a mutually nuclearized Middle East would not be true parity from an Israeli perspective. "The use of a nuclear bomb against Israel," Rafsanjani declared, "will leave nothing on the ground, whereas it will only damage the world of Islam."[12] That such a reminder came from an Iranian president only intensified Israelis' almost unbearable existential anxiety about Iran's pursuit of a nuclear capability. No matter how devastating Israel's nuclear retaliation could be, it would never outweigh the impact of an initial nuclear attack on Israel.[13]

In the aftermath of the Holocaust, the vow "never again" was incorporated into the Zionist ethos of national revival. This was a response to the helplessness of the Jewish communities in Europe and of the Jewish community and Zionist Palestine, the Yishuv, during the Holocaust.[14] Then, with the creation of Israel in 1948, local ethnic strife between Palestinian Arabs and Zionist settlers over land and natural resources escalated into a multistate regional conflict over national aspirations and rights. This conflict between Arabs and Israelis is still with us and shapes the face of the modern Middle East today.

What the Palestinians still refer to as the *Nakba* (in Arabic, "the catastrophe") has determined the Arabs' discourse on its side of the conflict. Since 1948, the yearning to bring about the "destruction of the Zionist entity" has captured the Arab psyche, reinforcing the Arabs' refusal to accept the reality and the legitimacy of the state of Israel.

This Arab-Israeli conflict, with existential avowals on both sides, led Israeli Prime Minister David Ben-Gurion to pursue the bomb. He concluded that without outside guarantees of Israel's existence, its future could be assured only through the fruits of the Jewish mind—science and technology—and that the vow "never again" meant that Israel must acquire "the nuclear option." By 1955, soon after Ben-Gurion came to power for the second time, this commitment was translated from a vision for the future into a series of concrete actions. By this time, realizing that Israel could not rely on the assurance of the world's big powers of Israel's territorial integrity, Ben-Gurion settled on the bomb as Israel's ultimate guarantee for survival in a hostile environment.[15] Ben-Gurion initiated the nuclear project during Israel's first decade, and the project's first products became available a decade later, on the eve of the 1967 Six-Day War. Today, almost universally, Israelis believe that this fateful decision was perhaps the wisest he ever made. (Some would argue that it was the second such decision, that the first one was the decision to declare independence in May 1948, against the counsel of those who wanted to delay such a declaration.)

Over time—the 1973 Yom Kippur War may have been the turning point—the rhetoric in most of the Arab world about the "destruction of Israel" has gradually been replaced by a more realistic and moderate discourse.[16] Some suggest that the advent of the Israeli bomb played an important, if unacknowledged, role in that development, making apparent that it no longer made sense to talk about the destruction of nuclear Israel by military means.

Although the old rhetoric is seldom heard in the mainstream Sunni Arab world, it has not entirely disappeared. Radical Islamist movements still speak of the "elimination of the Zionist entity." Within the Palestinian-Israeli conflict, the desire to undo Israel as a Jewish state fuels the ideological fervor of the Hamas movement, and outside that conflict, this same desire can be found in the "spider web" rhetoric of the Lebanese Shiite paramilitary movement Hezbollah. Indeed, the dissolution of the state of Israel is one of Hezbollah's stated goals, its leaders arguing that only the dissolution of Israel will bring peace to the Middle East.

Iran, Israel, and the Politics of Fear

Much of the antagonism toward Iranian President Mahmoud Ahmadinejad stems from two related themes—one about the past and the other about the future—which together highlight his extreme hostility to Israel as a Jewish state: his denial of the Holocaust and his desire (and prediction) to "wipe Israel off the world's map."[17] As the leader of a state openly committed to becoming "a nuclear power," Ahmadinejad has reawakened and heightened Israelis' existential dread.

In an editorial in the *Washington Post*, Charles Krauthammer explained the historical context of this fear about Ahmadinejad's statements.[18] He started with numbers, reminding us that Israel's current Jewish population has just passed 5.6 million, whereas the American Jewish population has declined to about 5.5 million, both demographic trends that are likely to continue. For the first time in nearly two millennia, since the exile of the Jews by the Romans in the first and second centuries CE after the destruction of the second Temple, more Jews are living in Israel than in any other country in the world. After the destruction of the European Jewish civilization in the Holocaust, only two centers of Jewish life remained intact: the very small Hebraic community in Palestine (about half a million in 1945) and the much larger Jewish community in the United States. Ever since the Holocaust, Israel has been positioning itself to replace the United States as the center of Jewish life and now, by its numbers, has done so.

With this demographic shift in mind, Israelis understandably have difficulty dismissing Ahmadinejad's comments as silly but empty rhetoric, as many people in the West do. Israeli intelligence officials have been closely monitoring the Iranian nuclear program at least since the early 1990s. But with the election of President Ahmadinejad in 2005, the Iranian nuclear issue now dominates Israel's national discourse.[19] After Israel's national election in 2009, the Iranian nuclear issue was tied more tightly to Israeli domestic politics.[20]

With the rise of a nuclear-capable Iran, a new generation of Israelis are reminded of what their parents and grandparents had recognized as a theoretical possibility but tended to dismiss as unreal: the vulnerability of Israel to nuclear attack. The old argument from the nuclear debate of the early 1960s about the inherent fragility and instability of a nuclear-deterrence regime in the Middle East has resurfaced and inaugurated a new politics of nuclear fear in Israel.

A poll published in Israel in September 2006 found that 79 percent of Israeli Jews believed that Iran posed a genuine threat to Israel's existence. Another poll, published two months later, found that 66 percent of Israeli Jews were convinced that Iran would develop a nuclear weapon and use it against Israel.[21] Consequently, a number of prominent Israelis have called on the international community to treat President Ahmadinejad as another Hitler.[22] In October 2006, based on this renewed fear, the editors of the daily Ha'aretz devoted seven pages in its weekly magazine to a project entitled "The Iranian Danger and You." The project centered on a question posed to a few Tel Aviv residents, including some well-known personalities: "What would you do if you knew Ahmadinejad was going to drop the bomb on Tel Aviv in two months?"[23] After noting the absurdity of the question, one prominent Israeli writer, Yoram Kanyuk, responded that he would stay; he would not run away from his beloved city. Another respondent, a well-known video artist who lives now in New York City, said that she would try to preserve and document as many "items" from Israel as possible and would send them off in boxes overseas. She then added, "It would have surely depressed me greatly because Israel is important to me. . . . I would have probably created a major show on Israel, calling it 'homage to Israel.'" Absurd questions tend to produce absurd responses.

This project was a nihilistic farce. In the abstract, it may have seemed intriguing to the editors, but in reality, the effort to make people think practically and prosaically about an Iranian-made nuclear holocaust was so surreal, so intolerable, that I called Ha'aretz's publisher, Amos Schocken, to express my outrage. As I began, he interrupted, saying, "You are totally right, this project was an inexcusable error on our part. We should not have published this."

A few days later, in early November 2006, I participated in a TV panel discussion by a number of experts and policymakers about the Iranian nuclear threat. One was the then Israeli deputy minister of defense, Dr. Ephraim Sneh. I had been aware for years of his alarmist outlook, but I was not prepared for his exceedingly dark view. Sneh argued that the political and psychological impact of the Iranian bomb on Israel would be devastating. Even if Iran never actually dropped a bomb on Israel, a nuclear-capable Iran would destroy Israel's sense of vitality and self-confidence. In Sneh's view, in this way a nuclear Iran already would have achieved some of its strategic goals. Sneh directly linked the Iranian bomb and the Holocaust, believing Jews simply would no longer tolerate living in the shadow of existential threat. He is convinced that the Iranian bomb would lead to a major wave of emigration by Israelis and that this in itself would fulfill Ahmadinejad's prophecy about wiping the Zionists off the map, but without his having to push a single button.[24]

Although the Israeli public is familiar with Sneh's worries about the Iranian bomb, Israel Dostrovsky's even more alarmist view is private and quiet. Dostrovsky is not a politician; he is one of Israel's most distinguished scientists, a former president of the Weizmann Institute, and the country's unofficial dean of atomic affairs. Moreover, Dostrovsky is the only living Israeli nuclear scientist who has seen it all: from 1948, when he founded and commanded HEMED GIMMEL (the predecessor of the Israel Atomic Energy Commission, IAEC); to the mid-1960s, when he was asked to overhaul the IAEC, and when, under his watch, Israel assembled its first nuclear devices on the eve of the 1967 war; until almost the present day, as he continues to advise the government on energy matters.[25]

Dostrovsky told me during a meeting in March 2006 that he is very uneasy about the Iranian situation. When our conversation turned to Iran's nuclear program, Dostrovsky commented—after noting that his views were not supported by hard data and were not based on privileged intelligence— that he personally believes Iran may already have some nuclear-weapons capability, if not actual bombs, then some sort of a nuclear device. In any case, in his view it was likely that Iran already may have secretly produced, outside the IAEA's safeguards, enough fissile material for a few bombs. Furthermore, Dostrovsky invoked the possibility that Iran could drop a bomb on Israel. It seems plausible to him that Iranian leaders may calculate that the cost of a loss of a few million Iranians would be worth destroying once and for all the Zionist enterprise. At the end of the conversation, Dostrovsky admitted to me that he has grave and continuous doubts about the future of the state of Israel, about whether Zionist Israel will survive the coming century.

The Israeli Bargain: Invisibility as Constraint

These reflections and observations lead us to the central theme of this book: Israel's unique bargain with the bomb. Each bargain reflects the special way that that state sets up its "contract" with the bomb. It determines how the state will handle its nuclear matters. The bargain is as much about the country's national identity as it is about nuclear affairs, and it is as much about politics, law, and society—images, symbols, prohibitions, and identities—as it is about nuclear-weapons technology and strategy. Although these nuclear-armed states resemble one another technologically, they vary in their bargain's political, social, legal, and cultural aspects.

By talking about bargain, I am referring to something broader than what we normally mean by "policy" or "strategy" or "posture," even though it includes elements of all three. I call it a bargain because it refers to the overall relations that a country establishes with the bomb, metaphorically speaking, realizing that such a bargain is always dynamic and changing. Such a bargain requires the national narrative to provide a rationale for why the country acquired, or did not acquire, nuclear weapons and what they mean for that country, as well as the level of salience or visibility of the bomb in that country's public life. Then there are the bargain makers: the individuals, institutions, and ethos that shape that nation's nuclear history. In nuclear democracies, the citizens, even if they did not initiate the bargain, must be made part of its ongoing acceptance. This bargain takes shape through a process of interactions, or "negotiations," between both domestic and international players.

In Israel's case, since about 1970 every educated newspaper reader has known that Israel was a nuclear-armed state, the first and only one in the Middle East. It is commonly believed that Israel's nuclear arsenal is both significant numerically and advanced in quality. Table 1, from a recent dossier produced by the International Institute for Strategic Studies, summarizes most of the known estimates. As the table shows, estimates of the arsenal's size range from fewer than one hundred to about two hundred or even more warheads. Recent leaks from classified U.S. intelligence sources reveal that since the 1990s, Israel has maintained a rather stable nuclear arsenal of about eighty to ninety warheads,[26] although former President Jimmy Carter contends that the figures are higher.[27]

Israel's nuclear conduct, however, has been different from that of all other nuclear-weapons states. First and foremost is the issue of acknowledgment.

TABLE 1   ESTIMATES OF ISRAEL'S NUCLEAR ARSENAL

Source	Estimate
Sunday Times (1986)	As many as 200 nuclear weapons.
Frank Barnaby (1989)	From 100 to 200 weapons' worth of plutonium and up to 35 thermonuclear weapons.
Seymour Hersh (1991)	Hundreds of nuclear weapons, ranging from low-yield, enhanced radiation "neutron" designs, mines, and artillery shells to thermonuclear weapons.
Anthony Cordesman (1996)	From 60 to 80 nuclear weapons.
Wisconsin Project on Nuclear Arms Control (1996)	Up to 175 bombs' worth of plutonium.
Jane's Intelligence Review (1997)	More than 400 nuclear weapons.
U.S. Defense Intelligence Agency (1999)	From 60 to 80 nuclear weapons.
David Albright, Institute for Science and International Security (2005)	From 510 to 650 kilograms of separated plutonium (by the end of 2003).
Stockholm International Peace Research Institute (2007)	From 100 to 200 warheads.

Source: International Institute for Strategic Studies, *Nuclear Programmes in the Middle East*, 2008.

All other nuclear-weapons states have publicly acknowledged their nuclear arsenals and openly demonstrated their nuclear capability. But Israel has not done so.[28] It has not sought at home or abroad the prestige, respect, or recognition that comes from possessing nuclear weapons. This remarkable commitment to self-restraint is a central tenet of Israel's nuclear bargain that affects every aspect of Israel's relationship with nuclear weapons. Israel treats its nuclear weapons as if they were outside the public sphere and not part of the country's arsenal of power and thus not available for political use.

Today, more than four decades after Israel crossed the nuclear threshold, the Israeli government still runs its nuclear program by virtually the same code of invisibility, treating any factual information about its nuclear activities as classified beyond the minimal acknowledgment that Israel operates two nuclear research centers, at Soreq and at Dimona, and that the latter is not subject to international safeguards.[29]

The Taboo

Taboo is derived from the Polynesian word *tabu* or *tapu*, meaning "prohibition," which social scientists use to refer to societal prohibitions observed through customs or rituals. What makes the taboo a powerful prohibition is the sense of fear or danger it entails; that is, breaking the prohibition could be dangerous because it means openly questioning authority. As Hutton Webster states in his book *Taboo: A Sociological Study*: "The authority of a taboo is unmatched by that of any other prohibition. There is no reflection on it, no reasoning about it, no discussion of it. A taboo amounts simply to an imperative 'thou-shalt-not' in the presence of the danger apprehended."[30]

The former American Secretary of State John Foster Dulles was the first to have borrowed the term *taboo* in reference to the unwritten prohibition of nuclear weapons. He is reported to have warned in a National Security Council meeting that "we must manage to remove the taboo from the use of these [nuclear] weapons,"[31] in order to make nuclear weapons more usable as integral battlefield weapons in the U.S. armed forces' arsenal. Later, both policymakers (like Robert McNamara and McGeorge Bundy) and scholars (like Thomas Schelling, Nina Tannenwald, Harald Müller, and T. V. Paul) have observed the existence of a taboolike prohibition against the use of nuclear weapons.[32]

While acknowledging that the prohibition against such use is not exactly the same as other social taboos, these scholars also emphasized that not using nuclear weapons nonetheless had a strong normative-moral component. I use the term "taboolike prohibition" because it is more than the outcome of successful deterrence or prudent calculations. For example, in 1983, in response to President Ronald Reagan's nuclear policies, which appeared to treat nuclear weapons as usable first-strike weapons, George Ball warned that a sense of revulsion "has enveloped nuclear weapons in a rigid taboo" and that a nation that broke that taboo "would suffer universal condemnation."[33] Two decades later, I suggested in an op-ed in the *New York Times* that Golda Meir's nuclear conduct during the 1973 war and her reluctance to consider seriously even a nuclear demonstration probably reflected her own instinctive sense of taboo regarding the use of nuclear weapons.[34]

My reference to Israel's nuclear taboo throughout this book is different from that used by these scholars, however. I do think that Israel's restrained nuclear conduct entails a taboolike prohibition on nuclear use, but I use "taboo" here to refer to Israel's deeper, all-encompassing societal prohibition against open acknowledgment, let alone discussion, of Israel's nuclear bargain. Israel's prohibition against discussing nuclear issues stems from a government policy that insists on lowering the salience of nuclear weapons by rendering them publicly invisible and unacknowledged. This prohibition is rigidly enforced by Israeli military censorship (the Censora), which bans any references to Israel's nuclear weapons in the Israeli media.

Israel's nuclear bargain, however, goes beyond governmental policy and its enforcement. As I argue in chapters 4 and 5, it comprises behavior and everyday discourse as well. Had the bargain been limited to government policy and conduct, it would not have been so successful or long lasting. It is this societywide taboo, a nongovernmental extension of government policy, that makes Israel's bargain with the bomb both exceptional and effective.

Although Israel's secret is not a real secret anymore, the ethos of secrecy and invisibility has survived. The Israeli public still respects the official secrecy and nonacknowledgment of the subject and so treats the matter as if it were off-limits. As commentator Yossi Klein has observed, Israelis talk a great deal about the dangers of the Iranian nuclear threat—what would happen if and when Iran gets the bomb—but they keep silent about their own bomb, their own ability to rain down destruction on the Middle East.[35]

Israel has erected formidable institutional and sociocultural walls of silence to separate itself from the nuclear reality. Living with the bomb has left almost no visible traces on the Israeli psyche, as was shown during the 1986 Mordechai Vanunu affair. Despite the gravity of Vanunu's revelations, their publication created nothing resembling a national nuclear debate, as hardly any Israelis asked fundamental questions about their country's nuclear program. This was not just a result of official censorship, although censorship tends to strengthen the prohibition. Rather, it was more a matter of self-censorship.[36]

Psychologically, this nuclear taboo spares, but also deprives, Israelis from having to deal with the issue of the bomb in a straightforward way. Except for a small pocket of debate and protest in the early 1960s, Israel has not had a full social engagement with the bomb, not even on an intellectual level where controversies concerning topics of mass destruction usually thrive. The taboo has thus exempted Israelis from having to confront their country's nuclear reality, and the military censor has given them an excuse not to feel accountable for their nation's nuclear status.

Democracy and the Bomb

Israel's nuclear bargain is at odds with its otherwise vibrant political culture of democratic governance. As Robert Dahl, one of America's most distinguished political scientists, noted, nuclear weapons pose "a tragic paradox" for the idea of liberal democracy. He observed that "no decisions can be more fateful for Americans, and for the world, than decisions about nuclear weapons. Yet, these decisions have largely escaped the control of democratic process." The rise of nuclear weapons, Dahl lamented, has testified to "a profound failure in the capacity of contemporary democratic institutions to achieve their purpose."[37] Richard Falk, another prominent contemporary political theorist, argues similarly that nuclear weapons create "structural necessities" that contradict the spirit of democratic governance.[38] Indeed, nuclear weapons tend to corrode and corrupt the very notion of democratic rule.

In sum, national decisions about nuclear weapons—their development, deployment, doctrine, command and control, safety, and, ultimately, use— are the most fateful that a nation can make. Moreover, these decisions have often been made, especially in the early stages of the nation's nuclear history, in secrecy, by a select few, and with very little participation by the general citizenry.

Israel has pushed this nondemocratic decision making in nuclear affairs to its limits. As I contend in chapters 6 and 7, Israel is probably the nuclear democracies' most extreme case of nondemocratic policymaking. In Israel, to this day, the gap between nuclear conduct and basic democratic norms of open debate, the public's right to know, public accountability, oversight, and transparency remains vast.

The American Role in the Israel's Bargain

Israel could never have fashioned its bargain without the support of the United States. Taboo at home and exceptionalism abroad, the two inseparable components of Israel's bargain, together constitute Israel's distinctive nuclear posture and culture.

The term *exceptionalism* that I use throughout this book in reference to the unique way the United States dealt with the Israeli nuclear case is a loaded term requiring conceptual refinement. One could argue that Israel is not the only exception to the United States' nonproliferation policy and that Israel is only one of several other cases of nuclear exceptionalism. One could even suggest that the history of the United States' nonproliferation policy contains all kinds of exceptions, some more publicly known than others, and that making exceptions to the general nonproliferation norm has been the hallmark of the policy's evolution.[39]

This may well be true. Still, we could counter that the Israeli nuclear case has some qualitative components that are missing in all or most of the other cases. Israel is probably the only case of proliferation that is close to being a matter of American political taboo. In his *The Samson Option*, Seymour Hersh documented many revealing examples over the decades of how the Israeli nuclear case was a taboo in American foreign policy.[40] I, too, have personally witnessed this phenomenon on many occasions.

It took four American administrations, from Eisenhower's to Nixon's, to accept the unavoidable reality of the Israeli bomb. These administrations, each in its own way, treated the Israeli nuclear reality as a no-win situation, the acknowledgment of which would have serious consequences for both global nonproliferation and domestic politics, regardless of U.S. actions.

The critical moment that gave rise to the Israeli bargain, as I elaborate in the first chapter, occurred in September 1969 when President Richard Nixon and Israeli Prime Minister Golda Meir arrived at a secret bilateral understanding on the Israeli nuclear issue. This secret understanding exempted Israel's nuclear weapons from the United States' nonproliferation policy as long as Israel kept these weapons invisible. Neither government has ever officially acknowledged the existence of that secret deal, and both are still formally committed to a policy of nonacknowledgment and secrecy on this matter.

Besides the distinctive taboolike character of the Israeli nuclear issue in America, a few other features of the Nixon-Meir nuclear accord of 1969 make the exemptions given to Israel qualitatively different from the United States' other bilateral nuclear understandings. First, the 1969 accord was, for all intents and purposes, a tacit American acquiescence in Israel's acquisition of nuclear weapons; none of the other states had this understanding with the United States. Second, the Nixon-Meir understanding—initially not in writing—had nothing to do with the Nuclear Nonproliferation Treaty or even with nuclear weapons per se. Rather, the understanding was essentially about what would count as the "introduction" of nuclear weapons into the region. In return for Israel's commitment not to take any public action that could lead to the introduction of nuclear weapons, President Nixon agreed to remove the Israeli nuclear issue from bilateral relations. Third, the 1969 accord tried to blur, even distort, the facts of the nuclear situation, not to clarify them. Finally, the United States actively supported the bargain, so American officials pretended not to know exactly what the status was of the Israeli nuclear program.

Finally, we should also note that the relationship between the United States and Israel is qualitatively different from the relationship between the United States and some of the other exceptional cases; that is, Japan, Germany, and South Korea, among others, have formal defense treaties with the United States, treaties that either explicitly or implicitly extend the United States' protective nuclear umbrella over these countries. The United States may have felt comfortable reaching understandings with these countries over nuclear matters because once under the U.S. nuclear umbrella, it was not likely that these countries would develop nuclear weapons of their own. Israel, however, had no formal defense treaty with the United States, and the United States has never offered such a treaty to Israel. In sum, it may be argued that in these other cases, the combination of U.S. exemptions and the U.S. nuclear umbrella served to persuade these countries not to develop nuclear weapons of their own. In the case of Israel, American understandings served to endorse and accept, albeit tacitly, Israel's acquisition of nuclear weapons.

Introducing Amimut

Amimut, the Hebrew word for "opacity" or "ambiguity," has a range of meanings that encompass Israel's interpretation of the nuclear issue. Amimut refers narrowly to Israel's official policy of nuclear opacity adopted with the 1969 Nixon-Meir deal, and it also refers, more broadly, to the taboolike social aspects of Israel's prohibitions and restraints in connection with its nuclear weapons. This policy has come to be prized as a successful tool of statecraft, to such an extent that the late Ze'ev Schiff, Israel's respected defense analyst, commented once that if Israel had a national prize for strategy, it should have been awarded to those who invented the strategy of amimut.[41]

As a national nuclear bargain, amimut is not an invention with a recognizable inventor.[42] Rather, as I argue in chapters 2 and 3, amimut evolved piecemeal as the outcome of political and strategic decisions, and at times improvisations, made in response to specific political and strategic needs. Although Ben-Gurion created the notion of a nuclear Israel and planted the seeds of amimut, he did not have, and could not have had, a deliberate strategic blueprint for its enduring future application. His focus instead was on the immediate strategic considerations of a nuclear option and not on its long-term implications.[43]

Nixon and Meir's understanding was decisive for policy, but not until the mid- to late-1970s did Shalheveth Freier and his team at the Israeli Atomic Energy Commission (IAEC) codify those ground rules and practices into a national doctrine of nuclear restraint. If any one person deserves credit for inventing amimut as a distinctive Israeli nuclear outlook, it is Freier, an extraordinary individual who headed the Israeli nuclear administration during the 1973 Yom Kippur War. Under his leadership in the 1970s, the IAEC developed an elaborate national concept of amimut and wrote it in doctrinal form. But even Freier did not invent amimut; rather, he articulated the logic and rationale for a policy and a code of conduct already in place.

Also in the early to mid-1970s, some Israeli academics, among them Yair Evron, Alan Dowty, and Avigdor Haselkorn, coined the English term *nuclear ambiguity*. Around the same time, Shlomo Aronson used the term *covert proliferation* to describe Israel's unique nuclear conduct.[44] Other academic students of proliferation, mostly outside Israel (such as William Potter and Harold Feiveson), used the term *latent proliferation* to describe the phenomenon of second-generation nuclear proliferation.[45]

Ze'ev Schiff's insight, however, best captures the Israeli appraisal that amimut has been the nation's most prudent and successful strategic achievement. Through the use of amimut and the subsequent role of the United States as a partner, Israel has created a precedent in the international affairs of a state considered by the international community as a nuclear-weapons nation, albeit without ever acknowledging its possession. All international players, friends and foes alike, consider this when shaping their strategic perceptions and actions.

Israel's nuclear bargain has many praiseworthy aspects. Through a prudent use of amimut, Israel has committed to both resolve and caution, thereby avoiding the either-or structure of the nuclear dilemma. Over time and through a great deal of restraint, Israel has created and maintained a nearly impossible and uniquely creative response to its nuclear dilemma. Its solution contains a sleight of hand that allows Israel to live in the best of all possible worlds by having the bomb but without having to deal with many of the negative consequences that such possession entails.

Through invisibility and nonacknowledgment, amimut has allowed Israel to separate the building of its nuclear capability (resolve) from the code of conduct necessary to handle this capability (caution). In doing so, Israel has lowered the salience of nuclear weapons without rejecting them. As a result, these weapons have become a mirage, a phantom, and a paradox. To wit, at one time, in two subsequent issues, *The Economist* referred to the Israeli bomb as being both "the world's worst kept secret" and "the bomb that never is."[46]

This strategic achievement has had a substantial democratic and normative cost. As long as Israel is committed to not acknowledging its possession of nuclear weapons or even that it has produced weapons-grade materials, it would be difficult, if not impossible, to engage with Israel in any meaningful arms control or other nuclear weapons–related diplomacy. Although these shortcomings initially appeared as virtues, as time goes by they have become increasingly apparent as flaws.

Here is one illustration. On the surface, the Israeli policy of amimut is distinguished by its continuity. For example, Israel has never changed its declaratory amimut formula, which originated in the mid-1960s ("Israel will not be first to introduce . . ."), or the parameters by which it runs the policy. The policy's essential function, however, has changed over time. In the early period, Israel was an emergent proliferator, a state attempting to build its nuclear capability without confronting the world. At the same time, the primary function of amimut was to provide political cover for its new nuclear program. Today, Israel is in a fundamentally different historical era. After forty years of possessing nuclear weapons, Israel is now a mature and cautious nuclear-weapons state. In recent speeches for international audiences, Israeli spokespersons have referred to "Israel's long-standing commitment to norms of security, responsibility, accountability and restraint in the nuclear domain."[47] Israeli nuclear chiefs now refer to Israel as "a responsible state with advanced nuclear technology," in much the same way that U.S. President George W. Bush referred to India as "a state that has conducted its civilian nuclear energy program in a safe and responsible way for decades," after signing into law a nuclear technology-sharing agreement between the two countries.[48]

Israel wants the kind of recognition and legitimacy that nuclear maturity deserves. India, which is a newer nuclear-weapons state than Israel, declared its nuclear capability through a series of tests in 1998, subsequently has acquired more weapons, and has been rewarded with peaceful nuclear cooperation with the United States. Israel, in contrast, had not received American diplomatic support when it explored being granted associate status with the Nuclear Suppliers Group (NSG). Indeed, given its logical structure, amimut makes it difficult, if not impossible, for Israel even to seek the recognition it deserves as a "responsible state with advanced nuclear technology."

This book has been researched and written during the decade when the Iranian nuclear problem finally has come to overshadow any discussion of the future of nuclear weapons. What started as a complex but abstract challenge to the integrity and future of the Nuclear Non-Proliferation Treaty (NPT) has developed into an increasingly tense impasse between Iran and the international community, especially Israel. Tensions have ebbed and flowed, and cycles of negotiations have resulted in temporary remedies and informal pauses, which now appear to be ending. As this book goes to press, Iran appears to have become more defiant and recalcitrant. The current impasse may soon become a crisis.

Whatever the outcome of the Iranian nuclear situation, it will have far-reaching repercussions for the global nuclear situation, and probably more so for the Israeli bargain. Given the volatility and unpredictability of the situation, the future of Israeli amimut is probably less certain, and it could look quite different in light of a decisive outcome of the Iranian nuclear issue, whether an act of creative diplomacy, a regime change in Tehran, military action against Iran, or, worst of all, acceptance by the world of a nuclear-armed Iran.

One thing is certain. Although today the issue of Israel's bargain with the bomb looks intellectually interesting but politically remote, abstract, and academic, tomorrow it may look very different. Should the Iranian nuclear issue be resolved, Israel will be under considerable pressures to rethink its bargain. The different theoretical possibilities regarding domestic and international reforms in the bargain that I raise in the last three chapters of this book thus are likely to become timely and relevant.

In sum, the nature of the Iranian challenge to the NPT and to Israel's amimut is such that almost any resolution of this challenge may be not a change *in* the nuclear proliferation game but a change *of* the game itself. The discourse of nuclear nonproliferation practices and norms may well be transformed by how the Iranian nuclear problem is resolved. If nonproliferation practices were to change, amimut in its present form is unlikely to survive.

As I argue throughout this book, amimut is increasingly at odds with both emerging international nuclear proliferation norms and with evolving

domestic Israeli expectations and preferences regarding democratic governance. A dramatic resolution of the Iranian crisis would reveal these tensions
between amimut and the international and domestic environments within
which it is practiced as outright contradictions. At that point the Israeli leadership and Israeli society as a whole may be called on to make another fateful
decision regarding the country's nuclear bargain.

(July 2010)

Abbreviations

ACDA	Arms Control and Disarmament Agency
ACRS	Arms Control and Regional Security
AEC	Atomic Energy Commission
AIPAC	American Israel Public Affairs Committee
AMAN	Agaf Modi'in (Israeli Military Intelligence)
CD	Conference on Disarmament
CEA	Commissariat a l'Énergie Atomique (Atomic Energy Commission)
CIA/OSI	Office of Scientific Intelligence at the Central Intelligence Agency
DCI	Director of Central Intelligence
DEFCON	Defense Condition
DFAC	Israeli Knesset's Defense and Foreign Affairs Committee
DOD	U.S. Department of Defense
DOE	U.S. Department of Energy
EMET	Agaf Mechkar Ve'Tichun (Research and Planning Division of the Israeli Ministry of Defense)
FMCT	Fissile Materials Cutoff Treaty
GSS	General Security Service (Israeli internal civilian security service)
HEMED	Ha'il Mada (Science Corps, a department of the Israel Defense Forces)
HEU	Highly Enriched Uranium
IAEA	International Atomic Energy Agency
IAEC	Israel Atomic Energy Commission

IAF	Israeli Air Force
IDF	Israel Defense Forces (Tzva Haganah Le'Israel)
KAMAG	Kirya Le'Mechkar Gariini (Israeli nuclear research center at Dimona)
LEKEM	Lishka Lekishrey Mada (Bureau of Science Relations)
LEU	Low-Enriched Uranium
MAD	Mutual Assured Destruction
MALMAB	Bureau of Security in the Israel Ministry of Defense
MAPAI	Land of Israel Workers Party
NATO	North Atlantic Treaty Organization
NIE	National Intelligence Estimate
NNSA	National Nuclear Security Administration
NPT	Nuclear Non-Proliferation Treaty
NPR	Nuclear Posture Review
NSAM	National Security Action Memorandum
NSC	National Security Council
NSDM	National Security Decision Memorandum
NSG	Nuclear Suppliers Group
NSSM	National Security Study Memorandum
NUMEC	Nuclear Materials and Equipment Company
NWFZ	Nuclear Weapons–Free Zone
RAFAEL	Rashut Le'Pituach Emtzaei Lechnima (Armaments and Development Authority)
SRG	Senior Review Group
UAR	United Arab Republic

THE WORST-KEPT SECRET

Chapter One

The Birth of Amimut

On September 9, 1969, a big brown envelope was hand-carried to the Oval Office on order of Richard Helms, director of the Central Intelligence Agency (CIA). On the envelope he had written, "For and to be opened only by the President, the White House." The content of the envelope is still unknown, but evidence suggests it held the latest intelligence on one of Washington's most secret foreign policy matters: Israel's nuclear program. The material apparently was so sensitive that the nation's spymaster was unwilling to share it with anybody but President Richard Nixon.[1]

Today, the now-empty envelope is at the Nixon Presidential Materials Project at the National Archives in College Park, Maryland, and is kept inside a two-folder set, labeled "NSSM 40." NSSM stands for National Security Study Memorandum, a series of policy studies initiated by National Security Adviser Henry Kissinger and produced by the national security bureaucracy for the Nixon White House. Except for a handful of administrative notes, the NSSM 40 files are almost completely bare, containing only "withdrawal sheets" for the many documents that remain classified.

In recent years, however, the Nixon Presidential Library and the U.S. National Archives and Records Administration jointly declassified and released more archival material on the NSSM 40 deliberations. With the aid of these recently declassified documents and interviews with some of the key figures of that era, we now know that NSSM 40 was the Nixon administration's effort to grapple with the policy implications of a nuclear-armed Israel. These documents offer insights into the deliberations in 1969, when the fate of the Nuclear Non-Proliferation Treaty (NPT) was still uncertain.

The climax of those deliberations was the meeting on September 26, 1969, at the White House, at which President Nixon and Israeli Prime Minister Golda Meir had a private conversation about Israel's nuclear weapons. No written record of or oral testimony about what transpired at that meeting is known to have survived, so what the leaders discussed still remains shrouded in mystery. In retrospect we can say that it was in this meeting that amimut as a strategic posture mutually supported by Israel and the United States came into being. That Nixon-Meir meeting is the birthplace of the bargain.

The Historical Context

The U.S.-Israel nuclear deal that Meir and Nixon reached in September 1969 had started a decade or so earlier. By 1958 Israel had secretly begun constructing the nuclear center at Dimona, but the United States did not find out the purpose of the site until December 1960. Within a few months the CIA estimated that Israel could produce nuclear weapons within the decade.[2]

Responding to the discovery of Dimona posed a challenge for American policymakers. Only fifteen years after the Holocaust and before international nuclear nonproliferation norms existed, Israel's founders believed they had a compelling case for acquiring nuclear weapons. From the American perspective, Israel was a small and friendly state that was surrounded by much larger enemies vowing to destroy it, and was outside the boundaries of America's system of global alliances and its containment policy. Moreover, Israel enjoyed unique domestic support in America. If the United States was not willing to guarantee Israel's borders, how could it deny Israel the ultimate defense?

Yet the idea of a nuclear-armed Israel was perceived as antithetical to American's global and regional interests. President John F. Kennedy was fearful that without decisive international action to curb nuclear proliferation, the number of nuclear-weapons states would inevitably rise to twenty or thirty within a decade or two. In the early 1960s, Israel stood at the divide between the uncontrolled nuclear proliferation of the past and the emerging international norm of nonproliferation. If the United States could not prevent small Israel from becoming a nuclear state, how could it persuade the Germans not to acquire nuclear weapons? And if the United States could not stop the Israelis or the Germans, how could it expect the Soviets to prevent China from acquiring nuclear weapons? Israel's development of a nuclear-weapons capability thus undermined U.S. efforts to establish a global order dedicated to nonproliferation.

President Kennedy was also concerned that Israeli nuclearization would lead to another Arab-Israeli war, with grave repercussions. A special national intelligence estimate (SNIE) that the CIA issued on May 8, 1963, entitled "The Advanced Weapons Programs of the UAR and Israel," details the political concern about Israel's nuclearization:

> If Nasser could not devise a counter to an Israeli nuclear threat on his own, he probably would turn to the USSR to try to ensure his protection, and the Arabs would blame the West, including the U.S. for the increased Israeli threat. Israel, likewise, would become increasingly activist in its dealings with the Arabs. . . . [A]s the advanced weapons progress, tensions will probably rise on both sides. In an atmosphere of this kind, there would always be the possibility that one or the other side would initiate hostile action to safeguard its ultimate security.[3]

As a result of these concerns, Kennedy insisted on annual U.S. access to Dimona in order to check up on the Israeli nuclear program. Although this was an unprecedented demand, deviating from international norms and inconsistent with the notion of sovereignty, Kennedy concluded that only a stringent monitoring of Israel's nuclear activities could halt that country's momentum toward constructing a bomb. In the spring of 1963, a few months before the Dimona reactor was scheduled to begin operation and after he learned that Israel had contracted with a French arms manufacturer to develop a nuclear-capable ballistic missile (the MD-620), Kennedy pressed to establish a long-term U.S. monitoring arrangement at Dimona, the closest possible arrangement to placing Dimona under a formal American inspection regime. In a series of toughly worded letters to Prime Ministers Ben-Gurion and Levi Eshkol, Kennedy indicated that American commitment to Israel's security and well-being "would be seriously jeopardized" if his inspection demands were not met.[4]

In August 1963, after weeks of intense internal deliberations, Prime Minister Eshkol accepted many of Kennedy's demands, or so it seemed, but it was up to Kennedy's successor, President Lyndon B. Johnson, to implement the terms of the agreement. Johnson—who was less adamant on nuclear nonproliferation in general and Israel's nuclear program in particular—preferred not to confront Prime Minister Eshkol on the details of U.S. inspections of Dimona. The American visits there were, we now know, ineffectual. Beyond Johnson's lack of enthusiasm, Israel made a concerted effort to limit the information that the American inspections could gather. By placing obstacles to the American visits, Israel eliminated their technical effectiveness. The U.S. visits were a nuisance to Israel, but they did not stop it from continuing its secret nuclear R&D efforts. Rather, the significance of the American visits was primarily political, as they demonstrated that Israel was politically committed to a nonnuclear stance.[5] Moreover, after March 1965, that political commitment was reinforced by Israel's private and public pledge "not to be the first to introduce nuclear weapons to the Middle East."[6] By late 1966, though, before the negotiations over the NPT were concluded, Israel had positioned itself just below the nuclear-weapons threshold. At that time Israel had completed the necessary R&D for building an atomic weapon, but had no intention of conducting an atomic test.

By early 1968 the U.S. government—or at least the State Department—still believed that Israel had "not embarked on a program to produce a nuclear weapon."[7] Throughout 1968, however, American assessments changed and by October 1968, both the State and Defense departments believed that Israel was changing its nuclear course. A recently declassified State Department memo indicates that by the fall of 1968, the United States realized that "Israel has made the policy decision and is moving rapidly toward obtaining and deploying strategic missiles."[8]

One major policy issue raised by the Israeli nuclear program involved the Nuclear Non-Proliferation Treaty (NPT). The NPT was the result of a complex negotiating process sponsored by two Democratic administrations seeking a strong international treaty establishing a nonproliferation norm. By July 1968, the NPT negotiations had been completed and submitted for signature to the participating states. Even though Israel's signature was essential to the treaty's success, Jerusalem did not rush to sign, saying that it needed time to study the treaty and its implications.

The U.S.-Israel negotiations over the sale of F-4 Phantom fighter-bombers in November became "America's last best chance" to halt a nuclear Israel and to get Israel to sign the NPT. Ultimately, Paul Warnke, the assistant secretary of defense for international security who conducted the negotiations, failed in his effort to persuade Israeli Ambassador Yitzhak Rabin to commit to stronger nonnuclear assurances. These negotiations did, however, highlight each side's different interpretations of the meaning of those assurances, particularly the meaning of Israel's "nonintroduction" pledge.[9]

At the end of these negotiations, it was clear that the United States and Israel—Warnke and Rabin—had two completely different ideas of what constituted both "nuclear weapons" and the "introduction" of such weapons into the Middle East. For Warnke, the possession of a nuclear weapon meant the physical presence of all the bomb's components, even if they were not fully assembled. That is, the physical presence of the weapon was equivalent to the act of introduction. Thus, Warnke's position equated the possession of the bomb's components with the possession of a weapon and the introduction of a weapon.

But for Rabin, a weapon was not a weapon until it had been successfully tested, and conducting a test was one of the activities that defined or constituted introduction. The other act that constituted "introducing" nuclear weapons was "public acknowledgment." Without a test and official publicity, there was no introduction.[10] According to these criteria, Israel had fulfilled its pledge not to be the first country to introduce nuclear weapons into the region.

When Warnke heard this, as he told me decades later, he realized that Israel already had the bomb and that the battle to deny it to Israel had failed.[11] It would be up to the Nixon administration to decide how to handle a nuclear Israel. As it turned out, these two aspects of "introduction," testing and publicity, that Rabin invoked in his exchange with Warnke played a major role in the deal that Nixon made with Meir less than a year later.

A New Era

On January 20, 1969, Richard M. Nixon succeeded Lyndon B. Johnson as the thirty-seventh president of the United States. A month later, on February 26, 1969, Prime Minister Levi Eshkol died, and three weeks later, Golda Meir was sworn in as Israel's fourth prime minister. Both leaders faced important decisions concerning Israel's nuclear program and the NPT. In the United States, Nixon had to decide about the ratification of the NPT, and in Israel, Meir had to make fateful decisions about Israel's own long-term nuclear policies, including the NPT.

The NPT was a product of two Democratic administrations, which were committed to the proposition that the spread of nuclear weapons was bad for American interests and bad for the world. This position implied that the United States should not distinguish between "friendly" and "hostile" nuclear proliferation because any instance of proliferation was harmful to future international stability. For the Democrats, the best way to combat nuclear proliferation was to establish a nonproliferation norm through a strong international treaty.

Nixon's view of the NPT was more nuanced and different from that of his immediate predecessors. In general, Republicans tend to be suspicious of universalistic and multilateral schemes and organizations, and accordingly, the Nixon team initially was skeptical of the NPT's effectiveness and desirability. As early as his presidential campaign in 1968, Nixon criticized the NPT for not permitting the transfer of "defensive nuclear weapons," especially after the Soviet invasion of Czechoslovakia in 1968. Furthermore, Nixon publicly opposed ratification of the NPT as long as Soviet troops were stationed on Czech soil. By late November 1968, more than seventy nations had signed the treaty, but only a few had ratified it. The momentum for signing the NPT had slowed because of the Soviet invasion and the American decision to delay ratification.

Nixon's reluctance made the U.S. arms-control community anxious about the NPT's fate. Israeli leaders and diplomats, aware of Nixon's and Kissinger's views, were heartened. In his memoirs Rabin wrote that he recognized that a Republican administration would be more sympathetic to Israel's security needs than the Johnson administration had been.[12] According to Rabin, Kissinger assured him when they met in late December—after Kissinger had been named the new national security adviser—that the United States would be receptive to Israel's requests for weapons and "that the Republican administration would be more relaxed on the nuclear issue."[13]

Morton Halperin, who served on the National Security Council staff during the early Nixon administration, recalled arms-control professionals' anxiety over whether Nixon would support ratification of the NPT. He remembered the distress after he and his associate Spurgeon Keeny went to see Kissinger to lobby for its ratification, when Kissinger told them that any country with major security problems would try to get the bomb and that the United States should not interfere with it.[14]

As skeptical as Nixon and Kissinger were about the NPT, the new administration found it politically necessary to resubmit the treaty to Congress for ratification. In a public statement, Nixon expressed support for the NPT, saying that the United States would urge other nations, including Germany and France, to sign it. The same day, however, national security adviser Henry Kissinger circulated National Security Decision Memorandum (NSDM) 6 to the executive bureaucracy, which significantly qualified the administration's public support for the treaty. According to the NSDM, "there should be no efforts by the U.S. Government to pressure any other nation, particularly the Federal Republic of Germany, 'to follow suit' in signing and ratifying the

NPT."[15] Although the NSDM did not specify any country except Germany, there are good reasons to believe that both Nixon and Kissinger saw Israel as an exception as well.[16]

While Nixon and Kissinger may have been inclined by the time they took office to accommodate Israel's nuclear ambitions, they had to find ways to manage those senior civil servants, primarily from the State Department and the Pentagon, whose views differed from that of the White House. Ever since the United States had discovered the Dimona facility a decade earlier, American regional and arms-control experts believed that Israel should be prevented from acquiring nuclear weapons. Acknowledgment—let alone acceptance—of Israel as a new member of the nuclear club was antithetical to the culture and assumptions of that establishment.

Israel, however, did not advocate changing its declaratory nuclear status, even after it had acquired nuclear-weapons capability. When Prime Minister Eshkol died in February 1969, the Israeli government still had no overall vision of what its grand nuclear strategy should be. Israeli policymakers were even less certain how to convey their interests to the United States. Under Eshkol, Israel had become so good at concealment and deception, fending off American pressure while secretly continuing R&D efforts, that it had lost sight of its own long-term goals. Since 1965, Israel had pledged its adherence to the principle of the "nonintroduction" of nuclear weapons. But when it reached the threshold of nuclearization, it did not have a clear sense of how to make its new military position strategically beneficial, let alone how to make it public.

The rapid deterioration in Prime Minister Eshkol's health in the second half of 1968 exacerbated the situation. At a time when new and bold decisions had to be made, Eshkol was not in a position to lead in making them. It soon became apparent that without a decisive national actor at the cabinet level, decision making would be allowed to drift, creating a situation of opacity concerning Israel's intentions. On the ground, meanwhile, a new reality was forming, independent of Israel's political actions.

New Intelligence and Policy Dilemmas

When the Nixon administration took office, growing but circumstantial intelligence evidence indicated that Israel's nuclear capabilities were rapidly progressing, and it was apparent that the new president would soon have to decide whether and how to adjust to the new situation. Documents prepared between February and April 1969 by key players in the bureaucracy indicate their awareness of the problem. Most of the raw intelligence that came to the attention of the principals in the national security bureaucracy—President Nixon, national security adviser Kissinger, Secretary of Defense Melvin Laird, Secretary of State William Rogers, and Director of Central Intelligence Richard Helms—is still classified, but it is evident that these officials believed that Israel's nuclear situation had changed and that U.S. policy must address it. The question was how.

In early February 1969, Henry Owen, chair of the Policy Planning Staff at the State Department, wrote to Secretary Rogers that

> intelligence indicates that Israel is rapidly developing a capability to produce and deploy nuclear weapons, and to deliver them by surface to surface missile or a plane. Recognizing the adverse repercussions of the disclosure, the Israelis are likely to work on their nuclear program clandestinely till they are ready to decide whether to deploy the weapons.[17]

That same month, on February 27, Secretary of Defense Laird advised Rogers, Kissinger, and Helms that based on intelligence information, he also believed that Israel was "developing both nuclear weapons and strategic missiles at a rapid pace and may have both this year." The next month, on March 17, Laird wrote again to the same senior officials that since his last letter, he had received additional evidence of activity that "would enhance Israel's capability in developing nuclear weapons." (Laird was referring to the purchase of two powerful CDC 6400 computers.) Most significantly, he urged the three senior officials to meet within days and exchange views on the "possible introduction of nuclear weapons into the Middle East."[18]

In early April 1969, Joseph Sisco, assistant secretary of state for Near East and South Asian affairs, echoed Laird's intelligence assessment, but he was even more specific, as he saw little "doubt that the green light has been given to Israeli technicians to develop the capability to build a bomb at short notice." It was possible, Sisco speculated, that Israel would follow a "last wire" concept, "whereby all the components for a weapon are at hand, awaiting only final assembly and testing."[19]

The intelligence reports that led senior officials to these conclusions are still classified, but we know of the many telltale signs showing that Israel was on the brink of a nuclear-weapons capability. Among the known evidence was its purchase of huge quantities of uranium, such as the 1968 "Plumbat affair," involving the diversion to Israel of a large quantity of yellowcake (i.e., uranium oxide).[20] Also telling was information about nuclear-related aerial exercises, the development of the MD-620 missile, and the sites that the Israelis had prepared for them. Top officials like Helms and Laird were convinced of the significance of intelligence about the alleged diversion of highly enriched uranium (HEU) to Israel from the Nuclear Materials and Equipment Company (NUMEC) of Pennsylvania.[21] Nevertheless, the intelligence was still tentative, partial, and less than conclusive.

Whether Israel was weeks or even days or hours away from having fully assembled and deliverable nuclear weapons remained unclear, but the policy implications of either case alarmed senior officials. As Laird wrote in late March, these "developments were not in the United States' interests and should, if at all possible, be stopped."[22] Sisco was not sure when or how Israel would "choose to display a nuclear weapon," but he agreed on the danger: a nuclear-armed Israel would have "far reaching and even dangerous implications for the U.S."[23]

Sisco shared Laird's sense of urgency about the problem and its far-reaching consequences but differed somewhat about what could be done about it. Laird clearly wanted the United States to use both carrots and sticks to stop Israel from further nuclearization. But Sisco was more dubious—some would say realistic—about what the Nixon administration could or should do about it. He found it unlikely that imposed diplomatic solutions, such as a comprehensive Middle East peace settlement, would lead to denuclearization. Another possibility was direct pressure: if the United States told Israel in unequivocal terms that "if it actually embarks on the manufacture of nuclear weapons, it would cause a fundamental change in the U.S.-Israel relationship." But that would require open pressure and extraordinary domestic political controversy. "Half-way measures," such as using weapons deliveries "as leverage," would be "futile and probably counter-productive."[24]

NSSM 40

One of Henry Kissinger's first priorities when he came to the White House in January 1969 was to work with President Nixon to establish tighter White House control over the foreign policy decision-making machinery. The two brought with them to the White House views and assumptions that combined to create a decision-making system concentrated in the hands of the president and his advisers. Nixon loathed the Eastern Establishment, particularly the State Department's senior civil servants and foreign service officers. And Kissinger, in his academic writing, developed the argument that the State Department was inherently incapable of developing and guiding a meaningful and coherent foreign policy for the United States.[25]

For this purpose, Kissinger, with Nixon's blessing, used the National Security Council as an oversight mechanism to assert the White House's supremacy in making foreign policy decisions. As part of the drive toward centralization, Kissinger ordered the various agencies involved in U.S. foreign policy to provide him with NSSMs, or interagency background studies of all the important foreign policy problems, from Vietnam to arms control to issues of strategic balance. Kissinger often chaired interagency meetings of what was called the Senior Review Group (SRG), which oversaw the production of the NSSMs. Sometimes the interagency responses to NSSMs led to a formal presidential decision in the form of a national security decision memorandum (NSDM), but often they produced a "quiet" presidential decision without a bureaucratic paper trail. The story of NSSM 40 is a good example of Nixon's and Kissinger's efforts to impose their agenda on the Eastern Establishment's formation of foreign policy.

Our knowledge of NSSM 40 is still fragmentary and, on some points, even conjectural. It remains unclear what exactly prompted President Nixon and national security adviser Kissinger to initiate the NSSM 40 process, but we do know that it started on or about April 10, 1969. It appears, as the memos from Laird and Sisco indicate, that new intelligence evidence (as well as the memos) prompted a sense of urgency at the White House on the Israeli nuclear issue. The National Security Council (NSC) staff, particularly Harold Saunders and Morton Halperin, coordinated the production of intelligence assessments, policy options, and scenarios by those foreign policy agencies within the administration that supplied the principals with the background for their deliberations.[26]

NSSM 40 itself and all the subsequent documents and deliberations it generated were classified as "Top Secret/Nodis,"[27] so it was distributed to a very small group of senior officials at the NSC, State, Defense, and the CIA. Notably, neither the Arms Control and Disarmament Agency (ACDA), with its responsibility for global nuclear proliferation issues, nor the Atomic Energy Commission (AEC), the agency whose personnel conducted the visits at Dimona and produced nuclear intelligence, was involved in the NSSM 40 deliberations. The reason may have been that Nixon did not trust their chiefs, Gerard C. Smith and Glenn Seaborg, holdovers from previous administrations (Smith from Kennedy's and Seaborg's from Johnson's).[28]

The White House asserted complete control over the policy review process, probably the most comprehensive review ever conducted for an American president on the subject of the Israeli nuclear program. The stakes were high: how should the United States respond to the emergence of a nuclear Israel? Even today, the contents of NSSM 40 are still highly sensitive; it is the only NSSM from the Nixon era whose title is still classified, and it is the only NSSM that cannot be accessed on the Internet through the Nixon Presidential Library, which describes it as "fully classified."[29]

Sometime after initiating the NSSM 40 process, Kissinger formed and chaired the SRG in charge of reviewing and preparing policy options for the president. Its membership was restricted to a few senior officials: Elliot L. Richardson (undersecretary of state), David Packard (deputy secretary of defense), General Earle Wheeler (chairman of the Joint Chiefs of Staff), and Richard Helms (director of the CIA). Morton Halperin recalls that initially, Harold Saunders and he attended the meetings on NSSM 40 until Kissinger suggested that it did not look good to have on such a sensitive committee three representatives from the NSC staff, two of them Jews.[30]

The SRG met twice in June as part of the NSSM 40 process. The available minutes of the second meeting suggest that the bureaucracy was willing to exert some pressure to halt Israel's nuclear program, although Kissinger voiced his reservations. During this meeting, on June 26, 1969, Deputy Secretary of Defense David Packard suggested that if Israel "signs the NPT and gives appropriate assurances on not deploying nuclear weapons, we could live with a secret research and development program." The apparent inconsistency of having both a public commitment to the NPT and a very advanced secret R&D weapons program did not raise any opposition. Others in the SRG accepted the approach, to seek assurance that Israel would agree "not to carry forward any further development in the [nuclear] weapons field." That is, Washington should seek assurance that Israel would not "develop a nuclear explosive device."

How much pressure the United States should exert remained an open question. Kissinger favored avoiding "direct confrontation," whereas Elliot Richardson was willing to exert direct pressure if a probe to determine Israel's intentions showed that it probably would not supply such assurance. In such a circumstance, the United States could tell the Israelis that the deliveries of the F-4 fighter-bombers would "have to be reconsidered." The missile issue received less than full consensus. Some suggested pressing Israel to dismantle its missiles, and others proposed an agreement not to deploy missiles but to store them clandestinely (the CIA representative, General Cushman, pointed out that "Israel already had eleven missiles and would have between 25 to 30 by the end of 1970, ten, reportedly, with nuclear warheads").[31]

There was broad consensus within the SRG on the preferred tactics and the appropriate context in which to employ them: the two deputies, Richardson and Packard, should summon Ambassador Rabin and, with reference to Israel's request to advance the delivery of its Phantom jets to August 1969, make the point that while reviewing the record of the F-4 sale, "we want to tie up loose ends," that is, clarify the exact meaning of Israel's pledge not to be the first to introduce nuclear weapons to the region. There was much less agreement, though, as to how much, and how explicitly, the United States should use the Phantoms sale as leverage to obtain its objectives: *the issue is whether we are prepared to imply—and to carry out if necessary—the threat not to deliver the Phantoms if Israel does not comply with our request*" (italics in the original).[32]

Everyone on the SRG supported some form of pressure by linking the F-4s' delivery schedule, originally slated to begin delivery in September, to Tel Aviv's responsiveness to the nuclear issue. In contrast to the direct approach advocated by Packard and Richardson and the graduated approach suggested by Sisco, Kissinger apparently favored a "gentle approach to minimize confrontation" but nevertheless to "leave little doubt that we are prepared to withhold conventional weapons to achieve our objective."[33]

In addition was the issue of the Israeli missile program and specifically what the United States should ask Israel to do with its program. Here, too, various options were mentioned, including asking Israel to halt its missile production, to dismantle its production line, and not to deploy whatever missiles it manufactured. The SRG recommended that the United States ask Israel not to deploy its missiles. Finally was the question of who should do the job. The State and Defense departments recommended an approach by the deputies, Richardson and Packard, to highlight the gravity of the matter and to imply the possible threat. This also was Kissinger's recommendation.

The two meetings ended with a general agreement that the national security adviser, Kissinger, would prepare, based on the SRG's discussion and recommendations, an "issues" paper for President Nixon that would spell out the various policy alternatives. On July 4, Kissinger wrote a one-page memo to President Nixon, informing him that "two very good meetings" of the

SRG on the Israeli nuclear program had taken place and "we are now ready for you to consider the problem." Kissinger proposed a special meeting of a restricted group of the National Security Council—with Secretaries Rogers and Laird, General Wheeler and CIA Director Helms, and possibly Undersecretary Richardson—to be held on July 16. The president approved Kissinger's proposal.

Kissinger's Memo to President Nixon

It is unclear whether that NSC meeting actually took place on July 16, as the archival record is still incomplete, but sometime on or around July 19, Kissinger issued a six-page memo for President Nixon entitled "Israeli Nuclear Program."[34] It is possible that both the memo and the briefing book were passed along for the president to sign. The memo was the primary item of a larger briefing book under this title that contains five attachments (tabs A to E), of which the most prominent is an eighteen-page paper (tab A) by Kissinger himself entitled "Summary of the Situation and Issues."

Kissinger started the memo with a brief factual account of the nuclear and missile situation. Although the first sentence is partially redacted, we can safely presume from viewing other, but related, documents that it states roughly that the U.S. intelligence believes that Israel had reached a weapons-capability threshold. The attached paper revealed that the United States' intelligence community was somewhat uncertain and divided as to the exact status of the Israeli nuclear program, especially whether or not Israel actually had assembled the bombs, but there was consensus that Israel had acquired an operational weapons capability.[35] Following the redacted sentence, the memo stated that the SRG believes that "the introduction of nuclear weapons into the Near East would increase the dangers in an already dangerous situation and therefore not be in our interest." In regard to the missile situation, the memo noted that "Israel has 12 surface to surface delivered from France" and that Israel "has set up a production line and plans by the end of 1970 to have a total force of 24–30, ten of which are programmed to carry nuclear warheads."[36]

The memo then outlined the problem by reminding Nixon that during the negotiations of the Phantoms sale with the Johnson administration in November of the previous year, when Ambassador Rabin pledged that Israel "will not be the first to introduce nuclear weapons into the near East," it was understood that Rabin viewed that pledge as consistent with Israel's possession of nuclear weapons that were not tested, deployed, or made public. (Kissinger was inaccurate here: in the negotiations over the sale of the F-4s, Rabin referred to testing and publicity but not to deployment.)

The memo continued that the Phantom negotiations were finalized through an exchange of letters in which the American side stated that "physical possession" constituted "introduction"; hence the current situation (as understood and defined by the American side) could be a reason for the United States to cancel the contract. The United States now believed that Israel's nuclear program had crossed the American definition of what constituted "introduction," and moreover, the delivery of the Phantoms was fast approaching. The scheduled delivery was supposed to begin in September, and because some of the planes would be available in August, Israel had asked that their delivery start right away. The issue for the president was how to respond to the Israelis' request and to the Phantom deal as a whole, given that Israel had crossed the American definition of "introduction." In fact, the policy issue was larger than the Phantom deal. It was the United States' position on a nuclear Israel.

By describing the situation in this way, the memo spelled out the American interest by highlighting "one *important distinction*" (italics added) central to the SRG: the distinction between public and secret knowledge. While Israel's possession of nuclear weapons increased the danger in the Middle East, the SRG recognized the huge difference between a secret and a public possession of nuclear weapons. According to the memo, "Public knowledge is almost as dangerous as possession itself. What this means is that while we might ideally like to halt actual Israeli possession, what we really want at a minimum may be just to keep Israeli possession from becoming an established international fact."[37] This distinction formed the essence of the Nixon-Meir amimut deal.

The memo noted that the SRG broadly agreed that "as a minimum," Israel should sign the NPT, and it provides an interesting rationale why the United States should press Israel hard on signing the NPT. "This is not because signing will make any difference in Israel's actual nuclear program because Israel could produce warhead[s] clandestinely. Israel's signature would, however, give us a publicly feasible issue to raise with the Israeli government . . . it would also publicly commit Israel not to acquire nuclear weapons." The memo also asserted that the SRG agreed that the United States "should try to get from Israel a bilateral understanding on Israel's nuclear intentions" and that the reason is that "the NPT is not precise enough and . . . the Phantom aircraft are potential nuclear weapons carriers." But "opinion was divided on the nature of the assurances we should seek and on the tactics of seeking them."[38]

The group agreed on the minimal objectives: Israel should sign and ratify the NPT; Israel should put in writing its pledge not to be the first to introduce nuclear weapons to the region; and it should agree that "possession" means "introduction." Notably, Kissinger maintained, "For our own internal purposes, we would decide that we could tolerate Israeli activity short of assembly of a completed nuclear device." Also, Israel should give the United States written assurance that it would not produce and deploy the Jericho missiles or any other nuclear-capable missiles. But Kissinger added his own reservations:

> Israel is sovereign in this decision, and I do not see how we can ask it not to produce a weapon just because we do not see it as an effective weapon without nuclear warheads. We might persuade them not to deploy what they produce on the grounds that the rest of the world will believe that the missile must have nuclear warheads.[39]

The memo described four different postures that the U.S. policymakers could take: they could initiate discussions now (July / August) and try to reach an understanding before the delivery of the F-4s became an active issue in September; they could initiate discussions when Prime Minister Meir came to Washington in late September and, in the meantime, permit the delivery to start; they could initiate discussions in September and not let the delivery start until an understanding was reached; or they could not raise the issue at all. Kissinger recommended, in partial agreement with the SRG, that the United States adopt the first posture in a two-stage approach. First, the two deputies, Richardson (State) and Packard (Defense), would summon Rabin and inform him that, in connection with Israel's request to advance the delivery date of the F-4s to August, the United States needed "to tie up some loose ends" involving the contract. Specifically, the United States wanted a common interpretation of the "nonintroduction" pledge under which "introduction" was equivalent to "actual possession." Hence, a commitment to "nonintroduction" would be a commitment to "nonpossession." This would allow, the memo noted, the United States to press Israel on the NPT: If Israel accepted the American interpretation of "nonintroduction," it should have no difficulty signing the NPT. The deputies would also press Rabin on prohibiting the production and deployment of the Jericho missiles, noting that the missile issue had left doubts about Israel's nuclear pledges. No explicit linkage between those issues and the delivery of the fighter-bombers was proposed for the first meeting.

If Rabin's reaction was negative, Kissinger suggested, then he himself would summon Rabin, stress the president's personal concerns about the NPT, and confirm that Israel would not "introduce" (defined as "possess") or deploy missiles. This avenue would be preferable because it would allow the United States to "take stock before committing ourselves on withholding the Phantoms."

Kissinger framed this problem as damned if we do and damned if we don't. As the memo put it:

> Our problem is that Israel will not take us seriously on the nuclear issue unless they believe we are prepared to withhold something they very much need—the Phantoms or, even more, their whole military supply relationship with us. On the other hand, if we withhold the Phantoms and they make this fact public in the United States, enormous political pressure will be mounted on us. We will be in an indefensible position if we cannot state why we are withholding the planes. Yet if we explain our position publicly we will be the ones to make Israel's possession of nuclear weapons public with all the international consequences it entails.

Although the attached paper (tab A) is long, Kissinger wrote in the memo, "I believe you will want to read through it because this is a complex matter."[40]

The paper reveals further the problem's complex international and domestic considerations, which at times were contradictory, leaving the United States very little room to maneuver. Virtually every aspect of the situation—its factual and conceptual nature, the dangers involved, the formulation and ranking of the American objectives, their feasibility, and the best way to introduce them—was ambiguous.

On the question of "the choice between recording a judgment that Israel may have nuclear weapons and recording only a general judgment as to Israel's capability," Kissinger's paper states that that the advantage of recording a general judgment

> is that it permits us the freedom of acting as if we believe Israel is still short of assembling a weapon and of leaving to Israel the choice of

whether to hide what it has or dismantle it. It also retains our freedom to press Israel to sign the NPT and prevent the USSR from reacting.

The disadvantage is that it "underscores the immediacy of the problem if we are called on in the Congress, for instance, to justify our position."

The paper struggles with the question of whether the United States could actually prevent Israel from acquiring nuclear weapons or, more precisely, "Could we persuade Israel to freeze its nuclear weapons where it is?" Kissinger acknowledged "that it is impossible to deprive Israel of the option to put together as operational nuclear capability." The paper notes that the Israeli nuclear program is "very near fruition" and that Israel already may have some weapons, so it would be

> impossible politically for an Israeli Prime Minister to give up completely an advantage deemed vital and achieved at considerable cost. . . . We have no way of forcing Israel to destroy any nuclear devices or components it may now have—much less the design data or the technical knowledge in people's minds.

While the United States had to acknowledge that it would be impossible to persuade Israel to give up its nuclear program, it might be difficult, but not impossible, to persuade Israel to "freeze" its nuclear program, that is, to halt it as an operational capability, a posture that Kissinger believed might even be consistent with the NPT. Still, Kissinger pointed out that even if the United States could persuade Israel politically to freeze its program, this commitment would be unverifiable. "It is unrealistic to think that such an agreement would mean that Israel had actually stopped. We would have no way of assuring compliance. . . . This is one program on which the Israelis have persistently deceived us—and might even have stolen from us." In fact, Kissinger reasoned, the United States may even be better off not talking to Israel about where its program stands because "putting this in the record leaves us vulnerable to the charge of complicity."

> Saying that we want to keep Israel's possession of nuclear weapons from becoming an established international fact may come very close to describing what we really want in this case. Our interest is in preventing Israel's possession of nuclear weapons. But since we cannot—and may not want to try—control the state of Israel's nuclear program and since

Israel may already have nuclear weapons, the one objective we might achieve is to persuade them to keep what they have secret. This would meet our objective because the international implications of an Israeli program are not triggered until it becomes public knowledge.

. . . We may want to differentiate between our private understanding of what we want and what we ask the Israelis for: we may want to consider saying to ourselves that our aim is to keep Israel's possession of nuclear weapons from becoming public knowledge and to do what we can to stop further proliferation. But in talking to the Israelis and for the record . . . we may want to state our position as opposing Israel's "possession" of nuclear weapons.[41]

Another undated document, entitled "The Issues for Decision" and enclosed with Kissinger's memo (tab C), reveals even more about the United States' limited ability to control Israel. Tab C describes the various options in each presidential decision on the matter and includes Kissinger's own comments on and recommendations for each option. On the question of what the United States really wants Israel to do, the document concedes that a "freeze" is not a real option because "we do not know exactly what this would mean since we are not sure whether they have weapons now or not." In regard to persuading Israel "not [to] assemble completed nuclear devices," Kissinger noted that this might be the best statement "of what we should ask for . . . but it may be illusive" because it is unverifiable. So the United States was left with a minimal goal: getting Israel to sign the NPT and keeping its nuclear activities secret.

The documents also underscore the American dilemma in communicating with Israel on this delicate subject: the more the United States split hairs in its effort to demarcate the exact status of the Israeli nuclear program, by defining the exact meaning of "nuclear possession," the more the United States would expose itself in the future to charges of complicity: "For our own purposes, 'possession' means the availability of a device that could be exploded on a short notice, but we do not want to get into a debate over how many hours or days short of actual assembly a nation could be without possession."

Kissinger's declassified memo does not have Nixon's initials on the decision lines, but other evidence, and especially the record of a meeting with Ambassador Rabin on July 29, indicates that Nixon authorized the course of action it proposed.[42] Recently declassified documents, including the four-page detailed "talking points" memo that Sisco prepared for Richardson, indicate that Nixon approved nearly all Kissinger's recommendations following the work of the NSSM 40 Advisory Group, which thus became presidential decisions. Nixon's only decision that differed from the SRG's recommendations was using the sale of the F-4s as leverage. On this issue, Nixon adopted Kissinger's "graduated approach" that did not explicitly link the two issues. By mid-July Nixon had decided that he was "leery" of using the planes as leverage.[43] Both implicitly and explicitly, all subsequent documents related to the issue avoid recommending the use of pressure, that is, linking the delivery of the F-4s to a satisfactory Israeli response to the probe. Subsequent developments indicate that Nixon opposed any use of pressure.

Summoning Rabin

On July 29, 1969, the two deputies, David Packard of the Defense Department and Elliot Richardson of the State Department summoned Ambassador Yitzhak Rabin (who came along with two aides, Shlomo Argov and Moshe Raviv) to probe him about Israel's nuclear program and intentions.[44] Richardson started the meeting with a reference to former Assistant Secretary Paul Warnke's discussions with Rabin regarding "the introduction of nuclear weapons to the Middle East." Given the subsequent progress toward ratifying the NPT, Richardson continued, the United States now wanted to review the status of this issue with Israel. The exchange of letters between Rabin and Warnke in late November had not made it clear because both countries used different interpretations of what was meant by the "introduction of nuclear weapons."

Rabin interrupted, pointing out that these were two different issues. First was the nuclear weapons in the Middle East, and second was the NPT, and Warnke had not discussed the latter. Which, then, Rabin asked, "Was the subject of today's talk?" Richardson replied that the United States saw the two issues as inseparable, and because the NPT issue had moved forward since those discussions, the United States wanted to review the two issues together.

Then, according to the script produced by the NSSM 40 deliberations and authorized by President Nixon, Richardson read a long (twelve paragraphs) formal statement. It began by expressing "deep concern" about Israel's nuclear program, particularly "the possibility that nuclear weapons and . . . their delivery systems will be introduced into the Middle East," which would be not only a "tragedy for the Middle East but a direct threat to United States national security," as well as Israel's troubling delay in signing the NPT. "For these reasons, Israel's nuclear policy is a subject of great interest to us . . . transcends considerations of purely bilateral significance to our two nations." At this point, Richardson linked Israel's "nonintroduction" commitment to the NPT, asserting that with the advent of the NPT, "unilateral assurances are no longer sufficient in themselves to give confidence that Israel does not intend to manufacture nuclear weapons." He also noted that Israel's delay in signing the NPT troubled the United States

> because Israel is not just another state that for one reason or another is delaying its adherence to the Treaty . . . unlike most other states Israel has the technical capability to build nuclear weapons . . . because of this proximity to the nuclear weapons threshold, Israel's attitude towards the NPT is being closely watched . . . and we therefore attach utmost importance to Israel's early signature and ratification of the NPT.[45]

After reading his statement, Richardson posed three issues for Ambassador Rabin: (1) the status of Israel's deliberations on the NPT issue, (2) assurances that "nonintroduction" actually meant "nonpossession" of nuclear weapons, and (3) assurances about the production and deployment status of the Jericho missile (MD-620).

Rabin, surprised by Richardson's demands and without any new instructions from Jerusalem, had nothing new to tell Richardson and Packard, and could only repeat old formulas. In regard to the NPT, Rabin stated that the issue was still "under study" and that he was unauthorized to comment beyond this before the study was completed. On the "nonintroduction" assurance, Rabin noted "parenthetically" that the scope of the formula referred to Middle Eastern states, not to the major powers that had already introduced nuclear weapons.

Insofar as his response to Warnke was analytical and in the form of a question, it was not meant to be a factual statement or even an authoritative Israeli definition of "introduction." Rabin observed that "he personally had no knowledge about nuclear weapon" and that it was only in response to Warnke's own definition (i.e., possession) that he asked him whether an untested nuclear weapon would be considered an effective weapon. Rabin also asked whether "Warnke [would] consider a weapon which had not been advertised and proven to be a weapon that could be used?" Rabin pointed out again that "he was seeking to learn the U.S. interpretation, not to represent an Israeli position."

Rabin thus was very careful—as he had been during his exchange with Warnke—not to acknowledge that Israel had a nuclear-weapons program (but also not to deny it). To make this point even more explicit, Rabin reiterated that "he was not [in fact] accepting the U.S. assumption that Israel has the capability to build nuclear weapons. He could say neither that Israel was capable nor that it was not."[46] But in alluding to the U.S. arrangement to visit Dimona, Rabin reminded Packard and Richardson that the United States had a unique arrangement with Israel that did not exist with any of the United States' other allies and that allowed the United States "a close look at what Israel is doing in the nuclear field."[47]

In response, Richardson pointed out that the purpose of the meeting was not to rehash the Warnke-Rabin exchange but to remind Rabin that the question of "nonintroduction" was still loosely defined. The United States sought confirmation that Israel's understanding of the concept concurred with the American understanding that "nonintroduction" meant that "the physical possession and control of nuclear arms by a Middle Eastern power would be deemed to constitute the introduction of nuclear weapons." In other words, Richardson wanted Israel to agree that the "nonintroduction" of nuclear weapons meant "nonpossession."

Rabin listened but said nothing in response. When the discussion turned back to the question of the NPT, Richardson pointed out that the United States had been discussing this with the Germans and the Japanese and that the time had come to raise it with Israel as well. Rabin's answer referred to President Nixon's European tour in which Nixon had said that the United States would not twist any arms in regard to signing the NPT and expressed sympathy for the difficulties the Germans may have in signing it before their election. In turn, Richardson stated that he would not engage in "a semantic discussion" but that the United States had been discussing the matter with both the Germans and the Japanese and expected that both would sign. Rabin remained noncommittal: "he was not saying that Israel would not sign, but he could not say it would."[48]

Rabin reminded Richardson that the United States had only recently visited Dimona "and that everything seemed to be working as agreed." Richardson said only that he did not wish to record any complaints during their conversation, thereby hinting that the United States might have had some. But he did make the general point that "Dimona visits do not obviate our concern about nuclear weapons, missiles and the NPT." When Rabin repeated that Israel had given assurances of its nuclear intentions, Richardson responded that

> bluntly speaking, those assurances had been hedged. If "nonintroduction" means only that the weapons will not be tested and advertised, we are on a brink of a serious situation. If "introduction" is defined in the narrowest possible sense, meaning that all but minimal final steps will have been taken, then the situation is dangerous and potentially destabilizing.

The meeting ended with Richardson reiterating the "seriousness" with which the United States viewed the matter of nuclear weapons in the Middle East and Israel's signature on the NPT. Rabin promised in return to convey the message to Jerusalem but gave no deadline for a reply from Jerusalem. Richardson notified Secretary Rogers (who was in Asia), Kissinger, and Sisco that the first step of the NSSM 40 exercise had been completed. Ambassador Walworth Barbour in Tel Aviv, who apparently had not participated in the NSSM exercise, received a limited account of the meeting and was told only about Rabin's request to advance the delivery of the F-4s.[49]

On August 1, Richardson prepared a two-page, top-secret memo for President Nixon reporting in a straightforward manner on the substance of his conversation with Rabin. Interestingly, the memo stated that "were Israel to possess nuclear weapons, we would see this as a direct threat to the national security of the United States since it would add a new dimension of danger to the risk of U.S.-Soviet confrontation."[50] As it turned out, it is far from clear that President Nixon saw things that way. Richardson ended his memo saying that if Israel did not reply within a week or so, the United States should remind the ambassador that it was waiting for a reply.[51]

Nixon's decision not to link the NSSM 40 probe to the deliveries of the F-4s (scheduled to start on September 5) turned out to be critical to the fate of the entire exercise. Packard and Richardson had not had a "big stick" to support their rhetoric. That is, they were not authorized by the White House to invoke the F-4s as leverage as they had wished (except to imply a loose linkage by refusing Rabin's request for an earlier delivery). Several weeks earlier, Richardson had advised Packard that "we should not explicitly state the threat," and he may have hoped to use that in a follow-up meeting.[52] While Richardson and Packard believed that greater pressure could be used later, President Nixon disagreed.

Rabin did not respond to the three items, instead notifying Richardson in late August that he understood that the nuclear issue would be "on the agenda" for Prime Minister Meir's visit on September 25 and 26. In answer to Richardson's query regarding whether he had anything new to add to the July 29 exchange, Rabin said that Israel would probably postpone its decision on the NPT until after the Israeli election in the fall.

Despite Richardson's stated wish to submit a démarche to Israel after one week, Rabin did not respond, and the Israeli government apparently did not press him to do so. Indeed, when Richardson brought up the matter again a month later (August 28), Rabin had a new reason for a delay: Israel's upcoming elections made the nuclear question a "difficult subject for his government." It therefore became evident to Richardson that Prime Minister Golda Meir would have to address the issue herself when she visited President Nixon at the White House on September 25 and 26.[53]

Even though Richardson and Packard recommended pressuring the Israelis on their nuclear program, Nixon's inclinations undercut them. By late August, the State Department learned that President Nixon had ruled out linking the delivery of the F-4s to the nuclear issue, and his subsequent actions showed his lack of desire to press the Israelis on nuclear nonproliferation.[54] In retrospect, this bureaucratic exercise and the NSSM that led to it accomplished nothing. The bureaucratic process was only a means of bringing the final decision to the "two partners in power" in the White House, who were sharing a "co-presidency," as historian Robert Dallek described the relationship between the president and his national security adviser.[55]

The Nixon-Meir Nuclear Accord

The one element that is missing so far from the narrative is also the most important and intriguing: President Nixon's views on the subject. The recently available archival material covers fairly well what others in the administration thought about the problem of a nuclear Israel but tells us almost nothing about Nixon's own thoughts on the issue. All we know for certain is by way of omission: Nixon refused to link the nuclear issue with the delivery of the F-4s (but he did not intervene to accelerate it, either), and he apparently endorsed the Israeli suggestion to leave the issue for his meeting with the prime minister.

The drama reached its climax—when both the United States and Israel managed to create new ground rules to deal with Israel's nuclear capability—

in a one-on-one meeting between President Nixon and Prime Minister Meir at the While House on September 26, 1969. Both governments still regard as top secret almost the entire paper trail relating to this meeting, before and after. Nixon later told U.S. Ambassador to Israel Walworth Barbour that he personally dictated a record of the meeting, but if that record exists, it has not come to light.[56] Meir also dictated notes of the meeting, but likewise it is unclear where these notes are. As of this writing, it appears that both national archives may be missing the original minutes of the conversation.[57]

Nonetheless, most of the large briefing book that the State Department had prepared for the visit is available and sheds some light on what the bureaucrats knew and how they wanted to brief the president for the meeting. Before Meir's visit, the State Department produced a new intelligence assessment of Israel's nuclear program, implying that it was fast becoming too late to push the Israelis to accept the "nonpossession" of nuclear weapons as the meaning of "nonintroduction." Background papers prepared by the State Department for the meetings with Meir, with intelligence updates with clearance by all the relevant agencies, including the CIA, the Pentagon, and the Atomic Energy Commission (AEC), further reinforced the view that "Israel might very well now have a nuclear bomb." Surely "Israel already had the technical ability and material resources to produce weapons-grade plutonium for a number of weapons." If that was true, it meant that events had overtaken the NSSM 40 exercise, meaning that Israel most likely possessed nuclear weapons, a development that the bureaucracy had originally wanted to contain.[58]

According to the new intelligence reports, Israel also already possessed several prototypes of the MD 620 missile. Moreover, Israel soon would be able to test-fire the Jericho, its own, domestically produced, version of the French missile. The new intelligence reports included evidence that "several sites providing operational launch capabilities" already were complete, which meant that the demand that Israel neither deploy nor produce the Jericho also was already moot.[59]

For the State Department, a nuclear Israel remained incompatible with U.S. interests, not least because if it "were to become known as a nuclear power, the United States would, however unjustly, be held responsible in the eyes of the great majority of the world community." While the State Department continued to advise Nixon to press Meir for assurances that "Israel would not possess nuclear weapons, would sign the NPT, and would not deploy missiles," it is unknown whether he adopted that approach during his conversation with the prime minister or even whether he shared the State Department's sense of danger. He probably did not.[60]

During her official two-day state visit at the White House, on September 25 and 26, the Israeli leader had two meetings with President Nixon (also a state dinner for her on the eve of September 25). But it was in her second, private meeting with President Nixon on September 26—which included a walk on the White House lawn—that the nuclear accord was reached.[61] At the time of that meeting, national security adviser Kissinger had his own meeting with Rabin and Rogers. Nixon later briefed Kissinger on the discussion, including the "private understandings" that the two reached, even though, from Kissinger's own subsequent memo (to Nixon), it is unclear to what extent he was told all the details.[62] Other senior officials with the need to know never found out exactly what Nixon and Meir had agreed to.[63] We do have some clues, though.

In her memoirs, Golda Meir did not discuss the substance of her private conversation with Nixon, saying only that "I could not quote him then, and I will not quote him now." Yet we know that since the early 1960s, she always had thought that "Israel should tell the United States the truth [on the nuclear issue] and explain why." In his memoirs, Yitzhak Rabin says merely that the discussions between Nixon and Meir were highly sensitive and that their understandings were not written or formal.[64] Some of them pertained to issues of procedure and communication, such as setting up direct channels of communication between their offices, thereby bypassing their foreign policy bureaucracies. But the most sensitive and substantive part of their meeting concerned the nuclear issue.

For many years, the significance of the nuclear aspect of the Nixon-Meir meeting remained a well-kept secret. The first public indication that something important on the nuclear front happened during the meeting came fifteen years later. In a 1984 book entitled *The Unnatural Alliance*, British author James Adams provided a few tips. According to Adams's tale, said to be based on Meir's report to the Israeli cabinet upon her return, as the two leaders walked on the lawn Nixon asked her whether Israel had any "dangerous toys," explaining in response to Meir's wonder that he referred to atomic weapons. Meir replied, "We do," to which she thought Nixon "seemed impressed." As she left the meeting, Nixon cautioned her to "be careful." Adams ends his account by noting that "she wryly remarked to the Israeli cabinet: 'I was just lucky that he did not ask how many bombs.'"[65]

Adams describes the climax of the meeting, but he missed the broader context. Whatever Meir told Nixon was in the larger context of a political problem the two leaders had to resolve. It took another decade until Israeli journalist Aluf Benn revealed that an unprecedented bargain on the Israeli nuclear issue was struck in that meeting.[66] Benn was the first to report the parameters of the accord, but he, too, was not aware of the tale of NSSM 40 that preceded it.

By now, even without a formal written record of that private meeting, we have sufficient information to place the meeting in its larger historical context. Prime Minister Meir almost certainly confided in Nixon that Israel already was in possession of the bomb, with the bomb assembled or otherwise. She must have explained the reasons why, something she always argued Israel should do, and Nixon did not quarrel with her presentation. Almost certainly he was already aware, from his own sources, of Israel's nuclear status, and he surely understood the reasons for Israel's decisions. That would have meant that pressing Israel to reverse its actions and to sign the NPT made no sense. Also, the Americans' annual visits to Dimona made no sense once it became evident that Israel had acquired the bomb. The two leaders probably agreed to end that arrangement, an arrangement that belonged to another era and now was no longer beneficial to either side. President Nixon, who had accepted that America could not—and should not—exert pressure on Israel, received a firm commitment from the prime minister that Israel would not change its declaratory pledge not to be the first country to introduce nuclear weapons to the region. This request followed Kissinger's memo to Nixon from July. Years later Nixon told CNN's Larry King that he knew that Israel had the bomb but would not reveal his source.[67] Meir also, most likely, assured Nixon that Israel regarded nuclear weapons as a deterrent and as weapons of last resort.

Decades later, reliable American sources unofficially confirmed that during that 1969 meeting, Meir told Nixon that Israel already had nuclear weapons and pledged to keep them invisible, that is, untested and undeclared. In return, Nixon agreed to end the United States' annual visits to the nuclear reactor at Dimona and apparently agreed not to pressure Israel to sign the NPT.[68] This practical agreement between the leaders became the foundation of the secret bilateral understanding of the nuclear issue.

Subsequent memoranda from Kissinger to Nixon confirmed this by providing a sense of what Kissinger thought happened at the meeting. In those memoranda, Kissinger mentioned that the president had emphasized to the prime minister that "our primary concern was that the Israelis make no visible introduction of nuclear weapons or undertake a nuclear test program." This means that Nixon had effectively asked Meir to abide by Rabin's interpretation that the "introduction of nuclear weapons" would mean a nuclear test or a formal declaration. Thus, Israel would be committed to keeping its nuclear activities secret. While Meir may have told Nixon informally that Israel was not likely to sign the NPT, for the record she told Nixon that the NPT issue would not be settled until after the elections and that missiles would not be deployed "for at least three years."[69]

Those understandings allowed Israel to maintain its secret nuclear program and allowed the United States to look the other way. Specifically, three well-defined understandings, based on the agreement between the leaders, became the foundation on which the Israeli bargain with the bomb rested. Those understandings constitute the constraints on its nuclear program that Israel accepted: no test, no declaration and publicity, no joining the NPT, and possibly a related understanding about what the commitment to "nonintroduction" meant operationally (i.e., keeping the weapons' cores unassembled and under the custodianship of the prime minister). According to one anonymous American source, these understandings were subsequently formalized in a secret exchange of letters between Kissinger and Rabin.

As noted earlier, it appears that no archival record exists that reveals what was agreed in the meeting or, more generally, what Nixon thought about the issue of a nuclear Israel. This is not surprising. Nonetheless, Nixon's opinions on the subject were not a mystery, either. Seymour M. Hersh summarized Nixon's (and Kissinger's) views in the following way: "Richard Nixon and Henry Kissinger approached inauguration day on January 20, 1969 convinced that Israel's nuclear ambitions were justified and understandable. Once in office, they went a step further: they endorsed Israel's nuclear ambitions."[70]

Hersh's account may be too sweeping, but it is likely close to the truth. In his *Nixon and Kissinger: Partners in Power*, historian Robert Dallek analyzes Nixon's and Meir's nuclear understanding primarily in the context of American domestic politics, but I would add that geopolitical and strategic considerations were equally important to Nixon's endorsement of a nuclear-capable Israel. Only two months earlier, in late July 1969, Nixon articulated his strategy in a speech he gave in Guam (which became known as the Nixon Doctrine or the Guam Doctrine). In that speech he emphasized that regional allies of the United States would be asked to, or would be allowed to, strengthen themselves militarily so that they could help the United States contain the Soviet Union even while the United States was reeling from the effects of the Vietnam War, effects that included rising domestic opposition to burdensome U.S. commitments abroad. The word often used at the time was *retrenchment*: Because the United States was lowering its global posture— or "retrenching"—as a result of Vietnam, other allies had to step in and pick up the slack. In this light, Kissinger's and Nixon's unwillingness to pressure Israel on the nuclear issue makes perfect sense.[71]

The Aftermath

Nixon's and Meir's understandings were secret and unwritten and tentative as to their full operational and diplomatic meanings. The senior American foreign policy bureaucracy was never properly told about them.

A week or so after the meeting between the leaders, Ambassador Rabin delivered to Kissinger the long-awaited replies to all three questions that Richardson had posed to him on July 29 and asked him whether they were satisfactory in light of the discussion between Meir and Nixon. On October 7, 1969, Kissinger reported in an internal memo on those questions and answers:

1. Q: Would the Israelis assure us that they would not "possess" nuclear weapons? A: Israel will not become a nuclear power.
2. Q: Would they be willing to affirm that they would not deploy strategic missiles? A: They will not deploy strategic missiles until at least 1972.
3. Q: Would they be willing to sign the NPT? A: The NPT will be considered by the new government.[72]

The next day Kissinger sent a six-page memo to President Nixon analyzing the meaning and the policy implications of Rabin's replies and proposing recommendations for the United States' reaction. On the memo's cover page, Kissinger wrote that the paper "is much longer than the one page analysis I had promised you but this issue is so sensitive and has been held to such a limited group of individuals that I believe that it is essential that you be presented with all nuances of the problem."[73] This cover note suggests that even Kissinger may have not been privy to all that was discussed and agreed between the two leaders.[74]

In regard to Rabin's first reply, Kissinger admitted that he did not understand why Israel preferred to define its assurance in terms of not becoming a nuclear power while leaving the issue of nuclear possession untouched. "When I asked [Rabin] how a nation could become a 'nuclear power' without 'possessing' nuclear weapons, he simply said they 'prefer' their formulation." Kissinger recommended that as vague as Rabin's formulation was, Nixon should accept it as a private Israeli commitment to language derived from the NPT because it sounded like an assurance roughly corresponding to article II of the treaty. Nixon approved that recommendation as well as the next, on the missile issue. Kissinger would tell the Israelis that their proposal was acceptable, provided they agreed to further discussion of the subject with the United States in 1971 or before any decision to deploy the Jericho.

On the NPT issue, Kissinger showed his uncertainty about the exact content of the Nixon-Meir talks by observing that "Mrs. Meir may have made some commitment to you privately that would give this statement significance."[75] His recommendation, which Nixon approved, was to tell Rabin that the president wished Meir to make "a vigorous personal effort to win cabinet approval" of the NPT. Kissinger finally suggested that on this complex issue, Nixon should take the "opportunity for second thoughts" and that this should be made known to the Israelis. Interestingly, Nixon left this recommendation unmarked.

After Kissinger communicated with Rabin, Rabin held a formal meeting with Richardson on October 15 in which he officially replied to the questions that he had been asked on July 29.[76] Rabin's formal answers substantially repeated what he told Kissinger, except that in regard to "introduction," Rabin asserted that it meant the "transformation from a non-nuclear-weapons country into a nuclear-weapons country." The strong language that Packard and Richardson had used in July apparently had had no impact, as Israel was rejecting any language that alluded to "possession."

When Kissinger briefed Nixon on the meeting, he pointed out that Rabin's language defining "nonintroduction" paralleled the NPT's distinction between nuclear-weapons states and nonnuclear-weapons states. This would allow Washington to be on record as if it had Israel's assurances that it would remain a nonnuclear-weapons state as defined in the NPT. Such assurances "would put on our internal record a rationale for standing down," that is, effectively ending the debate and discussion within the bureaucracy on pressuring Israel. Washington, Kissinger advised, had pushed the Israeli nuclear issue "as far as we constructively can," at least until a new government was formed. For Kissinger, the debate was, for all practical purposes, over.[77]

While the members of the SRG unanimously agreed that "at the minimum" the United States must pressure Israel on the matter of the NPT, in reality the NPT issue already was dead after the Nixon-Meir meeting. Formally, however, Kissinger still waited for Tel Aviv's formal response to the U.S. query on the treaty. That reply came on February 23, 1970, when Ambassador Rabin went alone to see Kissinger at his office. He told him that Richardson had just summoned him in regard to the NPT, and he wanted the president to know that in light of the conversation Nixon had had with Meir in September, "Israel has no intention to sign the NPT." Rabin, Kissinger wrote, "wanted also to make sure there was no misapprehension at the White House about Israel's current intentions." He also sought assurance that Washington would not link the NPT to arms sales to Israel. After summarizing what Rabin had said about other, unrelated issues, Kissinger ended his memo with one sentence: "I was non-committal and told him that his message would be transmitted to the President."[78]

That was it. After that tense and protracted effort to get Israel to sign the NPT—President Lyndon Johnson's numerous personal pleas to Prime Minister Levi Eshkol, the tough lecture that Secretary Dean Rusk gave to Deputy Prime Minister Yigal Allon and Foreign Minister Abba Eban in October 1968, the tough exchange Assistant Secretary Paul Warnke had had with Ambassador Yitzhak Rabin in November 1968 during the F-4 negotiations, the admonishment that Rabin had endured from the two deputy secretaries (Richardson and Packard) in July 1969, and finally, in October, Kissinger's request that Meir make a vigorous personal effort to win cabinet approval—Kissinger had nothing to say to Rabin, not even a statement of regret for the record, when he was told that Israel had no interest in signing the NPT. Kissinger simply promised to pass along Rabin's message to the president. The long effort to stop Israel's nuclear program through diplomacy and the NPT was finally over.

Ever since then, under the terms of the new understandings, the NPT has no longer been an active item on the U.S.-Israel bilateral agenda. This does not mean that America has dropped the issue of NPT universality as a policy objective but that for all practical purposes, Israel has received an exemption. Various diplomatic verbal conventions have been devised to minimize the tension between Israel's exceptionality and American support of universality.

The Lasting Legacy: A Unique Binational Bargain

That we still know so little today about the Nixon-Meir nuclear deal and that
the deal is still not officially acknowledged is not surprising. Both nations are
still committed to secrecy on this matter. Israel's nuclear ambitions were a
thorny issue for the Nixon administration, but it had to deal with it, as Israel was crossing the nuclear threshold. Unlike President Kennedy, Nixon had
little faith in the universality of nuclear nonproliferation as a matter of principle; he distinguished between friends and foes. Small Israel was indeed a
most difficult proliferation case. How could President Nixon (with Kissinger
on his side) deny Israel, a U.S. ally, the ultimate means for its survival given its
unique history? He could not.

Yet even as Nixon enabled Israel to flout the NPT, as a bureaucratic process
NSSM 40 allowed him to establish a "defensible record" for the administration.[79] In accordance with his typical modus operandi, Kissinger used NSSM 40
as a way to maintain bureaucratic control over key administration officials
who had concluded that something needed to be done about Israel's nuclear
problem. Whatever top administration officials like Secretary of State William Rogers or Secretary of Defense Melvin Laird knew or thought about the
secret deal—and apparently they knew initially nothing or very little about
it—they and those below them in the NSSM 40 group still believed that the
Israeli nuclear case was not completely lost and that some lines could and
must be drawn in the sand. For example, there is evidence that as late as June
1970, State and Defense officials participating in the NSSM 40 group were still
pushing for another inspection visit to Dimona, which, of course, was made
irrelevant by the Nixon-Meir understandings. In Laird's recollection, Kissinger would not let the SRG take up the issue of visiting Dimona.[80] The great
irony is that just a few weeks later, on July 17, 1970, the *New York Times* ran a
front-page story informing the public that for a year the "U.S. Assumes the
Israelis Have A-Bomb or Its Parts." Overnight, the world's most closely held
secret was turned into its worst-kept secret.

Politically, Nixon and Meir's "private nuclear understandings" allowed
both leaders to continue publicly with their old policies without being forced
to publicly acknowledge the new reality. On the most sensitive issue—the reality of the Israeli bomb—both leaders could be honest with each other, but
with everybody else they needed to maintain a certain degree of deniability
and ambiguity. As long as Israel kept the bomb in the basement, the United

States could live with Israel's "nonintroduction" pledge. Even in a classified congressional hearing as late as 1975, the State Department still refused to agree with CIA claims that Israel actually had nuclear weapons.[81]

In retrospect, the secret Nixon-Meir nuclear understandings became the foundation for a remarkable bilateral bargain, accompanied by a strict but tacit code of behavior to which both nations have closely adhered. The United States ended the inspection visits to Dimona, which were an expression of Kennedy's determination to actively force Israel to halt its nuclear development. This objective was no longer U.S. policy. Instead, the new amimut bargain was established, dependent on a "don't ask, don't tell" stance. The details of the new nuclear reality became off-limits even within the intimate confines of U.S.-Israel relations, as long as both countries adhered to their tacit understanding.

In Israel, the accord between Nixon and Meir is recognized as Meir's greatest strategic achievement. Israelis understand the bargain as an American pledge to shield the Israeli nuclear program. In return for this amimut, the United States gave Israel political cover in such forums as the IAEA and NPT review conferences. In the United States, however, the legacy of the secret accord is somewhat less clear-cut. When Jimmy Carter assumed the U.S. presidency in 1977, Israel was so concerned that the accord might not reach the new president that it asked Kissinger to personally brief him.[82] Since then, both Democratic and Republican administrations have accepted that Israel is, and should be, a special case for the United States' nonproliferation policy and that Israel's nuclear opacity is an American interest as well. At the same time, however, successive U.S. administrations have struggled to balance (and conceal) the incongruity between the United States' commitment to the NPT and upholding Israel's nuclear deterrent. While Republicans have generally cared more about Israel's deterrent, Democrats have been more willing to endorse the NPT. The United States and Israel recognize that Israel's nuclear issue is an existential matter that ideally should be set apart from all other bilateral political issues, especially the Israeli-Palestinian conflict. At the same time, they also recognize that treating Israel as an exceptional nuclear case is part of the "special relationship" between the United States and Israel.

Given the extreme secrecy and sensitivity of the Nixon-Meir nuclear accord, its quiet reaffirmation has become nearly a tradition in the first meeting between the Israeli prime minister and the American president.[83] In 1998, in the wake of President Bill Clinton's pressure on Israel regarding the fissile materials cutoff treaty (FMCT) in the Conference on Disarmament, Prime

Minister Benjamin Netanyahu urged the updating and formalizing of the old Nixon-Meir accord with a new presidential commitment. According to American and Israeli sources, as part (perhaps even as a condition) of the Wye River agreement in October 1998, Netanyahu asked for and received a signed secret letter from President Clinton. In this letter, Clinton committed to being sympathetic to Israel's preservation of its own "strategic deterrent capabilities"—a code word for Israel's nuclear weapons—and assured the Israeli prime minister that Israel would be consulted ahead of future U.S. arms-control initiatives relevant to Israel's strategic interests.[84] Netanyahu was concerned that the Clinton administration's push to negotiate the FMCT would ultimately create pressure on Israel to limit its nuclear-weapons program or, at least, to expose it more publicly. Clinton's letter was viewed as a reassurance of the Nixon-Meir accord's validity. A year later President Clinton signed an almost identical letter to Prime Minister Ehud Barak.[85]

By November 2008, as departing President George W. Bush met for a last meeting with departing Israeli Prime Minister Ehud Olmert at the White House, they reaffirmed the old Nixon-Meir accord once again. Olmert reportedly asked that the Bush White House pass along to President Barack Obama the updated version of the old Nixon-Meir nuclear understandings. It was important to the Israelis that the new president learn directly from his predecessor the unique and (largely) unwritten nature of American commitment to Israel's bargain with nuclear weapons.[86]

Chapter Two
The Case for Amimut

The fundamental question that nations face with regard to nuclear weapons is whether or not their possession would serve or harm the nation's national security.

From the nuclear-resolve perspective, the bomb is the most powerful deterrent available for a state. This is why the five great powers decided to acquire nuclear weapons during the early cold war. Their leaders thought that the acquisition of nuclear weapons would maximize their security and would confer other political benefits, such as prestige at home and abroad. For them, being a great power meant possessing the bomb. The ideal situation for any nation would be being the sole possessor of nuclear weapons, because then it would be completely safe and might even be able to aspire to hegemony. But if it is impossible for only one nation to have nuclear weapons, then the fallback position of realists (and also of some nonrealists) is that it is better to have nuclear weapons in the hands of a few great powers. This has two benefits: it reduces the number of wars among the great powers themselves and it also prevents or slows proliferation because these nuclear-armed powers can offer nuclear guarantees to their client states, persuading them not to develop their own nuclear weapons, thus preventing proliferation.

From the nuclear-caution perspective, however, the acquisition of nuclear weapons generates the risk of spreading nuclear weapons, thereby increasing the risk that nuclear weapons would be used. Nuclear weapons are existential threats to all nations. It is therefore in each nation's interest to ensure that there are no nuclear weapons, anywhere. These two perspectives resemble the academic debate between supporters and opponents of proliferation.[1]

The deal that Prime Minister Golda Meir and President Richard Nixon made in September 1969 proved fateful for Israel's handling of its nuclear dilemma. The Nixon-Meir agreement allowed Israel to finesse the dilemma it faced: it could "go nuclear" and, at the same time, exercise nuclear caution by "not introducing" nuclear weapons. Furthermore, amimut was a way of masking the contradictions inherent in this solution. By tolerating the Israeli bomb as long as it remained invisible (i.e., undeclared and untested), the United States effectively allowed Israel to enjoy the best of all possible worlds, resolve and caution.

The nuclear dilemma in Israel was acute, but the solution it has fashioned has become, over time, extraordinary. Because of the solution's "schizophrenic" nature, Israel has tried to enjoy the benefits of both nuclear resolve and nuclear caution and has refused to make a clear-cut choice of one or the other. Amimut is the outcome of this schizophrenic compromise.[2]

Israel has established a unique style of proliferation and a code of nuclear conduct that set it apart from other nuclear-weapons states. The result has been Israel's tacit national and international bargain with the bomb.

This chapter makes the strongest possible case for the amimut bargain. Amimut was the only way in which Israel could have addressed the nuclear issue, and it was also the only policy through which first the United States and gradually most of the rest of the world could accept Israel as a nuclear-armed state.

Nuclear Resolve

Israel's nuclear resolve was inspired by Israel's founding father, David Ben-Gurion. Influenced by the Holocaust, Ben-Gurion worried about Israel's long-term survival. His fear is derived from a sober, realistic view of the Arab-Israeli conflict. The basic tenets of Ben-Gurion's outlook, formed after the 1948 war, can be summarized as follows:[3]

A *deep conflict*. The Arab-Israeli conflict runs deep, as it is an existential conflict about land and the right to land, and it is one not amenable to conventional diplomatic settlement. Another round of Arab-Israeli hostilities was likely.

A *peaceful settlement unlikely anytime soon*. The Arabs would have difficulty reconciling themselves to and accepting the outcome of the 1948 war (and the 1949 cease-fire lines that came with it) as final and lasting. But only when the Arabs are convinced that the post-1948 reality cannot be changed by force, and that no military option is available to them to reverse that political reality, will they accept the post-1948 political outcome as final and lasting. Ben-Gurion knew this was not likely anytime soon.

The lesson from the Holocaust. For Ben-Gurion, the lesson from the Holocaust was that a small Jewish state without a formal alliance with an outside world power would have to create its own existential insurance policy. In his correspondence with President John F. Kennedy and other world leaders, Ben-Gurion argued that another holocaust could happen if Israel became vulnerable to such a threat.

Fear of a pan-Arab war coalition. Based on his understanding of demography and geography, Ben-Gurion believed that over time, the Israel Defense Forces (IDF) would have great difficulty deterring a pan-Arab war coalition through conventional means.

A need for unconventional deterrence. Given the geopolitical asymmetries of the Arab-Israeli conflict, Ben-Gurion believed Israel would not be able to compete in a conventional arms race with the Arabs. In the long run, conventional weapons would not be sufficient to give the Israelis a military victory or even a deterrent edge.

The "brain" factor. Only reliance on science and technology would allow Israel to compensate for its geopolitical disadvantages and overcome its inferiority in manpower, land, and resources.

This strategic outlook is crucial to explaining why Ben-Gurion responded so decisively and so early to Israel's nuclear dilemma.[4] For a small nation born from the ashes of the Holocaust, surrounded by neighbors devoted to its destruction, and without a security alliance with any world power, the rationale for pursuing the bomb was compelling.[5]

Ben-Gurion was pessimistic about Israel's long-term conventional capabilities vis-à-vis the Arabs, but he was optimistic about his country's technological capabilities. As Shimon Peres, his chief executive officer of the nuclear project in its formative years, put it many years later, "Ben-Gurion believed that Science could compensate us for what Nature has denied us."[6] Indeed, these words could be used to sum up Israel's nuclear project.

Ben-Gurion's outlook was anchored to the historical reality of the Israel of his time. That reality, however, no longer exists. A half a century later, we live in a different world with a different Middle East and a different Israel. Most contemporary Israelis, however, still see their nation's existential predicament somewhat as Ben-Gurion saw it. As long as the Palestinian-Israeli conflict— the core of the Arab-Israeli conflict—remains unresolved, the larger conflict built on it will last. And the Palestinian-Israeli conflict still appears unresolved to most Israelis. Accordingly, despite the "cold" peace with Egypt and Jordan, most Israelis still view their nation as an island in a hostile sea, and the rise of nuclear and implacably hostile Iran reinforces this outlook.

After more than half a century, the impact of the Holocaust on the Israeli psyche remains as powerful as ever. The Holocaust was a definitive experience in Jewish history, and for many Jews and non-Jews alike, it is the strongest justification for Israel's existence as a Jewish state. Israel's commitment to the promise "never again" is stronger now than ever before.[7]

Although the formation of a pan-Arab conventional-war coalition "to eliminate the Zionist entity" may no longer be an issue, it has been replaced by renewed threats to "wipe Israel off the map." In numerous public statements in recent years, Iran's President Mahmoud Ahmadinejad denied the Holocaust, questioned the legitimacy of Israel as a state, and predicted that it "will be wiped off the map" or from history.[8] Six decades after the Holocaust and after the founding of the state of Israel, Israelis are as beset by existential anxiety about their place in the world as they were during the Ben-Gurion era. Consequently, many Israelis today view Ben Gurion's nuclear initiative— his decision to embark on Israel's nuclear weapons project—as the best decision that any Israeli prime minister has ever made.[9]

Nuclear Caution

Israel's nuclear posture is constricted by a countervailing perspective that calls for nuclear caution and restraint. Just as the Holocaust is a key to understanding Israel's nuclear resolve—Israelis believe that their country's capability to inflict the horror of Hiroshima on its enemies will deter another Auschwitz—Hiroshima also is a strong argument *against* the introduction of nuclear weapons. Israel's geopolitical vulnerabilities mean that if Israel itself were to suffer a Hiroshima-like attack, it could mean holocaust-like consequences for Israel's population. For Israel to be responsible for another Auschwitz would be unthinkable.

Even when Israel was establishing a regional nuclear monopoly, it was always aware that its monopoly could eventually be lost and turn into parity. Under nuclear parity, small Israel would be many times more vulnerable than its Arab neighbors to the destructive effects of nuclear weapons. To wit, a recent assessment, based on standard U.S. calculations of the effects of nuclear weapons, found that one Hiroshima-type bomb (about 15 to 20 kilotons) dropped on the port of Jaffa (the southern side of Tel Aviv) would cause about a quarter million deaths and about half a million wounded, out of an urban population of about million and a half.[10] A more advanced fission bomb or a thermonuclear bomb would greatly increase the number of casualties. The existential security achieved by nuclear weapons could thus be reversed by the acquisition of a nuclear-weapons capacity by Iran or any other Middle Eastern state hostile to Israel. The inescapable conclusion therefore is that it is in Israel's interest to make sure that nuclear weapons are not introduced into the Middle East.[11]

This argument was articulated for the first time in the early 1960s, soon after the nuclear project had become known, by the leaders of the Achdut Ha'avodah Party, Israel Galili and Yigal Allon, as well as by a small group of antinuclear Israeli scientists and intellectuals. Their basic argument was that if Israel were to initiate a nuclear-weapons project, it would inevitably lead to similar projects on the Arab side, which would make Israel's security dramatically worse. Once the Arab-Israeli conflict had been elevated to the nuclear level, Israel's security predicament would quickly worsen. The fundamental asymmetries that pushed Israel toward the bomb would hurt it even more in a situation of nuclear parity. Given Israel's limited size, population, and resources, a situation of mutual nuclear deterrence would tend to be less stable and more dangerous than the nuclear balance of terror among the superpowers during the cold war. That is, mutual nuclear deterrence would work to Israel's disadvantage. Hence, the argument went, Israel's nuclear program embodied the seeds of its own futility. Its nuclear ambitions were self-defeating. Because its nuclear monopoly could not last, and mutual nuclear deterrence would be destabilizing, Israel's true interest was a Middle East free from nuclear weapons.

Various technological and financial arguments against the nuclear project have been forgotten over time, as they have proved to be more manageable than initially feared. The strategic argument, however, has survived, its relevance lying in the recognition that Israel's regional nuclear monopoly is fragile and temporary. Accordingly, Israel's true interest lies in nuclear disarmament, not nuclear armament.

The antinuclear campaign never gathered enough momentum to halt Israel's nuclear resolve. By the late 1960s Israel "quietly" crossed the nuclear threshold, and the small antinuclear movement faded from the Israeli public scene. After the 1967 war, Israel's political agenda began to change dramatically, and no one had an interest in campaigning against nuclear weapons any more. Egypt was no longer a major factor and the Nixon-Meir deal had resolved the NPT issue.

Even though the antinuclear movement had dissipated, the impulse for nuclear caution and its underlying argument did not disappear. Nuclear caution continued to influence both Israel's diplomacy and its nuclear posture, profoundly shaping how Israel has dealt with its nuclear monopoly.

Amimut

Instead of choosing between resolve (proliferation) and caution (nonproliferation), Israel has adopted a posture that incorporates both. This synthesis is Israel's long-standing policy of nuclear opacity.

Today, amimut is surrounded by an aura of inevitability, but this was not always the case. Ben-Gurion's resolve was apparent in his decision to build a nuclear infrastructure dedicated to producing weapons, but at the same time he steadfastly refused to allow Israel to adopt an open nuclear strategy (as Shimon Peres had advocated). Because his bold nuclear decisions involved such a huge gamble, nobody could have predicted whether the nuclear project would succeed and what the consequences of failure would be. Although these uncertainties did not deter him, they did determine the caution with which he pursued his vision. In turn, this caution determined Ben-Gurion's political commitments, especially those with the United States, and balanced his resolve that Israel become a nuclear-weapons power. Over time, this caution evolved into a specific code of conduct. Ben-Gurion's modus operandi served as a model for Israel's later nuclear ambivalence and culture of amimut.

Ben-Gurion's successor, Prime Minister Levi Eshkol, deepened this dual legacy. In his actions, Eshkol intensified the tension between (technological) resolve and (political) caution. On the caution side, Eshkol, as Ben-Gurion had, seemed to capitulate to President John F. Kennedy's demands. Although the U.S. administration understood his reply to Kennedy's letters as Israel's commitment not to acquire nuclear weapons, in reality he never abandoned Ben-Gurion's commitment to Israel's becoming a nuclear power. Under his watch, while American scientists visited Dimona, the infrastructure was completed and Israel reached the nuclear threshold. Eshkol generally avoided intervening in the project's work, but he made one important exception: he explicitly prohibited a full-yield test. Eshkol thus completed the nuclear-weapons infrastructure but left the project's long-term objectives undefined and undecided.

When Eshkol died in office in February 1969, Israel already was an emerging nuclear-weapons state. Yigal Allon, then the acting prime minister, still was hesitant about making a political decision about the NPT. Ideally, Israel would have liked to join the NPT as a nuclear-weapons state, but since this option was closed, Israel found itself in a predicament: It was a state in favor of an effective NPT as long as Israel itself was not bound by the treaty's prohibitions. Israel's reason was straightforward but could not be openly stated: Israel had acquired the bomb with great pain and effort, and as long as it faced existential threats, it was not willing to relinquish it. Israel wanted an effective NPT to deny proliferation to others but was not willing to give up the fruits of its own nuclear acquisition. This stance remains the essence of Israel's position to this day.[12]

The 1969 nuclear deal was meant to create a special code of restrained conduct that would conceal the built-in tension between resolve and caution. But it took at least a decade until this initially fragile deal became established firmly enough on both sides to become the foundation of Israel's long-term nuclear policy. This tension resurfaced during the 1973 Yom Kippur War and its aftermath. In retrospect, that war was the most challenging test of amimut. Although I discuss the 1973 war in chapter 3, I should note here that the Yom Kippur War—the most traumatic military action in Israel's history—almost shattered the veil of amimut. Amimut was saved—but just barely—by Prime Minister Golda Meir with the support of Ministers Yigal Allon and Israel Galili and her chief in charge of the nuclear establishment, Shalheveth Freier.

The Yom Kippur War ended in a manner that kept the 1969 Nixon-Meir understandings intact. Owing to the nerves, the wisdom, and the serenity of Golda Meir, the Israeli bomb remained in the basement. In return, Israel was rewarded with an immediate resupply of conventional weapons from the United States to keep a nuclear Israel from being cornered militarily.

Although amimut survived the 1973 war, it was not assured a long-term future. The 1969 Nixon-Meir deal had been informal, secretive, and fragile,[13] and after the Yom Kippur War, Israel was traumatized and the amimut deal was under pressure. Strong voices, inside and outside the government, were arguing that to prevent a similar surprise in the future, Israel must rely more explicitly on its nuclear option. In plain language, that meant Israel should disclose its possession of the bomb.[14]

This did not happen. Those suggestions were deliberated but ultimately were rejected by the governments of both Yitzhak Rabin and Menachem Begin. Israel's commitment to restraint was honored. Israel adopted once again a compromise similar to the way Ben-Gurion had handled the nuclear issue more than a decade earlier. Under Rabin's first term as prime minister (with Shimon Peres serving as minister of defense), the synthesis of technical resolve and political caution was renewed. The man who, as Israel's ambassador to the United States, had helped fashion the Nixon-Meir deal had become a national leader responsible for deepening Israel's commitment to amimut.

Against the background of strategic uncertainty that dominated Rabin's first term as prime minister (1974–1977), in which both peace and war seemed possible, Israel decided to hedge its nuclear position. On the side of nuclear resolve, Israel strengthened its nuclear commitment, advancing in both its nuclear capabilities and means of delivery, as well as setting up a robust command-and-control system. On the side of political caution, Israel did not change an iota in the public and private commitments it had made in the past but added new elements of nuclear caution and restraint. For the first time, Israel devised a nonproliferation diplomacy, which was separate from its improvised efforts to shield its own nuclear actions.[15]

By the mid-1970s, it became evident to Prime Minister Rabin and Foreign Minister Yigal Allon that the 1969 Nixon-Meir understanding was incapable of sustaining Israel's commitment to nuclear caution. The old nonintroduction formula was insufficient as a positive nonproliferation policy. Israel had to propose its own nonproliferation vision as an alternative to the NPT. It had to be a positive vision of disarmament but, at the same time, a vision that would not impose tangible restrictions on Israel's nuclear capability. This policy had to be a diplomatic instrument that would ease the pressure on Israel to sign the NPT, but without requiring a concrete commitment that could jeopardize its nuclear position. It had to be a disarmament vision that imposed no prohibitions whatsoever on Israel unless some substantial political requirements regarding Arab belligerency and recognition of Israel were met. Until that "long corridor" of concrete steps toward peace was crossed, Israel would accept no tangible limits on its freedom of action in the nuclear field. Unlike the NPT, Israel's vision of nuclear disarmament links the nuclear issue with the political questions of war and peace in the Middle East.[16]

Under the leadership of Shalheveth Freier as director general of Israel's Atomic Energy Commission (IAEC), the concept of amimut was articulated and codified as a basis for nuclear diplomacy.[17] Freier also formulated the Israeli vision of the Middle East as a nuclear weapons–free zone (NWFZ), with its emphasis on the "long corridor" required to make it a reality. The vision of a NWFZ was linked with Israel's long-standing demand for full and mutual political recognition by all the states of the region. This would be a way to show that Israel supported nonproliferation, despite its insistence that applying the NPT to the Middle East was inappropriate. Only under conditions of peaceful coexistence or after a formal peace had been achieved would Israel consider signing the NPT.

To Israel, the diplomatic advantages of the NWFZ initiative were obvious:

1. It allowed Israel to present itself as supporting the cause of nonproliferation, countering the image of its rejection of the NPT. Not only did the NWFZ present an alternative to the NPT, but it also allowed Israel to explain why it was compelled to reject the NPT without openly acknowledging its nuclear status and activities. That is, a state whose legitimacy is challenged by its neighbors and is exposed to existential threats cannot rely on the NPT for its existential security. This explanation allowed Israel also to justify publicly its decision to stay outside the NPT, not because of its own security needs, but because of deficiencies of the NPT safeguards system, which is not strong enough for regions with existential conflicts. Since the 1970s Israel has insisted that a rogue state could abuse the NPT safeguards system and develop nuclear weapons while staying within the framework of the treaty—or at least stay within that framework until the last minute before crossing the nuclear-weapons threshold.[18]

2. Israel's emphasis on a broad regional vision whose details ought to be directly negotiated by all relevant parties over time in order to become a real blueprint rather than a fixed treaty allowed it a great deal of political flexibility.

3. The vision of the NWFZ, unlike the NPT, allowed Israel to link the nuclear issue directly with the Arab-Israeli conflict and, in doing so, linked the nuclear problem to its cause: that is, issues of war and peace, recognition and legitimacy.

4. Perhaps most important, the NWFZ vision did not require Israel to do anything, in deed or in words, until the political arena changed substantially. Israel could remain a free agent in its nuclear activities as long as they were not

visible or public. Furthermore, Israel's notion of the NWFZ was designed to give it a long corridor of time before the country would actually be required to deliver on its commitment to the vision. The political process of making peace came first and would be followed by the nuclear issue. When and if this should change was solely Israel's decision. And conveniently, until such changes took place, Israel could continue with its code of conduct of amimut.

5. Endorsing the vision of NWFZ allowed Prime Minister Rabin (and subsequently Prime Minister Begin) to signal that Israel remained committed to its amimut policy. Despite the public calls made in 1976/1977 by the former minister of defense, Moshe Dayan, that Israel should adopt a stance of more explicit nuclear deterrence, Israel stuck to its old nonintroduction policy. This meant that Israel did not, and still does not, believe in open nuclear deterrence.

Amimut makes Israel a benign or constrained proliferator. Unlike all other nuclear-weapons states, Israel has resisted the temptation to make a public commitment to nuclear weapons. This is not meaningless. It is a mistake to consider amimut merely a semantic way of not acknowledging a reality known by all, for Israel's commitment to the vision of NWFZ is a real commitment to nuclear caution.

The Political Robustness of Amimut

By the 1980s it became apparent that amimut would remain Israel's nuclear posture for the foreseeable future. Amimut reflected the widespread consensus of Israel's national security elite that this was the most prudent way—indeed, the only possible way—Israel could conduct nuclear policy in light of its difficult situation.

Senior Israeli officials have made the point (always off the record) that the continuity of amimut is not automatic, that it is not a dogma that can be taken for granted. Rather, amimut is a policy that the Israeli government reviews occasionally, based on international developments. But each of these reviews has concluded that this policy is still the best response to Israel's nuclear situation. Indeed, these reviews have only strengthened the conviction that amimut best serves Israeli strategic interests and, absent any dramatic new developments, seems to have no viable alternative.

The nuclear tests in South Asia in May 1998 led to one of these policy reviews. Some Israeli strategists, both inside and outside the government, suggested that Israel should not be left alone behind India and Pakistan and insisted that the new nuclear reality in South Asia had created an opportunity for Israel to revise its own long-standing nuclear policy. The Israeli government had instructed those in charge of nuclear matters to make a quiet but comprehensive review of the nation's nuclear policies in light of the nuclear changes in South Asia and to study in particular whether or not Israel should modify its own policy of nuclear opacity. But that internal review process concluded that the events in South Asia only strengthened the case for maintaining the policy of amimut.[19]

The nuclear dynamics in South Asia created an opportunity to underscore the difference between Israel's cautious nuclear policy of amimut with India's and Pakistan's decisions to end the era of nuclear self-restraint and adopt one of nuclear deterrence. By contrast, Israel's stance conveyed a message of stability, continuity, and self-restraint.

For Israel, the fact that India and Pakistan had decided to abandon their semiopacity had little bearing on Israel's own strategic calculations. What really mattered for Israel was not India's and Pakistan's tests and declarations and the subsequent impact of their deeds on the global nuclear order. Rather, the issue would be the potential impact of a decision by Israel to deviate from its current nuclear practice on Middle East politics.

The intuitively obvious answer was that any deviation from Israel's policy of amimut could have catastrophic effects on the political dynamics of the Middle East, especially on the relations between Israel and the two states with which it maintained formal peace, Egypt and Jordan.[20] Furthermore, Israel did not need to reestablish its nuclear credentials because under amimut, it had already extracted all the benefits of existential deterrence. Nobody questioned the credibility of Israel's nuclear status.

Israel's, India's, and Pakistan's positions on nuclear affairs are quite different. At its core, Israel is truly ambivalent about nuclear weapons. It is determined to maintain existential deterrence as long as its existence is questioned, but it also is committed to preventing the nuclearization of the Middle East. India's abandonment of opacity was motivated by nationalistic ideology and its desire for great-power status. In Israel, however, such reasoning would be irrelevant, and also impossible.

In 2004, Prime Minister Ariel Sharon appointed a distinguished external review body, headed by Minister Dan Meridor, to examine Israel's national security concept and structure from the perspective of twenty-first-century developments.[21] The commission submitted its report in April 2006 following nearly two years of thorough study, and one of its central recommendations was that Israel should stick to its nuclear policy as long as possible. Short of the imminent advent of a new nuclear state in the region, Israel should do everything in its power to continue with the policy and practice of nuclear opacity.

Today, four decades after the policy was created, the Israeli national security elite still firmly believes that amimut as a national nuclear strategy has proved itself and that there is no viable alternative. In the late 1970s, Moshe Dayan tried to make his advocacy of open nuclear deterrence part of his political campaign, but today the consensus in Israel is that the wisdom of amimut should guide the conduct of the country's nuclear affairs.

While few Israelis know the name of Shalheveth Freier or exactly what the policy of amimut is, Israelis, like their leaders, support the policy Freier and his team wrote and codified. Even most educated Israelis are not familiar with the legal and political intricacies of the nonproliferation regime, nor do they care about understanding how amimut works, but they do believe that amimut is the key to Israel's possession of nuclear weapons. Without amimut, the United States would not have allowed Israel to acquire nuclear weapons. For this reason, Israelis regard compromising amimut as a direct threat to their national security.

Nonacknowledgment and Secrecy

Secrecy and nonacknowledgment are key ingredients in the idea of amimut and provide a crucial cultural underpinning for the government's nuclear policy. The two are closely related, partly overlapping, but conceptually distinct. Although a policy of amimut without strict secrecy is impossible, it is nonacknowledgment—not secrecy as such—that is the politically, culturally, and socially undergirding feature of amimut. Even if a secret were disclosed inadvertently, nonacknowledgment provides room to ignore it and deny its implications.[22]

Furthermore, acknowledgment implies accepting responsibility for an action; it suggests an act of recognition. Conversely, a refusal to acknowledge implies reluctance to accept political or moral responsibility; it is akin to dismissal. Nonacknowledgment is a way to insist that an issue is off-limits and outside the accepted discourse, as if the issue did not exist or did not merit discussion. Nonacknowledgment means a refusal to recognize something as a fact; it confers a mark of illegitimacy.

For amimut to be politically effective, it must be comprehensive and all-encompassing. This feature is manifested in the absolute official refusal to acknowledge anything factual about Israel's nuclear activities. One consequence is that amimut stifles all official fact-based discussions of nuclear matters whatsoever. From a strategic perspective, it is logical that the policy stresses nonacknowledgment, not simply secrecy. Indeed, the notion of total nuclear secrecy makes no strategic sense. If the other side did not know that Israel had nuclear weapons, there could be no deterrence. For this reason, the strategic objective of amimut was never total secrecy but partial and unconfirmed knowledge, with enough uncertainty on the margins to keep the issue of acknowledgment in the forefront.

In other words, there should be enough credible evidence to deter enemies but sufficient ambiguity and lack of acknowledgment to allow friends to look the other way. The underlying idea is that without authoritative acknowledgment, without confirmation, one cannot distinguish, at least politically, between information and disinformation, facts and speculations. Under amimut, even the definitional issue of what counts as possession of nuclear weapons is left unclear. The strategic objective of amimut was to create a policy that was credible enough to generate effects of deterrence but opaque enough to maintain political distance, even deniability.

According to the Israeli doctrine and practice, for amimut to be politically effective, it had to apply not only to present and past officials but to the entire Israeli national discourse, that is, to everyone writing on the nuclear issue in Israel. Furthermore, Israel has the legal and institutional means to enforce societal application: the Office of the Military Censor (Censora).

Accordingly, all Israeli publications and electronic media must adhere to the official discourse prescribed by amimut, with the result that Israel and everything published in Israel has only one perspective on the nuclear issue: the official discourse of amimut. This arrangement makes the Censora an essential bridge between government policy and societal taboo. Because no other state has a military censor as an institution in the way that Israel has, no other state can generate anything like the societal taboo that supports amimut.

Even though total secrecy is not the primary objective of amimut, it is essential from the guardians' perspective. The rationale for this is twofold. First, the logical linkage between nonacknowledgment and secrecy is that without tight and absolute secrecy, nonacknowledgment would be meaningless. Since the policy of amimut places a low bar for acknowledgment, this means that essentially almost everything concerning nuclear matters—no matter how trivial—is, by definition, a secret.

Second is the slippery slope concern: if amimut were ever relaxed, the pressure for more transparency would never end. In the eyes of the policy's guardians, only an all-encompassing and clearly delineated code of secrecy can prevent such a slippery slope. If the code of secrecy were not absolute, the policy would be compromised. Because many thousands of people have been involved in one or another classified aspect of Israel's nuclear program, its security policy must be broad as well as absolute.

As time passes, such a code of secrecy becomes more difficult to maintain. It is more difficult to treat Israel's nuclear capability as a total secret when the entire world regards it as an obvious fact. This is one reason that the guardians of amimut are so concerned with the slippery slope effect, because once Israel acknowledges its nuclear activity, it will be impossible to maintain secrecy.[23] Nonetheless, amimut cannot be airtight. In his very first interview as the president of Israel, Shimon Peres appeared to deviate from the official protocol of Israel's amimut policy by all but acknowledging that Israel was a nuclear state.[24]

Why Did Israelis Embrace Amimut?

Over time, amimut has become much more than a government policy; it has become Israel's way of thinking and dealing with nuclear weapons. It has become both the intellectual rationale and the social sanction that constitute Israel's bargain with the bomb. The following summary describes how the Israeli national security elite views the strategic and political advantages of amimut. This is not an "objective" assessment of amimut but the common Israeli view of why it has been so successful.

Existential Deterrence

Under amimut, Israel's nuclear resolve has been validated and vindicated, but in a cautious and unprovocative fashion. By now, Israel's possession of nuclear weapons is well known to friends and foes alike, yet Israel has been careful (and successful) not to issue direct nuclear threats to any state. This kind of nuclear politics has allowed Israel to extract virtually all the benefits of credible *existential* nuclear deterrence, but without the political, diplomatic, and moral difficulties (and most of the cost) that nuclear possession entails. For example, Israel used its nuclear deterrence posture effectively in the first Gulf War.[25] Israel thus has acquired the "extra" measure of security that Ben-Gurion had sought for the unlikely situations of "last resort."

Insulation and Freedom of Action

Amimut has permitted Israel's nuclear program to enjoy remarkable and perhaps unparalleled freedom of action. Total secrecy has insulated the nuclear program from the outside world. No one, neither at home nor abroad, could intervene because nobody knew clearly and exactly what was going on inside the country. Amimut has permitted the Israeli nuclear program to operate like a "black box." In chapters 6 and 7, I elaborate on the democratic deficiencies of this situation, so here I note only that it has created a most convenient situation for bureaucrats and administrators.[26]

The revelations in 1986 about Mordechai Vanunu illustrate this point. Although they revealed that the Israeli nuclear program was advanced, the relatively limited political reaction that followed also indicated the international community's lack of political interest in meddling in Israel's nuclear affairs. With the sole exception of Norway, where the opposition forced the government to take action on the issue of heavy water that Norway had supplied to Israel in the late 1950s, no Western government made a political issue out of those revelations. Even the official Arab response was relatively muted.[27]

The United States as a Tacit Partner

After a stormy decade in which Israel's nuclear program had been a continuous source of irritation and friction between the United States and Israel, the 1969 deal allowed the United States to live with nuclear-armed Israel. In essence, the United States would leave Israel alone in regard to nuclear matters as long as Israel kept its part of the deal. The only time when the United States challenged Israel on a nuclear issue ever since was in the context of the American global effort to advance the fissile materials cutoff treaty (FMCT).[28]

The importance of the deal to bilateral relations went beyond removing a source of tension, however, as it made the United States a real partner of Israel in the amimut policy. This had far-reaching ramifications because the United States was also the primary co-custodian of the nonproliferation regime. While the details of the Nixon-Meir agreement remained confidential for many years, the United States protected Israel's nuclear program in the international arena. Egypt started peace negotiations with Israel in 1977 under the shadow of the Israeli bomb, and it was the United States during the Camp David phase of the negotiations that told Egypt straightforwardly that any effort to introduce the nuclear issues into the peace negotiations, particularly Egypt's demand that Israel join the NPT, would be futile. Egypt dropped the effort.[29]

Israel gave the United States assurances of and commitments to its nuclear conduct—no test, no declaration, no transfer to others—and the United States has used its own influence to persuade others, Western and non-Western states alike, that the world can live with an Israeli bomb that is kept invisible.

Israel and the NPT Regime

Over time, the Nixon-Meir deal evolved into a working arrangement under which the United States has given Israel a great deal of diplomatic cover, and many Western and non-Western states have been persuaded to treat Israel as an exceptional case. Today, most nations view treating Israel tacitly as an exception under the ground rules of amimut—that is, accepting Israel's unique status outside the NPT—as the best of the available options.

Regional Stability and Peace

Against the concerns that Israel's possession of nuclear weapons would destabilize and polarize the region, the politics of amimut created a reality that was more benign than anybody expected. While it is difficult to quantify the political effects of amimut, it is commonly believed, especially by Israelis, that Israel's nuclear deterrence under amimut has contributed significantly to regional stability and has transformed the nature of the Arab-Israeli conflict. That is, the veiled presence of the Israeli bomb is believed to have been a significant factor in lowering the intensity of the Arab-Israeli conflict since the 1973 war and even may have contributed to achieving peace.

When Ben-Gurion initiated the nuclear project in the late 1950s, he did so against the background of the Arab countries' open declarations of intent regarding the "destruction of Israel and Zionism." Their defeat in the 1967 war, however, was important to starting the decline of this rhetoric. Then the 1973 Yom Kippur War, the bloodiest of all Arab-Israeli wars since 1948 and the last great Arab-Israeli war involving major armies in battle, took place under the shadow of the Israeli bomb and, as a result, led to two related developments. First, the Arabs' rhetoric about the "destruction of Israel" began to fade. Various comments made by Egyptian President Anwar Sadat during his 1977 visit to Jerusalem led those watching the developments to believe that the bomb had played some role in the diminishment of Arab discourse about the destruction of Israel and Egypt's (and subsequently other Arab states') acceptance of Israel as an ineradicable entity in the Middle East.[30] Second, the 1973 war initiated the view that the nuclear age could no longer tolerate big wars. Less than five years after the war, President Sadat visited Jerusalem and promised "no more war." It seems clear, then, from these two outcomes, that the subsequent Egyptian-Israeli 1978 peace treaty was signed under the shadow of the Israeli bomb.[31] Many Israelis view Israel's invisible bomb as the "quiet" anchor of the Egyptian-Israeli peace. Finally, the Arab League's endorsement of Saudi Arabia's 2002 peace plan, which calls for a two-state solution in resolving the Palestinian-Israeli conflict based on the 1949 lines in return for full recognition of Israel by the Arab world, highlights the remarkable change that took place in the Arab world toward Israel. Many Israelis believe that the presence of the "invisible" Israeli bomb contributed significantly to this development.

Impact on Arab Proliferation

The most serious concern in the 1960s was that the Israeli nuclear project would lead to a dangerous regional nuclear arms race and was the fear underlying the drive for nuclear caution. But some have argued that the regional consequences of the Israeli bomb under amimut proved to be more benign than had been feared, that amimut enabled Israel to maintain its monopoly without spurring an arms race.

On closer examination, however, the record here is mixed and incomplete. On five occasions, Israel faced the emergence of hostile nuclear programs: Egypt in the 1960s, Iraq (twice) in the 1970s and 1980s, Libya in the 1990s, Syria in the first decade of this century, and today, the most difficult case, Iran. In the first four instances, owing to a combination of both luck and policy, the hostile proliferator ultimately failed to reach its objectives. Israel's own amimut policy has probably been a moderating force, but it surely is not formidable enough to prevent cases of hostile proliferation entirely.[32]

The Slippery Slope Issue

The threat of outside pressure has been a concern that dominates Israeli nuclear thinking. That is, if Israel engages in nuclear discussions prematurely, before fundamental political changes take root, the other side would see this as an invitation to make more demands toward eroding Israel's nuclear capabilities. For this reason, Israelis have always viewed the fissile materials cutoff treaty (FMCT) with great suspicion, because it could be the first step to more and new, but premature, demands for Israel to move toward disarmament. The Arab states would argue that the FMCT was not an adequate acceptable substitute for a nuclear weapons–free zone, as it would tend to legitimate Israel's nuclear monopoly in the Middle East, which they could never accept. In sum, the Israelis fear that the Arabs would not appreciate an Israeli cutoff and that they would try to use the FMCT as a launching pad for further pressure on Israel to disarm.[33]

Nuclear Exceptionalism

The strength of amimut derives from the political judgment that Israel has no real alternative to this policy, that only through the conduct of amimut has Israel been able to build and maintain over the years its "exempt" status in nuclear affairs, first with the United States and subsequently with most of the international nonproliferation regime. It is the responsible conduct of amimut that has produced the political conditions that have made Israel's exceptionalism tolerable, if not acceptable.[34]

Israelis view the evolution of this exceptionalism as a great political asset, even though it has not awarded Israel a formal nuclear status. Given the rigid legal and political makeup of the nonproliferation regime, the Israeli national security elite see no realistic alternative to amimut. They see no way to accommodate Israel's nuclear status within the NPT regime, so by default, they prefer to keep the exceptionalism of amimut. It is one thing for nations to look the other way, but it is quite another to formally add another nuclear state to the system. Israelis understand the international situation and see the present situation as one without an alternative. Even if Israel could be formally recognized as a nuclear-weapons state—possibly by creating a new layer within the NPT regime, perhaps through the FMCT—Israelis most likely would still prefer the familiar landscape of amimut. It requires fewer commitments from

Israel than any other foreseeable arrangement. After all, the great virtue of this policy is that it is largely informal and almost free of cost.

Amimut and a Nuclear Israel

Israelis have embraced amimut for reasons beyond strategic considerations of nuclear deterrence. Israelis do not separate the two conceptually; for them, amimut and nuclear Israel are one and the same. Simply put, Israelis see amimut as the key for nuclear Israel, and they cherish the notion of nuclear Israel. Amimut was the only political modality for Israel under which it could have acquired nuclear weapons without alienating the rest of the world. Its benefits are therefore as much about identity as about strategy.

Some Israelis would argue that the benefits of amimut go far beyond merely providing Israel a national insurance policy at the existential level.[35] Such a policy is not simply about preventing another Holocaust; it is about making tangible and positive contributions to Israel's well-being. That is, the amimut bargain contributed to transcending Israeli identity in three important but, at the same time, subtle ways.

First, the Israeli bomb was instrumental in changing Israel's character: in particular, Israel is no longer referred to as a "garrison state" as it was during its early years.[36] Today, despite the continuation of the Arab-Israeli conflict, Israel is closer to Athens than to Sparta. The Israeli economy and culture could not have been so successful without the cover of stability that the bomb has provided. One could probably argue that since the late 1970s—the peace pact with Egypt could be viewed as a turning point—under the cover of its invisible bomb, Israel was able to attain sufficient calm to accelerate major internal societal changes. Most prominently, the ethos of *kdushat habitachon* (in Hebrew, the "sanctity of security") that reflected Israel's garrison state image has been in decline, and the civil ethos of the rule of law has been in ascendance. The irony, of course, is that the ethos of *kdushat habitachon* still wraps the Israeli bargain with the bomb.

Second, the bomb project under the cover of amimut probably contributed to making Israel a global high-tech hub. I qualify this statement with "probably" because amimut has precluded open and independent quantitative studies of the technological and scientific spin-offs of the larger nuclear project (i.e., including the missile project).[37] Notwithstanding this absence of hard data, it is virtually inevitable that the nuclear project generated major spin-offs for Israeli technology and science in a variety of fields.

Probably the missile project had more spin-offs than the nuclear project alone, but ultimately, the missile project was largely a derivative of the nuclear project. While both the nuclear and the missile projects initially received a great deal of technological assistance from France, within a few years Israel had to continue with both projects on its own. There is little doubt that these two related projects contributed significantly both to the development of a scientific, technological, and education infrastructure and to the development of Israel's high-tech industry.

Third, the amimut bargain has given Israel a certain international cachet: respect and prestige. Since 1970, not only has the world learned to view (and subsequently accept) Israel as the sixth de facto nuclear-weapons power, but both friends and foes appreciate the amimut modality as strategically and politically "smart": clear enough to deter foes and opaque enough to be tolerated. Ultimately, the mixture of respect and appreciation that the Israeli bomb generated in others had tangible results, even within the Arab world.

Since the 1980s, especially after the Vanunu revelations, the bomb has been important to Arab perceptions of Israel as a technological giant. At the same time, amimut has demonstrated to most Arab states the cautionary aspect of Israel's nuclear conduct and the role of the bomb as a guarantee of national survival, not an instrument of political advantage.

The advocacy of amimut has now gone beyond Israel itself. Over time, many outside policymakers and policy analysts have endorsed amimut. Initially, Israelis and Americans viewed the 1969 Nixon-Meir discussion as a secret interim arrangement for a thorny bilateral issue over which neither country wanted a confrontation. Now others in the international arena have also recognized the wisdom of amimut. As happens so often, the temporal becomes permanent, and the familiar becomes most convenient.[38]

Final Reflections

In a rare press briefing in July 2004 during a visit to Israel by Mohammed El-Baradei, then the director general of the International Atomic Energy Agency (IAEA), a senior Israeli nuclear official made some general remarks about the nation's nuclear policy. He told his audience that Israel had no intention of changing its long-standing amimut policy, one characterized by remarkable continuity and stability. In its essence, he noted obliquely, the policy is guided by two imperatives: respect for the lessons of Jewish history and a great deal of political caution.

Israel has acquired nuclear weapons, but very differently from how other states have done so. Some would argue (as did Paul Warnke in his exchange with Ambassador Yitzhak Rabin in 1968) that Israel's nuclear pledge is no more than verbal acrobatics designed to conceal a secret reality. But others would contend that Israel has been remarkably successful in establishing a unique nuclear posture and, in doing so, has set a special example for the entire nuclear age. George Perkovich expressed this view most eloquently:

> Today the United States, Russia, the United Kingdom, China, France, India and Pakistan are known to possess atomic arsenals. By treaty or declaration, these countries are formally committed to pursuing nuclear disarmament. But much of the world feels that, because these declared nuclear-armed powers refuse to take this objective seriously, they have no right to enforce nonproliferation rules on other countries. One way the Nuclear Eight could begin to show they are serious about disarmament would be to follow Israel's example and lower the salience of their weapons—putting them at the bottom of their national arsenals, refraining from pointing to them during crisis and declining to pull international rank because of them. Since such forbearance has not threatened the small, beleaguered Jewish state's security, the United States, Russia, Pakistan, and France increasingly have no excuse for relying as prominently as they do on nuclear weapons.[39]

Perkovich is correct, I believe.

Israel has taken a different path altogether. While Israel has left little doubt about its nuclear resolve, it has remained reluctant to seal its pact with the bomb in any public or societal way. Instead of joining the nuclear club—by conducting a test that technically Israel could have done as early as 1966 and that would have made it a nuclear-weapons state according to the NPT's legal criteria—Israel adopted a policy based on a low salience of nuclear weapons (to use Perkovich's phrase). In historical overview, the amimut posture has become a permanent posture for Israel, not merely an interim stage (as it was for India and Pakistan).

The core nuclear inhibition, I believe, is strategic and moral as well as political. A change in Israel's nuclear profile is seen as against its own vital interests and values. In 1966, when Prime Minister Levi Eshkol pledged Israel's commitment to the principle of nonintroduction, he truthfully stated Israel's desire to keep the Arab-Israeli conflict free from nuclear weapons.

This was the case then, and this probably remains the case now. Unlike the case between India and Pakistan, Israel truly opposes the nuclearization of its conflict with the Arabs. Furthermore, if Israel tried to openly legitimize its nuclear weapons, it would not be able to oppose the introduction of nuclear weapons by others.

Some people may regard my interpretation as too sanguine. In the end, they would argue, Israel's opacity is all about political expediency. What really counts is the reality on the ground, which is the reality of nuclear resolve. Israel, they would say, is not that different from France or India. In a small academic workshop, my commentator, a distinguished American scholar in international relations, responded to this account of Israel's nuclear portrait by saying, "There is no way to think of Israel as a reluctant proliferator. If anything, Israel is the most dedicated and determined of all proliferators; its public silence on the matter is only political expediency and PR."[40]

I agree with him that a great deal of Israel's inhibition and hesitancy in the nuclear field is politically driven. This is not surprising. This conclusion is derived from the realistic assessment that the "world" would not be willing to treat nuclear Israel like, say, France, or even India and Pakistan. Still, Israel's nuclear inhibitions cannot be reduced to political expediency or bureaucratic convenience. Ultimately, it comes down to the nation's fundamental outlook on nuclear weapons, and in this respect Perkovich is right in saying that Israel sees things quite differently from the other nuclear-weapons states.

Chapter Three
Israel's Nuclear Path
The Key Decisions

More than half a century after the initiation of the Israeli nuclear program, and more than forty years after Israel crossed the nuclear threshold, our historical understanding of Israel's key nuclear decisions is still murky, if not lacking.[1]

Ambiguity and secrecy were intrinsic to the making of Israel's nuclear decisions. Although this pattern was not unique to Israel, in no other country did it become the nation's trademark. Israel is the only nuclear-weapons state committed to a policy of *total* nonacknowledgment and secrecy. Even if all the primary historical sources were available to us, owing to Israel's opaque decision-making style, it would still be difficult to construct an accurate—let alone complete—account of the fundamental nuclear decisions. What is more, almost no primary sources bearing on Israel's nuclear history, including both documents and firsthand testimony, are available. From what we do know, there are reasons to believe that a few key decisions at a few crucial moments affected the evolution of Israel's nuclear posture and decision-making style. These early decisions, each of which could be viewed as a response to a specific dilemma, shaped the way Israel acts and thinks on nuclear matters to this day.

I am aware of the paradox here. If the historical evidence is that meager and ambiguous, how could historical reconstruction be possible? Two theoretical, or heuristic, tools are needed for this reconstruction effort. The first is the organizing principle by which one can identify those key junctures. The underlying idea is that any nuclear proliferator must confront a certain progressive sequence of proliferation decisions (what the early proliferation literature called the *proliferation ladder*) in order to become a nuclear-weapons state. Each decision is a response to a specific nuclear situation, fixed at a specific moment in a nation's nuclear history. The second guiding rule is the assumption spelled out in chapter 2, that each of Israel's nuclear dilemmas parallels its fundamental nuclear dilemma.

Project Initiation

The issue that every potential nuclear proliferator must consider first is *project initiation*: determining the desirability and feasibility of the nuclear program and the kind of program that is required. A response to the question of whether or not to embark on the nuclear path, and how to do so, reveals a great deal about the decision makers' intentions.

When Prime Minister David Ben-Gurion decided to launch Israel's nuclear project in the mid- to late 1950s, he made the decision virtually alone and in utmost secrecy. He did not share his thoughts with his cabinet, nor did he consult with any other independent elected or nonelected body. Israel thus began its nuclear project not as a result of a deliberative and orderly decision-making process but of a lonely decision by an authoritative leader who was determined to pursue his own vision with the assistance of a few loyal executives.

Initiating a national nuclear project, with an eye to the bomb, had been high on Ben-Gurion's agenda even before he returned to power in early 1955 from a year-long self-imposed exile.[2] By that time he already was convinced that Israel should embark on a nuclear project, but the practical concerns about the project's feasibility, concerns he had entertained earlier, remained.[3] Could Israel pursue a nuclear-weapons project on its own? If not, was there a foreign supplier who could provide the required technology? Could that foreign supplier be trusted, politically and technologically, to do so secretly and reliably?[4] By mid-1956, when it became evident that Israel could not develop the project within the framework of the Atoms for Peace program, its focus shifted to France as the foreign supplier.[5]

The scope of the Israeli request for French technological assistance, the details of which Shimon Peres spelled out in Paris in 1956/1957, was tantamount to a national proliferation commitment.[6] Enough is now known about the extent of the Dimona deal to appreciate how determined Ben-Gurion was to pursue it.[7] The Dimona nuclear complex was designed to include *all* the technological components required for a plutonium-based nuclear-weapons infrastructure. The project's scope and purpose were evident in the facility's sanctum sanctorum, the deeply dug underground reprocessing facility designed to extract plutonium from spent uranium rods. Nothing is more indicative of Israel's initial commitment to build a nuclear-weapons capability than this supersecret and costly facility. From the beginning, Israel hoped that within a decade or so to have enough fissile material to build its own nuclear device.

Ben-Gurion often expressed his confidence in the project by referring to his absolute faith in Israeli scientists. He used to say, "What Einstein, Oppenheimer, and Teller, the three of them are Jews, made for the United States, could also be done by scientists in Israel, for their own people." In reality, however, it was not the scientists who translated his nuclear vision into nuclear reality. Rather, it was an extraordinary engineer named Manes Pratt who did. He is remembered as the Dimona builder. Just as the qualities of General Leslie Groves made possible the Manhattan Project, Pratt's larger-than-life persona as a manager and leader made Dimona possible.[8]

Ben-Gurion was aware of the great risks involved in his decision to initiate the project.[9] They did not deter him but instead shaped how he would pursue the project. Even though his actions amounted to a long-term proliferation decision, he apparently presented them to his political colleagues cautiously, as if he were only exploring options for the future. Preserving this distance between the initiation of the project and its long-term strategic implications served a purpose. For even though this distance was artificial—decisions about nuclear infrastructure would make little sense without some reference to long-term objectives—it was beneficial politically to avoid long-term commitments.[10]

Viewed in this way, the initiation of the Dimona project was about creating "options" for "future leaders"; it was not about a commitment to build the bomb.[11] Years later, in a moment of historical reflection, Shimon Peres referred to Ben-Gurion's modus operandi as a reluctance to "nail down" the specifics of his nuclear vision, "for nailing down would have meant to identify specific objectives too early, and too fast, and that would have been too complicated."[12] Because those long-term objectives were left vague and undetermined, the technological resolve was moderated, at times even disguised, by political caution, and this caution was critical to Israel's path to amimut. Over time, these early initiation decisions were eclipsed by later decisions about Israel's technological infrastructure, but the spirit of technological resolve moderated by political caution never changed. None of the leaders of this secret project could have predicted in those early days how successful Israel would be in pursuing its nuclear project. Although the project's success was largely dependent on whether the world would tolerate Israel's nuclear resolve, the initiation commitment nevertheless created an implicit expectation by the project's leaders that by the end of the decade Israel would probably have some sort of "nuclear option." Even without top-down political guidance, which apparently was never formally issued, the developers considered it their mission to complete the R&D phase by decade's end, regardless of the declaratory stance that Israel would decide on. The reasoning was that as long as the R&D work could be conducted in secrecy, the declaratory policy would impose no constraints on it.

Another important Israeli nuclear legacy that should be attributed to how Ben-Gurion shaped the initiation phase is the notion that all nuclear-energy issues should be managed and controlled by civilians, primarily those with technological training and background, and not by military officers, with the prime minister as the highest authority.[13] It was an arrangement convenient to all involved. Just as the generals in the Israel Defense Forces (IDF) were initially skeptical of the supersecret project (because most of them thought the IDF had no need for it and therefore had no interest whatsoever in running it), so the civilian leaders of the nuclear project could not see themselves working on a military project and had no interest in reporting to the military. Neither side viewed the project's ultimate product—if such a product were indeed ever produced—as another type of weapon. From Ben-Gurion's perspective, it was *his* special project, not another military project. The nuclear project and the rest of the defense establishment maintained a strict budgetary separation. A great deal of this thinking and organizational separation has survived to this day.

The Disclosure Dilemma

Israel's second nuclear decision was how to present its nuclear project to the world. Throughout 1960 it became increasingly evident that the secret nuclear project could no longer remain completely secret and that sooner or later, Israel would have to address it publicly. There were two choices available for dealing with the problem: Israel could adopt a cautious strategy, claiming that the project was strictly civilian and peaceful; or it could adopt a bolder approach, acknowledging that the project concerned defense. Whatever was said, it would have a profound effect on what Israel could or could not do or say in the future.

Israel's disclosure problem had a context. Already in early-mid 1960, before U.S. intelligence knew much about Dimona, Israel was having problems with France over the secret nuclear issue. After France changed its national leadership when Charles de Gaulle became president in 1959, its "unprecedented" nuclear deal with Israel turned sour. France's new president decided to end, and to reveal, its nuclear partnership with Israel. Not only did de Gaulle decide to halt France's involvement, but he also insisted that Israel declare the Dimona project peaceful and place it under safeguards.[14] A hastily arranged summit between Ben-Gurion and de Gaulle did not produce a solution.[15] In Israeli eyes, this was a fight over the survival of the Dimona project.

From Peres's perspective, the impasse with France was not a policy dispute but a challenge of necessity. He therefore sought to devise a compromise allowing Israel to complete Dimona on its own, without the French government's involvement. Two issues were critical. First, some French technical assistance was necessary. Second, some aspects of the project needed to remain secret. The kind of compromise Israel could achieve with France was also important to Israel's relations with the United States. If no compromise could be found and if the French revealed Israel's secret, Israel's relationship with the United States might be damaged.[16] In late November, Shimon Peres told the French that Ben-Gurion would soon issue a public statement about Dimona, pledging that the project was peaceful.[17] According to Peres's biographer, this compromise "saved the Israeli nuclear project from a total disaster."[18]

A few days later, the Dimona project was revealed. The high-profile American disclosure, along with the press's speculations that Dimona meant an Israeli bomb project, created a problem for Israel: How should it react to the disclosure? How much should Israel tell? Could Israel tell the U.S. government one thing in private and something else to the world in public? Should Israel make a commitment to a peaceful nuclear endeavor for the future? Simply put, should Israel choose the path of truth or the path of ambiguity?

Ben-Gurion chose the path of ambiguity. On December 21, 1960, he delivered the first (and only) public statement in the Knesset in which he referred to the Dimona project as a strictly civilian nuclear research center. The Dimona reactor, Ben-Gurion stated, was "exclusively for peaceful purposes." In addition, the Israeli government privately provided the United States with additional information about the nuclear project that was consistent with the public statement.[19] The United States accepted this as a commitment that "Israel has no plans for the production of atomic weapons."[20] Neither the public statement nor the additional clarifications referred to Dimona's security-related dimension.

Ben-Gurion's public statement was not the whole truth, to say the least, but at stake was not only truth but the fate of the project.[21] The prime minister apparently decided to adopt the ambiguous strategy for its obvious short-term benefits, that is, avoiding a public showdown with the United States, lessening American pressure on Israel, and calming the political waters.[22]

But those short-term benefits now had to be weighed against their long-term disadvantages. For example, declaring that the Dimona project was exclusively peaceful while secretly continuing to work on its true mission set Israel on a future route of deception with the United States. Such a strategy opened the door to more American demands to verify the exclusively peaceful pledge, such as additional requests to visit the Dimona site and, ultimately, demands to place Dimona under international safeguards. If Dimona was exclusively peaceful, why worry about visitors or safeguards?

Moreover, the logic of this strategy of ambiguity made it difficult for Israel to gain the security benefits from its nuclear investment. Even if Israel were able not to be caught in its untruth, it would likely end up with a secret nuclear capability that could not provide security benefits. Since this disclosure strategy did not allow Israel to present Dimona as a security asset, the country would have difficulty in the future using Dimona's potential to bargain for other security assets. Most important, this strategy made it more difficult for Israel to join the nuclear club at a later time.

In retrospect, Ben-Gurion's endorsement of this disclosure strategy had a lasting effect. It imposed political and technological inhibitions on Israel's freedom of action in the nuclear field. Accordingly, after Ben-Gurion's address in the Knesset, Israel was formally committed to the "peaceful use" of its nuclear technology. Moreover, Israel was forced to allow the United States to visit in order to verify its peaceful commitment and thus had to pursue its nuclear program under concealment and deception. Israel was not even in a position to demand American security guarantees for concession on the nuclear issue.

Ben-Gurion's response to the disclosure dilemma in December 1960 was eclipsed by subsequent decisions, but this initial declaratory strategy shaped the political space in which those later decisions were made. Much of the nuclear dialogue between the United States and Israel throughout the 1960s took place under the shadow of this strategy: the May 1961 meeting between President John F. Kennedy and Ben-Gurion; Kennedy's letters to Ben-Gurion and Eshkol in the spring and summer of 1963; the Kennedy-Eshkol deal in August 1963, which led to annual U.S. visits to Dimona; and Eshkol's 1965 nonintroduction pledge, which was at the heart of the Nixon-Meir 1969 deal.

American efforts to halt Israel's nuclear progress failed, but they helped shape the restraint and caution under which Israel created a special bargain with the bomb. Although the United States was not in a position to reverse Israel's nuclear resolve, it was influential in determining the restraints under which Israel became a nuclear power.

Some people may argue that it is unfair to treat the disclosure decision as an authentic dilemma because Ben-Gurion had no real alternatives to the course of action he chose. But such a claim is untrue. Even Ben-Gurion's own foreign minister, Golda Meir, saw room for alternatives, believing that Israel should "tell [the United States] the truth, and explain why."[23] Had Israel adopted Meir's suggestion, it might have ended up with a different nuclear bargain.

Nuclear Versus Conventional Weapons

The next rung on the proliferation ladder was the strategic role of the nuclear program within Israel's overall national security posture. In general, there is no exact timeline when such deliberations should be initiated, and it varies from one case to another, but logic suggests that such deliberations should take place sometime before the R&D phase is completed.

Such high-level deliberations must include the nuclear program's strategic fundamentals: its role in the nation's overall national security posture, its strategic vision, the ratio of conventional to nuclear components, and the program's specific products or capabilities. Basic issues like national security doctrine, deterrence, force structure, the military utility of nuclear weapons, defense budgets, civil-military relations, and organizational structure had to be introduced into the overall picture.

Israel was decisive on the issue of the infrastructure but slow and tentative on the other decisions, which reflects Ben-Gurion's reluctance to make long-term decisions, along with his tendency to leave Israel's nuclear intentions ambiguous and unstated. He also had concrete reasons to delay his decisions on long-term issues. In 1960/1961, the survival of the Dimona project was still in doubt due to France's reverse in policy and the Kennedy administration's opposition. Moreover, Ben-Gurion's cautious declaratory strategy made it difficult even to bring the topic up for negotiation. At home, Ben-Gurion's leadership was bitterly challenged in generational infighting within his own party (as a result of what became known as the Lavon affair) that consumed his political energy and eventually led to his downfall. Given all this, from Ben-Gurion's perspective, this was not the time to start raising sensitive, long-term questions about the nuclear project.

New developments in 1962, abroad and at home, however, forced the issue. On July 21, 1962, Egypt announced its successful test firing of four ballistic missiles, thereby proclaiming the existence of a missile project aimed to hit any target "south of Beirut." Israel was stunned. The Mossad (Institute for Intelligence and Special Operations) issued an alarming report about hundreds of West German scientists and engineers who were developing a variety of technological projects in Egypt, including ballistic missiles and unconventional weaponry. The Israeli media were spreading horrific stories whose central theme was that fifteen years after the Holocaust, West German scientists were working on weapons to perpetuate another Holocaust against the Jews.[24] Almost overnight, Israel was engulfed in a debate over what its strategic response to the news from Egypt should be.[25]

At home, Ben-Gurion's junior coalition partners, the leaders of the Achdut Ha'avodah Party, Yigal Allon and Israel Galili, had their own concerns about the atomic project. They asked to discuss the nuclear issue with the prime minister and to register their concern. After joining his government in October 1961, the two had already inserted a clause in their coalition agreement, stating that a ministerial committee must be responsible for decisions on "the development of [a] new weapons system to be deployed by the IDF."[26]

The result was the first closed-door leadership conference in which the nuclear project's strategic fundamentals were debated by the nation's top politicians with defense credentials.[27] The minutes of that meeting, if they exist at all, are not available; it is not even clear who attended it. According to Arnan Azaryahu, Galili's aide who prepared a memo for that conference, it was essentially a debate between the advocates and the opponents of nuclear deterrence.[28] The meeting apparently took place in the second half of 1962, for which both sides prepared position papers.[29] For contemporary academic audiences, the debate anticipated many of the arguments that international security theorists like Kenneth Waltz and Scott Sagan would debate many decades later concerning the spread of nuclear weapons.[30]

The advocates of nuclear deterrence were the former chief of staff and then minister of agriculture, Moshe Dayan, and the deputy minister of defense, Shimon Peres (who was directly responsible for the nuclear program). They argued that over the long run, Israel could not afford a conventional arms race, for financial and other reasons. Only advanced technological weaponry—atomic weapons and ballistic missiles—could give Israel the deterrence edge it needed. Not only was the bomb the most effective and least expensive deterrent, it also could eventually convince the Arabs to accept the reality of Israel. Without external security guarantees, the bomb would have to be Israel's own ultimate deterrent. They promoted the view that the IDF should be reorganized "as an army of deterrence and decisive victory by relying on the anticipated achievements in science and technology of the 1970s."[31] They called their advocacy "the doctrine of self-reliance," an Israeli version of the French contemporary doctrine of *force de frappe*.[32]

The counterview, represented by Galili and Allon, started with deep skepticism of nuclear deterrence based on the superpowers' nuclear balance of terror. They rejected all three presumptions of the nuclear advocates: questioning the inevitability of the global spread of nuclear weapons, dismissing the view that the bomb was the only cost-effective solution to Israel's long-term security, and, most important, raising doubts about the applicability of a nuclear deterrence to the Middle East. Although Galili and Allon doubted the inevitability of the spread of nuclear weapons, they did think that the introduction of Israeli nuclear weapons to the Middle East would most likely lead to their proliferation in the region. They maintained that an Israeli nuclear monopoly would be short lived and that both sides of the Arab-Israeli conflict would eventually acquire atomic weapons. Given the geopolitical and demographic asymmetries of the Arab-Israeli conflict, Israel's national interest naturally was to oppose the region's nuclearization. Israel's strategic preference was for a nonnuclear Middle East.

Furthermore, investment in a costly nuclear-weapons program would weaken the IDF and was likely to encourage the Arabs to wage a preemptive war against Israel.[33] Galili and Allon did not believe that Israel should avoid all nuclear and missile R&D. They realized that Israel had to maintain its lead in nuclear R&D over its Arab adversaries but that Israel needed to be careful that its own actions would not trigger a nuclear arms race in the region. Israel's paramount interest was to keep the Middle East free of nuclear weapons.

Without a public record, it is not clear how Ben-Gurion concluded the conference and what, if any, operational decisions were issued. But the annals of Achdut Ha'avodah recount the meeting as their victory in the nuclear debate. Galili and Allon believed that they had been able to persuade Ben-Gurion that a nuclearized Middle East would be against Israeli interests and that the IDF must remain conventional.[34] They believed that they had been able to persuade Ben-Gurion to reject Peres's call to move the IDF toward a nuclear-capable force, in the way that France was moving its own military toward nuclear capability. They thought they had succeeded in blocking Peres's dream of making Israel a member of the nuclear club.[35]

Ben-Gurion's perspective was probably more pragmatic and less ideological, seeing the debate as more political than operational. It was a way to release political steam on a most sensitive subject that until then had never been debated by politicians. Ben-Gurion probably wanted to assure Galili and Allon that he was not rushing the IDF into a nuclear posture without proper consultations. Because Ben-Gurion had initiated the nuclear project on his own, without democratic consent, it was important to him to maintain a consensus on it.

While Ben-Gurion was interested in the "bomb" as a national insurance policy, by 1962 he may have concluded that Israel was not in a political position to join the nuclear club. After all, he had given his word to President Kennedy a year earlier that Israel would not acquire nuclear weapons. Besides, Ben-Gurion still maintained that making fateful and long-term decisions on this subject was premature and unnecessary. The nuclear program was too young and uncertain to warrant making any major changes in the IDF. In 1962 Ben-Gurion had no desire to impose changes on the IDF against the will of his top generals. To preserve the IDF's conventional doctrine—of which Ben-Gurion himself was the prime author—was the practical and obvious thing to do. One could speculate that these considerations, and not lofty considerations against nuclear deterrence, led him to support Galili and Allon.[36] This was also a way to assure the IDF leadership—which had little interest in nuclear affairs—that the secret project at the Ministry of Defense was not a threat to their own turf.

During his last year in office (1962/1963) Ben-Gurion supported proposals from both sides of the nuclear debate. He approved the initiation of a big Israeli missile project in cooperation with the French firm Marcel Dassault, as Israel had to respond to the challenge of an Egyptian missile project with a missile project of its own.[37] This decision strengthened the nuclear commitment because the missile project made little sense in a nonnuclear context. Although the missile project was not a platform that could change the IDF's organizational structure and doctrine, a small missile-planning unit was established at the headquarters of the Israeli air force (IAF). Over time, that small air force unit became a liaison with the joint Israeli-French nuclear project, and decades later, it evolved into a wing base, the home of Israel's missile squadrons.

At the same time, Ben-Gurion rejected proposals to put more funds into the nuclear project at the expense of the conventional army. Instead, as a show of his continued support of Israel's conventional forces, he authorized creating a new regular armored brigade in the IDF.[38] All doctrinal and organizational issues were postponed, pending the completion of the missile program in the late 1960s.

How should we assess the historical significance of the 1962 conference? It probably was more an advisory meeting than a real executive meeting. It most likely was a deft political move that allowed Allon and Galili to register their concerns on the nuclear issue without gaining any real political victory. But in a long-term historical outlook, we could argue that the 1962 nuclear conference was probably instrumental in creating the following important legacies that shaped the way Israel acted and thought on nuclear matters:

- The IDF remains a conventional army in its basic orientation (i.e., force structure and doctrine) as long as Israel faces conventional threats.
- The nuclear program has been treated as a national asset, a sort of national security insurance policy under the control of the prime minister, not as just another military weapons system in competition with other military weapons systems.
- Israel remains politically committed not to introduce nuclear weapons into the Middle East.
- The utility of the nuclear program is viewed largely in political and psychological, not military, terms.
- The nuclear program has been handled with extreme caution by its political and professional custodians, and it has not become a vehicle through which to change the IDF and not a platform on which to economize national security.
- Because the nuclear issue needs to be handled with extraordinary secrecy and discretion by the prime minister and because democratic procedures have had to be bypassed, national consensus needs to be maintained.

Not until the mid- to late 1970s, under the inspiration of IAEC Director General Shalheveth Freier, were these insights incorporated into a national nuclear outlook that has become almost legally formalized and culturally sacrosanct. But the 1962 conference was the moment that initiated the insights that led to amimut as a policy and a long-term posture. Even though Ben-Gurion apparently left no written record of his thinking on the nuclear issue, it would be historically fair to treat the results just enumerated as part of his unwritten nuclear legacy, much of which still stands.

The idea that Israel should shift its IDF conventional doctrine to an overt nuclear doctrine was no longer seriously proposed after 1962. Even after the trauma of the 1973 Yom Kippur War, when some prominent Israeli defense intellectuals advocated a certain—but still very limited—role for nuclear weapons in Israel's military doctrine, the idea soon faded away.[39] It became an Israeli article of faith that as long as the conflict remained conventional, Israel's military doctrine must remain conventional as well.

The 1962 nuclear debate was the last time that matters involving nuclear strategy were debated by senior Israeli political leaders. From that point on, such sensitive issues were debated only in professional forums by nuclear experts. Even when Prime Minister Golda Meir made her own fateful nuclear decisions in 1969/1970 (see chapter 1 and later in this chapter), with direct involvement of the same leaders who had been present in the 1962 conference (Dayan, Allon, Galili, and Zur), it was not like the gathering in 1962. While the nuclear divide between the two camps lasted for many more years—in fact, Dayan and Allon saw nuclear matters very differently until the end of their political careers—it produced no more explicitly articulated showdowns.

The Post-R&D Dilemma and the 1967 War

By 1966, under Prime Minister Levi Eshkol, a new set of nuclear decisions started to accumulate. They all were related to one key development: Israel was approaching the nuclear-weapons threshold as the R&D phase neared completion.[40] The convergence of the two major partners of the divided project proved to be a thorny process, involving bureaucratic, technological, and personnel mismatches.[41] A new administration to take charge of all aspects of the project became imperative. In mid-1966, therefore, after a long dormant period, the Israel Atomic Energy Commission (IAEC) was reorganized as the new executive body, with Professor Israel Dostrovsky of the Weizmann Institute as its director general. Prime Minister Eshkol appointed himself as the IAEC chairman, making it clear that nuclear affairs were the sole responsibility of the prime minister.[42] These organizational changes were vital to completing the R&D phase, but they could not by themselves provide the necessary political guidance. Now new decisions were needed regarding the depth of Israel's nuclear commitment, but Eshkol was hesitant about the direction he should take.[43]

The R&D phase for all previous nuclear proliferators had ended with a full-yield nuclear test. Such a test accomplished more than demonstrating technical capability; it meant membership in the nuclear club, a way to announce the state's new international status. As was evident in the cases of India and Pakistan, the latest confirmed additions to the nuclear club, testing was an occasion for governments to issue a public statement highlighting their national nuclear commitment.

Had its leaders chosen to do so, Israel would likely have been in a position to conduct a full-yield test of a nuclear device in the second half of 1966. If Israel had conducted a test that year, even a so-called peaceful nuclear explosion, it could have declared itself the world's sixth nuclear state, and subsequently it could have joined the Nuclear Non-Proliferation Treaty (NPT) as a declared nuclear-weapons state. As a matter of international law, there was nothing illegal about following that path. China and France had done this just a few years earlier. But Israel's strategic situation and its commitments to the United States made it impossible to follow this course, and Israel's political leaders were uncertain what the nation's intentions and commitments should be.

One thing was clear: Prime Minister Eshkol categorically ruled out, on political grounds, conducting a nuclear test. "Do you think that the world would congratulate us for our achievement?" he used to ask sarcastically those people around him who entertained the idea of a test.[44] He had good reasons to reject a test outright.

First, Eshkol knew that a nuclear test would violate his public and private pledge that Israel would not be the first to introduce nuclear weapons to the Middle East. While Israel left the exact meaning of "nuclear introduction" vague, it was unquestionably clear that this commitment was incompatible with a nuclear test.[45] Second, Eshkol was aware that the superpowers were conducting intense negotiations on a global treaty aimed at preventing the proliferation of nuclear weapons. Conducting a nuclear test would be not only a catastrophe for U.S.-Israel bilateral relations—relations in which Eshkol had invested a great deal of political capital to cultivate—but also an act of defiance directed against the entire world community. Third, the prohibition against nuclear testing meant more than merely a commitment to the United States. It was also a domestic promise that Eshkol willingly made to his close political allies, Galili and Allon. For them, the nonintroduction commitment was viewed as a genuine Israeli strategic interest, not as a concession to the United States. They firmly opposed nuclear testing. Finally, there was Egypt. Eshkol knew that an Israeli test would have serious regional repercussions, particularly in light of the likely Egyptian response. In fact, an Israeli test could very well provoke Egypt and possibly the Soviets into hostilities toward Israel, possibly resulting in an all-out war.

Apart from the test issue, Israel needed to figure out its response to a new set of complicated and interrelated issues involving the future of its nuclear project. Simply put, Israel had to define, in operational and political terms, the *meaning* of its nuclear commitment:

- What should be the strategic role of the nation's nuclear program for the post-R&D period?
- What should be Israel's real national security interest: to possess nuclear weapons secretly or to obtain the political assets that declared nuclear weapons could buy?
- How could Israel extract deterrence value from its secret weapons?
- Could the nuclear program be used as a bargaining chip in a larger political deal, with either the United States or Egypt? Should Israel pursue such a bargain?
- What did Israel actually mean when it committed itself to the nonintroduction of nuclear weapons? Was this a genuine Israeli interest or just a convenient formula to deflect American pressure?
- How should Israel use its nuclear option? Should it include weaponization and deployment?
- Should Israel turn the Dimona nuclear infrastructure into a nuclear-weapons facility? Would that be compatible with its declaration of nonintroduction?
- What should be the future of the missile project?

Based on answers to these questions, Israel should have fashioned a nuclear posture that would preserve a viable "nuclear-weapons option" but would still be compatible with its commitment to nonintroduction. Between 1966 and 1969, Israel faced its moment of truth for its nuclear project.

Arguing on behalf of resolve were the project's leaders, who naturally pushed for moving forward. For them, it was nearly inconceivable to pause at such a critical juncture. As they understood it, a nuclear option meant an *operational* capability available for the existential moment of last resort. Freezing the project in a nondeployable mode thus would defeat the logic of the whole enterprise. Israel had to retain a real nuclear posture, not something virtual and amorphous. In sum, the leaders felt that the inertia of the project was simply too strong to counteract.[46]

On the side of caution were arguments emphasizing Israel's commitment not to be the first to introduce nuclear weapons to the region. This formula apparently had been used first in 1962 by David Ben-Gurion and a year later by his deputy minister of defense, Shimon Peres, who gave it as a response to a query by President John F. Kennedy. But it was Prime Minister Eshkol himself, in a memorandum of understanding that he signed with the United States in March 1965, who made it a pillar of U.S.-Israel security relations.[47] Israel left the exact meaning of its commitment vague—it never explained the operational meaning of this pledge, and the United States did not press at that time for clarification—but it was implicitly understood that "nonintroduction" meant, at a minimum, the nontesting and nonpossession of nuclear weapons. Indeed, in his speech to the Knesset in May 1966, Eshkol stated that Israel had no nuclear weapons and would not be the first to introduce them to the region.[48]

New evidence suggests that in the months before the Six-Day War, Prime Minister Eshkol and his senior military officers were anxious about the nuclear project. First, they were concerned about Egypt's reaction to the completion of the Dimona complex, especially if Egypt concluded that Israel was developing nuclear weapons. The Israeli leadership imagined a scenario in which Egypt launched a surprise aerial attack on Israel's nuclear facilities. Those worries had a profound impact on the thinking of Chief of Staff General Yitzhak Rabin and Chief of Intelligence General Aharon Yariv.[49]

Egyptian President Gamal Abdel Nasser's threat of preemptive war against the Israeli nuclear project, issued in February 1966, reinforced this apprehension. While the threat of an all-out preemptive war was not viewed as plausible (as long as much of the Egyptian army was still stuck in Yemen), a limited aerial attack on Dimona was considered a possibility.[50] On one occasion, in late 1966, Rabin cited these worries in arguing that Israel should limit its military actions against Syria. "There is one vital object in the south [Dimona],"

Rabin told his colleagues, "which is an ideal object for a limited attack, and of which Egypt may have the support of the entire world."[51]

There are other indications of Israeli anxiety over Dimona. In the year and a half before the Six-Day War, the chief of the Mossad, General Meir Amit, promoted an initiative to establish a secret, direct channel of communication with Egypt. It started as a humanitarian effort—releasing imprisoned Israeli spies—but Amit tried to turn the probe into a diplomatic channel aimed at no less than transforming the relations between the two states. While the nuclear issue was surely not what led to the "Ikaros" initiative (its code name) in 1965–1967, it apparently was a factor in Amit's overall motivation. By 1966 Amit recognized that Israel was fast approaching the nuclear threshold and understood the implications of a nuclearized Middle East. He knew that Israel's advanced nuclear capability could create a dangerous situation with the potential for war or, alternatively, could give the Soviets reason to offer a nuclear umbrella to Egypt. Given Israel's nuclear development, the period between 1966 and 1968 was a critical time, perhaps offering the last chance for Israel to reach out to Egyptian leaders before the nuclear situation became irreversible. The Ikaros initiative gained momentum when Amit was invited to a secret visit in Cairo, including a possible meeting with Nasser. The Eshkol government, however, was fearful of the risks involved, so the visit never was authorized. Although Amit continued his efforts to keep Ikaros alive until the 1967 war, he was unsuccessful.[52]

Israel's nervousness on the nuclear matter was further demonstrated when the Dimona project faced its first internal crisis. In December 1966, there was a serious industrial accident in a sensitive area in the Dimona complex. An employee was killed, and a working area was contaminated. It took weeks of cleanup until the damaged area was declared decontaminated. The accident left Israel's nuclear chiefs, including Prime Minister Eshkol, shaken.[53] A month later, in a cable to Washington, U.S. Ambassador Walworth Barbour noted that he never saw Eshkol so uncertain about the future of the nuclear project, suggesting that it was time for innovative American diplomacy on this issue. In another correspondence from that period (March 1967), Barbour dismissed U.S. intelligence reports asserting that Israel was only weeks from the bomb and noted that Dimona was "not running at full blast."[54]

I found the final piece of evidence of Israeli hesitancy on the nuclear issue in an interview I conducted in 1996 with Dr. Floyd Culler, the team leader of most of the United States' annual visits to Dimona in the mid- to late 1960s.

In that interview Culler revealed that at the end of his last visit to Dimona in April 1967, Professor Amos De-Shalit, the official Israeli host for the visit, took him aside to raise some "unconventional" ideas about preventing nuclearization in the Middle East. Culler refused to tell me what exactly those ideas were but noted that they prompted him to write a special report to the State Department. Although De-Shalit presented his ideas as "private," Culler understood his initiative as a probe launched on behalf of Eshkol.[55]

With this anxiety in the air, by early 1967 Eshkol appeared to be more open than ever to creative ideas that would allow him to avoid crossing the nuclear threshold, or possibly just to slow Israel's approach to it. Then, however, the crisis leading up to the 1967 Six-Day War caused Eshkol to overcome his hesitation. The new and unexpected developments during those crucial days changed the entire situation. Without making any political resolution regarding the nuclear dilemma—and no such resolution was forthcoming— the dynamics of the crisis generated new dramatic facts and a new frame of mind.

As Israel faced the worst crisis in its history—the massing of Egyptian troops in the Sinai peninsula and the possibility of a surprise aerial attack— the nuclear project was transformed, almost overnight, into the nation's ultimate insurance policy. At a time when Israel was preparing temporary burial sites for thousands of soldiers, it was unthinkable that the leaders of the nuclear project would sit idle. If Israel's nuclear-weapons capability could be made available, it must be made available. Prime Minister Eshkol was not in a position to stop them, and he must have authorized special emergency activity.[56]

In the few days before the war, Israel did something it had never done before. In an intensive crash effort, Israeli teams improvised the assembly of the nation's first nuclear explosive devices. As Israeli scientists and technicians were "tickling the dragon's tail," meaning assembling the first nuclear cores for those devices, only a few of them were aware that there was even a military contingency plan in the works. As Israeli leaders contemplated the worst scenarios—in particular, the failure of the Israeli air force to destroy the Arab air forces and/or the extensive use by Egypt of chemical weapons against Israeli cities—authority was given for preliminary contingency planning for "demonstrating" Israel's nuclear capability. The idea was to create the technical possibility of demonstrating Israel's nuclear capability over some remote desert area as a political signal, not to actually use the devices militarily.[57] Israel wanted to be in a position to send a signal to Egypt and to the superpowers that if all else failed and Israel's existence was in peril, Israel would have a doomsday capability to inflict great harm on Egypt. The final step in the assembly process, arming the devices, was never taken.[58]

These were most dramatic moments for those who involved, especially the project's leaders. To them, the assembly of those devices meant an extraordinary historical moment in the life of the project and the nation as a whole. It was seen as the moment when Israel actually became a nuclear power.[59] From their perspective, it also was an irreversible moment, as they could no longer conceive of a future Israeli prime minister who would give up this capability for any reason, except, perhaps, a real peace.

Prime Minister Eshkol may not have made a formal decision on the nuclear question. As already noted, before the Six-Day War, he was hesitant, ambivalent, unsure. Yet even without a formal decision, in those dramatic days of May and June 1967 the balance between the forces of resolve and caution tipped toward resolve. Although Eshkol may have been leaning toward caution, he was overtaken by the facts on the ground. Israel had effectively made a commitment to possess nuclear weapons.

The NPT Dilemma

While the significance of the new facts on the ground had to be reckoned with, Israel still had to respond in a comprehensive manner to the many outstanding issues that constituted its post-R&D nuclear dilemma. Israel still needed to define in operational and political terms the meaning of its nuclear commitment. Eshkol's task was further complicated by the political and personnel changes created by the Six-Day War.

Until the war, Eshkol held the dual portfolio of prime minister and minister of defense and, as such, was the sole overseer of the nuclear project. After the war and after Moshe Dayan had been appointed minister of defense on the eve of the war, they had to share responsibility for certain aspects of the nuclear project.[60] Furthermore, Zvi Dinstein, Eshkol's right-hand man on the nuclear project, was no longer the deputy minister of defense. His executive responsibility was transferred to Dayan's top civilian aide, the former chief of staff, Zvi Zur, who was friendlier to the needs of the nuclear project than Dinstein. Moreover, the cabinet was now reinforced by a minister of defense who was himself a nuclear advocate.[61]

Eshkol and Dayan, however, were not interested or did not have the political will to open the nuclear issue to the cabinet for discussion. Neither wanted a repeat of the 1962 debate.[62] Eshkol's plate was full after the war, and by mid-1968 his health was fast deteriorating. He died in office in February 1969 not knowing what Israel's nuclear future would be. The problem of determining Israel's nuclear future thus was passed to Israel's new leader, Prime Minister Golda Meir.

After 1967, Israel's nuclear dilemma was reframed and dominated by a new factor, Israel's stance on the Nuclear Non-Proliferation Treaty (NPT). The completion of the NPT negotiations and Israel's completion of its R&D phase took place at virtually the same time, as if they were racing with each other. Each development took nearly a decade to come to fruition, and the completion of each meant the end of an era. The two developments also represented opposite nuclear trends that contradicted each other, but until late 1968, few in Israel (or the United States) understood the depth of the conflict.[63] Israel now had to make up its mind, and a decision on this issue would determine many of the other nuclear issues. Israel spent a long time resolving the NPT dilemma. In the meantime, the nuclear program was drifting slowly toward the threshold without a formal political decision from the top. In response to this vacuum, various civilian and military government agencies made their own strategic assumptions about the future, sometimes in bureaucratic isolation and in secret.[64] Nuclear ambiguity prevailed in those days, toward the United States but also within the Israeli bureaucracy itself.

By the spring of 1968 the conventional wisdom in the United States and Israel was that Israel would eventually join the NPT.[65] By late May Israeli sources agreed that their country would soon sign the NPT.[66] Even without access to internal deliberations, it is possible to reconstruct the logic behind this reasoning. Obtaining Israel's signature to the NPT was assumed to be more important to the United States than it was to Israel to stay outside the treaty. In Israel, rejecting the NPT was understood as an act of defiance on an issue important to America's global interests. We should recall that in 1968 Israel was anxiously anticipating a fundamental transformation in its security relations with the United States, as America was about to replace France as Israel's primary defense supplier. Israelis believed that in return for the Phantoms that Eshkol had officially requested during his visit in January, Israel would sign the NPT.[67]

Equally important was the early view that signing the NPT was not incompatible with Israel's previous nuclear commitments, particularly its pledge regarding nonintroduction. Signing the NPT was viewed by some to add little, perhaps nothing, to what Israel had already committed not to do. After all, Israel had already committed not to introduce nuclear weapons, and signing the NPT would still allow Israel to keep a posture of advanced "nuclear pregnancy." The common view was that even after a nation had signed and ratified the NPT, it still would be allowed to proceed with a full array of "dual-use" activities, ostensibly for peaceful purposes but with an implicit military meaning.[68]

These early expectations all proved to be wrong. The NPT was presented for signature on July 1, 1968. Sixty-five nations signed it on that day, but Israel was not among them.[69] The more that Israel studied the legal and political implications of the NPT, the more doubts it had. By the fall of 1968, Israel had publicly raised various concerns about the applicability of the NPT to its security situation, especially that the NPT lacked sufficient guarantees against aggression by a nuclear power (e.g., the Soviet Union) against a nonnuclear state. Despite these admitted concerns, though, Israel's real problem with the NPT could not be openly stated.[70] We can assume, however, that the NPT issue forced the Israeli government to take a hard look at the entire nuclear issue, something it had been reluctant to do for a long time.

The late Professor Yuval Ne'eman recalled that sometime after Golda Meir became prime minister, she chaired a meeting of the Israel's top political leadership to discuss the future of the nuclear project. The meeting was held at Dimona. Among the participants, in addition to the prime minister herself, were Minister of Defense Moshe Dayan, Deputy Prime Minister Yigal Allon, Minister Israel Galili, as well as the appointed leaders of the nuclear project. Nothing was ever written about the meeting, but Ne'eman, who attended the meeting as a member of the IAEC, recalled the meeting for Dayan's remarkable performance. When Dayan's turn came, he started to talk about issues that first appeared totally unrelated to the subject of the meeting. He recited recent intelligence reports about torture in the Arab world and provided graphic accounts of how Arab leaders tortured their political opponents. A few minutes into his talk, according to Ne'eman, Meir interrupted him by saying, "Enough with this. I made up my mind. We will proceed."

In Ne'eman's account, this was Dayan's brilliant way of reminding his colleagues of the kind of neighborhood in which Israel lived. While Ministers Allon and Galili were willing to put some unspecified limits on the nuclear program, possibly on the production of fissile material, Meir was convinced that Israel must proceed with the full program. This was a key political decision that preceded Israel's final negative decision on the NPT.[71]

Israel under Golda Meir must have recognized that signing the NPT meant a solemn legal obligation not to acquire nuclear weapons. Some officials had warned that signing the NPT was utterly incompatible with Israel's newly acquired nuclear capability. Taking the NPT seriously would have legally required rolling back those capabilities. But Israel could not convey this to the United States, as doing so would have been admitting that for years Israel had been playing games with its nuclear pledges, in particular manipulating American visits to Dimona. Israel therefore formally maintained that the NPT was still "under active study."

As detailed in chapter 1, by 1969 it became apparent that Israel first had to quietly work out new nuclear understandings with the United States at the highest level. In September 1969 Prime Minister Meir laid the groundwork for Israel's negative decision on the NPT, but she still promised a formal reply after her new cabinet had discussed the issue. As detailed in chapter 1, it took four more months until Ambassador Rabin informed national security adviser Henry Kissinger in February 1970 that Israel had decided not to sign the NPT. Rabin provided no further explanation but merely asked Kissinger to notify President Nixon of Israel's decision. In turn, Kissinger did not ask Rabin for any explanation, nor for the record, did he express any regret.

The Nixon-Meir understandings enabled Israel to formally decide not to sign the NPT and to move into a real nuclear-deployment posture. This outcome meant a great deal to Israel, as it gave it wide latitude in what it could and could not do in the nuclear field. Because secrecy was essential to the deal, it left Israel with a freedom of action that it would not otherwise have had.

After years of hesitancy and inhibition, Israel had finally made up its mind to choose resolution over caution. This decision was perhaps equal in importance to Ben-Gurion's initial decision to develop an atomic weapon in 1957. The U.S.-Israel deal of 1969 put to rest Israel's nuclear dilemma regarding domestic disclosure of the nation's nuclear status when Israel committed to a policy of nonacknowledgment, both internationally and domestically. All subsequent Israeli prime ministers have endorsed the legacy of the Nixon-Meir deal.

The Dilemma of Use

A nation that develops nuclear weapons must grapple with the dilemma of when and under what circumstances they could be used. In order to design a militarily meaningful posture, the military utility of those weapons must be considered. Even if the thinking about the purpose of the nuclear program is primarily political—that is, projecting existential deterrence and overall strength—weaponization necessitates thinking about military use.

The very idea of deterrence is built on credibility, and credibility is based on the feasibility of use. If the products of the nuclear program are in non-weaponized form, their deterrent value may be diminished because they may be perceived as less credible. Alternatively, it could be argued, leaving the products of the nuclear program presumed but unacknowledged can still have an effective deterrent value.

In the mid- to late 1960s, Israeli defense intellectuals were asked to grapple systematically with these issues. Initially, those discussions were couched in quasi-theoretical terms: If Israel were to develop and acquire nuclear weapons, under what circumstances could they be used? What kind of nuclear weapons would best serve Israel's needs? What kind of arsenal might Israel need? Note that it was not the IDF that initiated this brainstorming; it was initiated by Eshkol and Deputy Defense Minister Zvi Dinstein in coordination with Chiefs of Staff Yitzhak Rabin and Chaim Bar-Lev and IAF commander Mordechai Hod. These discussions arrived at the conclusion that Israel's commitment to nuclear resolve must, at a minimum, reach the level of full or near-full weaponization. If Israel took the pains to develop a nuclear capability as a national insurance policy for the purpose of projecting deterrence, that capability must be operational, not virtual. Such a view was influential in the Israeli government under Golda Meir when it made its final decisions on the nuclear issue in 1969/1970.

These early deliberations produced the first articulation of the underlying concept of Israel's use doctrine. The idea was to define certain existential "red lines" that, if crossed, could trigger the use of nuclear weapons. Those red lines gave operational meaning to the qualitative idea of "last resort." Specifically, four different scenarios—all of them considered theoretical and unlikely—could invoke such use: (1) a successful Arab military penetration of populated areas within Israel's 1949 cease-fire lines; (2) the destruction of the IAF; (3) the exposure of Israeli centers of population to massive and continuous air attacks or to major chemical or biological attacks; and (4) the use of nuclear weapons or other unconventional weaponry against Israeli territory. Each of these scenarios was defined as an existential threat to the state of Israel against which the nation would be politically, militarily, and morally justified in defending itself by means of atomic weapons.[72]

From the start, however, it was evident that finding a sensible use for nuclear weapons in the Arab-Israeli theater would be problematic. Analysis of the notion of last resort, especially under circumstances in which the capability was unacknowledged and unintroduced, revealed a paradox. Using a nuclear bomb *after* a massive Arab army had already penetrated Israel's 1949 borders could be too late to be militarily effective, perhaps even impossible because of the proximity of Israeli troops or citizens. Conversely, using nuclear weapons to preempt Arab army troops on their way to the border was deemed too early to justify use; that is, it would be politically unacceptable. Israeli strategists had encountered a problem similar to the one that NATO faced throughout much of the cold war: the difficulty of defining the militarily and politically proper moment to use nuclear weapons effectively to stop a conventionally superior enemy attack.[73]

Another realization that emerged in those discussions, in part in response to this dilemma, was that it would be inconceivable for Israel to resort to using nuclear weapons without an explicit prior and proper warning. There was a consensus that Israel's first nuclear detonation had to be a *demonstration* for deterrence purposes. After all, deterrence will work only if the capability and the willingness to use it are clearly conveyed to the other side. But how can a state establish deterrence effects in a strategic situation of nuclear ambiguity? This dilemma becomes even more complicated when a nation is committed to a declaratory posture of nonintroduction, which logically *appears* to imply no first use. A nuclear demonstration has two important purposes: it is the equivalent to issuing a deterrent statement, and it is an act of both acknowledgment and resolve, whereas a demonstration can be conducted earlier than the actual crossing of those red lines.

These considerations were put to the test in 1967, 1973, and 1991. On the eve of the 1967 war, Israel's nuclear-weapons capability was barely operational. Although the country had almost completed the R&D phase, it had no nuclear weapons. Under the gravity of the crisis, Israel improvised the nearly complete assembly of a handful of nuclear devices, something that it had never done before, and it was done not for deterrence but as an emergency contingency plan.[74] As I understand it, this was not done in response to a specific political or military request from the top or to a specific operational need. It was done because it would have been inconceivable not to do it and the political leadership could not resist it.[75]

It was clear from the start that the use of atomic weapons was incompatible with the IDF's operational plans, all of which were based on aerial preemption to be followed by an armor attack deep into the Sinai. The efforts to rationalize scenarios of atomic use illustrate the oddity of thinking about the unthinkable. The various doomsday scenarios assumed some sort of colossal failure by the IDF (perhaps due to an intelligence leak) in its preemption and/or a decisive strategic surprise attack by Egypt, including the massive use of missiles tipped with chemical warheads against Israeli cities (there was no complete clarity on the status of the Egyptian missile force). Yet all of Israel's contingency plans were based on the idea of first deploying the capability politically through a demonstration.[76]

None of these worst-case scenarios materialized. Israel's success in 1967 using a conventional preemptive attack demonstrated the soundness of the conventionalist school in the 1962 debate. Israel had strong enough conventional weapons to defeat three Arab armies in six days. One important lesson might have been that the nuclear issue was primarily about politics and psychology, not about military utility.

The nuclear issue had proved irrelevant in 1967. Israel's improvised nuclear devices turned out to have no deterrence value whatsoever. Shimon Peres, who in 1967 was outside the government, proposed that Israel take advantage of Egypt's massing of troops to introduce its nuclear capability by conducting a nuclear demonstration explosion.[77] His thinking must have been that the new circumstances that Egypt created offered an opportunity for Israel to move away from its pledge to President Kennedy and to introduce and legitimize its nuclear status. Peres's suggestion was ignored by the Eshkol government.

Another strategic lesson that Israel probably learned from the 1967 nuclear incident was the difficulty of extracting deterrence value from a situation in which the very capability itself was unacknowledged. The credibility of nuclear deterrence under a nonacknowledgment posture depends on perception, so the perception would have to be manipulated if nuclear capabilities could not be "introduced" officially.

We might think of nuclear deterrence as an epistemic ladder that starts with unconfirmed rumors and speculations and ends with an official declaration accompanied by a test. In this image, Israel stands on, or just above, the first rung of that ladder. Israel's nuclear deterrence under a nonacknowledgment posture has rested on the presumption, which is periodically supported by credible leaks, that Israel actually has the bomb and, under conditions of existential threat, would use it. Furthermore after the 1967 war, in the case of an emergency, Israel needed to be ready to move quickly up the deterrence ladder, which meant that it needed to have on very short notice the technical capabilities to demonstrate its nuclear capability.[78]

Perhaps the most dramatic moment in Israel's nuclear history took place during the early stages of the 1973 war. Unlike the situation in 1967, in 1973 Israel appeared to be on the brink of military collapse. Its defense lines on both fronts, the Suez Canal and the Golan Heights, were overwhelmed by huge advancing columns of armor and infantry, backed up by hundreds of pieces of artillery. Hundreds of Israeli soldiers died in the early hours of the war as many regular army units were decimated. It was the closest to a military collapse that Israel had faced. Israeli Defense Minister Moshe Dayan, who apparently was close to a mental breakdown, was mumbling about "the demise of the Third Temple," reportedly proposed or suggested in a number of contexts the use of Israel's ultimate weapons. By the end of the first week, Israel had lost about a quarter of its combat-ready planes. By that time the commander of the air force, General Benny Peled, warned that at such a rate of losses, the IAF would have to limit its activities. Dayan feared that Israel was approaching a point of no return, and he evidently wanted the United States to take notice that Israel had reached that point.[79]

No authoritative record has surfaced as to what exactly Dayan proposed and what activities took place on the ground, but rumors referred to various scenarios that Dayan could have invoked. According to one person's testimony, at the end of the war cabinet meeting in the late morning of October 9, a day after the IDF had failed miserably in its first counterattack in the Egyptian frontier, Dayan suggested discussing some options involving a nuclear demonstration. On hand was Shalheveth Freier, the IAEC's director general, who was waiting to provide a briefing. As soon as Dayan made his suggestion, Ministers Allon and Galili told the prime minister that such a discussion was premature and uncalled for. The prime minister agreed with them and Freier did not address the forum.[80]

It also appeared that on two or three occasions during the war, a "strategic alert" (a euphemism for nuclear alert) was declared, twice in the first week of the war and the third on October 17 or 18 in response to a state of alert of Soviet SCUD missiles in Egypt.[81] It is believed that those state of alerts involved certain readiness "dispositions" such as mobilizing the Jericho missiles from their shelters, fueling them, and other related activities. Such activities require the authorization of the prime minister and the minister of defense but apparently do not require a formal decision by the war cabinet. These activities were supervised personally by representatives of both the prime minister and the minister of defense. Decades later, in a conference in Washington, D.C., William Quandt (who then was an aide at the National Security Council) recalled how profound the impact of American intelligence reports of these "dispositions" was on Henry Kissinger. Quandt believes those reports were critical to the American decision to initiate the airlift to Israel.

The bottom line is that Prime Minister Golda Meir refused to permit the military use of nuclear weapons. Ultimately, it was she, the prime minister, who had to make the decision. She apparently had strong inhibitions against the use of nuclear weapons, including in a demonstration, in a situation short of last resort. As was the case with John F. Kennedy during the Cuban missile crisis a decade earlier, Golda Meir contemplated the use of nuclear weapons and firmly rejected that option.[82]

After more than four decades and three major wars during which Israel has been "thinking the unthinkable," little has changed. If anything, the experience of the wars deepened the basic Israeli outlook that nuclear weapons may have important symbolic and political value but lack genuine military value and should not be recognized as military weapons systems. Generations of Israeli defense intellectuals rediscover the same lesson: how difficult—indeed, nearly impossible—it is to construe realistic military scenarios that could call for, let alone justify, the use of nuclear weapons. As Israel recognized in the 1967 war, nuclear thinking is at odds with the principles of Israel's conventional warfare strategy. Even in the 1973 war, the only war that brought Israel truly close to the brink, it would have been extremely difficult to construe a scenario in which nuclear weapons could be used sensibly. Israel has no military reason to "introduce" nuclear weapons, and it has many political reasons not to do so. The chief political role of nuclear weapons is to enforce the realization that any call for the "destruction of Israel" is irrational. Short of a nuclear attack, it is inconceivable that Israel would ever use nuclear weapons to defend itself against any military threats. The legacy of Israel's nuclear weapons is that they are truly unusable.[83]

Subsequent Dilemmas: Advanced Weaponry and Posture Design

Countries must make new types of nuclear decisions as they move from initiation to maturity. These subsequent decisions involve matters such as posture and arsenal design, that is, how broad and advanced their nuclear commitment should be. Each of the first five nuclear-weapons states developed, within a decade or so, advanced nuclear weaponry, especially thermonuclear weapons.

There are indications (e.g., Vanunu's testimony) that after the 1973 war Israel followed suit and significantly strengthened its nuclear commitment. It is believed that in the mid-late 1970s Israel took the path of its predecessors and built an arsenal that is qualitatively advanced and consists primarily of two-stage thermonuclear weapons. This may shed a new light on one of the greatest mysteries in the history of proliferation: whether the "double flash" that was detected by an American Vela Hotel satellite at dawn September 22, 1979, over a remote swath of the Indian Ocean nearly halfway between South Africa and Antarctica, was produced by a low-yield nuclear test.[84] Israel was the only country in 1979 that had a strong motivation to conduct such a test. If Israel was moving at that time toward an advanced two-stage arsenal, Israel had to test it somewhere. The technical complexity of two-stage weapons, in particular the working of the trigger (the primary), requires a test. A nation cannot launch such an ambitious program without conducting a final test. If this story is true, then it is another indication of Israeli technological resolve.

About the same time, however, it appears that Israel also made a key decision on the side of caution. Israel decided against developing tactical battlefield nuclear weapons. Unlike the other declared nuclear-weapons states, except for China, which have developed, manufactured, and deployed tactical nuclear weapons, Israel apparently decided against their production and deployment (even though it completed the necessary R&D phase of their development). The reasons behind that decision were many—political, strategic, and operational—but they all manifested the concern about blurring the distinction between nuclear and conventional weapons and whether the dissemination of tactical nuclear weapons would undermine some of the fundamental aspects of amimut. Given the traumatic experience of the 1973 war, this was a bold strategic decision. Once again, resolve (two-stage weapons) and caution (no tactical weapons) were coexisting.

Finally, the size of the Israeli nuclear arsenal is not known.[85] Following Mordechai Vanunu's revelations, it was common to hear claims that Israel might have one hundred to two hundred nuclear weapons. Seymour Hersh claimed that Israel might have three hundred nuclear weapons or even more, both tactical and strategic.[86] More contemporary estimates, based on leaks attributed to sources in the U.S. intelligence community, are of a much smaller arsenal, perhaps around one hundred weapons and possibly fewer.[87]

If these more conservative claims are true, the development of Israel's nuclear posture was guided by strategic considerations derived from Israel's nuclear doctrine, and not by technological or bureaucratic inertia, as some feared in the wake of the Vanunu revelations in 1986. It also suggests that Israel dealt with its subsequent nuclear dilemmas using a careful calibration between resolve and caution. This suggestion is consistent with Israel's other strategic decision in the mid- to late 1970s, to develop a longer-range and more accurate nuclear-tipped ballistic missile, the Jericho II, to replace the outdated Jericho I. Israel reportedly tested the Jericho II in the late 1980s and deployed it in the early 1990s.

If Israel decided not to produce and deploy tactical nuclear weapons and also to keep the size of its arsenal relatively small, this would indicate that unlike the historical trend of most other nuclear nations, Israel treats its nuclear arsenal in existential terms. If true, these decisions agree with Israel's previous decisions to maintain the conventional orientation of the Israeli army, as well as the related requirements of a regime of opacity.

Since the early 1980s (and possibly earlier), the Israeli navy, with the support of other government agencies, promoted the idea that Israel should build a small fleet of modern conventional (diesel) submarines for "strategic purposes," an Israeli euphemism for a sea-launched nuclear capability. After complex negotiations in which a deal was almost signed with a German shipyard in early 1990, General Ehud Barak vetoed it on the basis of cost, as well as on Israeli policymakers' prevailing sense of nuclear caution.

After the 1991 Gulf War, Israel's strategic picture changed fundamentally. Israel decided to reverse its earlier decision and to establish a sea-based strategic arm. Moreover, it enthusiastically accepted the German government's offer to finance the purchase of two large diesel submarines and to share in the financing of a third, presumably because of the role of German industries in the development of Iraq's unconventional weaponry. The strategic developments throughout the 1990s in both Iraq and Iran, compounded by the failure of Western intelligence agencies to detect Iraq's nuclear program, were critical to Israel's decision to boost its strategic capabilities. Nuclear resolve had taken the lead. Although details about the specific capabilities of those submarines are classified, the new, sea-based strategic arm is presumed to have a second-strike nuclear component. The most sensitive aspects of the submarine project, the cruise-missile technology that makes these diesel submarines dually capable (nuclear and conventional) launching platforms, are believed to have been developed and built in Israel. Last, the Israeli-made cruise missiles are thought to be capable of hitting strategic targets within a range of more than nine hundred miles.[88]

By July 2000, Israel had taken delivery of all three Dolphin-class submarines it had ordered from Germany. In doing so, Israel has moved toward acquiring a survivable second-strike nuclear capability and is now on its way to restructuring its nuclear forces into a triad form, like that of all the other five declared nuclear-weapons states. A fleet of three submarines was initially believed the smallest fleet that Israeli needed to deploy at sea one nuclear-armed submarine at all times. Then in 2006 Israel placed an order for two more submarines. A survivable deterrent fleet of five is now perceived as necessary because of Israel's unique geopolitical and demographic vulnerability to nuclear attack, and one that no potential nuclear enemy of Israel could ignore.

Final Reflections

Proliferation decisions are never final and fixed commitments. It takes nations many years, a decade or longer since the advent of the first bomb, to establish a full nuclear-weapons capability.[89] Given this time frame and the complexity of the proliferation landscape, proliferation decisions are intrinsically tentative. The long-term vision is often left implicit and vague, best understood as less a firm plan and more a hedge with regard to an uncertain future. Consequently, historians have difficulty pinpointing the key moments of nuclear decision making.

All initial proliferation decisions are revised, and sometimes they are scrapped altogether. This was the case in Sweden, which made a series of tentative (but significant) proliferation decisions—more hedging than a commitment—but a decade later decided to reverse them gradually as the political environment changed. Even when all the proliferation decisions have been made, the final dilemma of whether to cross the nuclear-weapons threshold remains. France spent a long time making its final proliferation decision. India and Pakistan each sat on the fence (each in its own way and style) for more than a decade, drifting slowly from an "option" to actual weapons, but without making a full and public disclosure.

Even after the infrastructure has been built and weapons have been manufactured, a nation's nuclear posture commitments are still subject to periodic reevaluation. Under certain political circumstances, states may even decide to roll back their entire commitment to nuclear weapons, as South Africa did in the early 1990s. (I should point out, however, that the white apartheid regime, which decided to dismantle South Africa's six or seven assembled nuclear bombs and scrap the country's nuclear-weapons infrastructure, did so only after it had decided to move toward black majority rule in the country. This meant that the then-radical African National Congress [ANC] would rule the country, and even if many white South Africans grudgingly accepted the logic and necessity of majority rule, they thought it would be imprudent to have an ANC regime armed with nuclear weapons.) All nations with nuclear weapons periodically conduct posture reviews of their entire nuclear complex, usually once or twice in a decade. Nuclear commitments are, in short, dynamic.

Owing to its use of amimut, the Israeli nuclear case has pushed many of these historical patterns to their limits. All the methodological difficulties of reconstructing nuclear decisions are compounded in the Israeli case. Even though I believe that the narrative I present here reflects real nuclear dilemmas with which real Israeli decision makers had to grapple, I also concede that the available evidence is too indirect and too incomplete to recount exactly those dilemmas and their related decision-making process. To overcome the scarcity of evidence, I have had to rely on historical reconstruction using certain theoretical presumptions, interpretative reasoning, and, ultimately, educated guesses.[90] Nonetheless, I still believe that enough historical evidence exists, some of it public, other parts off the record, to reconstruct the basic events.

In the Israeli case, reconstructing the Israeli nuclear program rests on three separate policy decisions. Just as David Ben-Gurion was firmly committed to establishing an Israeli nuclear option, he also was cautious about making long-term nuclear commitments. His immediate successor, Levi Eshkol, pushed the tension even further. Under his leadership, Israel's nuclear capability was completed, but he died in office not knowing what route Israel should (or would) take. His successor, Golda Meir, made the required decisions, but those decisions kept the nuclear issue invisible, with no public face. It was during her term in office that amimut became the nation's permanent nuclear signature.

Two of those key decisions expressed nuclear resolve, and the other two expressed caution. Israel initiated its nuclear program in the late 1950s with an extraordinary commitment to technological resolve, but afterward it realized that this resolve had to be checked by a commitment to constraint. Even Ben-Gurion recognized this, and his next two major nuclear legacies were on the side of caution. First, his disclosure strategy set the stage for Israel's non-introduction pledge, which to this day has remained an important pillar of its nuclear policy. Second, Ben-Gurion promised in 1962 not to change the IDF's conventional doctrine and so adopted a covert nuclear posture. That decision meant ruling out Peres's vision of Israel as a member of the nuclear club. These two decisions shaped Israel's bargain with the bomb. Finally, when Golda Meir chose nuclear resolve in 1969/1970, almost all the elements of Israel's amimut policy were in place. Little in the basic outlook has changed since. Over the years, various review panels have examined the Israeli bargain, but they all have recommended keeping the basic outlook in place. This is a remarkable record of continuity.

Israel's current nuclear policy was not inevitable. On the contrary, until Golda Meir made her nuclear decisions in 1969/1970, the fate of Israel's nuclear future was still largely undetermined. Three key events between 1967 and 1969 determined the choices that Israel made in 1969/1970: the Six-Day War (1967), the NPT (1968), and the appointment of Golda Meir as prime minister (1969). Had these developments not occurred as they did, Israel's nuclear history could have taken a different turn.

Before the 1967 Six-Day War, Prime Minister Eshkol was uncertain about the direction of the nation's nuclear project after achieving the "nuclear option" threshold. He and his associates sought creative ways of using the nuclear program as a tool to transform Israel's political relations in the Middle East. Eshkol was aware of the risks involved in crossing the weapons threshold. He knew that the Israeli bomb, as either a reality or a presumption, could provoke Nasser to start a war. Eshkol also was aware that a global nonproliferation movement was progressing, and he assumed that Israel eventually would join it. Keeping the Middle East free from nuclear weapons was good for Israel if it could use its nuclear program to bargain for a major security and economic package.

But the 1967 war made all that impossible, for three reasons. First, Israel crossed the weapons threshold in May/June 1967. Second, Egypt lost the war and, with it, much of its leverage to affect Israel's nuclear behavior. Third, Moshe Dayan, an advocate of nuclear weapons, became the minister of defense and thus had some say on the nuclear issue; Eshkol was no longer the sole decision maker. With these changes, the pendulum swung from caution to resolve.

Had the NPT been completed and signed only two years earlier, say in 1966 and not in 1968, Israel would likely have signed it. Israel would have secretly completed the R&D phase, forming a weapons option, but probably would not have moved much beyond it (i.e., to produce or deploy weapons). Israel would have considered halting its nuclear program short of possessing actual weapons, at the threshold point. In this counterfactual scenario, Israel might have informed the United States that it had developed a nuclear option and negotiated from a position of strength, probably asking the United States for formal certain security commitments and assistance in building a major nuclear-power program as a condition for its NPT signature. It is almost certain that the United States would have given Israel a nuclear-power package and security assurances for its signing the NPT. Israel still would have had a highly developed nuclear option, along with a civil nuclear-power program, but without actual nuclear weapons. But NPT came two years too late, and *after* the Six-Day War.

Prime Minister Eshkol died in office on February 26, 1969, after many months of illness that had prevented him from governing effectively. Until early to mid-1968, Eshkol was leaning toward signing the NPT, believing that Israel could not defy the United States. By mid-1968 Eshkol had gradually shifted his position on the NPT, probably under the influence or pressure of Israel's nuclear custodians, believing that Israel should postpone any commitment to scale back its nuclear program. Meir, his successor, took a few months to form her answers to Israel's nuclear issues, but her decisions solidified Israel's final move toward amimut. The Nixon-Meir deal was, to a large extent, her creation, reflecting her own political instincts and style.

Amimut is a crucial aspect of Israeli society and polity and reflects this dual history of both strong resolve toward the acquisition and development of nuclear weapons, and a matching awareness that nuclear weapons demand almost absolute nuclear caution that forbids all formal acknowledgment of this important part of Israeli national life.

Chapter Four
The Infrastructure of Amimut

In chapter 2, I described Israel's response to its nuclear dilemma as the adoption of a declaratory opaque policy that allowed it to maximize the benefits of both nuclear resolve and nuclear caution while incurring the lowest costs possible. But this is not the whole story of amimut. Opacity as a declaratory policy is only one layer within the larger fabric of amimut. To grasp the robustness of the Israeli bargain with the bomb, one must examine the entire infrastructure of amimut.

The infrastructure of amimut has three distinct institutional layers. At the core is the Israel Atomic Energy Commission (IAEC), Israel's primary atomic secret maker and the "midwife" of amimut. This core is wrapped in a second layer, the MALMAB (Office of Security at the Ministry of Defense), which is amimut's security guard. The last layer is the Office of the Military Censor, or, in colloquial Hebrew, the Censora, whose mission is to control public discourse and enforce amimut. Together, these three organizations are the guardians of amimut. Each has its own bureaucratic function and identity, and they often appear to have a certain bureaucratic friction with one another, but ultimately they complement one another in this task, and the enduring success of amimut is proof of their effectiveness.

Exposing this infrastructure is a tricky business, as much of it is invisible to the naked eye; in fact, much of it is technically classified. Even the apolitical professionals who manage the infrastructure are largely unknown to the Israeli public. Amimut insists on concealing its inner working mechanism with a thin visible cover at the top obscuring most of the structure below. My exposition therefore is inevitably incomplete, reconstructive, and interpretative.

THE IAEC: The Secret Maker

At the institutional core of Israel's bargain with the bomb, at the center of the amimut bureaucracy, is the Israel Atomic Energy Commission (IAEC), the agency that has overall responsibility for Israel's nuclear affairs. The IAEC is the *sanctum sanctorum*—the holy of holies—of Israel's secret nuclear republic. It is here where most of Israel's nuclear secrets are manufactured, where the vision of amimut was conceived, developed and codified, and where the current state of amimut is monitored.

The IAEC is probably Israel's most secretive government agency. Virtually every aspect of its operations is considered classified, including its real mandate, organizational structure, budget, relations with other (military and civilian) government agencies, and even most of its oversight procedures. Its various physical facilities are among the most guarded sites in Israel, with most unmarked and unknown. Its personnel must pass frequent top-secret security clearances, and its senior officials are required to pass the highest standards of security checks available in Israel, including periodic polygraph tests. With the exception of director general and spokesperson, the identities of its senior personnel are not publicly known.

The IAEC is also one of Israel's most insulated governmental agencies. Its internal code of secrecy is more restricted than that of the two other secret organizations also under the direct control of the prime minister: the Mossad (Israel's foreign intelligence service) and the General Security Services (GSS, Israel's domestic intelligence service).[1] For example, both the Mossad's[2] and the GSS's[3] official Web sites contain mission statements describing their missions. The IAEC's Web site does not, however, contain a mission statement. To illustrate, we might compare the IAEC Web site with that of its American counterpart, the National Nuclear Security Administration (NNSA), the semiautonomous agency within the Department of Energy (DOE) that is in charge of the U.S. nuclear-weapons complex.[4] The NNSA's elaborate Web site, however, has a six-point mission statement:

1. To enhance U.S. national security through the military application of nuclear energy.
2. To maintain and enhance the safety, reliability, and performance of the U.S. nuclear weapons stockpile, including the ability to design, produce, and test, in order to meet national security requirements.

3. To provide the U.S. Navy with safe, militarily effective nuclear propulsion plants and to ensure the safe and reliable operation of those plants.
4. To promote international nuclear safety and nonproliferation.
5. To reduce global danger from weapons of mass destruction.
6. To support U.S. leadership in science and technology.[5]

In comparison, the IAEC's extremely spare Web site—posted on the Web in early 2004 after reportedly long months of bureaucratic bickering within the IAEC itself and with MALMAB—does not have even a single explicit reference to or even hint of national security, let alone of nuclear weapons. Instead, the IAEC Web site contains the following innocuous (but empty) description of the organization:

> The IAEC advises the Government of Israel in areas of nuclear policy and in setting priorities in nuclear research and development. The commission implements governmental policies and represents the State of Israel in international organizations in the nuclear field, such as the International Atomic Energy Agency. The IAEC maintains relations with relevant national authorities of other states.[6]

The reason for the difference is obvious: the IAEC's mandate is classified.

A Brief History

In the beginning, there was secrecy. The IAEC came into existence on June 13, 1952, through a secret executive order issued by Prime Minister David Ben-Gurion,[7] but it took two more years for it to become officially (but inadvertently) acknowledged.[8] Professor Ernst David Bergmann was the IAEC's founder and chair until 1966, which made him a man with two, and sometimes even more, hats.[9] This duality of titles and administrative affiliations, mimicking Ben-Gurion's dual portfolios as both prime minister and minister of defense, shaped the split identity of the organization he created. From the beginning, the IAEC was established as a civilian agency with two identities, and its external identity has continued to serve as a public veneer to conceal its more secretive and substantive internal identity.

The public reference to the "Israel Atomic Energy Commission" mimicked the organizational concept of the national civil control of atomic energy, a concept under which other leading countries, such as the United States and France, had organized their national nuclear affairs in the 1940s and 1950s. Nevertheless, Israel recognized early on that this organizational concept was useful for concealing activities and intentions. Publicly, the IAEC was presented as a coordinating and advisory scientific semiautonomous body that resided administratively in the prime minister's office to advise the government in implementing its national commitment to nuclear energy. The commission's membership was made up of the nation's best-known scientists. Calling it a public scientific commission allowed Israel's nuclear scientists to apply for membership in international scientific bodies, to participate in training overseas, and to publish their unclassified research in respectable scientific journals.

This respectable civil identity was intended also to conceal the fact that in the mind of its creators, the IAEC's primary mission was to lay the foundation for a future Israeli nuclear project with military applications. This veneer was designed to obscure the existence of a secret nuclear research center, named in the early to mid-1950s "Machon 4," which operated, and was budgeted, as a research unit within the Research and Planning Division (EMET) at the Ministry of Defense (MOD).

In those early days, the IAEC's public front had a life of its own. The national commission occasionally convened and debated ideas and plans for atomic energy research without being fully aware that the real decision-making process was actually taking place elsewhere, at the MOD. Members of the commission clearly suspected that the IAEC's chair, Ernst Bergmann, quietly promoted a more ambitious defense-related agenda of his own, often making important decisions on behalf of the IAEC without informing them, but most of them did not realize how decisive and determined he actually was. Whereas most of the commission members envisioned an actual scientific commission that promoted basic academic research, Bergmann dreamed of a national nuclear project that would ultimately lead to the bomb.[10] Amimut and secrecy were needed from the very start to keep Bergmann's vision concealed from his own fellow commissioners.

Until the Dimona project became a reality in the late 1950s, though, people in the IAEC's main facility, known as Machon 4, did more dreaming about the future than actually working on the project. Nevertheless, the ethos of secrecy was prevalent long before there were any real atomic secrets to guard. Although there was little to show for those ambitious dreams for the future, except a few buildings on a hill adjacent to the Weizmann

Institute, Machon 4 already was one of Israel's most guarded facilities. A few years later, when the Dimona facility was established, the academic commissioners were outraged that Chairman Bergmann had not briefed them—let alone consulted with them—on the new project. They collectively resigned for not being consulted, leaving a chair without fellow commissioners.

The commissioners did not realize that Bergmann himself and the IAEC were only marginally involved in the creation of the Dimona project. In fact, the Dimona project was a setback to the IAEC as an institution because it was not established by the IAEC. Rather, the secret project was set up and run by a new independent and highly compartmentalized group within the MOD headed by the director general and later the deputy minister of defense, Shimon Peres. Peres in turn assigned the task of building Dimona to a colonel in the Ordnance Corps named Emanuel (Manes) Pratt. Pratt was given the authority to become Dimona's czar, Israel's version of General Leslie Groves, the all-powerful commander of the Manhattan Project. Pratt reported directly to Shimon Peres (not to IAEC Chair Bergmann), and Peres reported to Prime Minister Ben-Gurion. Under that arrangement, Peres was directly in charge of all aspects of the nuclear project, including its policies. The role of the IAEC as an organization was marginalized and its chair sidelined in the decision-making process. In those days, the IAEC and its chair also were kept in the dark about many aspects of the new nuclear project.

By the mid-1960s the Dimona and RAFAEL (Armaments Development Authority) branches of the nuclear project had to be merged, and the IAEC had to be reestablished as the overall executive technological authority in charge of all aspects of the nuclear project. Without establishing such new executive authority, it became apparent that it would be impossible to finalize the project. Bergmann himself was aware of this and sought a new technological leader who could merge all aspects of the project into a product, a nuclear explosive device.

In 1966, Bergmann resigned and Prime Minister Levi Eshkol (along with his deputy, Zvi Dinstein, who replaced Peres) decided to appoint another scientist with a long history of wearing two hats, Professor Israel Dostrovsky, a distinguished chemist who specialized in isotope research. Soon after returning to Israel from England in 1948, Dostrovsky founded and commanded HEMED GIMMEL, the geological unit within the Science Corps that conducted the geological survey of the Negev. Since then, Dostrovsky divided his time between academic and defense research.

Bergmann's resignation offered a chance to reestablish the IAEC in its new role as the administration in charge of all aspects of the nuclear project. Dostrovsky was appointed as the new-old IAEC's first director general and Prime Minister Eshkol appointed himself as its chair. Ever since, Israel's prime minister has been, ex officio, the IAEC chair.

What was publicly visible was a very limited part of the action. A dual identity continued to characterize the organizational structure of the new nuclear administration, publicly known as the new IAEC. This arrangement was based on a similar organizational principle used for the original IAEC in 1952: a thin public layer (the IAEC) and, behind it, a classified scientific administration (in Hebrew, *ha-minhal madaii*), which was founded within the MOD as the headquarters of Israel's entire nuclear-weapons complex. The new entity's chief was publicly the IAEC's director general and functioned also as the head of the most secretive administration within the MOD. He also had two channels of reporting: for policy and oversight, the responsibility for the IAEC resided with the prime minister, but for budget and administration, the *minhal* was an entity within the defense bureaucracy.

Nuclear Governance Under Amimut

Since 1966, the ministerial responsibility for Israel's nuclear affairs is publicly acknowledged to reside with the prime minister. As the IAEC chair, the prime minister appoints the IAEC's chief and the directors of the two nuclear research centers (at Dimona and Soreq), as well as the IAEC's board members. The IAEC's director general holds, ex officio, the rank of ambassador and serves as the head of the Israeli delegation to the International Atomic Energy Agency (IAEA)'s annual conferences. A senior official from the IAEC usually serves as Israel's permanent ambassador to the IAEA. For all practical purposes, the IAEC, not the Foreign Ministry, takes the lead in Israel's nuclear diplomacy, although in recent years there has been more coordination between the two organizations.

All nuclear matters in Israel are the prime minister's responsibility, but this does not tell the entire story. As noted, the involvement of the MOD in nuclear affairs is invisible. No public information is available about the organizational linkages between the IAEC and the MOD. But an examination of the experience of other nuclear weapons states may highlight Israel's unique arrangement under amimut.[11]

In the United States, the current division of labor between the Department of Energy (DOE) and the Department of Defense (DOD) on nuclear-weapons matters is drawn roughly along the lines of producer versus consumer. The DOE (through the NNSA) has overall responsibility for the nuclear-weapons complex (i.e., research, development, maintenance, and dismantlement) as the producer of nuclear weapons. The DOD maintains operational and custodial functions as the consumer of nuclear weapons that either are in DOD stockpiles or are actually deployed by the armed services. As a consumer, the DOD is in charge of the deployment and employment aspects of the nuclear systems, that is, matters related to delivery platforms, command and control, security, and doctrine. At the deployment stage, the responsibility and custodianship are transferred from civilian leadership to the military, namely, to the air force and the navy. Similar arrangements between producer and consumer exist in all other nuclear-weapons states because these two roles are generic elements of a nuclear posture.

This division of labor is murkier in the United States on matters of strategy and planning, in which both sides of the division, as well as other federal agencies, must coordinate in making national policy. In general, maintaining a coherent nuclear posture requires a great deal of coordination and cooperation between these two bureaucracies on a variety of practical issues, such as the life cycles of warheads, the safety and security of weapons, classification and declassification issues, and the long-term strategic planning of the United States' nuclear posture.[12] On matters of nuclear diplomacy, especially nonproliferation issues, the State Department also is a major player in policy. In the U.S. presidential system, the executive branch sets overall policies and goals, and the legislative branch authorizes funding and provides independent oversight. Because nuclear weapons require a great deal of interagency activity, the United States, and presumably other nuclear-weapons states, has a nuclear weapons council, or a similarly high-level professional forum, in which the relevant bureaucracies discuss nuclear policies.

In contrast, there is no public information on how Israel governs the bomb. But we must assume that in committing itself to nuclear weapons, Israel had to devise its own functional arrangement between its nuclear producers and consumers reflecting the constraints of amimut. The fact that the responsibility for all nuclear matters in Israel resides with the prime minister must have been critical to the design of Israel's system of nuclear governance. We should presume that *unlike* the United States, the custodianship of all nuclear assets rests in Israel with the prime minister, not with the minister of defense.

If so, Israel's nuclear bureaucracy has (relatively speaking) more authority over and responsibility for nuclear affairs than does its American counterpart, the NNSA under the DOE.

Designing the strategic and operational parameters of Israel's nuclear posture under amimut must have been a challenge. Given the constraints of amimut, logic suggests that Israel designed a nuclear governance system based on the separation (physical and probably organizational as well) of the nuclear assets (such as the nuclear cores) from their means of delivery. Or the nuclear agency may have been designed with double and parallel lines of command, one to the prime minister and the other to the minister of defense. We should also presume that Israel has a high-level interagency council for nuclear affairs. In a sense, the anonymous members of such a council would be Israel's "guardians of the arsenal," the ultimate guardians of amimut.

The "Constitution"

Israel's system of nuclear governance was launched in 1966 with the overhaul of the IAEC. A highly classified document, signed by Prime Minister Eshkol and drafted by Deputy Minister of Defense Zvi Dinstein (with the direct involvement of Minister Without Portfolio Israel Galili) apparently was issued, detailing the structure of the new-old nuclear agency. Little is known about that initiation document, but it probably was in the form of a short executive order.[13] Presumably, the executive order announced the subordination of the new IAEC to the prime minister.

This new-old bureaucracy was created at a time when the prime minister served also as the minister of defense, so the "sharing" aspect of the arrangement was not perceived as problematic. Prime Minister Levi Eshkol was in charge of the new agency, but his new deputy in the MOD, Zvi Dinstein, was effectively the new agency's real boss. Dostrovsky reported to Dinstein (who was much less familiar with nuclear affairs than was his predecessor, Shimon Peres). In 1966 Israel did not yet have nuclear weapons, and it was not even clear whether it would actually build them. In a sense, the IAEC's mission was opaque from the beginning. (This jurisdictional issue is discussed further in chapter 7.)

On the eve of the 1967 war, when Moshe Dayan joined the government as the new minister of defense, Prime Minister Eshkol asked former Chief of Staff Yigal Yadin and Minister Israel Galili to draft an agreement document that would specify the division of responsibilities between the prime minister and the minister of defense. This reportedly was a short document, only two paragraphs long. The first specified those military actions that the defense minister could not take without the explicit approval of the prime minister. Apparently that paragraph asserted that the minister of defense could not initiate any use of unconventional weaponry without the approval of the prime minister. The second paragraph stipulated those defense personnel that the prime minister, with the knowledge of the minister of defense, could invite to solicit information. To what extent this paragraph referred explicitly to personnel within the nuclear system is not known.[14]

Later, particularly after Golda Meir became prime minister, it became increasingly evident that the two-paragraph document had not addressed the complex reality of the division of responsibility between the prime minister and the minister of defense. It left too many holes and ambiguities. Already during Prime Minister Eshkol's final year, Dayan and his colleagues seemed to be doing things that the prime minister had not approved (see chapter 7). The recognition of the Yadin-Galili document's inadequacy prompted the military secretaries of the prime minister and the minister of defense (Yisrael Lior and Yehoshua Raviv, respectively), with the direct involvement of Minister Galili on behalf of the prime minister, to draw up a more detailed document. This document, or series of documents, which was subsequently formalized in an exchange of letters between Prime Minister Meir and Minister of Defense Dayan, was also brought to the attention of the chief of staff, Lieutenant General Chaim Bar-Lev.[15]

This series of documents became known informally as "the constitution." They outlined the type of activities that the minister of defense was authorized to approve on his own, those that the prime minister had to approve, and those operations that had to be submitted for the approval of the cabinet or the defense ministerial committee. One segment of "the constitution," apparently the most sensitive, dealt with the division of authorities and responsibilities between the two regarding the nuclear organization and its products. Details of the document remain unknown, but it is understood to have been short and to have confirmed the primacy of the prime minister in all policy and operational aspects of the shared arrangement.

This document was fundamental to the way that Israel developed its nuclear command-and-control system, under the personal involvement of Chief of Staff Bar-Lev. The system was designed to be consistent with the special role of the prime minister as preeminent in nuclear affairs. According to Israeli nuclear lore, this document has remained valid and unchanged for decades. Its custodians considered it almost sacred, the embodiment of the Israeli idea of governing the bomb. Even when new systems were introduced, technologically and operationally, they were reluctant to tamper with this quasi-"constitutional" document, worrying that it was so sensitive, so classified, that any effort to reopen and renegotiate it would bring more trouble than benefits.

We must presume that the Israeli command-and-control system has remained faithful to the principle that no single individual, or even organization, would have the final power to activate the system, that is, to mobilize the system into an operational mode (the reference is not only to the actual use of nuclear weapons but also to assembling and arming the weapons). According to the U.S.-based investigative journalist Seymour Hersh, "At one early stage it was agreed that no nuclear weapon could be armed or fired without authorization from the prime minister, minister of defense and army chief of staff. The rules of engagement were subsequently modified to include the head of the Israeli air force." Hersh also suggested that the warheads were "maintained in preassembled units in special secure boxes that could be opened only with three keys to be supplied by the representatives of the top civilian and military leadership."[16]

The system presumably was designed so that even the prime minister could not initiate any nuclear activity on his or her own. Over the years, the Israeli authorities must have designed, executed, and formalized a detailed system of procedures pertaining to how the system could be activated during a state of emergency. Israel most likely has developed its own system of various states of alert, similar to the American system of nuclear alert, which during the cold war had five modalities (DEFCON) of nuclear alert.[17] Indeed, senior Israeli officials have given private assurances overseas that Israel's nuclear system is securely protected against accidental or unauthorized use.

Well-established facts are lacking, but it has been suggested that certain features of the double-key command-and-control system also shape the organizational chart of the nuclear bureaucracy. If so, the nuclear agency is shared in some fashion by the prime minister, who functions as the ultimate authority, and the minister of defense, who has certain responsibilities for some of the system's operational aspects and functions.

A new and expanded "constitutional" document is believed to have been introduced recently to replace the old one. The new document probably addresses the most current reality, including new topics, responsibilities, and concerns not covered in the old document. If Israel is currently engaged in building second-strike nuclear capability, based on new sea-based nuclear systems, this probably has necessitated rewriting some aspects of the constitution as applied to the new command-and-control structure.[18]

Although the IAEC is the primary civilian agency responsible for Israel's nuclear affairs, other agencies are important as well. In 1991, after the Gulf War, Minister of Defense Moshe Arens decided to set up a new highly classified division at the Ministry of Defense under the obscure bureaucratic title "Special Means" (in Hebrew, Emtzaim Meyuchadim [Amam], a reference to unconventional-weapons issues). Nothing authoritative is publicly known about Amam's responsibilities, but it is presumed to be concerned with coordinating Israel's readiness to launch (and respond to) an unconventional attack. Like a few other units in the defense establishment, this directorate operates under both the minister of defense and the chief of staff.[19]

The Nuclear Chief

The director general of the IAEC is one of Israel's most sensitive and responsible civil service positions. As of this writing, only six Israelis have held this post since Israel Dostrovsky overhauled the nuclear agency in 1966. They all were selected and appointed by the prime minister after consultations with the nation's nuclear guardians and the minister of defense (who apparently can veto the prime minister's choice).[20] From the prime minister's perspective, the nuclear chief's most important job is allow the prime minister do his business without worrying about the nation's nuclear assets. Any nuclear incident, let alone an accident, not only could cause physical damage and casualties but also could unravel amimut as a national policy.

The IAEC's director general is more than merely an executor of a policy or the custodian of the nation's nuclear assets. He plays a very important role in shaping and determining the country's nuclear policies and activities.[21] Furthermore, for a variety of reasons (which I explain in chapter 7), the IAEC's directors general in the past may have been subjected to less ministerial supervision and parliamentary oversight than almost any other high-ranking official in the security apparatus, including the chief of staff of the army, the inspector general of the police, and even the intelligence chiefs.

The Israeli nuclear establishment has been aware of, and at times concerned with, the lack of ministerial oversight over nuclear affairs. Accordingly, as a way to compensate for this shortcoming, the IAEC institutionalized its own system of internal checks and balances by creating layers of semiautonomous oversight bodies. This system of internal oversight was put in place during Israel Dostrovsky's tenure and was improved further during Shalheveth Freier's term in the 1970s. The prime minister appointed various subcommittees, all made up of experienced and professional individuals (often former senior employees) with the highest security clearance to act as independent supervisors and reviewers throughout the entire nuclear system, all of whom then reported to the prime minister and the director general. Freier even set up a procedure that allowed any senior IAEC personnel to meet directly with the prime minister without the presence of the director general, to enable employees to raise their concerns openly and freely. According to Freier, however, this system was hardly ever used, and his successors subsequently discontinued the procedure.[22]

Also during Freier's tenure a protocol was set up regarding the proper relations between the prime minister and the IAEC director general. The protocol stated that the IAEC chief should have a face-to-face working meeting with the prime minister at least once a month and that once a year, the prime minister should chair a plenary meeting of the commission's board members. Prime Minister Yitzhak Rabin, for example, under whose watch the protocol was written, made an effort to comply with the guidelines.[23] Other prime ministers were more flexible. Benjamin Netanyahu, for example, who was not privy to most of Israel's nuclear secrets until his first term as prime minister in 1996, was eager to exert his control over the nation's nuclear affairs. Netanyahu visited Dimona, met with nuclear experts, channeled funds into the system, and wrote the toughest letters that any Israeli prime minister has ever written to an American president (Clinton) on the nuclear issue. Ehud Barak, in contrast, who had been privy to Israel's nuclear secrets during his previous military posts, met with his nuclear chief only twice during his eighteen-month term in office, never convened the board of the commission, and never visited Dimona.[24]

Gideon Frank was the longest-serving and one of the most influential IAEC directors general (nearly fifteen years, from 1993 to 2007). Even after relinquishing his position on September 2, 2007, to Vice Admiral (Ret.) Dr. Shaul Horev, Frank has continued to retain influence on nuclear matters. On the very day he left his job as IAEC director general, Prime Minister Ehud Olmert appointed him vice chair of the IAEC, a position that had not previously existed.[25] Despite the awkwardness of this appointment—after all, in a hierarchical organization like the IAEC there is no room for two chief executives—it reflected Olmert's desire to ensure a smooth transition and good oversight in the nuclear domain. While it was understood that the unusual appointment is temporary, it remains unclear how long this unconventional arrangement will continue.

Frank was the first IAEC chief who spent his entire professional career inside this secret organization. He belongs to the second generation of IAEC leaders.[26] As director general, Frank was a skillful bureaucrat and diplomat as well as a hands-on manager. During his long tenure as IAEC chief, Frank emphasized the introduction of new management techniques to improve efficiency and productivity. He also made efforts to improve the international face of his agency, in particular to build relations with similar professional bodies in the world, including the IAEA. His long service as both director general and vice chair of the IAEC, reporting to six different prime ministers, gave him special stature in the Israeli national security bureaucracy. His involvement in his own organization was vast, and it is rumored that he personally approved every important document sent out of his organization during his tenure as director general. Although in his subsequent role as vice chair, Frank is not expected to be involved in the day-to-day management of the organization, he remains engaged in matters of policy.

It is interesting to consider Frank's legacy in historical terms by comparing him with the founding fathers of the organization. Israel Dostrovsky built the organization almost from scratch, the scientist-executive who took over the ailing agency and overhauled it technologically and organizationally to suit its new missions. Under his watch Israel crossed the nuclear threshold and became a de facto nuclear-weapons state. Shalheveth Freier, his immediate successor, was the thinker-diplomat who codified amimut as a unique national concept and policy. He wrote down Israel's special bargain with the bomb. Gideon Frank inherited from them all the fundamentals of the bargain. His job was to preserve it at a time when its exceptionalist nature had become increasingly incompatible with contemporary norms, both at home and abroad.

Secrecy and amimut were in those early days enforceable and acceptable. But they are much less so today. Frank faced the challenge to preserve an organization and ethos in a changing external environment in Israel and the world at large, an environment that is much less receptive to such an ethos. His challenge was to initiate a quiet, almost invisible, reform in the identity of the organization yet without changing the bargain of amimut.

Apparently Frank did not see the challenge in his early years in office, but he became increasingly aware of it during his latter years. Frank, along with his deputy for policy for his last five years, Dr. Ariel E. Levite, a policymaker and defense intellectual who came from academia, tried to set in motion a guarded reform process in the organization. The idea was to transform the organization's identity and culture gradually from within: from a secret organization that used to operate as a state within a state into a more normal national security agency governed by the rule of law. All this was to be done without changing the overall commitment to amimut.

On various occasions, both at home and abroad, the two gave their audience the impression that they hoped to lead the secret agency into a new era characterized by more compliance with the democratic values of the rule of law at home and, to the greatest extent possible, by compliance with international nonproliferation norms. In both arenas, they promoted the notion that Israel would conduct itself as "a democratic and responsible state with advanced nuclear technology." This new terminology hinted at, without explicitly acknowledging, Israel's nuclear capability while underscoring and promoting its credentials of nuclear responsibility and caution.

This has not been easy. In a sense, it is similar to the challenge that other Israeli secret organizations, notably the GSS and the Mossad, have confronted, but in another sense it is a much more difficult and complicated challenge. It is more difficult because the bargain is so different and also involves amimut. Whereas the other two intelligence organizations are secret but not opaque about their national missions; the IAEC is both secret and opaque about its mission.

MALMAB: The Guardian of Secrets

In conjunction with the organization that creates Israel's nuclear secrets is the organization that guards them. This organization is MALMAB, an acronym that stands for the Office (or Directorate) of Security for the Israeli Defense Establishment (the official English-language acronym used for the MALMAB's chief is DSDE, Director of Security of the Defense Establishment). MALMAB, and the ethos of secrecy that it has cultivated, is the second layer in Israel's nuclear-intelligence infrastructure.

MALMAB is one of the most secretive and autonomous agencies in Israel's Ministry of Defense (MOD). Even the origins and the exact meaning of the acronym MALMAB, let alone the precise definition of its mission, are a matter of historical mystery. MALMAB's longest-serving chief, Yechiel Horev (1986–2007), was once cited as even being uncertain himself about the meaning of the agency's name.[27] Even after the names of both the Mossad and GSS chiefs became public in the early 1990s, Horev insisted that his own identity as the MALMAB's chief must remain secret. In fact, until a few years ago, the military censor forbade any reference to MALMAB and its chief. Ironically, the secrecy of his identity was compromised by his own overzealous conduct, particularly his frequent involvement in a number of high-profile legal cases.[28]

To understand the power of the current MALMAB, we must begin by looking at the role of secrecy in the Zionist ethos of defense. From the early days of Zionist paramilitary activity, first under the Turks and then under the British, matters of defense—especially the acquisition and manufacture of weapons—were treated as both secret and sacred. Most Jewish paramilitary activities were illegal under the British rule in Palestine (the exception was a limited policing and defensive role allowed for the Haganah, the military arm of the Jewish Agency, to defend Jewish settlements against Arab attacks), so secrecy was essential. The Hebrew phrase *kdushat habitachon* (in Hebrew, the "sanctity of security") highlights this ethos. This tradition of secrecy characterized the activities of HEMED (the Science Corps) during Israel's war of independence, especially its branches dealing with unconventional warfare. Israel's nuclear pursuit, which can be traced to HEMED GIMMEL, which turned into Machon 4 (whose public face was the IAEC), cultivated that ethos. Even when there were no real secrets yet to guard, the very act of dreaming was secret.

In 1958, when the nuclear project was initiated, Shimon Peres, the project's chief, asked Benjamin Blumberg (nicknamed "Benny" or "Bibi"), then the MOD's security chief, to set up a security shop for the new Dimona project. Soon Blumberg added to his portfolio another security mission: not only guarding Israel's nuclear secrets but also spying on other countries' nuclear secrets. Guided by the idea that Israel did not have to reinvent the wheel, Peres instructed Blumberg to create a small and autonomous intelligence office within the nuclear project to collect scientific information. The secret office tried out various names and titles until it came to be known as the Bureau for Science Relations (Lishka Lekishrey Mada, or LEKEM in its Hebrew acronym). LEKEM became the headquarters of Israel's scientific intelligence.[29]

For about fifteen years, Blumberg served as the nuclear project's security and intelligence czar. Even though thousands of people, including hundreds of foreign employees, were involved in building the Dimona complex—the biggest construction site in Israel at the time—its true nature was kept out of the public domain from 1958 through 1960 well after the digging had begun. This was critical because when the United States finally realized that Israel was constructing a major nuclear facility, it was too late to stop it. Even then, only part of the secret was disclosed. The project's most secret element, the underground reprocessing plant, remained a secret for two more decades until it was finally revealed by Mordechai Vanunu in 1986.[30]

Blumberg designed and managed the security apparatus that made the Israeli nuclear project a republic of secrecy. He compartmentalized the republic into smaller provinces, which seldom communicated with one another and sometimes were not even aware of the other's existence. Blumberg himself was often the only intermediary between those secret provinces, as he was the only one who knew about all of them. He knew all the secrets, he was everywhere, but he was not a policymaker; he was merely the security officer who executed the policymakers' decisions.

Today, decades after Blumberg set up his relatively small security shop within the nuclear project, MALMAB—the successor to Blumberg's shop—has evolved into a large intelligence organization involved in policy matters. When the secrets were truly secrets, a small security shop was sufficient, but once Israel's nuclear secrets became known worldwide and amimut became practically a fiction, that infrastructure turned into an empire.

Yechiel Horev

Enter Yechiel Horev. More than any individual, it was Horev, the second and longest-serving MALMAB head, who was responsible for transforming MALMAB into Israel's de facto fourth intelligence organization. He elevated MALMAB's status and power to that of a formidable and distinct player in Israel's intelligence community.

Horev began his long career in 1969 as a junior guardian of Israel's nuclear secrets when he was a security officer in one of the IAEC's most highly classified field units. In 1974, as part of the MOD's bureaucratic overhaul and against the background of the 1973 Yom Kippur War, MALMAB became the headquarters for all the security shops in the defense establishment.[31] Horev was named the head of the unit in charge of physical security for all the secret facilities and sites under MALMAB's jurisdiction, including the Dimona nuclear facility. By then, he already had acquired a reputation as a skillful bureaucrat with an eye for detail, and he was promoted quickly through the ranks. In 1984, Horev became deputy to MALMAB's first chief, Chaim

Carmon, but soon afterward took two years of leave for academic studies. This was, in retrospect, fortunate for his future career.

The mid-1980s was a bad time for all of Israel's secret services, as almost all of them were beset by major scandals. During this time, Jonathan Pollard was recruited and subsequently caught spying in the United States, which led to the dismantlement of LEKEM as an independent intelligence organization. It was then that Israel's involvement in the Iran-Contra scandal was revealed, poisoning the relations between the intelligence organizations of the United States and Israel. Also during this time, the internal security service, the GSS, endured its worst scandal, the so-called Bus 300 affair, in which GSS forces executed two Palestinian detainees, leading to a political scandal following the media exposure of the murder and cover-up.[32] This scandal led to sweeping changes in the GSS leadership. Finally, for the IAEC and MALMAB, this period was defined by its own worst failure: the treason case of Mordechai Vanunu (on the case itself, see chapter 5).

It is not widely known that Vanunu's conduct had attracted the interest of the security authorities in Dimona (and elsewhere, including GSS and the MALMAB headquarters) some four years before his story appeared in the London *Sunday Times*. Vanunu had been monitored by the security officials at Dimona since 1982 when the security services learned about his political views and odd personal conduct. Sometime in 1983 Vanunu was officially classified as a "security risk," which meant that no action regarding his employment, including firing, could be taken without security approval. Around that time Vanunu was summoned for questioning at the GSS headquarters in Tel Aviv. He did not deny that his political opinions were critical of Israeli policy vis-à-vis the Palestinians but assured the security officials that his views would not compromise his formal security obligations at Dimona.[33]

In retrospect, however, the security officials failed to recognize the huge potential risk that Vanunu presented. Ambiguities about jurisdiction also added to the failure, as it was unclear which specific security agency within the tangled security bureaucracy had the final responsibility for the case, Dimona's local security management, the GSS, or the MALMAB. Sometime in 1984, owing to the lack of confidence by the MALMAB's chief (Carmon) in the Dimona security authorities, Horev was asked to keep a close watch on the Dimona security shop. But Horev soon went on academic leave, and a year later, sometime in the summer of 1985, the Dimona managers decided unilaterally to remove Vanunu from his sensitive position at Machon Bet, apparently without clearing the matter with security. In response,

Vanunu asked to leave, and by October 1985, he was fired. Weeks later, he left Israel.[34]

On the very day in the summer of 1986 when Horev returned from his leave to resume his old job at the MALMAB headquarters, Mossad informed his office about Vanunu and its impending operation to capture him. Because MALMAB Chief Carmon was abroad, Horev, as his deputy, became the MALMAB representative in an interagency team that had been formed to deal with the affair. Then, after Vanunu was kidnapped and returned to Israel, the MALMAB and the GSS appointed a two-man senior investigative committee to find out what the various security agencies had done wrong.

Neither organization, however, appears to have had any real interest in uncovering the security agencies' missteps. Once again, Horev was appointed by MALMAB Chief Carmon to be the organization's representative in that investigative body, but Horev did not disclose to his fellow GSS investigator that he had been asked to oversee the security in Dimona two years earlier. The two members of the team wrote a classified report focusing on the jurisdictional ambiguities and the lack of coordination among the various security bodies but refraining from blaming any one person or organization. Soon after, Carmon was eased "upstairs" and became the MOD's deputy director general, responsible for security and other portfolios. Horev became the MALMAB's chief. The irony is evident: Horev "owes" his career to Vanunu.[35]

For an ambitious chief like Horev, there could have been no better time to rebuild the MALMAB. The MOD's director general, former Air Force Commander General David Ivry, was sympathetic to Horev's argument that the "control stick" (as Horev termed the chain of command within the security apparatus) must be shortened because it made no sense to separate responsibility from authority. Within a short time, Horev bypassed his old boss, Carmon, and reported directly to Ivry. At the same time, largely due to the Bus 300 affair, the GSS sank to its lowest point as an organization. The institutional weakness of the GSS, coupled with the support of Ivry and Minister of Defense Yitzhak Rabin, both of whom wanted a strong and autonomous MOD, allowed Horev to expand the MALMAB and to make it more independent and powerful.

The GSS's leadership crisis permitted Horev to identify new emerging security challenges and seize new responsibilities. For example, he recognized the significance of information technology as a security issue and obtained funds to establish an infrastructure to address the issue. In 1988, after Yaakov Peri was appointed the GSS's chief, he and Horev met to redefine the two organizations' boundaries and responsibilities. Peri, whose primary mission was to restore and rebuild the GSS as the nation's domestic intelligence organization in the wake of the Bus 300 affair, was not interested in retaining formal security responsibility over matters like the nuclear program, which were not central to his organization's primary mission and not really under his control anyway. This was his lesson from the Vanunu affair. These negotiations led to a change in the MALMAB's status. It no longer was a unit of the GSS at the MOD but now was an autonomous division in the MOD whose head coordinated with the GSS but was not subordinate to it.[36]

This was not merely a formal or technical change but one that permitted Horev to redefine and expand the entire MALMAB structure. Under Horev's leadership, the MALMAB was transformed from a relatively small and highly fragmented security unit of the MOD, which was subordinated to the GSS, to a large and highly centralized intelligence organization that provided security services to the entire civilian defense establishment (with the exception of other intelligence organizations). Over time, the MALMAB grew to have a strong interdisciplinary staff of more than three hundred people, and Horev himself became one of Israel's most powerful security bureaucrats. Seven prime ministers and six ministers of defense came and went, but Yechiel Horev remained in his sensitive position for more than two decades.

The Vanunu affair gave Horev an opportunity to reduce the authority of the local security officers stationed in the various facilities of the civilian defense establishment, which until then had been formidable, and to strengthen instead the central authority of the MALMAB headquarters. For example, all correspondence on security clearance issuances had to be approved by the MALMAB headquarters, not the GSS headquarters. All the field security officers reported to the MALMAB headquarters, not to the GSS. Even though the MALMAB chief is administratively only a division head at the MOD, in reality Horev had autonomy and authority superior to that of any other senior official at the ministry. Because all appointments in the ministry had to have security clearances, the MALMAB acquired enormous power. Nobody in the ministry could challenge Horev on matters of security, and the MOD became the only ministry with a security apparatus of its own.

In time, Horev demanded that due to his organization's unique and broad mission, the MALMAB's status should be equal to that of the other secret services and that he should be made a member of the chiefs' club, the council of all the heads of Israel's intelligence services. A high-level governmental committee set up to explore the issue decided in 2000 to reject Horev's request.[37]

Still, not merely bureaucratic skills can explain the MALMAB's unique institutional power and authority.

Amimut as a Bureaucratic Asset

As a sacred national policy, amimut was central to Horev's claim that the MALMAB's function was unique, exclusive, and distinct from that of Israel's four intelligence organizations. Indeed, amimut's special security requirements were a great platform from which to insist that the MALMAB must be independent and autonomous. Horev was persuasive in presenting the MALMAB, and himself as its chief, as the true guardian of Israel's most sacred assets. More than the MALMAB's responsibility for the nuclear program's physical and information security was its security responsibility for amimut as a policy. Given the unique status of amimut in Israel's national security, one can see why Horev's claim was persuasive.

This claim gave the MALMAB unique voice of authority and judgment on a highly sensitive subject. It has made the MALMAB the final security authority for everything in the nuclear program, operation and policy alike. Inevitably, there were sporadic turf wars between the MALMAB and the nuclear professionals, including the IAEC's chief, which, on a few occasions, had to be resolved by the prime minister.

Being the ultimate guardian of amimut gave Horev two special and remarkable bureaucratic assets. First, he had direct and exclusive access to the ultimate policymaker in charge of the nuclear program, the prime minister, sometimes in a one-on-one setting. Second, Horev had veto power in decisions on most nuclear matters. Hence, amimut granted the MALMAB a mandate that went far beyond the traditional tasks of a chief of security. Unlike Blumberg and Carmon before him, Horev was able to identify the bureaucratic benefits of amimut as a platform on which to build a fourth independent national intelligence organization.

Horev's "ownership" of this issue gave him a unique status and prestige in Israel's governmental establishment, and his opinion on nuclear matters came to be perceived by many as the voice of national security. Oddly, it is unclear who or what body had formally appointed the MALMAB to be the chief guardian of amimut and under what authority they had done so. Horev himself used to claim that an old and highly classified cabinet decision had given him special authority, although some questioned the all-encompassing nature of such a decision, or even if such a cabinet decision had ever been made. In

2004, in response to direct questions about this matter by the investigative journalist Ronen Bergman, Horev responded that his special nuclear mandate had been granted by a joint decision of the prime minister and the minister of defense. He claimed that he had a letter signed by both that granted that authority to the MALMAB but did not make clear which prime minister and minister of defense had written the letter or what the exact language of the letter was.[38] The legal standing of that letter also remains unclear (see the discussion of the legality issue in chapters 7 and 8). Like everything else concerning definitions of authority and responsibility for Israel's nuclear issue, all is classified, all is opaque.

As the chief guardian of amimut, Horev was credited with many successes, especially in the international arena, which reinforced the belief that a strict policy of amimut still made political sense. One such success was in South Africa, where the MALMAB had a permanent presence on the ground and had taken measures to prevent a compromising situation that would reveal Israel's nuclear secrets. The result was that no major Israeli secrets fell into the wrong hands during the transition of power in the early 1990s. Another major MALMAB success, this time in the United States, presumably with the assistance of the American Israel Public Affairs Committee (AIPAC), was preventing the publication of high-resolution satellite photos of sensitive sites in Israel, primarily nuclear-related sites.[39]

Horev's Legacy

On July 31, 2007, Yechiel Horev, by then the MALMAB's longest-serving chief and the acting director general of the Ministry of Defense, retired. In a high-profile farewell ceremony at the MOD headquarters, Prime Minister Ehud Olmert, along with Minister of Defense Ehud Barak, warmly thanked Horev for his long and extraordinary contribution to the country's defense, referring to him as Israel's "Mr. Security."[40]

The truth was more complicated, however. Prime Minister Olmert had been forced to dismiss Horev after the U.S. government (specifically, the Department of Defense) made it clear that it considered Horev persona non grata for his involvement in Israel's transfer of sensitive American technology to China. That is, because the U.S. government refused to cooperate with Horev, effectively banning him, Olmert had no choice but to let Horev retire.

The Pentagon identified Horev as one of several Israeli defense officials who not only were involved in an illegal transfer of sensitive American defense technology to China but also actively sought to hide the truth. Ironically, the chief guardian of Israel's amimut policy became unacceptable to the United States for his insistence on keeping the Israeli-Chinese connection secret. In the American view, Horev's concealment was a cover for plain deception.

Probably no other Israeli defense bureaucrat in recent times was as influential and controversial as Horev. He often has been compared with J. Edgar Hoover, the long-serving director of the Federal Bureau of Investigation. Like Hoover, Horev was a long-serving bureaucrat who built an extraordinary national security empire almost from scratch, with virtually no democratic oversight. Like Hoover, Horev outlasted a long list of elected officials, from both the right and the left, making clear that on matters of national security, the bureaucracy of secrecy, not the elected officials, was what mattered. Whether or not Horev held files on all his political bosses, as it was rumored, it appeared that they were reluctant to initiate a confrontation with him. More than any other civil servant, Horev knew how to elevate and manipulate the MALMAB into a source of bureaucratic power.

Ultimately, however, Horev was intoxicated by the ethos of *kdushat habitachon* and amimut. Despite being a keen observer of the Israeli domestic and legal scene, he failed to notice the deeper changes taking place in the Israeli society. After decades of living out of the public eye he became visible and public and too controversial, thus ultimately unacceptable.

The Censora: Amimut's Enforcer

The third and final layer in amimut's infrastructure is also the smallest, the Office of the Military Censor, commonly known in Israel as the "Censora." If the first two organizations, the IAEC and the MALMAB, operate almost invisibly within the inner walls of officialdom, the Censora is the gatekeeper between the state's secrets and the external world. The Censora conducts prepublication reviews of items whose publication might damage national security. On the nuclear issue, the Censora enforces the discourse of amimut.

As an organization, the Censora now is a rather small military unit, consisting of a modest headquarters that supervises two regional offices, in Tel Aviv and Jerusalem. Currently, the Censora has a peacetime staff of twenty-eight full-time censors who work in sessions around the clock.[41] The chief censor is an active-duty senior military officer (in the past, a brigadier general but currently a colonel) appointed to head the agency by the minister of defense. Since the role of the Censora is more prominent during an emergency, it maintains a staff of dozens of reservists who can be mobilized to active duty on short notice.

Today Israel is the only Western democracy that maintains an active military censorship institution. In theory, the Censora's legal authority and scope are almost limitless. Virtually any media item about Israel's defense and foreign affairs is required to be submitted to the Censora for a prepublication review, not only the print and electronic media (including foreign media based in Israel) but also any books (even fiction), professional newsletters, and even postings on the Internet.[42] In practice, however, only a small fraction of printed material in Israel is actually submitted to the Censora, as only certain material falling into specific categories requires prepublication review. Israel's nuclear issue remains the most highly scrutinized of them all.

A Brief History of the Censora

The origins of Israel's Censora, like those of the MALMAB, can be traced to the Zionist ethos of *kdushat habitachon*, the "sanctity of security," which prevailed in the prestate (Yishuv) era.

In those days, the Zionist press regarded itself as a partner in building a Jewish homeland in Palestine. Guided by the *kdushat habitachon* ethos, censorship was viewed as necessary for the good of the community. By 1942, the mainstream Zionist newspapers in Palestine had created the first voluntary censorship mechanism via a committee of the editors in chief, named the Response Committee, which served as a liaison between the Yishuv's press and the political leadership. One of its functions was to give the press guidance on handling sensitive issues, such as illegal immigration. Another function was serving as a line of direct communication between the press and the Zionist leadership. Both functions later became the foundation for the relations between the Israeli media and the Censora. Unlike British censorship, which was strictly formal, the Zionist press was controlled by means of a semivoluntary and self-imposed arrangement.[43]

In late February 1948, as Arab-Jewish hostilities escalated and war became imminent, the first semiformal censorship agreement was concluded between the editors of the Zionist newspapers and the Haganah (the Jewish mainstream paramilitary organization). The agreement included a list of sixteen security-related topics to be prohibited from publication. By the time the state of Israel was constituted on May 14, 1948, a rudimentary Censora system already was in place.[44] Within days after Israel declared its independence, the new nation enacted the legal system it had inherited from the British Mandate authorities, specifically the 1945 British "Emergency Regulations," to create an Israeli censorship office with wartime authority. Prepublication submission of security-related news was mandatory, and penalties for violations were severe and immediate. Indeed, in August 1948 the military censor shut down two daily newspapers for a few days for censorship violations. Prime Minister David Ben-Gurion then promised that after the end of the war, the state would legislate a censorship law to ensure that only true security matters, not political matters, would be subject to state censorship.[45]

Ben-Gurion's pledge has yet to be realized. In fact, the historical record indicates that both the state and the media in Israel actually have opposed legislating a formal censorship law. Instead, the British Emergency Regulations became the legal basis for the Censora as an institution. The press found it easier to maintain the Censora through the prestate provisional Emergency Regulations than to legislate a permanent Israeli law. In addition to these mandatory regulations, a series of agreements between the press and the state regulate the practical aspects of these agreements.[46]

After long negotiations, the first Censora agreement was concluded in December 1949 in the form of a letter from a senior officer in the Israel Defense Forces (IDF) to the head of the editors' committee. The letter defined the purpose of the Censora as a mechanism to "prevent the leaking of information that could benefit the enemy or damage the defense of the state."[47] The presumption was that the Censora was an unavoidable, communal arrangement that benefited both parties, the state and the press, because it served the common good by protecting state secrets. The letter also outlined a three-man Censora tribunal to resolve quietly any disputes between the censor and the press without resorting to the public court system. This arrangement ensured secrecy as well as a way to settle disputes "within the family." This agreement, which was amended in 1951, laid the foundation for the Censora's daily operation.

In the Israel's early days, the Censora was used as a state instrument to enforce control of the press on behalf of *kdushat habitachon*. Virtually every item of military information was regarded in those days as classified and therefore had to be banned.[48] The idea of *kdushat habitachon* was so comprehensive that it covered all sorts of issues, some of them far beyond strictly military matters.

In July 1966, as part of Prime Minister Levi Eshkol's liberalization policy, a new Censora agreement was concluded that reflected a new balance between freedom of the press and national security. It established more objective, criteria-based principles for the Censora's work. Instead of the broad definition of national security that covered practically everything, the 1966 agreement listed sixty-eight subjects that required the Censora's prepublication review. The agreement stated explicitly that domestic political matters should be off-limits to the Censora, which meant that opinion and commentary would no longer be censored unless they contained—or implied—factual assertions whose publication would damage national security. The agreement included a mechanism for appeal to a tribunal made up of a public figure, a representative of the press, and a representative of the defense establishment. Nonetheless, the 1966 agreement failed to specify limits on the Censora's judgment and thus guaranteed that its rulings would be final, that is, would not be subjected to any criteria-based constraints or other limitations.[49]

The 1966 arrangement regulated the Censora for three decades (during which it was slightly amended twice), a period when its power was at its peak. This also was the golden age of the chief editors' committee, the other part of the Censora deal. One key feature of that deal was its elitist undertones: the editors enjoyed exclusive access to privileged information—they often received confidential briefings from the prime minister or the minister of defense—but this information was not to be shared with the public. This made the editors also guardians of a sort, a crucial element in the *kdushat habitachon* cooperative.

The Censora as the Enforcer of Amimut

Of all the subjects in the Censora's official list of topics, the nuclear issue has remained above and apart from all the rest. The amimut policy is often cited as the primary reason why Israeli democracy still needs the institution of the Censora. As long as Israel relies on amimut, the Censora will be its guard. It is important to recognize, however, that the connection between the Censora and the nuclear issue preceded amimut as a policy. From the start, the Censora did not just enforce total nuclear secrecy but had an important but unwritten role in elevating the nuclear issue to the level of a national taboo. In those early days the Censora's policy was simple: all *factual* items on the nation's nuclear program were considered secret and therefore had to be censored. During the construction of Dimona, when thousands of laborers (including hundreds of French personnel) made the construction an open secret in Beer Sheba, the Censora prohibited any leaks to the press.[50] After the initial disclosure and after Ben-Gurion stated that the project was peaceful, the Censora banned any items, news or opinion, that questioned Ben-Gurion's statement. Because the project was domestically controversial and its decision making was undemocratic, Ben-Gurion was determined at all costs to keep the nuclear issue out of the media. Shimon Peres, Ben-Gurion's deputy at the MOD and the nuclear project CEO, was committed to suppress public debate of Israel's nuclear issue. At times he appealed to *kdushat habitachon* as a patriotic argument to convince editors that the nuclear issue was too sensitive to be debated openly in the press. At other times he used the Censora (and other state security organs) simply to block public debate.[51]

At that time the Censora's restrictions covered virtually all factual aspects of the nuclear issue, including political and diplomatic matters. For example, in the spring and summer of 1963 the Censora prohibited any information about President Kennedy's correspondence with Prime Ministers Ben-Gurion and Eshkol over the nuclear issue. Both countries treated those exchanges as secret, leaving both publics ignorant of Kennedy's nuclear ultimatum to Israel. While the Censora allowed references to Ben-Gurion's letters about Israel's security situation, it banned any explicit links between the letters and the nuclear issue. The Censora also prohibited reporting the crisis that Kennedy's letters evoked in Jerusalem, as well as how Eshkol eventually responded to the American president's demands.[52] At best, the Censora allowed vague references to certain Israeli "development plans" that were at the core of a mysterious dispute with the United States.[53] Another prohibition by the Censora in the 1960s was banning articles or analysis that highlighted the danger that the nuclear issue could lead to a military confrontation with Egypt. Although this was a major concern of the Israeli intelligence agencies, the Israeli public was not allowed to know about it.[54]

Over time, the Censora adopted a somewhat more liberal approach to diplomatic issues, but it insisted that foreign press reports should be Israelis' sole information source about their nation's nuclear project. This required not only that Israeli policymakers keep total silence on the subject but also that Israeli analysts not discuss it. Not until the mid-1970s did the IAEC's director general, Shalheveth Freier, and his team translate the 1969 deal concerning amimut into an operational policy. In those discussions it became evident that the Censora could—and should—play an important role in enforcing the policy of amimut.

The fact that Israel had in place a Censora mechanism based on prepublication review created an opportunity for amimut to become not simply a governmental policy but also a vehicle for generating and enforcing a national Israeli discourse on nuclear affairs. The real challenge was fashioning a national discourse on nuclear matters that allowed effects of existential deterrence but without compromising the requirements of secrecy and non-acknowledgment. The solution was to modify the Censora's guidelines on the nuclear issue in order to incorporate the Censora as an element of the amimut policy itself. In this way, the Censora became an integral component of Israel's overall nuclear policy, not just a security tool to guard secrets.

The details of how the Censora was integrated into amimut policy were decided in strategy sessions in the 1970s by the IAEC, the MALMAB, and the Censora. To this day, the chief censor consults closely on nuclear matters with senior officials of the IAEC (on the policy itself) and the MALMAB (on the security aspects of the policy). Technically, the chiefs of the IAEC and the MALMAB are the censor's senior advisers on the nuclear issue. In reality, however, at least during the tenure of Yechiel Horev as the MALMAB's chief, the MALMAB almost always called the shots regarding the censor's conduct on the issue of amimut.

Three basic principles govern how the Censora promotes amimut as a national nuclear discourse. First, as it did in the past, the Censora bans any Israeli-originated information about the nation's nuclear activities. Second, also consistent with old practice, Israelis must cite foreign press sources in any factual reference to the Israeli nuclear program, and they must do it explicitly. As a general rule, any factual reference to the Israeli nuclear program must have an identifiable attribution to the foreign media. In addition, the Censora routinely adds the phrase "according to foreign sources," at times excessively, in the text.

Third, and here a fresh element was introduced, the Censora actively edits submitted texts to conform to the national discourse of amimut. Specifically, the censor insists that certain words and phrases be replaced with other, "softer" words. Certain words are thus forbidden, treated as a taboo. At the core of the taboo lies the bomb itself, that is, any words or phrases that imply Israel's actual possession or deployment of nuclear weapons. Phrases like *nuclear weapons*, let alone the word *bomb*, must be replaced by more ambiguous and softer phrases like *nuclear option, capability,* or *potential*. At times, the censor's editorial changes are silly, for example, replacing the forbidden phrase *nuclear weapons* with a permissible phrase like *strategic weapons* or *doomsday weapons*.

Compliance with these guidelines defines the Israeli national discourse of amimut. The two ideas governing the Censora's practice are "slippery slope" and "confirmation." That is, once ordinary Israelis begin talking about their country's possession of nuclear weapons as a fact, it amounts to a confirmation that would make the official amimut policy impossible. Even if officials continued to adhere to the official discourse of amimut, it would lose its credibility in public discourse that did not use amimut-supporting terminology. Knowing Israeli political sociology, once the barriers of amimut are limited to officials, the policy would lose much of its grip. Therefore, if Israel is committed to a credible policy of amimut, the Censora must be its public enforcer, the bargain's guardian.

The Decline of the Censora and the Nuclear Issue

Since the mid- to late 1980s, although the Censora still exists as an institution and continues to monitor and regulate security-related publications in Israel, it has become significantly weaker and smaller than what it was at its peak.[55] Even though the legal differences between the current and the two previous Censora agreements are insignificant, in its daily practice as the nation's security guardian, the Censora has lost a great deal of its authority and resources.[56] Many legal, social, and technological reasons underlie this steadily downward trajectory.

The definitive event symbolizing this decline was the 1989 ruling of the Supreme Court (680/88) on the Schnitzer case. A few months earlier, Meir Schnitzer, then the editor of a Tel Aviv weekly magazine *Ha'ir* (which was not a party to the 1966 editors' agreement) petitioned for a formal judicial review of the censor's decision regarding an article about the Mossad) submitted by his paper, claiming that the censor's deletions were excessive and unjustified.[57] This was the first time that an Israeli media outlet decided to submit the censor's decision for judicial review rather than seek a quiet, out-of-court resolution through the tribunal mechanism that the Censora agreement created. In a precedent-making ruling, the Supreme Court placed substantial legal constraints on the chief censor's judgment: Only that information whose publication is deemed, with a probability of "near certainty," to cause "grievous harm" to national security justifies a censor's intervention.[58]

This landmark ruling, written primarily by then Chief Justice Aharon Barak, became Israel's new balance between the requirements of national security and the rights of a free press. The "near certainty" of "grievous harm" requirement has become the legal criterion against which to measure the Censora's legitimate scope. At least in theory, the near-certainty threshold is significantly higher than the "classified" bar (i.e., the fact that information is classified is no longer sufficient to prevent its publication). The censor now must demonstrate that the publication of classified information would cause, with "near certainty," tangible harm to national security. The ruling thus allows some leaks to pass the Censora even if they entail classified information. The Schnitzer ruling clearly separated the realm of the classified from the realm of the censored: the censor was no longer the branch of field security responsible for preventing classified material from being leaked to the press.

Many people interpreted the Supreme Court ruling as testimony to the deep changes that had taken place in Israel and to the emergence of a new Israel with a different ethos and self-image. Some described the shift in Israel's self-image as a departure from that of a monolithic Spartan society that sees itself as living by its sword, to a more pluralistic, liberal, and relaxed Athens. One aspect of this change is the devaluation of the Zionist ethos of *kdushat habitachon*. As the Supreme Court ruling showed, the requirements of national security were no longer the overriding considerations in Israel; rather, those considerations needed to be carefully balanced against the values of open civil society and its citizens' right to know.

Four decades after becoming a state, Israel has signed a new contract with *kdushat habitachon*. Security is still at the forefront of the Israeli psyche, but it is no longer the dominant issue. *Kdushat habitachon* is no longer a blank check for the nation's national security guardians, such as the military censor, to make unchecked judgments. The Supreme Court's ruling, which reshaped the very fundamentals of the Censora's work, may have been the tipping point in the decline of the Censora as an institution. As the current chief censor, Colonel Sima Vaknin-Gil, openly acknowledged in her 2006 testimony before the Vinograd Commission, since that 1989 ruling, the extent of the Censora's intervention has significantly decreased. Indeed, her sworn testimony opened a rare window on the current state of the Censora:

Over the years, if you look into those agreements [the agreements between the Censora and the press], and there were five of them so far, each subsequent agreement meant more freedom of expression in the state of Israel, which is, of course, a fundamental right, and I will be the last to question that fundamental right. I think that in a democratic country that's the way it should be. Still, it is important to recognize that as a statutory institution, it is only us [the Censora] that have lost power, not the press.[59]

In another section of her testimony, Colonel Vaknin-Gil observed,

Over the years our manpower has been cut by a half, from seventy to thirty-five people, of which only twenty-eight are censors. When there were seventy of us, there were only three newspapers, maybe four. These days, there is Internet, television, radio, and local papers. We were twenty-eight people, with no reservists, and it is impossible to do more. If these are the standards Israel expects from the military censorship, it is welcome to leave it as it is.[60]

It is important to note that the decline in the Censora was more a societal normative phenomenon than a legal process. For example, until two decades ago, through the Censora, the Israeli air force prohibited the revelation of any data about its air accidents. Information about such accidents, especially about losses of aircraft during training flights, was considered classified information that the Censora had to keep off-limits. Likewise, names and locations of military bases and units were classified, and the identification of intelligence units also was strictly forbidden. Now, though, none of these old prohibitions is enforced any longer. Such matters are now public knowledge, without worries about damaging national security. These new trends, coming from both inside and outside the defense establishment, have elevated the tolerance threshold for the Censora's intervention. It was not that the 1989 Schnitzer ruling suddenly changed the rules for the Censora but that the court legitimized trends and attitudes that were already emerging in Israeli society. One thing is evident to observers: what constitutes "near certainty" is not fixed but changes over time.

These changes also have been affected by the changes introduced, before and after the Schnitzer case, into the craft of news production. New technological innovations that enhance speed and transparency, such as satellite imaging, the Internet, and mobile phones, have made the job of the Censora in controlling news information much more difficult and more anachronistic. For example, satellite images of Israel's most sensitive strategic sites, including its unacknowledged missile base, are now available commercially, as well as on various Internet sites. News production is no longer limited to a few established media outlets, such as newspapers, but instead is open to anyone with access to the Internet. As a result, the censor's old job of being the state's guardian of secrecy has become more problematic than ever before.

The Current Situation

Like the two other guardians of amimut, the IAEC and the MALMAB, the Censora finds itself at a historic junction. For the last two decades it has been in a steady decline, culminating in its weakness throughout the Second Lebanon War in the summer of 2006. The report on how the Israeli government conducted the war by the Vinograd Commission determined that the Censora's decline may have gone too far and that it may have lost too much of its power. If Israel still needs an effective security guardian, the Censora needs to be reinvigorated, with new powers and resources. But such a reverse may not be feasible, given the state of the media.

In any case, many contemporary Israeli journalists (perhaps the majority) view the Censora as an obsolete institutional irritant: a tamed beast that sooner or later will go away (in its present form). Other journalists refer to it as a necessary evil, but the kind with which the Israeli press can easily live without betraying its (the press's) mission. Virtually no one in the Israeli media actively favors abolishing the Censora. On the contrary, the Israeli media want to keep the Censora as long as it does not become too bothersome. In current practice, foreign journalists are usually left alone "as long as they don't violate the censorship rules too egregiously."[61] While conflicts between the Censora and the media are natural and common, we should note that those frictions rarely lead to a real legal fight. Almost all such disagreements are resolved through some sort of compromise, and in most cases, journalists are able to say most of what they really want to say.

Retired Justice Dr. Eliyahu Vinograd, who in 2004/2005 chaired another panel that examined the state of the Censora, made the following observations in his introduction to the testimony of Chief Military Censor Colonel Vaknin-Gil:

> The present agreement [between the Censora and the press] was signed after numerous concessions were made, all to accommodate the press. Someone who reads the agreement may think that the press does a favor

to the State in its willingness to agree that state secrets should remain secret. Second, the three-man arbitration body, which is not a statutory body and it is not anchored in the law, is authorized to null a decision of the censor. This, to me, is incomprehensible, that the arbitration body has the power to make the censor's decision void and null, because the censor is fully independent in his judgments, not even accountable to the chief of staff.[62]

Many people have pointed out that since the 1989 Supreme Court Schnitzer ruling, the Censora has changed much of its own self-image and ethos. It now views itself less as the government's keeper of secrets and more as a unique Israeli institution whose responsibility to the Israeli public is maintaining a delicate balance between the requirements of national security and the freedom of the press. Since that 1989 ruling, essentially all the Censora's chiefs—first the long-serving Yitzhak Shani and then his three successors, Rachel Dolev, Miri Regev, and Sima Vaknin-Gil—have made efforts to internalize the norm that the Censora's involvement must be limited to no more intervention than necessary. On its own blue and white posters distributed to foreign journalists, listing the thirty-eight topics currently subject to censorship, is also written the Censora's motto: "The Censor: The Freedom to Express Yourself Responsibly."[63]

Against these historical trends—the long decline of the Censora, along with the growing societal and technological trends toward transparency and openness—the nuclear issue still stands as a unique exception. On this issue, perhaps the only one, the Censora seems nearly as powerful as it was in its glory days.

Final Reflections

All three organizations discussed in this chapter—the IAEC, the MALMAB, and the Censora—still function together as the institutional backbone of Israel's bargain with the bomb.

This institutional infrastructure was constructed more than thirty years ago, when amimut as a national nuclear doctrine was codified. The IAEC, the producer of secrets, stands at the center, guarded by the MALMAB, and the Censora, the outer layer, stands behind them, shielding both from the public eye. This architecture proved to be vital to the survival of amimut. Except in the case of Mordechai Vanunu, amimut has worked remarkably well, at home and abroad. The system has changed little since that division of labor was made, and even today, nearly two generations later, it is still an impressive infrastructure.

On the surface, all three components seem to be as integrated as they were two generations ago. Below the surface, however, can be found signs, some more visible than others, that this infrastructure is under growing stress. It is not crumbling, and surely it will not collapse overnight, but there are indications that the old practice of amimut may have become increasingly burdensome and outdated and is being challenged by the advent of new international and domestic norms and trends. New winds of democratic practice and the future of nuclear weapons may have started to erode the old infrastructure and practice of amimut.

Chapter Five

The Citizenry
The Taboo Keepers

A multilayered institutional infrastructure supports and sustains amimut, including the Censora, the gatekeeper of Israel's atomic secrets. This infrastructure, however, cannot by itself explain the robustness of amimut. Rather, Israeli society and culture turned the formal prohibitions of amimut into a national taboo. Indeed, amimut would have been impossible without a powerful but tacit consensus by Israeli citizens to exclude the subject of possession of nuclear weapons from Israel's otherwise vibrant domestic political arena. The "magic" of amimut lies not in the institutional infrastructure but in society itself. Amimut is a societal taboo that has been internalized and into which members of the Israeli society are acculturated, creating a culture of supreme silence on nuclear matters. How did this happen? My explanation combines politics, history, and sociology. From the beginning, Israelis treated the nuclear project as the nation's holiest of holies, viewing it in existential terms as a matter of national survival. The nuclear project constitutes a link between two fundamental notions in the Zionist narrative: *Shoah* (Holocaust) and *Tekumah* (National Revival). Even those people who hold opposing viewpoints on the merits of nuclear proliferation recognize this linkage. For its proponents, only the bomb ensures that no other *Shoah* could ever happen again to the Jewish people, thus making it an instrument to guarantee *Tekumah*. For the bomb's opponents, it is the other way around: only the bomb could cause another *Shoah*, thereby undermining *Tekumah*.

Beyond their disagreement, however, all Israelis agree that the nuclear issue is so sensitive that it must be handled with extraordinary care. The proponents do not want any public debate at all, while the opponents want a muted and limited debate. The media are comfortable with the constraints of the Censora, and over time those limits have defined the parameters of the public discussion. The Israeli public has accepted that the nuclear subject is inappropriate for public discussion. The ethos of *kdushat habitachon* (the "sanctity of security") is paramount in Israel's culture, and no other security matter expresses this ethos so closely. The societal-cultural component makes the Israeli bargain with the bomb sui generis and creates a congruence between a policy and society. In this chapter, I revisit four historical landmarks in the development of Israel's nuclear taboo. Three of these landmarks are cases of individuals who struggled with the nuclear issue: Eliezer Livneh, Mordechai Vanunu, and General Yitzhak Yaakov. The fourth landmark is a three-year period (1967 to 1970) in which Israel was stumbling in its bid for nuclear weapons while the press said nothing. Then, on the sociological side, I examine how all the Israeli democratic watchdogs, especially the media, have reinforced the culture and silence of amimut.

My selection of Livneh, Vanunu, and Yaakov does not mean that they are a representative sample of a larger number of cases questioning or protesting the nuclear path Israel has chosen. They are not, in other words, the best examples of antinuclear sentiment in Israel, but, leaving my own case aside, they are the only significant examples. Unlike the history of other nuclear democracies, Israel has not produced an antinuclear protest movement or a nuclear disarmament movement. Outsiders may be surprised to learn that in the five decades since Israel embarked on the nuclear path, few Israelis have raised serious questions about Israel's nuclear choices and about amimut. A deeper sociological appreciation of amimut's hold on the Israeli psyche, however, would tell us that we should not be so surprised.

The Case of Citizen Eliezer Livneh

If anybody had the intellectual and political credentials to initiate a nuclear debate in Israel in early 1960s, it was Eliezer Livneh (1902–1974). Livneh was one of the brightest and most influential public figures of his generation. Born in Poland in 1902, he moved to Palestine in 1921 as a social-Zionist pioneer and kibbutz founder and emerged as a special kind of politician, a combination of an intellectual and a strategic thinker. With the outbreak of World War II, Livneh became a defense intellectual at the Haganah headquarters, where he founded *Ma'archot*, the first Hebrew periodical focusing on strategic and military affairs.

In the early years of the Israeli state, Livneh was a political insider. He founded and edited *Eshnav*, a small publication that served as the voice of the activist circle within MAPAI (David Ben-Gurion's majority party, the Land of Israel Workers Party). Days before Ben-Gurion declared the establishment of the state of Israel, he sent Livneh to Menachem Begin, the leader of the Irgun, a militant right-wing Zionist group, to seek his cooperation with the provisional government. Livneh later was elected a member of the Knesset from MAPAI for two terms (1949–1955) and served as an influential member on the Defense and Foreign Affairs Committee. Known as an independent thinker and increasingly critical of the MAPAI's leadership, Livneh was not reelected by his party to the Third Knesset. In November 1957, Livneh resigned from the MAPAI Party ostensibly for what he termed a disagreement with its leadership. In fact, however, Livneh resigned after questions were raised about the sources of funds he used to buy a luxurious apartment in Jerusalem.[1]

Livneh's resignation took place a few weeks after Shimon Peres signed the secret Dimona pact in Paris. Whether he actually knew something about the secret deal is not known, but four years later, some time after Dimona became public, the nuclear issue became the new focus of his public life. In January 1962, in an article in the daily *Ha'aretz* entitled "Warning in the Last Moment," Livneh raised the question of Israel's future national security doctrine: Should Israel change its military doctrine to rely on nuclear weapons and ballistic missiles? His answer was negative: the nuclearization of the Arab-Israeli conflict would be catastrophic to the region, and even more so to Israel itself. Israel thus must try to prevent the introduction of nuclear weapons into the region.[2]

Two months later, Livneh organized a small group of distinguished Israelis to sign a public petition urging the Israeli government to take a diplomatic initiative to ban the introduction of nuclear weapons to the region. Among the signers were such prominent intellectuals and scholars as Martin Buber, Ephraim Auerbach, and Yeshayahu Leibowitz; Gabriel Stein and Franz Olendorf, two former members of the Israel Atomic Energy Commission (IAEC) who had resigned in 1958; religious leaders; and one member of the Knesset, Shlomo Zalman Abramov of the General Zionist Party. The group presented itself as nonpartisan, as it was composed of prominent Zionist Jews from both the left and the right, whose common interest was opposing the bomb.[3]

This petition was the first act of nuclear public protest in Israel. The government issued no official response. Unofficially, however, the Ministry of Defense tried to delegitimize the group, insinuating that its activity was unpatriotic and damaged national security.[4] A few months later, in the wake of Egypt's test of ballistic rockets in July 1962, Deputy Minister of Defense Shimon Peres referred publicly to the need to revise Israel's security doctrine.[5] The Egyptians' test allowed Peres to express publicly his advocacy for a technological revolution in Israel's military doctrine.[6] Without explicitly advocating the bomb, Peres argued on a variety of public occasions that Israel must develop new and powerful "deterrent weapons" not only to win the war but also to prevent wars in the future.[7] He even hinted that Israel might soon be forced to adopt a new "military doctrine" in view of the new weapons in Arab hands.[8] With a veiled reference to Livneh and his antinuclear group, Peres attacked those calling for nuclear disarmament. Disarmament, he stressed, must relate to all weapons. As long as the Arabs preached the destruction of Israel, Israel must be prepared.[9]

Countering Peres's rhetoric about deterrence and technology—code words for the nuclear issue—Livneh escalated his antinuclear campaign. In the summer of 1962, Livneh founded the first (only and last) antinuclear lobby with the quiet support of Nahum Goldman, the president of the World Zionist Organization, and named it the Israeli Committee for the Denuclearization of the Middle East. From the start, the committee operated as a small, elite, citizen lobby. Its active membership was small, no more than a few dozen active supporters. Often only ten to twenty people attended its meetings, which were normally held in the residence of one of the participants.[10] Ultimately the committee was Livneh himself, and he aimed its activity at the leaders of the Zionist political parties and the Israeli intelligentsia at large, hoping to inform the public of the dangers of nuclear weapons.[11] Given the scientific and political weight of the committee's members, they had access to prominent political figures in both the governing coalition and opposition parties.[12]

The committee argued that the atomic bomb was the only weapon that could destroy the Zionist enterprise. Given Israel's geopolitical and demographic vulnerabilities, it could not, and should not, tolerate the nuclearization of the Arab-Israeli conflict. Israel would never be safe if nuclear weapons were in hostile hands. The presumption was that any Israeli advantage in the nuclear field would be short lived. The only way to prevent the region's nuclearization was through a political agreement by the region's states to create a Middle East free from nuclear weapons.[13]

Although the committee framed its public opposition to the bomb in regional terms, the context and focus were clearly domestic. Concerned that important decisions had already been made and that others were soon to be made, Livneh and his associates tried to alert the Zionist political parties of the significance of those decisions. Given the dynamics of technology, Livneh and his activists were aware of the short path from a nuclear "option" to producing a bomb once the nuclear infrastructure had been completed. They knew that the infrastructure was nearing completion—indeed, the Dimona reactor had been activated in early 1964, and the secret reprocessing plant had been completed a year later—and they were concerned that under the shroud of secrecy and without parliamentary oversight, Ben-Gurion and Peres could make critical decisions on their own.[14] In sum, they were concerned that Israel would soon have the bomb without ever engaging in a democratic discussion.[15]

For two years (1962–1964), the committee was engaged in efforts, some of which were politically awkward, to communicate its concerns to Knesset members and the public and force the issue into some sort of parliamentary or even public debate. In historical perspective, the committee's activities were the closest that Israel has ever come to an actual antinuclear protest.

This antinuclear campaign failed, however, and by analyzing its failure, we can trace the early indicators of what became Israel's special bargain with the bomb. Livneh's committee faced obstacles in expressing its concerns to the public. Both external pressure from the Censora and a self-imposed societal sense of *kdushat habitachon* made a public nuclear debate very tricky, nearly impossible. Neither side in the debate was able or willing to speak out frankly and freely about its real concerns and objectives. Officially, no Israeli nuclear weapons program existed, and the Censora prohibited any suggestion of it, so both sides had to use certain code words and phrases, like "new deterrent weapons" and "regional denuclearization" to express their message. This difficulty, however, applied to only the antinuclear camp seeking a public debate, whereas the other side could promote its objectives quietly.[16]

Livneh and his colleagues found themselves in an awkward position, not being able to state their real concerns. To do so would have violated the Censora by revealing state secrets, and it would have undermined their patriotic credentials. Committee members had to be mindful of how far they could push their critique without crossing the line, both legally and politically. They were under the quiet but effective surveillance of the Shin Bet, the country's domestic intelligence service, and Livneh was aware of it.[17] Aware of this risk, the committee's leader, Livneh, insisted on using only public information to make its case, which significantly weakened its position. The committee's ostensible objective, regional efforts toward denuclearization, looked hypothetical, as its members could not state publicly their real worry: that Ben-Gurion and Peres would push Israel and the region to become nuclearized.[18]

From the perspective of the nuclear project's guardians, the antinuclear lobby group was no more than an irritant. Peres initially tried to silence Livneh and his committee through the Censora, but this proved difficult because Livneh's articles tested its limits. Livneh himself had no direct access to classified information and avoided making factual claims, even when he implied that Dimona's purpose was to attain nuclear weapons and that it had not been built for research on basic science, health, or agriculture, as Ben-Gurion publicly claimed. Although Livneh was unable to say this explicitly, he insisted on his right to argue strategically against the applicability of nuclear weapons to the Middle East situation. The Censora had no legal case for banning his articles. Then, in early 1962, Peres tried to use patriotic persuasion to pressure Ha'aretz's editors not to publish Livneh's contributions, but his efforts backfired. In 1964, after a yearlong dispute with the Censora, Livneh and his associates published an edited collection of articles that examined the strategic, political, and economic aspects of the introduction of nuclear weapons.[19]

Livneh and his colleagues were not the only people in Israel at the time with reservations about the nuclear project. In 1961/1962, significant elements within the Israeli body politic, including some prominent figures in the MAPAI, as well as the leadership of Achdut ha'avodah (Ben-Gurion's junior coalition partner), also had quiet concerns about the nuclear project. Some of those concerns were strategic (in the case of Achdut ha'avodah), and others were political, financial, and even democratic. Ben-Gurion was aware of those reservations and thus tried to create a political climate that effectively precluded public nuclear debate.

First, from the start, Ben-Gurion adopted the public position that the nuclear project was peaceful. Such a strategy not only prevented a showdown with President John F. Kennedy's administration, but it also made it nearly impossible for his domestic opponents to argue publicly against him. That is, in order to call his bluff, challengers would have to violate their patriotic commitment to kdushat habitachon. Furthermore, the Censora did not allow him to say it in public.

Second, in 1962, in response to suggestions that he acted undemocratically, Ben-Gurion created a secret Knesset subcommittee, known as the Committee of Seven and made up of the leaders of main Zionist parties, and gave it extremely sensitive information regarding Israel's nuclear endeavor. In fact, the information shared with the Committee of Seven was so secret that its members were not allowed to take any notes, and in return for being privy to the secrets, they had to demonstrate their loyalty. The effective outcome was that Ben-Gurion created a highly secret political forum that ensured there would be no political debate. The guardians of the public interest were co-opted and transformed into guardians of the nuclear secret.

Third, by mid-1962 Ben-Gurion decided to open the nuclear issue for a strategic discussion, and for the first time he invited the leadership of Achdut ha'avodah, a party known for its hawkish, security-oriented approach, to be part of that discussion. As I elaborated in chapter 3, this discussion marked a critical juncture in Israel's nuclear history because it was the first actual closed door to debate among those who advocated Israel's joining the nuclear club: the technological school led by Shimon Peres and Moshe Dayan and the conventional school led by the Achdut ha'avodah leaders, Israel Galili and Yigal Allon. For the first time, Ben-Gurion was seeking a national consensus on this project, and he endorsed a compromise based on the strategic insight of the conventional school, that Israel should continue to build a nuclear option but that the Israel Defense Forces (IDF) must remain a conventional army.

Under these political circumstances, when it became apparent that Ben-Gurion was willing to listen to the bomb's critics and restrain Peres's and Dayan's nuclear ambitions, it also became clear that the leaders of the Achdut ha'avodah would accept Ben-Gurion's word and not push for a public debate. Ben-Gurion thus guaranteed that the leaders of the Achdut ha'avodah, the only political party with its own strategic doctrine, which questioned the wisdom of Israel's becoming a nuclear power, would not publicly protest against the bomb. Ben-Gurion's actions also guaranteed that the Achdut ha'avodah's leaders would not join forces with Livneh's committee. Livneh was thus left alone and out of politics in his public antinuclear crusade.

The strategic discussions with Ben-Gurion in 1962 were critical to the creation of a dual domestic consensus on the subject of nuclear weapons. First, without a national consensus, national political decisions on nuclear weapons could not be made. Second, a consensus also laid the groundwork for ambiguity as a compromise between the two sides to the debate. There had to be a consensus about the need for consensus. The compromise made in those 1962 discussions led to a combination of a basic conventional outlook with a strong nuclear option. Domestically this attitude was crucial to the willingness of virtually all politicians to keep the nuclear issue from becoming a matter of public debate. With the compromise of 1962, the path toward the policy and culture of amimut was cleared.

The legacy of Livneh's committee is mixed. Evidently, the committee failed to engender a national debate over the nuclear issue and to incorporate it into the nation's overall security agenda. The public was not interested in the subject, recognizing that a public debate would not serve the national interest. The failure was not simply because the committee was silenced but because the Israeli public itself, especially its body politic, was not interested in public engagement on the nuclear issue. Over time, these domestic attitudes grew into the special bargain that Israel made with the atom.

Despite the committee's failure, some of its core ideas remain relevant to this day. Among them are the convictions that Israel's fundamental interest is against introducing nuclear weapons into the region, that Israel must not adopt a nuclear strategy, and that a nuclear Middle East would be dangerous and unstable. All these convictions constitute the pillar of caution in Israel's policy of amimut.

Livneh and his colleagues saw Israel's nuclear dilemma in either/or terms: either Israel acquired the bomb and the region became nuclear, or Israel abstained from possessing nuclear weapons and kept the region denuclearized. They could not have imagined Israel's dual nuclear posture, in which it would possess nuclear weapons but not acknowledge them, by adopting a policy of nuclear opacity. Using amimut, Israel has been able to avoid the either/or decision concerning its nuclear dilemma and have the best of both worlds.

Eliezer Livneh and his comrades' antinuclear campaign was short lived, lasting for only two years, from 1962 to 1964. The book that the committee published in early 1964, after a yearlong struggle with the Censora, was among its last accomplishments. After its publication, Livneh began to lose his interest in publicly dealing with the nuclear subject, but he never explained why. It seems likely, though that once Levi Eshkol became prime minister—Livneh was always on friendly terms with Eshkol—Livneh worried less about the nuclear issue. He probably learned of Kennedy's pressure on the issue of Dimona, as well as Eshkol's subsequent response. He likely took Eshkol at his word when the latter pledged that Israel would not introduce nuclear weapons to the region. Livneh thus came to understand that public discussion was not the most effective way to promote his concerns.

By 1965 Livneh had stopped writing opinion articles on the nuclear issue. With Livneh ceasing to be active, his committee also faded from the public eye. Nobody in Israel continued to fight the nuclear cause, at least not by debating the issue openly and democratically. Two years later, weeks after the 1967 war, Livneh was among the founding fathers of a new nationalistic ideological movement named the Movement for Greater Israel, which called for Israel to annex the territories occupied during the Six-Day War.

The Citizenry and the Birth of Amimut

Ever since the United Kingdom exploded its first nuclear device in October 1952, nuclear testing became the act by which states commonly announced their crossing the nuclear threshold. It was the case with France in 1960, China in 1964, India and Pakistan in 1998, and, most recently, North Korea in 2006. For all these states, testing a nuclear device signified more than a demonstration of technological capability; it was a public political act of claiming nuclear status. Both at home and abroad, testing was a way to give the national nuclear program public legitimacy.

Israel did not follow this pattern. Although sometime in late 1966 Israel reached the technological stage that allowed for conducting a nuclear test on short notice, Prime Minister Eshkol ruled out a test for political reasons. Eshkol was committed to the nonintroduction stance, which was incompatible with testing. Hence, instead of moving to a posture of nuclear visibility and clarity, Israel remained faithful to secrecy and nonacknowledgment. This course of action is also critical to understanding the rise of amimut as a societal attitude.

To begin with, it is not natural for the Israeli democratic citizenry to follow such a nondemocratic pattern of total silence and secrecy. By its nature, the Israeli public is engaged, opinionated, and curious, especially on fundamental national issues. A good example is the full-blown public debate that swept Israel almost immediately after the 1967 war over the future of the conquered territories. While the Israeli government hesitated, the public took the lead on this issue.

It is fair to say that the nuclear issue was as important to the future of Israel as was the future of the occupied territories. In the late 1960s Israelis had good reasons to think about the future of their nation's nuclear project. Israel had to decide whether to maintain only an "option" or to actually build, possess, and deploy nuclear weapons. Two new developments complicated these decisions. First, the Nuclear Non-Proliferation Treaty (NPT) was introduced in 1968, and Israel's decision about the NPT was tantamount to a decision about its nuclear future. A number of technologically advanced countries, like West Germany and Sweden, viewed joining the NPT as a referendum on the nuclear issue. Israel was a key state for the new treaty, and President Lyndon B. Johnson's administration was pressing Israel hard to sign it.[20] Second, Israel's 1967 victory created a new strategic environment, which merited rethinking its objectives with regard to its nuclear program. Both developments should have prompted the Israeli public to debate their nation's nuclear future.

Furthermore, by the late 1960s, a great many Israelis—politicians, scientists, journalists, and others—recognized that their country had reached the nuclear-weapons threshold and had to make major decisions about its nuclear future. The foreign press (which was always cited in Israel) was reporting in 1969 that Israel either already had the bomb or was close to having it.[21] Nonetheless, the public greeted the nuclear issue with complete silence. The silence was deafening. An examination of the Israeli press in 1968/1969 shows no editorials on the nuclear issue, only citations from the world press. The NPT was reported and discussed by Israeli pundits almost as if it were an international issue not involving important questions for Israel.

Some scholars would note that in the late 1960s the Censora still had enough power to enforce this silence on behalf of the government. But the Censora had no legal authority to block opinion pieces and editorials (it could ban only those editorials that contained certain information); it could not block commentaries that argued hypothetically for one policy or another. The only way to ban a subject was through a personal plea by the prime minister, the minister of defense, or the chief of staff to the editors in chief to avoid publication on a certain subject for reasons of national security. This was not the case in 1968/1969. It was the editors and writers who decided on their own not to write on the nuclear issue, convinced that *kdushat habitachon* required silence.

After 1967 a few secret ministerial consultations were held on the nuclear issue, but they were part of top-secret executive decisions taken by the government, not a genuine, public, political debate. Had these consultations taken place today, they most likely would have been leaked, but at the time the public knew nothing. Furthermore, unlike the situation between 1961 and 1963 when the leadership of Achdut ha'avodah wanted to prevent Peres from making Israel a nuclear-weapons state, the ministerial consultations in 1968 to 1970 appeared more practical. By that time, Eshkol had already solidified Ben-Gurion's 1962 commitment to keep Israel outside the nuclear club by pledging that it would not be the first to introduce nuclear weapons to the region.

Ultimately, it was Prime Minister Golda Meir who made the critical decisions in 1969. She decided in 1969/1970 that Israel should not sign the NPT, should maintain "a bomb in the basement" posture, and should make an amimut deal with President Richard M. Nixon. Even the Achdut ha'avodah ministers, Yigal Allon and Israel Galili, who may have had reservations about her decisions, could live with them as long as Israel was officially still pledging "not to be the first to introduce nuclear weapons to the region." Above all, they agreed that the issue must be handled outside the public sphere. Nothing about her decisions was leaked to the press, let alone debated in public. The same is true about her meeting with President Nixon.

From that time forward, nobody in the Israeli democratic polity, including all its watchdogs, has raised direct or hard questions about the country's nuclear policy. Whenever international rumors flood the press, the Israeli public looks the other way. Had the citizenry not endorsed amimut, the policy could not have survived. The two next cases were criminal cases in which efforts to raise the nuclear issue broke the law.

The Vanunu Affair

During the half century since Israel initiated its nuclear project, many thousands of Israelis have been involved in one aspect or another of the nation's greatest secret. Since the nuclear project was perceived as ensuring national survival and preventing another holocaust, no Israeli has dared to break that taboo, including critics like Eliezer Livneh. The one exception was an Israeli citizen who decided for ideological reasons to violate that collective sacred secrecy. His name is Mordechai Vanunu.

The Vanunu case is now well known, with books, films, and plays produced about it, so I do not need to repeat the details here.[22] Rather, I will reflect on the affair's lessons, as they shed light on Israel's special bargain with the bomb. Amimut faced its most severe challenge in 1986 when Vanunu, a former technician at Dimona, told the London Sunday Times all he knew about the nuclear complex. He had worked in Dimona's most sensitive part, the underground reprocessing plant. Israel's guardians feared that because amimut's credibility depended on secrecy, Vanunu's revelations would render amimut no longer politically viable as a national nuclear posture.

These fears did not materialize. It turned out that Vanunu's revelations were politically insufficient to shatter amimut. Despite their journalistic visibility, his revelations lacked the political force, both inside and outside Israel, to affect the policy of amimut. On the contrary, except for Norway, the international community apparently was not willing to translate Vanunu's disclosure into the language of international relations. Even in the Arab world, where the sensational revelations received a great deal of media attention, the governments were ambivalent about making the issue a political case. Despite being treated as a sensational cloak-and-dagger affair, the Vanunu affair failed to become a political issue.[23] Israel's amimut had survived its most severe challenge.

The state of Israel promptly dealt with the affair. Mossad operatives in England "honey-trapped" Vanunu to Italy, drugged him, and brought him back to Israel to face Israeli justice. He was tried and convicted in February 1988 by the district court in Jerusalem on the most severe national security offenses in Israeli law: treason and severe espionage. Vanunu was sentenced to eighteen years in prison, twelve of which he spent in solitary confinement.

An equally interesting aspect of the Vanunu affair was the reaction by the Israeli public. First, the public was shocked by the gravity and the precedent-setting nature of the case. Then it supported—and was proud of—the government's clandestine action to bring Vanunu home to trial for treason. Most important, the public was firm in its reluctance to look into the forbidden area that Vanunu's revelations opened up. The Israeli media and the public at large ignored the affair's policy implications, as to do otherwise would mean being complicit in Vanunu's treacherous act. Evidently, the Israeli public was not interested in shattering amimut and the societal taboo it represented.

Although the media were curious about the human and the operational aspects of the Vanunu affair—the tale of betrayal, the cloak-and-dagger operation, and so on—they completely ignored its policy implications. The mainstream Israeli media outlets did not dare to defy the quiet appeal of Prime Minister Shimon Peres to the editors in chief on behalf of kdushat habitachon to ignore these policy issues. The editors complied with Peres's request because they agreed with him that in this case, kdushat habitachon outweighed any other journalistic or democratic consideration, including the public's right to know.

This remarkable societal reaction was not the result of formal censorship demands or Peres's authoritative plea to the editors. Rather, it was an authentic expression of the media's own commitment to kdushat habitachon. When they perceived the fate of amimut to be at stake, the Israeli media would do its best, independent of all journalistic values of disclosure and truth, to save this national security asset.

In late 1986, only weeks after the Vanunu story broke in the world press, I wrote my first article for the *Bulletin of the Atomic Scientists*, which compared the Israeli nuclear situation with the nuclear situation in the West:

> The nuclear debate that has gripped Western societies in the last several years has found no echo whatsoever in Israel. Even now, in stark contrast to the seriousness of Vanunu's revelations, there has been no debate or serious questioning of Israel's nuclear program. Once again, an event that should have sparked national questioning has been quickly and effectively stifled. This is not, however, just a result of official censorship; it is more a matter of self-censorship, a product of the culture of denial and secrecy.[24]

While Israeli officials have always recognized that the Vanunu revelations were beneficial strategically to Israel, because Vanunu contributed to the credibility of Israel's nuclear deterrence more than any other individual had done before and after, they have always treated the case as the first, and most abhorrent, act of treason in the country's history.

Mordechai Vanunu completed his eighteen years of imprisonment for treason and espionage in April 2004; by law, he was supposed to be a free man who had paid his debt to society. Vanunu himself dreamed of leaving Israel for good, raising a family, and beginning a new life. Norway, where his actions had received widespread support, was willing to accept him. But the Israeli government was determined to continue harassing the man who dared to betray Israel's most sacred of secrets, using, of course, the appeal to *kdushat habitachon* as a pretext for its actions.[25]

Using the claim that Vanunu still knew a great deal of sensitive information, the MALMAB chief, Yechiel Horev, persuaded the government to create a ministerial committee to approve a broad package of administrative restrictions and prohibitions on his fundamental freedoms, particularly speech and movement. The military Home Front Command chief, relying on the 1945 British Mandate Emergency Regulations, also signed off on some restrictions. The ministers of interior and justice signed other prohibitions, which banned Vanunu from leaving the country. These restrictions have been formally extended every year since then. Even though ministers with different outlooks come and go—even the MALMAB chief Horev has since left—they all remain firm on the Vanunu case. As of this writing (July 2009), they have renewed for the sixth time the administrative order forbidding Vanunu from leaving Israel.[26]

Just as the government of Israel has refused to ease up on Vanunu, he has remained defiant in his own actions. Vanunu has rejected the legitimacy of the government's restrictions, and since his release in 2004 he has been arrested briefly several times for violating those restrictions, primarily for giving interviews to foreign journalists. In early 2005 the Israeli government finally charged him with twenty-one counts of "contravening a lawful direction," and in April 2007 he was convicted by the Jerusalem Magistrate Court of violating the order barring foreign contacts and traveling outside Jerusalem. Two months later, he was sentenced to six months of jail, which was subsequently reduced to three months.[27] After a series of appeals, first in the Jerusalem district court and then in Israel's supreme court, on July 6, 2009, Vanunu's attorney, Avigdor Feldman, made a deal with the state that after six months, pending a review of his conduct, Vanunu would be able to ask for the restrictions to be lifted and be allowed to travel abroad.

As Israeli journalist Yossi Melman explained in an editorial in *Ha'aretz*, "Vanunu's harassment by the Israel government is unprecedented and represents a distortion of every accepted legal norm."[28] Melman touched on the depth of the Israeli nuclear taboo in describing the situation:

> It is unpopular to defend Vanunu, one of the most reviled people in Israel. Cabinet ministers, most Knesset members, and senior officials, including the attorney general, have remained silent. Since Vanunu's release from prison, there have been four justice ministers: Yosef Lapid, Tzipi Livni, Haim Ramon, and now Daniel Friedmann. Not one has attempted even to question to what degree the state has shown inhumanity, injustice, and foolishness in this painful chapter.
>
> Leading the campaign to confine Vanunu to Israel is the Defense Ministry's chief security officer [MALMAB], who is in charge of the security of the nuclear project. . . . The security chief's main argument, which the cabinet ministers and senior officials accepted at face value, was that Vanunu continues to threaten the country's security. In other words, he ostensibly possesses secrets that he could publicize if he were allowed to leave the country. This assumption is problematic. In the intelligence business, one has to assume the worst-case scenario, mean-

ing that Vanunu told the *Times* everything he knew. By the state's logic, Vanunu will remain a security risk forever, and the restrictions will never be lifted.

One might have expected Friedmann, who seeks to correct injustices in the justice system, to at least question the conduct of the defense establishment. He did not respond to a request by *Ha'aretz* for his position on the matter. The new Defense Ministry security chief, Amir Kain, refused to respond when asked how long Vanunu would continue to be punished.[29]

The Yatza Affair

On March 28, 2001, seventy-five-year-old retired Israeli Brigadier General Yitzhak Yaakov (known in Israel as Yatza) was arrested at Ben-Gurion Airport as he was about to board a flight to Turkey. Yatza was held under secret arrest and interrogated by the MALMAB about "secret information" that he had shared with "unauthorized people." The arrest was the beginning of an extraordinary tale known in Israel as the Yatza affair.[30]

Yatza's career had given him extensive access to a number of vital state secrets. He had served as the top weapons developer in the Israel Defense Forces (IDF) in the 1960s and early 1970s, a job that also made him the senior liaison between the IDF and all the defense R&D organizations, including the nuclear project. On the eve of the 1967 Six-Day War, Yatza was at the center of an extraordinary activity as its initiator, planner, and promoter. Although that operation was never carried out, and its story was never told, its preparations have left profound memories among those very few who were privy to its secrets.[31]

In the fall of 1973, just two weeks before the Yom Kippur War broke out, Yatza retired from active duty. He became the chief scientist in the Ministry of Trade and Commerce, a job involved with promotion of Israeli high-tech industry. A few years later, he moved to New York City and became an international high-tech entrepreneur.[32] For decades, that old memory from 1967 remained dormant in his mind, but thirty years later, it somehow came back to life. By the late 1990s, Yatza was haunted by that forbidden memory, referring to it as "my legacy." He wanted to share it with others, especially his own family, but was not sure how. So he wrote it down in two forms, one fictional and the other a memoir.

It was in the summer of 1999 that I met Yatza in New York City for the first time. During that summer, I traveled to New York several times just to hear his story in more detail. While Yatza's memory fascinated me, I also recognized that his subjective memory was only a partial version of the whole story. I remained uncertain as to what exactly did or did not happen in 1967. Some months later, I introduced him to Israeli journalist Ronen Bergman, who asked him for an interview for *Yediot Achronot*. That connection and the interview that followed were the starting point of the Yatza affair.[33]

Defying Amimut

When the chief military censor, Brigadier General Rachel Dolev, handed a transcript of Bergman's interview with Yatza to the MALMAB chief, Yechiel Horev, Horev was stunned.[34] For him, the interview meant a direct threat to Israel's policy of amimut, a challenge that had to be squelched beyond merely banning the interview. Within hours, Horev had set up a small task force of senior security and legal officials to address Yatza's challenge. At first they considered arresting him when he arrived in Israel, but when they learned about his high-profile seventy-fifth birthday party scheduled days later, they decided to arrest him upon his departure. Israel's political and legal leadership was briefed and approved Horev's course of action. A judge signed an arrest order. Yatza was placed under the MALMAB's surveillance.[35]

It took nearly four weeks for Yatza's arrest to become known. On April 22, 2001, London's *Sunday Times* revealed the arrest as a news item.[36] In Israel, a court-issued gag order prohibited the press from publishing anything about the case, not even citing the *Sunday Times* story (something that the Censora normally permits). But the daily *Ha'aretz* defied the gag order and published the *Sunday Times* story without adding anything to it.[37] Within hours, the rest of the Israeli press violated the gag order as well. The Israeli papers' headlines were exclusively about the former general who was secretly arrested only days after many prominent members of the defense and high-tech elite celebrated his birthday in recognition of his contribution to the state's well-being.

By the next day, the Tel Aviv district court partially lifted the gag order, and the arrest of General Yaakov on suspicion of threatening national security was confirmed.[38] The state acknowledged that the case concerned passing "secret information" to "unauthorized people" and noted that it was extremely grave due to the special nature of those secrets. Although the state did not link them to nuclear matters, the foreign press did, speculating that the case was about nuclear secrets.[39]

Yatza's secret arrest was exceptional for many reasons. First, such a lengthy secret arrest was truly unthinkable in contemporary Israel. Moreover, the level of secrecy used in the case was unheard of, involving two layers of secrecy, the Censora and a court gag order.[40] Second, Israel's top political and legal leadership had been informed and had authorized the arrest: Prime Minister Ariel Sharon, Defense Minister Binyamin Ben-Eliezer, State Prosecutor Edna Arbel, and Attorney General Elyakim Rubinstein. Third, the MALMAB chief, Yechiel Horev, received the authority to lead the investigation, even though the GSS should be the appropriate security agency to deal with national security investigations. Finally, the case was all about guarding amimut. In a sense, this feature encompassed the uniqueness of the whole case.

Although Yatza's case was formally about the disclosure of classified information, it was actually about the legal standing of amimut. What was for Yatza a personal memory was for the MALMAB chief a state secret whose disclosure could shatter Israel's policy of amimut. As long as the state of Israel was committed to amimut, Horev apparently argued, the state must provide its guardians the power to prosecute and penalize those who threatened it. Horev insisted that the case was an egregious offense against amimut, which had to be made a precedent for the future. Arbel, the state prosecutor, and Dvora Chen, the case prosecutor, were persuaded that the case deserved the strongest possible indictment. As he was in the Vanunu case, Horev was determined to achieve a victory in court that would serve as a deterrent to all other potential threats to amimut.[41]

Reconfirming Amimut

Three weeks after the arrest became public, an indictment was filed at the Tel Aviv district court, charging Yatza on two related counts of article 113, "severe espionage," in the Israeli criminal code. The first charge was disclosing secret information with intent to damage state security, which carries a maximum penalty of life imprisonment (113/b), and the second, a lighter backup charge, of disclosing secret information to unauthorized people (113/a).[42] Apart from the article pertaining to treason, Yatza's indictment was legally similar to that filed against Vanunu in 1986. It was assumed that, owing to the special status of amimut, no Israeli court would reject the claim that Yatza must have been aware of the harm to the state entailed in his disclosure. This awareness constituted the "intent" to harm national security.

The indictment was extraordinary, however, in at least two senses that made problematic any comparison with the Vanunu case. First, Israel had never had an espionage case based only on the offense of disclosing secret information to unauthorized people. Nobody had ever been prosecuted in Israel for such an offense. The Yatza case was even more unusual because that secret information was evidently obsolete and had no current intelligence value. Most important, this information never became public because it was banned by the Censora. Hence, even under worst-case assumptions, the nation's security could not have been damaged.

Second, the case involved no actual espionage, no foreign agents, and no demonstration of damage to national security, and yet it was treated as if it were a case of espionage. The indictment referred specifically to Yatza's two manuscripts that he had shared with unauthorized people, as well as his interview with Bergman.

The trial took place behind closed doors in the fall and winter of 2001/2002. The public learned about its proceedings only from selected uncensored portions of the testimonies released by the court. In May 2002, more than a year after Yatza was arrested, the three-judge panel issued a 140-page verdict (only a portion of which was available to the public). Two members of the panel found Yatza not guilty on the major charge of disclosing classified information with intent to harm state security (113/b), but he was convicted on the lighter, more narrow charge of passing such information without authorization (113/a). A month later, a majority of the panel sentenced Yatza to two years' probation, noting as reasons for leniency his imprisonment for more than a year, his medical condition, and his extraordinary contribution to the security and economy of the state. Effectively, the sentence meant that Yatza was immediately released.

Ironically, probably the biggest loser of the Yatza affair was not Yatza but the MALMAB chief, Yechiel Horev. Throughout the affair, the Israeli press criticized his conduct as abusive, extreme, and overbearing. Horev's treatment of Yatza like a spy, as a major security risk that required custody, continued throughout the trial and was characterized by his insistence that Yatza deserved a Vanunu-like indictment. Horev's reply to all his critics was simply "wait for the trial," implying that he expected the trial to vindicate him completely.

The outcome of the trial demonstrated how mistaken Horev's assumptions were. While the verdict formally justified the legal proceeding against Yatza, it did not vindicate Horev's conduct. Even before the trial, Horev had been losing credibility, not only with the media, but also with the case prosecutor, Dvora Chen. The more that Chen explored the intricacies of the case (as opposed to merely hearing allegations from Horev), the more she realized how vindictive Horev's judgments were.[43]

The verdict in Yatza's case provided further support for the criticism against Horev that the media had been making for months by pointing out how different the Yatza case was from the Vanunu case. Historically, the Yatza affair was probably the tipping point in Horev's long career as the chief guardian of Israel's nuclear program. Since that case, the Israeli media have portrayed Horev as a zealot, overbearing, vindictive, and paranoid (keep in mind that only a few years earlier he was still an anonymous figure). The verdict only strengthened this criticism. Horev was painted as the Israeli version of J. Edgar Hoover, a devoted security chief who lacked the judgment to use his power properly.[44] In the eyes of many people, the Yatza affair made Horev the embodiment of the antidemocratic risks inherent in the commitment to amimut.[45]

The Yatza case was the first and only legal case in Israel in which amimut played the central role. This case was not about espionage; it was not even about disclosure; it was about amimut and, more accurately, how closely it had to be protected. Even the censored public version of the verdict made clear that the case was about amimut when it alluded to the fact that Yatza broke the sanctity of that "special secret information," a violation that itself justified bringing the case to court. The verdict makes it clear that the court affirmed, even sanctioned, the special status of amimut. Yatza's initial effort to argue that amimut made little sense when the world already knew that Israel was a nuclear-weapons state made no impression on the court. At the same time, however, the court did not tolerate the abuse of the sanctity of amimut in order to inflate the case's severity.

Equally interesting was the public's, and the media's, reaction to the affair. Soon after Yatza's secret arrest became public, the media started to question Horev's conduct, noting that the days when citizens could disappear for weeks or months were gone and unacceptable in a democracy.[46] Questions about Israel's legal structure that permitted such an abuse of power were raised, and within two months, a legislative process was initiated and subsequently passed in the Knesset to modify Israel's draconian espionage law.[47]

The Media and Amimut

In the previous chapter, I noted that on the nuclear issue, the Censora still functions as a powerful state institution to control public discussion. This is remarkable, especially in view of the steady decline in the Censora's overall power as a state institution since the 1970s, counterbalanced by the media's becoming more aggressive in their demand for open information. This creates a puzzle: How is it that the Censora's authority has been diminishing steadily, but on the nuclear issue, it remains so authoritative and effective? I hinted in the previous chapter that the explanation of this puzzle lies not in the weakened Censora but in the unchanging fundamental attitudes of the public toward the nuclear issue, especially toward amimut, which allows the Censora to remain an effective force in this field. I suggested that the nuclear issue is probably the only area in which *kdushat habitachon* still maintains its old cultural dominance.

In this chapter I substantiate this claim by exploring the role of the media in amimut. The Israeli media are a good barometer by which to assess how Israelis deal with amimut. Apart from public polls (which are a relatively recent phenomenon in Israel), the media are the only available indicators that allow us to monitor and interpret the Israeli public's attitudes toward the nuclear issue. When contrasted with the major transformations of the Israeli media in the past few decades, the almost unchanged practices in their coverage of the nuclear issue are striking.

In the country's first two or three decades, the Israeli media were primarily print, comprising a dozen or so Hebrew daily newspapers and a handful of smaller, non-Hebrew papers. Most papers were organs of political parties, which often subsidized them.[48] In those days, Israel had one, state-run, broadcasting authority, which controlled the nation's air, radio, and TV (in 1968, the first year of Israeli national TV, the broadcast was one hour a day). Israel had no significant regional media outlets, and Tel Aviv was the nation's media capital. In accordance with its ethos, the Israeli media were, with the possible exception of the newspapers published by the Israeli Communist Party and the papers published in the Arab sector, both nationalistic and ideological. The media identified themselves proudly and openly as a Zionist press (the motto of *Al Hamishmar*, the most left-wing newspaper in Israel except for *Kol Ha'am*, the newspaper of the Communist Party, was "For Zionism, Socialism, and the Brotherhood of Peoples"). Security was the overarching concern, as the notion of *kdushat habitachon* reflected the Zionist commitment to security and was shared by all.

All this is no longer valid today. Within two or three decades, new media emerged in Israel, differing in both trade and ethos. Israel's present-day media are a sizable, market-driven, national and regional industry. The ideological overtones of the past have largely disappeared, and Israel no longer has a party-based newspaper system (except in the orthodox religious sector). The Israeli media have little need to wave their Zionist credentials. Instead, the leading Israeli media view themselves as the nation's democratic watchdogs, champions of transparency and openness. They are investigative, critical, and even cynical about governmental claims.

These trends are even more apparent in the area of national security. As I pointed out in chapter 4, the effectiveness of the Censora depends largely on its public support. The Censora's gradually shrinking scope since the 1970s reflects the public view that Israel now needs a less intrusive and weaker Censora than it did in the early days. Moreover, the Israeli media now have fewer inhibitions in dealing with national security than at any other time, as was evident during Israel's war with Hezbollah in July and August 2006.[49] The very phrase *kdushat habitachon,* which was pervasive in the first two decades of Israel life, has almost disappeared from sight, and to contemporary Hebrew ears, the phrase sounds anachronistic, even patronizing. The current leading national security journalists like Aluf Benn, Ronen Bergman, Yossi Melman, Ofer Shelach, and Amir Oren, to mention only a few, redrew the boundaries about what can and cannot be said about matters of national security in Israel. They all have contributed to the diminution in the Censora's power and authority.[50]

That said, there is one exception to this generally continuous trend: the nuclear issue. On this issue the Israeli media ignore their new self-image as democracy's watchdogs, and they have no interest in transparency and openness. The nuclear issue has remained the embodiment of *kdushat habitachon.* The old boundaries remain virtually unchanged because the Israeli public wants them unchanged.

To be sure, the nuclear issue is not completely frozen, and certain limited changes can be discerned. The public is more aware of environmental and health issues in relation to the nuclear complex than it was a generation ago. For example, in January 2002, Israel's Channel 2 presented an unprecedented twenty-seven-minute exposé by correspondent Chaim Rivlin on the subject of cancer found in the employees of the Dimona complex.[51] Such an exposé would have been impossible a generation ago. The Censora would not have permitted it, and no reporter would have had the ability or the courage to produce such a piece.

Nowadays, more information is available as well about the diplomatic aspects of Israel's nuclear situation. Another example of this happened in 2000, when *Ha'aretz* writer Aluf Benn revealed the contents of the correspondence between Prime Minister Benjamin Netanyahu and President Bill Clinton on the fissile materials cutoff issue.[52] This, too, would have been impossible two decades earlier.

These journalistic items are nonetheless rare; they are exceptions. Because of their rarity, they serve to highlight the continuity of the old tradition of absence and taboo. In almost a tacit consensus, the Israel media have avoided raising factual or even conceptual questions about the future of the Israeli nuclear complex in any of its aspects: strategic-political, economic, and environmental.[53] Not only is information about this subject not available, but such questions have never been raised, not even in a purely hypothetical form.

The same holds true about investigative journalism regarding any aspects of the nation's nuclear complex. Investigations are rarely initiated by the Israeli media themselves, and when they are, they (almost) always are in response to an external event, such as a news story overseas, court case, or slip of the tongue by the prime minister. This is consistent with the old reality: the Israeli media treat the nuclear subject as almost nonexistent.

How can the nuclear issue remain the only subject over which *kdushat habitachon* still maintains its old cultural dominance? For one thing, it is objectively much more difficult for the Israeli media to penetrate the inside of the nuclear complex than, say, to socialize with the leaders of the intelligence community. The nuclear establishment still treats outsiders, especially the media, with a great deal of suspicion and unease, and ultimately perceives itself as the guardian of the nation's greatest secret.

Like the rest of society, members of the media view amimut as something that must be supported and protected. Ze'ev Schiff, Israel's dean of national security media, reflected this attitude in almost anything he wrote or spoke on the nuclear issue.[54] Despite the generational difference between Schiff and today's leading journalists, Schiff's attitude that "amimut is *kdushat habitachon*" still represents the conventional wisdom of today's national security press corps.

The Israeli media have never formally questioned, let alone confronted, the seemingly arbitrary ground rules by which the Censora regulates the amimut discourse.[55] Members of the media have never directly challenged the legality of those ground rules, for example, through a petition to Israel's supreme court to determine whether ignoring these rules would constitute, in the court's view, a "near certainty" of harm to Israeli national security. For example, they could argue that the Censora's practice of banning all those direct references to nuclear weapons (or, alternatively, requiring "according to foreign sources" to be added to any direct reference to Israel's nuclear weapons) go beyond the "near-certainty" criterion that the Supreme Court introduced in its 1989 ruling. It would be difficult to conceive how using those taboo words, which in themselves do not reveal any new facts, could damage Israel's national security. Still, to this day, no news organization has ever been daring enough to challenge this practice in the supreme court.[56]

The Israeli media have been faithful and willing allies of the amimut policy. They not only have accepted the off-limits status of the nuclear issue but also have helped strengthen it. The existence of the Censora allows the press to resolve its own discomfort with the nuclear issue. It relieves the media from the otherwise inevitable job of making editorial decisions on these sensitive matters. Instead, there is an outside government authority, the Censora, whose job is to tell them what to do. The Censora policy on amimut could not have survived—let alone be successful for so long—had it not been a policy that the Israeli media supported for reasons ingrained in national cultural life.[57]

These patterns of complicity and duplicity illuminate one deep truth: on the nuclear issue, the Israeli public prefers not to exercise its democratic right to know. Israelis are fully aware that their country possesses nuclear weapons, but it goes along with amimut in the sense that they prefer not to know more. Whether for strategic or psychological reasons, they prefer to keep public discussion of nuclear weapons vague and opaque. It is not that Israelis have been deprived by their government of their democratic right to know but that they have willingly and actively given up this right in deference to the government's own institutions of oversight and accountability.

The Israeli Body Politic and the Knesset

The systematic exclusion of the nuclear issue from public discourse affects the Israeli body politic as well. Here, too, the basic patterns were formed early on and have changed little. Ever since Dimona became public, the Israeli body politic has treated the nuclear issue as separate from all other public-political issues, something that stands beyond the public sphere, off-limits to domestic politics.

Prime Minister Ben-Gurion delivered the first statement on the Dimona project in a Knesset plenary session in December 1960, and this was the first and last occasion in Israel's history in which a prime minister—or the government in general—made a factual statement about the nuclear issue. Later, in the 1960s, on a few rare occasions, Prime Minister Eshkol responded obliquely to nuclear questions by Knesset members in a plenary session. In July 1966 he incorporated the nonintroduction pledge into a political speech he delivered in the Knesset. Since the 1970s, though, the nuclear issue has not been broached in any open session of the Knesset. An unwritten tradition has developed that it is improper to discuss the nuclear issue in open parliamentary session, and for decades, no member has dared challenge that tradition.[58]

Another, parallel, parliamentary pattern has evolved as well. All necessary parliamentary dealings with the nuclear issue, such as budgetary approval and oversight, have been restricted to small and highly classified bodies. As early as in 1962, following a demand from opposition leaders, Prime Minister Ben-Gurion agreed to add the Knesset to the small and privileged club of public officials who shared the nuclear project's secrets. It was a way to turn a political necessity into a virtue. By sharing classified information with senior political leaders, Ben-Gurion made them part of the secret. The result was the establishment of a distinguished, secret, parliamentarian body, known only as the Committee of Seven, whose members were leaders of all the main Zionist parties, to fulfill the parliamentary requirements of overseeing the activities of the executive branch.

The Committee of Seven was so secretive that its members were not allowed to take notes during sessions and were never given written briefings. All briefings were oral, and even their existence was unacknowledged. Four decades later, an aide to Knesset Member Israel Galili, the leader of the Achdut ha'avodah who served on that body from 1962 to 1965, acknowledged that Galili used to write some information on the palm of his hand, under the table, and sometimes shared it with him after the session.[59] While the seven-member committee received a fair amount of information from the government about the construction of Dimona, they were given no technical assistance in understanding the details that they heard. The committee was also not a forum in which to discuss strategy and the long-term objectives of nuclear policy.

Since the 1970s, the Knesset has responded to the nuclear challenge by prohibiting discussion of the subject in any open parliamentary forum while, at the same time, setting up special, small, and classified bodies to fulfill its formal parliamentary oversight responsibilities (more on this in chapter 7). Likewise, except for a series of legal exemptions that the Knesset has made for the IAEC's facilities in a number of labor and environmental laws, the nuclear issue is absent from Israeli jurisprudence.

Overall, the Knesset has treated the nuclear subject as nonexistent. On the few rare occasions when a left-wing member of the Knesset—usually an Arab—tried to place the nuclear issue on the agenda, the Knesset leadership blocked open debate, ensuring that the motion died during a closed-door session of the Foreign Affairs and Defense Committee. The motions became meaningless and, for a long time, were no longer made. Then, in January 2002, an Arab Knesset member, Issam Mahoul, a member of the predominantly Arab Communist Party Hadash, who for some years had expressed an interest in the nuclear issue, filed a motion to debate the nuclear issue. Knesset Speaker Avrum Burg was about to handle the request in the usual manner, but Mahoul threatened to challenge the procedure in the Israeli High Court of Justice. To avoid that constitutional embarrassment and after considerable consultation, Burg decided to allow Mahoul to present his motion in open session. Burg's decision was described by the Israeli media as "historic."

In reality, however, the fifty-two-minute "debate" that occurred on February 2, 2002, was a farce. A shouting match ensued between Mahoul and his critics about the legitimacy of the debate itself, marked by a barrage of verbal attacks on Mahoul, the removal of four other Arab members who had interrupted a response by the government representative, Minister Haim Ramon, and a protest walkout by right-wing members. A vote the following week on whether to hold a wider debate was defeated sixty-one to sixteen. The historic debate was over. No major party with influence in the mainstream Jewish and Zionist public raised this important topic. It was left exclusively to Hadash, an Arab anti-Zionist party, and was therefore perceived as unpatriotic.[60]

The government's response, represented by Minister Ramon, was a series of assertions about the security of the state and the value of patriotism and secrecy, with no serious explanation as to why in 2002 Israel retained the same ostrichlike policy it had in the 1960s and 1970s. On February 4, 2002, a Ha'aretz editorial criticized the parliamentary spectacle and called for opening the nuclear issue to a real public debate: "Israeli society is mature enough to open its nuclear 'black box' with all due caution and look inside."[61] Even *Ha'aretz* fell back on Israel's policy of amimut: distinguishing between amimut as a national strategy, to be supported and preserved for strategic reasons, and its resulting system of outright censorship that needed to be modified.

Final Reflections

Evidently, the Israeli taboo regarding nuclear matters has weakened in recent years, as the story of the Yatza affair suggests, and yet it is still pervasive and persistent. Its continuity with the past is more impressive than the small apparent changes, as shown by the Vanunu affair. The vindictiveness of Israeli society (and its institutions) toward Vanunu has hardly changed to this day.

Amimut performs a great psychological-cultural function. Along with its political and strategic functions, it enables the Israeli public to maintain a certain distance from a politically complex and psychologically uncomfortable reality. It allows them to sustain a dual attitude toward the nuclear issue: a peculiar condition of knowing and not knowing at the same time. It permits Israelis to live in denial of and, consequently, with a lack of accountability for, a reality they tacitly acknowledge, all the while insisting that the public arena is not an appropriate forum for its discussion. This paralyzed state of knowing denial constitutes the fundamental Israeli nuclear dilemma.

Amimut has become more than a government policy; it has become for Israel what Émile Durkheim called *conscience collective*, a collective way of thinking and dealing with its nuclear weapons. This national attitude now functions independently of, even as it remains central to, Israel's national security ethos. Amimut is now inextricably woven into the fabric of the fundamental values, attitudes, and norms of Israeli culture of national security, and it is passed on through education and socialization to all newcomers initiated into that culture. The lack of any perceived alternative policy compatible with Israel's survival has become part of Israeli national identity. Israel's strategic community firmly believes that only through the cautious practice of amimut has the country been able to maintain its unique exemption in nuclear affairs, first with the United States and subsequently with most of the international nonproliferation regime. The responsible conduct of amimut has produced the political conditions making Israel's exceptionalism tolerable, if not accepted.

Chapter Six
The Democratic Cost of Amimut
The Impact on the Citizenry

When the atomic bomb and the cold war converged, few decisions became more important than those regarding nuclear weapons. But these decisions have tended to bypass the check-and-balance mechanisms integral to a liberal democracy, thus creating a new challenge to democratic governance.

Democratic governance relies on two related sets of principles and considerations, substance and procedures. The substantive component of democracy is rooted in the liberal thinking of the Enlightenment: human beings are endowed with reason and natural rights, among which are the right to life and happiness. The procedural element posits that human beings are entitled to participate in decisions affecting their lives and happiness, a right ensured by free elections, open dialogue, and transparency in the decision making of their elected representatives.

The philosophical argument regarding the incompatibility between nuclear weapons and the idea of liberal democracy can also be divided with reference to substance and procedures. In regard to substance, nuclear weapons are unique in their capacity to generate destruction by a magnitude many times larger than anything humanity has previously known. In regard to procedures, nuclear weapons necessitate a level of secrecy never before known to liberal democracies. Such secrecy obviates fundamental democratic values like transparency, oversight, public deliberations, and the public's right to know.

The substantive democratic argument against nuclear weapons played a significant, if tacit, role at several important junctures in the nuclear age. From 1945 to 1947, it was at the core of the popular call to outlaw nuclear weapons. Then, after this failed, it was a strong impetus in the evolution of the taboo-like prohibition against the use of nuclear weapons during the cold war. It also played a role in advancing the vision of the Nuclear Non-Proliferation Treaty (NPT), particularly article VI, which obligates all nuclear-weapons states to strive toward nuclear disarmament.

Both governments and the public in nuclear-weapons states have ignored the procedural democratic arguments against nuclear weapons. Once nuclear weapons were legitimized, nondemocratic guardianship came with it. The democratic procedure thereby gave way to the requirements of guardianship, secrecy, and security required by nuclear weapons.

Against this history, how should we construe the relation between Israeli amimut and the values and norms of liberal democracy? What is the democratic cost that Israel pays to maintain its unique bargain with the bomb? How high is the Israeli democratic premium paid for its opaque monopoly compared with that of declared nuclear-weapons states? In a conversation I had with Shalheveth Freier, the director general of the Israel Atomic Energy Commission (IAEC) in the early to mid-1970s, he noted that the issue of democracy and the atom was his biggest challenge. "This is a fascinating subject," he told me more than once, "but unfortunately the Israeli case, perhaps the most difficult case, cannot be studied."

These questions have hardly been asked, let alone studied and debated, in Israel. Indeed, the social-cultural makeup of amimut itself makes asking these questions in Israel seem almost unpatriotic. The Israeli public considers asking such questions as undermining the special bargain the country has struck with the bomb, and finding empirical data on these questions is difficult.

In chapter 4 I elaborated on the complex governmental edifice created over the years to shield amimut, and in chapter 5 I examined the role of the society and some of its agents in defending the policy by means of a taboolike social prohibition. In the next two chapters I look at the democratic cost that Israel must pay to maintain its bargain with the bomb. This chapter discusses the democratic cost to the Israeli public, and the next chapter focuses on the cost to democratic governance as a whole.

The Background of Nuclear Weapons

The recognition that nuclear weapons present a new and special challenge to democratic governance is as old as the nuclear age itself. The United States, the world's first nuclear democracy, created the Manhattan Project as a supersecret, wartime, military organization. From the beginning, total military secrecy was considered necessary for the nuclear project.

However, even before the bomb was actually built, the Manhattan Project's leaders (especially the top civilian in charge, Secretary of War Henry Stimson) recognized that in American democracy, postwar control of the new nuclear complex would have to be civilian. They also agreed that the transfer of control from military to civilian hands would have to be through an act of Congress.[1] The Atomic Energy Act of 1946, known also as the McMahon Act, was signed by President Harry S. Truman on August 1, 1946, and established the Atomic Energy Commission (AEC) as the government civilian agency in charge of the atomic complex.[2] This legislation was the first democratic effort to deal with the new challenge. It recognized that new and unprecedented standards of guardianship, secrecy, and security were required.

The Atomic Energy Act led to a new system of tight civilian guardianship that was alien to the spirit and practice of governance in America. For example, this system means that all nuclear weapons–related information, both in the legislation and through the practice it generated, is inherently "classified" and thus off-limits to the public unless or until declassified.[3] The "government of the atom" was a result of democratic legislation.

All this took place against the backdrop of the onset of the cold war. The bomb and the cold war not only came at the same time, but there was an affinity, even a reciprocity, between them. The United States had an intense domestic debate over whether to outlaw the bomb, but it was short lived (1945 to 1947) and ultimately was overwhelmed by the onset of the cold war. When the so-called Baruch Plan collapsed at the United Nations in mid-1947, the United States quickly endorsed the atomic bomb as the ultimate weapon of the free world against its enemies.[4] The bomb may have been secretly invented during World War II, but it was publicly introduced in big numbers as the ultimate weapon of the cold war. Secrecy was intrinsic to the bomb, but the cold war shaped and amplified the legal and societal norms and attitudes surrounding nuclear secrecy.[5]

With the founding of the North Atlantic Treaty Organization (NATO) in 1949, a "bargain" was made between the Western public and the bomb: if nuclear weapons were indispensable to defend Western democracy against communism, then nuclear guardianship outweighed democratic openness. The democratic cost of nuclear guardianship was seen by the Western public as both necessary and relatively benign, given the reality of the cold war, while the security and stability benefits were considerable. The very presence of the bomb created stability. It permitted keeping the conventional armies of the Western European members of NATO relatively small, in both manpower and finance expenditure, hence allocating funds instead to postwar economic recovery and social needs. Above all, the bomb created an enormous military deterrent without the cost of keeping a militarized society. In Secretary of State John Foster Dulles's words, it provided the most bang for the buck. Issues like an economic recovery and liberal education were viewed as the antidote to a return of fascism to Europe, and relying on nuclear weapons allowed European governments to invest money in this antidote. In sum, the bomb was viewed as providing a net democratic value.[6]

At the same time, a pattern of "distancing" evolved between the public and the bomb, which proved convenient to both the uninformed public and the informed guardians. This pattern of reciprocal distancing on nuclear matters took form in the late 1940s when it became evident that the presence of nuclear weapons was permanent, and it was cultivated throughout the cold war.

When large numbers of nuclear weapons were transferred from the United States and stationed in the territories of the NATO states in the 1950s and 1960s, Western Europe, too, subscribed to the notion that nuclear matters should be off-limits to common democratic procedures and codes of behavior. Nuclear-weapons decisions were to be left to a small priesthood, hidden behind government secrecy.

The key to understanding this special bargain was the existence of an external, existential, security threat. Nuclear weapons were introduced and perceived as the "friends" of Western liberal democracies in their struggle against global communism. They allowed the West to contain and deter the Soviet Union without the economic and political military and human expenditures of maintaining huge conventional forces. The presence of nuclear weapons would prevent old-fashioned European militarism. Hence, as long as the defense of the West was linked to nuclear deterrence, meaningful domestic opposition to nuclear weapons could not be easily sustained.

Toward the end of the cold war, people started to pay attention to the challenge that nuclear weapons posed to democracy. In the mid- to late 1980s, after the antinuclear movement's campaign against nuclear deterrence, intellectuals started to discuss the normative and empirical aspects of the democratic cost of nuclear deterrence. A prime trigger for the debate was President Ronald Reagan administration's massive nuclear buildup coupled with statements from high administration officials that a nuclear war with the Soviet

Union could not only be fought but also won.[7] Secretary of Defense Caspar Weinberger and others insisted, furthermore, that there would be a meaningful difference between winners and losers in an all-out nuclear war with the Soviet Union.[8]

In his 1985 *Controlling Nuclear Weapons*, Robert Dahl observed that nuclear weapons pose "a tragic paradox" for liberal democracy. He lamented that "no decisions can be more fateful for Americans, and for the world, than decisions about nuclear weapons. Yet, these decisions have largely escaped the control of democratic process." The rise of nuclear weapons, Dahl argued, has led to "a profound failure in the capacity of contemporary democratic institutions to achieve their purpose."[9] Richard Falk argued similarly around the same time that nuclear weapons create "structural necessities" that contradict the spirit of democratic governance.[10] For both Dahl and Falk, nuclear weapons corrode and corrupt the very notion of democratic rule.

In the late 1980s, in parallel with those critiques, academics and journalists started to ask empirical questions about the democratic control of nuclear weapons. One of the pioneer works in this area was Hugh Miall's *Nuclear Weapons: Who's in Charge?*, perhaps the first sociopolitical study of the details of the guardianship of nuclear weapons in the British democratic system. Miall looked into the structure of the British nuclear establishment—the weapons laboratories, the defense contractors, the military, and the civilian defense bureaucracy—and its relations with British democracy.[11]

In response, other intellectuals articulated an "elitist" counterargument warning of the dangers inherent in the "democratization" of the atom. George Perkovich, for example, developed the argument that decisions about, and the management of, nuclear weapons are, by their very nature, inherently incompatible with the spirit of the populist democratic governance. It was not an accident that all states that have dealt with nuclear weapons have had to create bureaucratic guardianship structures that bypassed democratic procedure in one way or another.[12]

Perkovich's concerns that decisions about nuclear matters should not be delegated to the public reflect a long-standing elitist tendency of American leaders. After World War I, President Woodrow Wilson stated that the task of enlightened statesmanship is "to make the world safe for democracy." In the 1950s, Henry Kissinger rephrased this by suggesting that in the nuclear age, the task of enlightened statesmanship is "to make democracy safe for the world." Kissinger was afraid of the emotional, uninformed, and unsteady state of mind of the masses, masses that could fall prey to demagogues and manipulators. Kissinger often spoke of the difficulties of a democratic super-power in conducting its affairs as a superpower: public opinion naturally swings between periods of euphoria and introspection, but a superpower's foreign policy must hold steady. Kissinger, George Kennan, and other cold war realists thus believed that public opinion in a nuclear democracy was just not informed, nuanced, supple, or flexible enough to deal with the intricacies of nuclear matters.

In essence, the general elitist argument is that control of the bomb needs to be delegated to councils of guardians that function as the enterprise's board of trustees. Their ultimate loyalty is to the enterprise itself, not the populace. While in theory the nation's top political leadership is in charge of the atom, in practice it is the guardians—senior administrators, scientists, strategists, and senior military officers—who actually are in control. The top political leaders, those who legally sign and approve these decisions, usually have only a superficial and thin understanding of the issues at stake. Because nuclear-weapons issues are technically complex, strategically uncomfortable, and highly classified, nuclear weapons are difficult to supervise and manage.

Both the democratic and the elitist arguments originate from two oppos-ing concerns, but they are not mutually exclusive. Both implicitly accept the tension between the requirements of nuclear guardianship and the norms of democracy. The challenge for nuclear democracies is to strike the proper balance between the two concerns. It may be inevitable that the governance of the atom must be a regime of guardianship, but it is also imperative in a democracy to maintain some democratic public control over the atomic guardians. This would be what Dahl refers to as the process of "delegating" control over nuclear weapons, rather than "alienating" such control from the democratic process completely.[13]

Finally, the balance between guardianship and democracy is not fixed and timeless. It has shifted over the years in all nuclear democracies. In the United States, for example, during the initiation stage, when the nuclear program was young and the need for secrecy was high, the compromise heavily fa-vored the elitist side, but over time as the nuclear program became more ma-ture and secrecy was less stringent, the compromise became more balanced. This shift toward the democracy side was reinforced further by the end of the cold war. The end of the bipolar order, based so heavily on nuclear deter-rence as the ultimate equalizer, has eroded heavily the old realist argument that nuclear matters are too intricate and sensitive to be left and decided by a democratic citizenry.

Amimut and Liberal Democracy

The tension between the requirements of nuclear weapons and the values and norms of a liberal democracy is not unique to Israel, but in no other nuclear democracy has this tension been as absolute and lasting. More than half a century after Israel made its first nuclear decision and more than two generations after it crossed the nuclear threshold, it has not even acknowledged its status as a nuclear-weapons state.

The uniqueness of the Israeli nuclear bargain is not that it endorses ambiguity as part of its nuclear posture. All other nuclear-armed states use ambiguity as well; no nuclear state is fully transparent. Britain, for example, which now is probably the most transparent of all nuclear-weapons states, openly emphasizes, even praises, the advantage of ambiguity in enhancing its own nuclear-deterrence capabilities. Rather, the uniqueness of the Israeli bargain is its almost total reluctance to acknowledge its nuclear reality; its deliberate and continued refusal to discuss the subject; its effort to treat the subject as illegitimate; and its insistence that the state has the right to avoid any discussion about its nuclear status, posture, and capability. No other nuclear-weapons state endorses such all-encompassing silence.

Another feature of the Israeli bargain's uniqueness is that in all nuclear democracies, the newly installed systems of nuclear guardianship initially conflicted with the spirit of democratic public and governance.[14] But once these nations attained weapons status, an act symbolized by a full-yield atomic test, they replaced their total nuclear secrecy with a more moderate policy of functional nuclear secrecy. The full-yield test thus is an act of public *introduction* signifying that the bomb is now being placed openly on the national and international agenda. Even after a long period of nuclear hesitancy and ambiguity, India and Pakistan ultimately followed this familiar path. This act of introduction tends to significantly reduce the tension between nuclear guardianship and democratic governance, as it permits a discussion of nuclear weapons at home and the negotiation of a national bargain with the bomb.

Israel never took that path but chose instead to obscure the nuclear divide: to blur as much as possible the distinction between possession and nonpossession and evade any questions about its nuclear reality. When Prime Minister Golda Meir privately acknowledged to President Richard Nixon in September 1969 that Israel already had the bomb but pledged to keep it invisible and undeclared and not to make Israel a nuclear power (as discussed in chapter 1), she cared little about the democratic consequences of the bargain she had just made. All that Prime Minister Meir wanted was a top-level understanding with the United States that would preserve the Israeli bomb and end the visits of American scientists to Dimona. But this amimut deal did have profound democratic consequences. The bargain was conditioned on the strict enforcement of a policy of absolute secrecy and nonacknowledgment, which stood in stark opposition to democratic values and principles.

To clarify the opposition between amimut and liberal democracy, we must look at the intellectual origins, or the political theory, of amimut. As a political practice, amimut is a product of the Hobbesian image of the world. According to that image, the state is the supreme political organ, the source of all (domestic) law, even though the state itself resides above the law. This outlook views the international system as essentially anarchic, a form of the Hobbesian "state of nature," and thus has little appreciation for international law, norms, rules of conduct, and the like. Domestic law has little bearing on the state's international conduct. What is commonly referred to as "reasons of state" is the state's prerogative to pursue its interests as it finds fit, especially in matters related to its survival.

This instrumentalist and amoralistic view of the international system cultivates secrecy as proper and natural in the conduct of states on matters of national security. Truth is neither an intrinsic value of the international system nor an obligation of the state, as liberal thinkers see it, but should be regarded as instrumental. Sometimes states are required to evade, blur, or even manipulate the truth.

Domestically, this Hobbesian outlook stands in tension with the spirit of liberal democracy. The source of domestic power is the sovereign, who receives power from the people, who surrender their own power in order to have security. Since these matters are conducted largely outside the public eye, the public is not even in a position to fully comprehend, let alone judge, such matters. According to this outlook, the government has no domestic obligation whatsoever to the public to be transparent or to tell the truth, and surely not on matters of nuclear weapons. From this perspective, there is nothing wrong in Israel's following an amimut policy as long as it considers that it is serving its national interest.

Israel is by now a liberal democracy in its own self-image and in most aspects of its public civil life, but on matters of supreme national interests, and most prominently on the nuclear issue, Israel subscribes to the Hobbesian outlook. This explains why the trend toward the rule of law has not reached the frontiers of Israeli national security (see more on this in chapters 7 and 8). Nothing represents this Hobbesian outlook as much as the nuclear issue.

Amimut has costs for democracy, with some more obvious than others. To address them, we must move beyond generalities and discuss the costs' concrete dimensions. In this chapter I focus on the public dimension. However, there is a catch here: to make this democratic critique concrete, I would have to use empirical evidence of how amimut affects the public, but much of the evidence is not available or is opaque. Accordingly, in the following I point to concrete dimensions of the problem, but the analysis is inevitably more theoretical than empirical.

The Citizenry and the Right to Know

Under amimut, the Israeli public is deprived of both knowledge of and participation in national decisions on its nuclear program. Among the necessary conditions for democratic participation, citizens' access to knowledge and their ability to participate in national decisions are at the forefront. Lacking both, however, the Israeli public (and even most of its elected representatives) have never been a party to any of the nation's big nuclear decisions. The public was ignored when Prime Minister David Ben-Gurion, in consultation with a few of his aides, made the decision to go nuclear in the mid- to late 1950s.

Few Israelis are aware that since Ben-Gurion delivered his two-paragraph statement to the Knesset on December 23, 1960, acknowledging that a twenty-four-megawatt research reactor "for peaceful purposes" was under construction, the Israeli government has never issued another official factual statement on the subject.[15] We know now that this statement was inaccurate and incomplete, that it was intended to evade the truth. Ever since that speech, all that Israelis have been told about the subject has been filtered through the lens of "foreign sources."

As noted in earlier chapters, Israelis appear not to see their lack of knowledge about and participation in the nuclear issue as a democratic problem that needs to be fixed. Even most of those few who admit that amimut is incompatible with democracy would say that when the nation's existential security is at stake, democracy is a luxury that the country cannot afford. This attitude is not that different from the Western public's view of the bomb during most of the cold war.[16] The difference is that during the cold war, the American bomb was public knowledge, whereas under amimut, the Israeli bomb is known but not acknowledged.

Some Israelis argue that the democratic cost of amimut is not much greater than that paid in other nuclear democracies. Nobody has articulated this point of view better than the late Ze'ev Schiff, Israel's dean of defense journalism. I had long discussions, mostly in private, with Schiff on the business of amimut, including its impact on democracy. In response to my arguments about the democratically deprived public, Schiff used to counter that despite all the formal restrictions of amimut on the freedom of the press, one can still say publicly in Israel (notwithstanding the Censora) a surprisingly "great deal" on the nuclear issue.[17] Almost all the important things that the public should know, I recall Schiff arguing, can be said "creatively," as long as the writer or the speaker is willing to respect the formalities of the amimut discourse.

Schiff used to illustrate this argument with some specific examples based on his own experience. He was proud to say that almost everything he really considered important for the Israeli public to know about the nuclear issue he managed to publish by means of "creative" methods.[18] By "creative," he meant primarily working "wisely" through the Censora's restrictions and pressing the Censora hard at the high level. According to its guidelines, the Censora can officially ban only factual assertions and must avoid banning mere opinions, especially if they are expressed in a hypothetical or semitheoretical fashion. Using the guise of opinion and aided by semitheoretical discourse, Schiff claimed that he was able to assert quite significant "things" in a manner that (usually) was (after negotiation) acceptable to the Censora.[19] Schiff insisted that not only was amimut indispensable to Israel's existential security but also that the democratic cost of its security benefits was less than most people thought.

Schiff made this argument, for example, in an article he wrote in *Ha'aretz* in March 2000 entitled "Why Nobody Debates the Nuclear Issue." First, he pointed out that "censorship on the issue is today far less strict than it was in the past" and that he actually published "plenty" of articles on the nuclear issue. In fact, 165 articles on the nuclear subject were published in the Israeli media in 1999. At the same time, though, Schiff admitted that despite the many articles, the Israeli media had not really debated the nuclear issue. He then focused on the media and the public itself:

> The conclusion is that public discussion of nuclear issues in Israel is only in its infancy, not because of security censorship but because those discussing it, including in the academic world, have failed to foster effec-

tive debate. It is not that there are no publications, but that there are not enough high-quality ones.[20]

I agree with Schiff on some of the facts, but my outlook on these matters is different. I agree that the Israeli press may well bear some responsibility for the absence of a serious nuclear debate. But this absence is not unrelated to amimut, for it is partially a function of the public's general lack of interest in nuclear matters. It is a reflection of the extent to which an embedded culture of cognitive dissonance about the nuclear program—amimut—has permeated Israeli society. Part of the Israeli bargain requires that the public voluntarily surrender its right to knowledge about Israel's nuclear program and accept the ground rules of amimut.

Furthermore, once there is a strict prohibition on any factual aspects of the issue, it is difficult, if not impossible, to conduct a meaningful public debate. Schiff was able to disguise certain information as opinion because he happened to have access to this classified information. For example, Schiff could not have written the "opinion" piece in 1998 regarding his concern about Prime Minister Benjamin Netanyahu's control of Israel's nuclear program if Schiff had not learned of certain sensitive (and classified) information about Netanyahu's conduct.[21]

Others agree with Schiff. Professor Uzi Arad, for example, also made the point that even under amimut, it was still possible in Israel to have a theoretical but meaningful debate on nuclear matters.[22] I disagree. Such a theoretical debate is not a substitute for a debate on concrete nuclear issues. A theoretical debate that is not anchored on concrete facts is sterile and hence meaningless. The citizen's right to know is not merely a right to discuss abstract principles; the public's access to factual information is a condition for a viable and engaged public. Knowledge that is accessible to the public is a basis for a true democratic public. This point was made by John Stuart Mill in his *On Liberty* some 140 years ago and has remained valid ever since.[23]

Only if the public has access to reliable public information and to independent experts who can discuss and explain openly the issues at stake can a genuine debate be possible. A ban on factual information guarantees that most journalists will remain uninformed and that the public will adopt a dogmatic and uninformed outlook. In short, a public whose right to knowledge is substantially compromised cannot fulfill the responsibilities essential to a democracy. By accepting amimut, Israelis have effectively deprived themselves of one of their most important democratic rights.

Furthermore, from a methodological point of view, to blame the absence of nuclear debate on the Israeli public and its media, as Schiff does, explains nothing. In particular, it does not explain why a public that otherwise is highly engaged on every public issue, especially in matters of national security, has chosen to be silent on the nuclear issue and has accepted without reservation that the subject is "off-limits" for public discussion. This is an anomaly and cannot be explained without appealing to the prohibitive power of the nuclear taboo, which is the cultural manifestation of amimut.

Amimut and the State's Obligation to Tell the Truth

Another democratic and moral dimension of Israel's nuclear bargain is the matter of truth. At heart the normative question is whether or not a liberal democracy is obligated to tell the truth concerning its nuclear status; whether the possession of the bomb is so important and fundamental that a country, any country, must openly acknowledge it. After all, acknowledgment is a public act of government that is fundamental to the spirit of liberal democracy. The act of acknowledgment by a liberal democratic government entails telling the truth and accepting political accountability for the deed. Without public acknowledgment, and the acceptance of responsibility that comes with it, the government cannot be held accountable.

This point becomes critical when a government acquires the bomb. If a democratically elected state is compelled to acquire the bomb, it must acknowledge it, to its own citizens and to the world. Nuclear weapons are not the kinds of weapons that states acquire without taking full responsibility; their possession is not like a special operation whose success is dependent on secrecy. All democratic nuclear-weapons states have made public their acquisition, at least by testing them, which by definition is a public act. The point is as much moral as it is political.

I noted earlier in this chapter that amimut is a manifestation of the Hobbesian paradigm. The issue of acknowledgment and truth as a value highlights the contrast between the Hobbesian tradition and the spirit of liberal democracy. Truth, acknowledgment, and transparency are intrinsic values for a liberal democracy, which requires that the state conduct itself truthfully and transparently under the rule of law. Although in the practice of international relations, democratic states often appeal to "reasons of state" as justifying national security secrecy, in recent decades the public (and the legislation) in Western liberal democracies has become increasingly critical of using excessive secrecy. The trend in liberal democracies now has been to reduce the appeal to secrecy on matters of foreign policy and national security.

In the United States, for example, pressure is mounting to limit the scope of national security classification. There is an expectation that even some of the most sensitive national security matters, from electronic surveillance to intelligence interrogation, should be subject to public oversight and discussion. While such expectations are inconsistently fulfilled, intelligence estimates of highly sensitive matters, such as Iran's nuclear weapons–related activities, have been released in unclassified, summary form. This trend toward more transparency is especially apparent in areas of national security policy pertaining to domestic debate and the right of the public to be engaged.[24]

On nuclear issues, the demand for transparency on some key policy issues has become a norm. For example, for decades nuclear-posture reviews were produced under total secrecy, with the process and the final product in the form of a highly classified document. But this attitude has changed in recent years as the U.S. Congress has taken control of the process. As a legal requirement, every administration in its first year must conduct a full interagency nuclear posture review and, at least in principle, the results must be published in a public, unclassified document stating the administration's views of nuclear-weapons policies. Britain has a similar approach.

There are no global norms about nuclear transparency, but one could make the legal case that by the virtue of the near universality of the NPT and the conduct of India and Pakistan, there are de facto global norms of transparency regarding nuclear possession. With only the exception of Israel, all nations treat the possession of nuclear weapons as something that must be openly acknowledged. I should stress again that the policy of amimut regarding such a large and lasting issue of nuclear possession is different from silence on specific operational matters as, for instance, the kind of blackout Israel imposed after its air raid on a Syrian nuclear reactor on September 6, 2007.[25] That blackout served a specific goal. Amimut, in contrast, is a policy of evading the truth over a vast area of activity with decades of national commitment, even though everyone knows what the truth is.

I heard a version of this democratic argument against amimut for the first time in 1992 when McGeorge Bundy delivered a keynote speech to a small group of Americans and Israelis in a workshop at MIT that Marvin Miller and I organized.[26] I remember vividly that Bundy's call for Israel to "come clean" on the nuclear issue appeared to me then as a moralistic cover for a political position. I thought it was an interesting way to promote a political objective, but I did not then comprehend the depth of his *moral* point about the importance of telling the truth on such matters. It took me many more years of reflecting on this issue to realize that much of my own discontent with the conduct of amimut was derived from the moral judgment that telling the truth on such issues is sacred to liberal democracy.

Amimut poses uncomfortable questions about what is and what is not right for a state to do regarding its nuclear policies: Does nonacknowledgment of the truth tacitly imply that the government of Israel views its posture of possessing nuclear weapons as sinful or shameful? Does it serve Israel's interest to appear to be conveying such a message? If Israel found itself compelled to rely on existential nuclear deterrence, could it not handle this truth? Is Israel more sinful than the other declared nuclear-weapons states on the nuclear question? Does a policy of evading the truth about such a fundamental matter fit Israel's image as a liberal democracy? By its very nature, amimut does not encourage asking such questions.

The bottom line is that amimut is costly for the democratic spirit, not only because it constitutes reluctance by the government to take public responsibility for its actions, but also because it sends the wrong signal about how the government ought to conduct its most existential affairs. It permits the government to claim that the public should trust it, without discussion or debate, to do what is best for the country. Doing so is a rejection of the democratic spirit.

Amimut and the Deprivation of History

Another unappreciated dimension of the democratic cost of amimut is the deprivation of history. Because amimut prohibits the acknowledgment of Israel's nuclear status, anything that details the history of the nuclear program, explicitly or implicitly, no matter how far into the past, also must remain sealed. In compliance with this policy, Israel prohibits the public's access to any historical documents that could undermine amimut.

Israel State Archives are not only a faithful servant of the country's amimut policy but also its victim. In violation of Israel's State Archives Law, a law that the archives help to enforce, the Israel Atomic Energy Committee (IAEC) has never transferred any of its archival materials to the custodianship of Israel's state archives, nor does it accept the oversight authority of the Israel State Archives in handling its archival material. A supreme court petition submitted in 2007 by the daily *Yediot Achronot* and journalist

Ronen Bergman against Israel's state archivist (and the heads of all those secret agencies) alleged that the IAEC was in breach of the State Archives Law
by establishing its own illegal archives in order to maintain full custodianship
over its material. At the same time, the petition alleged, Israel State Archives,
which also are under the administrative oversight of the prime minister's office, had failed for years in its obligation to enforce the archives law pertaining to these governmental agencies. As of this writing, after a long series of
delays and efforts to resolve the issue without formal ruling, the petition still
had no resolution.[27]

The real concern about the way that amimut undermines history is deeper
than the right of the public to access its country's archives. That is, amimut
makes the Israeli public historically ignorant. Denial of access to history is an
infringement on the public's right to know its national history, to form educated opinions, and to participate in national affairs. The democratic consequence of this prohibition on history is that Israelis cannot form an educated
opinion on the subject. Without knowing history, we are denied an understanding of the present.

The denial of Israel's nuclear history is more troubling than merely missing an important but well-defined classified chapter of military history. It also
is not merely an affront to an academic interest in history. Israel's nuclear
history touches broad existential themes of the Israeli national narrative. Its
absence thus deprives the Israeli public from being able to understand and
assess the effect of the bomb on contemporary Israel's historical place in the
Middle East, its national security, and, most significantly, the dynamics of
peace and war in the area.

Furthermore, amimut has made the empirical data on the nuclear issue
opaque and uncertain. For example, to this day we are not clear what role,
and to what extent, the nuclear issue had in shaping the decision by President
Anwar Sadat of Egypt to initiate his peace offensive in 1977. More generally,
the nuclear issue is ignored in most narratives of the history of the Egyptian-
Israeli peace process. Many people assume that Israel's nuclear weapons must
have played a role in Sadat's decision to go to Jerusalem. Sadat himself reportedly implied this in his conversations during his visit with Minister of
Defense Ezer Weizman and Deputy Prime Minister Yigal Yadin, but this has
never been determined definitively. I know of no open study of the peace
process that has empirically explored seriously the role of the nuclear issue.

Not only are the empirical data under amimut foggy, but they also generate a systematic cognitive bias that overlooks the significance of the nuclear

issue. Even though Israel has had nuclear weapons during all Arab-Israeli wars since 1967, mainstream Israeli historiography tends to minimize, if not ignore, the nuclear dimension. Despite contemporary historians' growing recognition that the nuclear issue must have played a role in the events leading to the 1967 Six-Day War, especially in stimulating the Soviet misinformation that triggered the crisis, mainstream historiography still tends to ignore the nuclear issue.[28] With regard to the run-up to both the 1967 and the 1973 wars, the nuclear issue is either ignored or, at best, treated as a speculative side issue.

Amimut makes Israel's nuclear history a "black box" not only to ordinary citizens but even to insiders. I recall the words of caution I heard some twenty years ago from two former IAEC heads and legendary figures of the Israeli nuclear establishment, Professor Israel Dostrovsky and Shalheveth Freier. Both seemed to discredit the official classified history collected and produced by the IAEC. Dostrovsky, who was there from the start, commented that much of that history (particularly the history of the major decisions) is conspicuously absent from the archive. There was a built-in reluctance in the early days, he told me, to spell out in writing the concrete motivations and objectives. Furthermore, Dostrovsky stressed, when things went well, according to the common plan, little was recorded. Only when things went wrong or when there were internal disagreements were memos written and distributed. Often these memos were written primarily for the sake of history, but sometimes they were destroyed when an agreement was reached.[29]

Freier, the third chief of the IAEC, seemed to agree with Dostrovsky that the IAEC's existing classified documentation is limited and partial and that much of the real drama may have escaped historical documentation. He told me, for example, that on the early morning of October 6, 1973, when General Zvi Zur (Chera) told him that a war was about to break out, Freier immediately ordered his subordinates that no written papers of any kind would be allowed to leave the agency without his permission. He also told me that in the early 1990s, when he was a member of the IAEC's steering committee on history, he realized that often there was no direct connection between the paper trail in the archives and the actual decisions and actions taken by Israel's nuclear complex. For example, Professor Ernst D. Bergmann, the founder of the IAEC, left a great deal of documentation about his visions for nuclear energy in Israel's future, but those visions were not anchored in any concrete reality. Another early commissioner, Professor Shmuel Sambursky, wrote volumes disputing Bergmann's vision; his papers, too, reveal little about what was actually happening.[30]

The Burden of Secrecy

Another neglected dimension of amimut's cost to democracy involves secrecy. Not only is secrecy itself costly to a democracy because it makes the public uninformed and disengaged, but secrecy also tends to generate more secrecy, which, in turn, requires the creation of a special secret bureaucracy to guard the initial secrecy. This bureaucracy of secrecy has its own, additional, democratic cost.[31]

In chapter 4, I described the MALMAB, the Ministry of Defense's security organization, one responsibility of which is to guard the country's atomic secrets. Little is known about MALMAB. Figures on the size and the cost of the MALMAB's activities are secret. In the United States, however, using the U.S. Department of Energy's calculations, it is estimated that about 20 percent of the entire budget of the nuclear-weapons complex is spent on secrecy and security.[32] This estimate may be useful for speculating about the financial cost of the MALMAB's nuclear activities, but it ignores the financial and democratic cost of the *special* security requirements of amimut. After all, the MALMAB has the exclusive responsibility for the security and secrecy requirements of amimut. We do not know how this extraordinary requirement has shaped the MALMAB's organizational and financial structure, but logic suggests that it must have had some impact.

The secrecy surrounding Israel's nuclear program therefore must be especially tight, as the MALMAB's security apparatus must be powerful and encompassing enough to address all aspects of information security and physical security. Even though the secrecy system greatly relies on the self-sustained ethos of secrecy, it must be sufficiently intrusive and formidable to prevent either accidental or deliberate leaks of classified information. Given amimut's absolutist nature as a policy, its security system must be equally absolute. This explains, for example, why Israeli nuclear guardians insisted that Vanunu be captured and brought to trial in 1986, as well as the way he has been treated since he was captured (chapter 5). This also explains why the MALMAB's chief, Yechiel Horev, dealt so harshly with a former insider like Yatza in 2001 (chapter 5).

The guardianship system under amimut must be an effective intelligence and counterintelligence organization with surveillance capabilities that allow the security monitoring of personnel with access to the nation's nuclear secrets. The system should be sufficiently invasive to detect all sorts of personnel problems that may compromise security. Just on the personnel issue alone, we could speculate that at any given time, thousands of Israelis need a security clearance of one type or another, which requires a bureaucratic security system to monitor the system's personnel.

Oversight of secret intelligence services is notoriously problematic in any democracy because intelligence services act covertly and often are exempt from the scrutiny of the law. Of all Israel's intelligence services, the MALMAB is apparently under the weakest democratic control. To symbolize its role as the guardian of Israel's atomic secrets, Horev promoted the idea that the MALMAB's chief should have a permanent seat on the prestigious council of the heads of Israel's intelligence services. But because of the stiff opposition of some members of the council, Horev was never offered that seat.[33] The result is troubling from a democratic point of view. While the MALMAB does function practically as Israel's fourth national intelligence organization (in addition to the Mossad, AMAN [Israeli Military Intelligence], and the GSS [General Security Services]), it is not subject to the same (parliamentary and other) requirements of democratic control and oversight as the other three secret services.

For many years, until the cases of Vanunu and Yatza (and, perhaps to a lesser extent, my own case), the Israeli public was not aware of how pervasive, intrusive, and powerful the bureaucracy of secrecy dedicated to guard amimut actually was. Even the identity of the MALMAB's chief was not made public until the late 1990s. Ordinary Israelis still know virtually nothing about the MALMAB's operations, so it is not surprising that they are not concerned about the democratic cost of those operations.

The democratic cost of amimut thus goes beyond the consequences of keeping the public uninformed and disengaged. Amimut necessitates the creation of powerful state organs to maintain nuclear secrecy. But because these organizations are instruments of state secrecy and most of their work takes place outside the public eye, they are prone to abuse and misuse. Accordingly, the democratic costs of amimut are not theoretical; they undermine Israel's democratic landscape.[34]

Democracy, Amimut, and Human Fallibility

Thus far, my critique of amimut has been predicated primarily on the value of an open and informed public in a liberal democracy, regardless of security considerations. I have framed my argument in terms of the intrinsic tension between nuclear weapons and democracy, which in itself is a special case of the larger "democracy versus national security" debate. Much of the rich academic literature on the subject frames this debate as a dilemma in which democratic nations are challenged to strike a fair balance between the two. Such a trade-off is the presumption of theorist Robert Dahl when he refers to the conflict between nuclear guardianship and democratic values as a "tragic paradox," since it involves a sacrifice of democracy in favor of national survival.[35] Viewed through the lens of either/or, democratic values and norms appear as a luxury when the nation's survival is at stake.

Israelis see the issue of amimut almost exclusively through this exclusive dichotomy. For decades, the very limited debate regarding amimut in Israel has been framed in terms of a zero-sum trade-off between democracy and amimut, between lofty democratic principles, on the one hand, and more concrete matters of existential deterrence and national survival, on the other. The great majority of Israelis believe that amimut is indispensable to the country's political ability to possess nuclear weapons, which most Israelis view as essential to their country's survival.[36] Only amimut can provide Israel the benefit of existential deterrence, and therefore democracy must yield.

This exclusive either/or dilemma between democracy and amimut may be flawed. On the political-empirical level, the dichotomy may beg the very question it asks, as it presumes (1) that Israel's possession of nuclear weapons must rely on amimut (the 1969 Nixon-Meir deal), (2) that amimut is an either/or policy and has no conceptual alternatives or modifications whatsoever, and (3) that without amimut, Israel will lose its ultimate insurance policy. As I elaborate in chapters 9 and 10, all these presumptions may have outlived their usefulness and are probably not valid anymore. Amimut may have become obsolete, and there are ways to diminish amimut without causing political damage.

On the more theoretical level, we also could argue that construing the relations between democracy and national security in exclusively either/or terms is conceptually misleading. Rather, we should argue that a policy of total secrecy is harmful not only to democracy but also to security. Even if amimut has provided Israel with the political cover to keep its nuclear weapons and to guarantee its survival, it also has removed many of the public mechanisms of democratic oversight and accountability that are critical to the nation's security as well. Especially when *kdushat habitachon* dominates, a system of open and independent checks and balances to prevent the risks of flawed decisions by political leaders, civilian guardians, or military leaders is needed.

One feature of democracy is the recognition that decision makers are inherently fallible and that therefore their decisions may be flawed. A democracy responds to this recognition by establishing a public system of checks and balances that can reverse earlier decisions. That is, the fallibility of human beings is compensated by relying on a larger system of open debate, which means that long-term decisions are never fixed and final but are subject (in most cases) to changes and modifications. The public nature of the process is critical to the existence of democratic debate.

If all human beings (and decision makers are human beings) are fallible, then what can we assume about a tiny nuclear priesthood that makes its decisions with no exposure to public checks and balances? This is a generic concern about all nuclear weapons–related decisions in all nuclear-weapons states, but it is magnified in Israel's nuclear situation. Indeed, the Israeli nuclear elite may be even more vulnerable to these flaws, as their complete isolation and insulation from the public eye is more likely to give rise to insular groupthink, negative information feedback, and other biases plaguing those who exercise power in an extremely sensitive environment with almost no feedback from the outside (for more on this, see the next chapter).

This should not be taken to mean a denigration of the apolitical and professional character of Israel's nuclear priesthood, as they may very well be acting in what they consider to be the best interest of the state. Rather, the concern here is about the integrity of the process: Who guards the guardians? How do we know whether what Israel's nuclear priesthood consider to be good for the country is, in fact, good for the country? For these reasons, a democratic state must subject its decision makers to oversight mechanisms, especially in existential matters.

Owing to the special conditions of the Israeli bargain with the bomb, and especially the insistence on absolute secrecy, the system under amimut reduces its awareness of its own flaws. Consequently, it has produced an isolated environment in which poorly made fateful decisions can be made by faceless bureaucrats without effective oversight, and it negates the ability of the public to intervene on its own behalf, since it does not even know what decisions have been made.

Final Reflections

I began this chapter by noting that by their very nature, nuclear weapons present an extraordinary challenge to a liberal democracy. As long as the democratic citizenry accepts the legitimacy of nuclear weapons, there will be fundamental features of governance that defy its idea of liberal democracy. Given this inevitable tension between democracy and nuclear guardianship, I also stated that the challenge is striking the proper balance between the two concerns.

Some might see my views as one sided, even naïve. It is true that human beings are fallible, they would argue, but this applies to a democratic public as well. In fact, some people might say that the fallibility argument applies to the general public even more than to an experienced and calm nuclear elite. In his *The Future of Freedom*, Fareed Zakaria contends that the American occupation with "democracy" could be, at times, dangerous and naïve.[37]

As I noted earlier, I am well aware that particularly on nuclear matters the elitist/guardianship view is persuasive and that one should be wary of the passions of the masses on these matters. Edward Teller and his supporters used the anticommunist hysteria of the early 1950s to paint as anti-American Robert Oppenheimer's views on what kinds of nuclear weapons the United States needed.[38] Richard Rhodes and Lawrence Friedman (and others) revealed that U.S. politicians opted to buy more and more powerful nuclear weapons out of all proportion for any military needs, only for the purpose of appearing patriotic and tougher on communism than the other politicians.

Here, however, I am addressing the unique case of Israel, which is radically different. Israel is an extreme case, a democratic state that refuses to acknowledge anything factual about the nuclear issue. This democratic critique of amimut should not be interpreted as a call to let the public decide these "fateful" issues. Indeed, the democratic public in Israel has almost no part in any other big defense decision. Nor do I believe or propose that the public should replace the nuclear priesthood. But I do propose that total amimut is an insult to Israel's democracy.

Israel's bargain with the bomb was born and cultivated in an undemocratic, elitist, guardianship ethos dominated by secrecy. Israel's nuclear project was initially designed and managed as a secret state within a state, exempt from practically any form of democratic control. Determined to keep secrecy tight and avoid controversy, Ben-Gurion and Shimon Peres devised unorthodox, and undemocratic, means to fund and guard the project, bypassing the traditional channels of state control.[39]

In a global historical context, however, this secrecy was not that different from what other Western democratic states—including Sweden, Norway,

Italy, Canada, and Australia—used in the early stages of their bargains with nuclear weapons. In none of these countries did the leadership tell anything to its public.

Israel initiated its nuclear-weapons program only a decade after both Auschwitz and Hiroshima, when the Holocaust was still a fresh memory and tight nuclear secrecy was common. Even the Manhattan Project was initially paid from special funds outside the normal channels of state funding (although unlike Israel's nuclear project, the Manhattan Project was never funded by donations of wealthy Americans). In retrospect, Israel's insistence on absolute secrecy and state-within-state guardianship was not at odds with the general attitude toward the bomb in the West during much of the cold war. In America, the two principal cold war legislative acts in the late 1940s— the Atomic Energy Act of 1946, which established the broad code of secrecy regarding nuclear weapons, and the National Security Act of 1947, which established the institutional edifice of U.S. national security—determined for decades the balance between the national security requirement for secrecy and the public's right to know.[40] For many years the American Atomic Energy Commission also functioned as a self-regulated state within a state. In those days, democracy was viewed as a luxury when survival was at stake.

Israel reached the nuclear threshold in the mid- to late 1960s, around the time of the arrival of the NPT, in a world that still had few international norms concerning nuclear proliferation, let alone domestic norms concerning transparency. It was natural for Israel to pursue its nuclear ambitions in total secrecy. France and China conducted their own nuclear tests only to signal their crossing the nuclear threshold after moving from a phase of near-total secrecy to functional secrecy, but Israel was compelled to take a different path. Tiny Israel—then with a population of fewer than two million—lacked the status and political resources of France and China. Technically, Israel probably could have tested its first nuclear device as early as late 1966. Instead, after a few years of quiet hesitancy, Israel struck its bargain of amimut with the United States in 1969.[41]

In retrospect, the democratic exceptionality of Israel's nuclear bargain took a distinctive path when several aspects of that 1969 bargain generated long-term democratic consequences. When amimut turned into Israel's permanent nuclear posture, some people recognized that it meant a long-term national commitment to absolute secrecy, that it would inevitably affect a variety of democratic issues. But those democratic issues were not on anybody's agenda. The Israeli leadership was delighted to have found a solution that would allow Israel to continue quietly with its nuclear program. Their next mission was to build a reliable command-and-control system consistent with the bargain. The focus was, notably, on safety and security, expediency, and reliability, not on democracy. Although a few recognized that amimut would exact a cost on democracy, they saw no way out.

That the Israeli public endorsed the bargain is even more intriguing. The bomb remained outside the public eye, and the public was more than happy to leave it there. Only at the end of the cold war did the consequences of relying on nuclear deterrence become more apparent. Nuclear deterrence then came to be viewed as inherently in conflict with the democratic rights of the public. When Robert Dahl and others began articulating their democratic critique of nuclear deterrence in the mid-1980s, it was with a renewed global interest in advancing new democratic norms regarding a transparent and accountable government. This renewed interest—in governmental transparency, the value of the freedom of information, the right of the public to know, and the like—was a new global phenomenon. These issues were introduced into the United States' democratic vocabulary, at both the scholarly and the public levels, mainly in the last two or three decades of the twentieth century.[42] This new intellectual and political interest in open democracy was to a large extent a consequence of the information revolution. By making the tension between nuclear deterrence and democracy more prominent, this interest led to the question of the democratic control of nuclear weapons, which was different from the more traditional question about the executive control of nuclear weapons raised by security-oriented students of nuclear weapons.[43]

Viewed through the lens of a new interest in democratic openness, the Israeli bargain of amimut appears anachronistic and inappropriate. Once the issue of democratic control of nuclear weapons has been defined in terms of open procedures, norms and measures of transparency, and the level of knowledge and involvement of the democratic public, the Israeli bargain of amimut is seen as contradicting these new democratic values and norms. From this perspective, any significant visible change between the Israeli bargain then and now is virtually indiscernible.

A national commitment to amimut as currently practiced in Israel entails significant democratic costs. It creates an coterie with existential responsibilities that is insulated from the rest of the society. The existence of such a coterie inevitably corrodes the commitment to the fundamental democratic values of an open society: the public's right to know, the public's right to discuss important national issues, and, ultimately, the norms of an open society. The democratic cost of amimut, then, is the cultivation of a willfully ignorant public that has been deprived of its basic democratic rights and that is complicit in that deprivation.

Chapter Seven

The Democratic Cost of Amimut

Governance

Thus far I have focused on the democratic cost of amimut imposed on the citizenry: the denial of the right to information and participation, blocking access to history, degrading the value of telling the truth, and imposing the stifling burden of secrecy. But the democratic price of the amimut bargain goes beyond mere infringements on the public. A policy of amimut rooted in total secrecy and nonacknowledgment harms and sometimes even undermines the integrity of governance itself.

As Robert Dahl and others observed, the requirements of nuclear weapons are different from the requirements of democratic governance.[1] The level of secrecy involved in early nuclear decisions challenges the ideals associated with democracy and the rule of law. But Israeli amimut as a *permanent* posture further bolsters that initial challenge. It is a symptom of both growing pains and a lifelong illness.

Other intrinsic factors in the Israeli situation worsen the problem. First, the policy of amimut is incorporated in a dual-identity organizational structure designed to obscure the truth. Second, the democratic price of amimut is exacerbated by structural deficiencies of the Israeli government in general and in the area of national security in particular. Third, all three organizations that constitute the guardianship infrastructure of amimut (as discussed in chapter 4)—the IAEC (Israel Atomic Energy Commission), the MALMAB (Office of Security at the Ministry of Defense), and the Censora (Office of the Military Censor)—are tainted because their power and authority are not firmly anchored in law; indeed, even their missions and powers are poorly defined.

Amimut is incompatible with the ideals of good democratic governance, understood to be a system of public accountability, due process, rule of law, and transparent government deliberations. My argument is not based merely on abstract legal reasoning. Rather, it reflects a real criticism I have heard many times over the years from civil servants who faithfully served amimut. Virtually all of them still believe that amimut has been—and maybe is—politically indispensable to Israel's security, but they also learned that the policy generated its own pitfalls: it is difficult to contain amimut. They also pointed out that Israel's basic system of government, a parliamentary system that diffuses executive power, tends to highlight and magnify these same deficiencies. The principal drawback of amimut, they argue, is that it leaves too much ambiguity as to who is in charge. This ambiguity tends to erode accountability and due process. Ultimately, then, the victim of amimut is not just the citizenry but the integrity of the democratic process.

Because the empirical evidence for this claim is largely hidden or at least publicly inaccessible, historical anecdotes can only hint at the democratic pitfalls of amimut. Some of these anecdotes may seem too old to apply to the current situation, but they still point to continuing areas and principles of concern. Finally, the critique of amimut presented here is about principles of governance, not about details.

Jurisdictional Confusion

In the summer of 1954, in response to internal disputes within the IAEC, Prime Minister Moshe Sharet wrote to his predecessor, former Prime Minister David Ben-Gurion, asking him to clarify under which ministerial jurisdiction he had established the IAEC two years earlier. At that time, Ben-Gurion had been serving as both prime minister and minister of defense: Had he set up the IAEC in his capacity as minister of defense or as prime minister? Ten days later Ben-Gurion responded, admitting that the IAEC's statuary status lacked jurisdictional clarity, and he noted, "It is difficult for me to answer your question because at the time I did not ask myself if I was acting in my capacity as prime minister or minister of defense. It makes more sense to me now that I did it on behalf of the prime minister's office."[2]

When he made his decision, Ben-Gurion had no practical reason to be concerned about the capacity in which he was acting because combining the two portfolios was a way to solidify his national authority and power while deliberately blurring the boundaries between the two. This allowed him to control all aspects of national security. Only when he retired in December 1953 (this was his first retirement; he came back to power in January 1955 and then retired permanently in 1963) and only after the two positions were separated did Ben-Gurion decide that the two civilian intelligence agencies, known today as the Mossad and the Shabak (General Security Service, GSS), should be formally under the prime minister's office, not the Ministry of Defense.[3] Apparently, though, no such explicit decision was made for the newly established IAEC.

Sharet, who served only in the capacity of prime minister, had a practical need to determine which ministry had jurisdiction over Israel's nuclear affairs. The confusion about the IAEC's status was a matter of both politics and security considerations, which had stemmed largely from a deliberate effort to obscure the bureaucratic linkage between the Ministry of Defense and nuclear energy. For this reason (as I explained in chapter 4), the IAEC had two roles, one classified and the other unclassified. As a classified executive agency, the IAEC resided within, and was funded by, the Ministry of Defense (MOD), but as an unclassified advisory commission, it was under control of the prime minister's office. Given Ben-Gurion's dual portfolio, his powerful authority, and his fondness for "constructive ambiguity," the question of formal jurisdiction meant little.[4] Not only was this arrangement supportive of Israel's security needs, but in those early days there was little interest in the formalities of due process.

In 1955 Ben-Gurion returned to power and to his two old jobs. A few years later, when the Dimona project started in earnest, it was subordinated bureaucratically to the MOD (but outside the IAEC's bureaucracy). The reasons were primarily issues of personnel: Peres wanted an executive czar to build Dimona, Manes Pratt, and it was evident that the IAEC chairman, Bergmann, lacked the skills to be in charge of the project. The other side of the project, the weaponization mission, was conducted at another bureaucratic entity (RAFAEL, the Hebrew acronym for the Armaments Development Authority) under the MOD's jurisdiction. Shimon Peres controlled all aspects of the nuclear project from his office at the MOD (first as director general and, after 1959, as deputy minister).

In 1966, after Peres's forced departure from the MOD and his replacement by Zvi Dinstein, Prime Minister Levi Eshkol decided to overhaul the old IAEC in order to reorganize the entire nuclear project. By that time, the need to combine the two centers of nuclear activity into a coherent mode of production was apparent. The IAEC, which until then had been sidelined by Peres's direct management, had to be reestablished as the executive administration serving as the headquarters for all nuclear activities (see chapter 4). As part of this overhaul, Eshkol and Dinstein decided to reassert the prime minister's jurisdiction over the nation's nuclear affairs by making the prime minister the ex-officio chairman of the IAEC.[5] Similar to the civilian intelligence agencies, all nuclear affairs in Israel must be conducted under the political authority of the prime minister. Still, key aspects of the IAEC's operations, such as budget and security, remain bureaucratically subordinated to the MOD. So even if the overall ministerial authority over the IAEC resides with the prime minister, he must share the MOD's assets and resources in order to activate his authority. The challenge was designing a system of governance that affirmed the prime minister's authority but also recognized the MOD's key role in managing the IAEC.

The governing concept of the renewed IAEC remained a variant of the old dual-identity organizing concept. In its thin public identity, the IAEC is a rather amorphous entity under the prime minister, but behind this veneer it functions as an executive nuclear administration (*minhal madaii*). As I pointed out in chapter 4, a highly classified executive order was drafted in 1966 to spell out the complex organizational and jurisdictional aspects of the new-old agency.[6]

This new arrangement was bureaucratically awkward and constitutionally ill defined from the beginning. While authority was declared to be in the hands of the prime minister, executive control remained within the MOD. In 1966, however, this lack of clarity did not matter much because Prime Minister Eshkol was also the minister of defense and thus held full ministerial control over both portfolios. As the prime minister he was the chair of the IAEC, and his deputy at the MOD, Zevi Dinstein, executed his policy.

But a year later, on the eve of the Six-Day War, this arrangement was abruptly disrupted with the appointment of Moshe Dayan as the minister of defense. Although Eshkol remained prime minister and, as such, was formally in control of the nuclear project, in reality the newly appointed minister of defense, Dayan, controlled the *minhal*. A day after taking over the MOD, Dayan fired Eshkol's deputy minister, Zvi Dinstein, and installed his former chief of staff, Zvi Zur (Chera), as his senior civilian aide (and in direct charge of all the defense industries under the ministry), thereby assuming Dinstein's role as the prime minister's eyes and ears for the secret nuclear

project. Within a short time Zur chaired all the relevant committees overseeing the nuclear project. On the eve of the war, Israel put together an improvised nuclear device (discussed in chapter 3).

In anticipation of war, a basic agreement was drafted to divide the powers of the prime minister and minister of defense. The Yadin document was
short, only two brief paragraphs. The first paragraph specified the military
actions that the minister of defense could not take without the prior approval
of the prime minister. Among those prohibitions was the use of unconventional weapons, the only implicit reference to the nuclear issue. The other
paragraph dealt with the defense personnel whom the prime minister could
consult.[7] Notwithstanding the importance of the document, it was a voluntary agreement without reference to any mechanism or body to resolve disagreements. It was legally nonbinding.[8]

This preliminary document says nothing explicit about the nuclear issue.
Sometime after the war, the military secretaries of the prime minister and the
minister of defense, with the ministerial assistance of Minister Israel Galili,
drafted a more elaborated document that is commonly known as "the constitution," which outlined the ministerial division of labor and lines of authority between the prime minister and minister of defense.[9] Since this first constitution was drafted and approved, it has become customary for each new
cabinet to approve the document in one of its first sessions.[10] It is assumed
that the division of responsibilities, outlined in the constitution, between
the prime minister and the defense minister with regard to nuclear issues
complements the 1966 executive order under which the new IAEC came into
being.

To this day, the exact history of how, and under whose authority, Israel
opaquely and incrementally crossed the nuclear threshold between 1967 and
1969 has not been told. Prime Minister Eshkol was reportedly still reluctant to
make a major long-term nuclear commitment, but there is much anecdotal
evidence suggesting that facts were created on the ground, owing more to
unauthorized drift generated at Dayan's MOD than to an explicit decision by
Eshkol or any other authorized body of the government (such as a ministerial committee). Israeli historian Tom Segev, based on Eshkol's aide's (Yaakov
Hertzog's) diaries, writes: "The rivalry between Dayan and Eshkol affected
almost every political and military issue, including the nuclear project and
the talks with Arabs in the territories. . . . In one incident Dayan gave orders
concerning the Dimona project, and only afterward instructed that Eshkol be
asked whether he had any objections."[11]

One way to think about Hertzog's entry goes as follows: Eshkol was incapable in the second half of 1968 of imposing his statuary authority over the nuclear project (the result of both the new reality at the MOD and his deteriorating health). Most decisions involving the nuclear project were made and executed by Zur at the MOD. The prime minister was not adequately informed as to the political meaning of those decisions. Subsequently, new facts were created that were not backed up by political decisions by the prime minister. The intrinsic and incompletely defined shared arrangement between Eshkol and Dayan, compounded by the political sensitivity of the subject and the reluctance of all sides to bring it to the cabinet for a decision, created the conditions for "constructive ambiguity," which allowed Dayan and Zur to advance their nuclear agenda in incremental steps in the absence of an overall decision. Accordingly, under the cover of political and jurisdictional ambiguity, Israel moved to a nuclear posture without making a cabinet-level decision to do so. But for all practical purposes, Israel actually had crossed the nuclear threshold on the eve of the 1967 war without the cabinet's being informed of that fact.

Even though Prime Minister Golda Meir presumably restored the prime minister's final authority over nuclear issues, the secret deal she struck with President Richard Nixon a few months after she assumed office did not help to clarify matters. On the contrary, amimut's requirements—in particular, the pledge that "Israel would not be the first to introduce nuclear weapons" and the need to maintain extreme measures of secrecy—made it inherently difficult to address the nuclear issue by the normal procedures of due process governance. And as long as the issue was not anchored in legislation, ambiguity about who is in charge has remained systemic and lasting.

Logic suggests that these inherent ambiguities would become more troubling after the state crossed the nuclear threshold. The separation between political authority and executive control (in which the prime minister has the authority but the minister of defense and the IDF [Israel Defense Forces] have much of the control) tends to generate jurisdictional ambiguities over areas of responsibility. Furthermore, those ambiguities are likely to be magnified when the political leadership is politically reluctant to make big political decisions. In this case, the small, incremental decisions made by the professionals determined the reality. Decisions covering a variety of semitechnical issues, such as modes of deployment, custody, and command-and-control systems, become the meaningful decisions if the political level is reluctant to make an overall decision at the political level.

The highly classified executive order initiating this governing arrangement in 1966, before Israel actually had nuclear devices, has been revised only once or twice since then. There was a natural reluctance to open up such a sensitive and secretive system of governance. We must assume that this system of governance functions well as long as all the key players—the prime minister, the minister of defense, the IAEC director general, and a few others—agree on the fundamentals or do not care to debate their differences. But how are these issues resolved when the prime minister and the minister of defense disagree?

Formal authority may lie with the prime minister, but in reality this may not amount to much. As already noted, in 1968 Minister of Defense Dayan used his ministry resources to create facts, presumably without Prime Minister Eshkol's authorization, that effectively closed Israel's political options concerning the Nuclear Non-Proliferation Treaty (NPT), even though the prime minister remained politically uncommitted on the matter. Even without judging its merits, this action presumably violated the principle of the prime minister's supremacy on nuclear policy.

Moreover, to this day we do not really know how big the gap between authority and control was during the 1973 war (this issue is discussed more fully in chapter 3). There was a rumor that after the 1973 war, Ministers Alon and Galili demanded an investigation of the nuclear aspects of the war, particularly whether Minister of Defense Dayan had breached his authority, but apparently Prime Minister Meir refused such an investigation. Later, in 1976, the IAEC's director general, Shalheveth Freier, was fired after a policy dispute with Minister of Defense Shimon Peres. According to Freier, even though Prime Minister Yitzhak Rabin fired him (Freier), his (Freier's) position on that matter of dispute (Freier refused to reveal what that matter was) was closer to Rabin's. But Rabin apparently regarded Freier (and perhaps the issue itself) as a political liability in his rivalry with Peres.[12] Freier added that the circumstances surrounding his firing were hushed and were never even shared with the Knesset's Foreign Affairs and Defense Committee, the parliamentary body that is supposed to oversee the defense system. Freier was never asked to testify before any state oversight body in regard to his firing.[13]

There are only three historical references to situations of jurisdictional ambiguity on the nuclear issue that came to the surface despite the secrecy. There may have been others. The general point is this: Amimut amplifies the problems of governance in such cases in two ways. First, it obscures the jurisdictional boundaries of responsibility for nuclear matters by generating an arrangement that divides and confuses authority with control. Second, it creates an environment that makes it difficult to investigate such incidents.[14]

Confusion over Accountability

More than fifteen years ago when I was conducting research for my book *Israel and the Bomb*, one of my interviewees told me an intriguing anecdote about the subtle nexus between amimut and accountability. Although the interviewee wanted me to know the story, he asked me not to use its details. Now, however, my source is no longer alive, and I believe his story should be told. Before writing this section, I consulted my original 1992 interview notes that the interviewee had read and approved.

This source was Professor Avraham Hermony, a chemist turned defense scientist. During the early to mid-1960s, Hermony was a technical director in RAFAEL, one of three serving as the technological eyes and ears for RAFAEL's boss, Munya Mardor. Hermony's area of responsibility was overseeing RAFAEL's role in the nuclear project, which was under the overall responsibility of Shimon Peres, then the deputy minister of defense.

But what, exactly, was RAFAEL's role supposed to be? In those years, since the project's future was somewhat unclear, that uncertainty spilled over to the technical level as well. According to Hermony, RAFAEL received no clear guidance from the Ministry of Defense, specifically from Peres, as to what the ultimate product and its specific requirements should be. "On projects with political significance," Hermony told me cautiously in that 1992 series of long extensive interviews, "the political level consistently avoided providing us—the developers—guidance, let alone specifications, beyond the principal decision."[15]

As time passed, Hermony became increasingly concerned about this lack of guidance. When it became evident that it would not be forthcoming, he decided on his own (and in fact against the advice of his boss, Munya Mardor) to force clarity on their political bosses in Tel Aviv. Sometime around 1964/1965, as he recalled nearly thirty years later, he wrote a memo to Shimon Peres, the project's overall chief executive, asking him for guidance. Specifically, Hermony listed three technological options, with each describing a particular technical product that the project could work toward. Hermony remembered that memo vividly because he considered it one of the most important he had ever written. Although Hermony refused in 1992 to be too specific as to what those options were, he left me with the understanding that they ranged from a crude nuclear explosive device to a fully deliverable weapons system (a bomb). His question to Peres was, in essence, How far should Israel go with its nuclear option? What should the developers ultimately aim for?

Moreover, the memo stated that in the absence of explicit guidance RAFAEL would follow a specified course of action (which he identified in the memo but again refused to tell me). Technical and strategic reasons and specifications were provided in the memo. Hermony anticipated that he might not receive a formal written reply from Peres, so one purpose of the memo was to put in writing RAFAEL's position (i.e., his position) on the matter. Hermony understood that the lack of guidance was not accidental but reflected the political uncertainty and ambiguity under which Peres had run the project. Insiders in those days knew that Peres had wanted to turn Israel into a full member of the nuclear club, but they also knew that he had no political mandate to do that. Hermony understood that Peres had wanted the developers to make their "technical" decisions on their own, relieving the political level (i.e. himself) from providing political instruction beyond the general authorization to work on "research and development."

Hermony prepared himself for not receiving an explicit answer from Peres, but he did not anticipate a specific request to regard the memo as if it had never been written. Not only did Peres himself ignore the request for guidance, but the memo also was returned to Hermony unsigned, via Hermony's boss, RAFAEL director Munya Mardor, with an oral demand to treat the memo as if it had never been sent. As it turned out, the lack of a reply did not slow the project's progress. As Hermony put it in 1992, "The project leaders knew how to proceed, and their superiors had no problems with the path they chose."

Hermony's story shows how the environment of ambiguity undermined accountability, responsibility, and due process. He acknowledged that when he had written that memo, there was no immediate technical need to determine the specific modality for the development. Indeed, budgets for the nuclear project were approved (by Peres) in a haphazard and tentative fashion, on a year-by-year basis, without making a long-term budgetary commitment. But Hermony wrote the memo because he felt (maybe naïvely, he added) that a certain political and strategic clarity was needed to ensure the integrity of the scientific and technical development activities.

Hermony reconstructed, from a 1992 perspective, three reasons that probably led him to seek such clarity. First, he wanted to be sure that what the developers (including himself) were thinking was in sync with what the political level wanted them to accomplish. Second, he wanted to be reassured that somebody higher up at the MOD (Peres and Eshkol) would be held accountable for this secret project. Third, he wanted to understand what strategic concepts, if any, actually guided those higher-ups who were politically responsible for the nuclear project, and he felt that those strategic concepts should be known to the developers. According to Hermony, the developers may have presumed that the nuclear project entailed giving Israel existential deterrence, and not manufacturing another weapons system for the IDF. But for the technical leaders in RAFAEL, translating this abstract strategic idea into the language of technical specifications was not a trivial matter. They hoped to find out what the leadership thought of the project in operational terms. (Only later did they realize that the political leadership was unwilling to formulate the project's operational goals.)

Although Hermony never said so explicitly, I got the impression that he also was concerned that maybe one day in the future, based on the absence of a paper trail, historians would say that those RAFAEL scientists exceeded their authorized mandate and gave Israel the atomic bomb without being formally authorized to do so, that the atomic project was a rogue operation of a few senior scientists who had been asked to develop an "option" but instead built the real thing. I sensed that Hermony wanted me to know (and even to appreciate) that he had been concerned about accountability and responsibility and that the climate of amimut allowed leaders to avoid both of them.

Whether or not my interpretation is fair, Hermony wanted a written document from Peres proving that RAFAEL had been instructed to do what it did, or at least that RAFAEL had informed Peres what they were about to do. Peres, however, was reluctant to provide any instructions. We can only speculate about his perspective and motives. Evidently, Peres was not authorized to make such a decision alone because if a decision is treated as not technical but political, it requires a political decision-making process. We also must assume that Peres did not want to engage Eshkol on such a matter, especially if such a decision was not necessary, because it would have forced Eshkol to open the nuclear issue. Eshkol himself recognized that he had no political mandate to make such a decision on his own. Therefore, to address the issue, Eshkol would have had to bring the issue to the cabinet, or at least to the defense ministerial committee, but this was the last thing he wanted to do. It was easier for all involved to leave those decisions to the technical level at RAFAEL.

Although Hermony's testimony is explicit, I have heard similar anecdotes about the refusal of the political level to be involved in nuclear-related decisions.[16] In the early days, security-related amimut enabled, even encouraged, ambiguities that allowed the political level to escape formal responsibility and accountability. We could speculate that the classified record indicates that Israel became a nuclear-weapons state without authorized orders from the appropriate governing body.[17]

Some critics may agree that amimut did undermine due process in the early years of the nuclear program but that these were "growing pains." Only over time, after Israel crossed the nuclear threshold, checks and balances were introduced into the system to make such anecdotes impossible. In today's practice, the argument goes, governance under amimut should not be that different from the governance of any other classified area of national security. That is, amimut is not inherently incompatible with the norms of governance under secrecy.

My response to such claims is twofold. First, we can only hope that such old anecdotes reflect the growing pains of the past and do not apply *in any way* to the present situation. But we do not know whether this is the case. Second, and more important, even if such anecdotes are outdated and no longer relevant, the ambiguities of accountability and responsibility are rooted in deeper legal-constitutional and structural deficiencies in the Israeli national security decision-making system. The amimut bargain only heightens these two problems.

Legal-Constitutional Confusion

The legal-constitutional confusion that amimut has generated over the nuclear issue is one of the bargain's most disturbing domestic features. Simply put, amimut has made the Israeli legal system incapable of adequately addressing the implications of the country's possession of nuclear weapons. Under amimut, the Israeli legal system cannot acknowledge the reality of nuclear weapons and thus cannot address its legal consequences. Amimut creates a legal reality in which the rule of law is not applied to one of the most important features of Israeli national security. The many legal concerns critical to the executive control of the nuclear complex cannot be dealt with adequately because most of them cannot even be stated.

Although amimut does not create the ambience of legal confusion, it exacerbates an already flawed situation. To begin with, there is an old Israeli tradition of how the state should run its secret national security organizations. According to that tradition, Israel has exempted its national security secret organizations from the law because in matters of intelligence and unconventional weaponry, the government must be able to act without encumbrances, that is, without legal constraints.

Constitutionally, the legality of these secret organizations is established through a short clause (only one and a half lines), known as the government's "residual power clause," which is now clause 32 in Israel's Basic Law: The Government.[18] This clause gives the government far-reaching legal power: the authority to act on behalf of the state in any way it finds fit, as long as that authority is not conferred by existing law to any other entity and does not challenge any supreme court ruling. It is a magical legal device that declares the impossibility of legal vacuum in regard to government action.[19] Israel's supreme court has determined that the clause gives the government sole and full authority to act in each and any area not covered by any existing law.[20]

The political theory supporting this law is the (Hobbesian) outlook that views the legality of the state's secret organizations as derived directly from the legality of the state itself.[21] One obvious function of the residual-power clause is to create constitutional legality for those state organizations and activities that the government wants to keep invisible and unacknowledged. Under the legal cover of this clause, Prime Minister David Ben-Gurion created Israel's triad of national security organizations: Israel's domestic intelligence service, the General Security Services (GSS), the foreign intelligence organization (the Mossad); and the state nuclear organization (the IAEC). Their legality was not derived from a specific law, as is that of the IDF, but from the residual-power clause.

Although this constitutional outlook dominated Israeli thinking and practice on matters of national security for a long time, it has declined over the last few decades. The decline was instigated by new societal and legal ideas about the rule of law in democracy as well as by actual severe misconduct within the secret organizations, demonstrating the need for legislation to govern the nation's secret organizations. Most prominent among those events was the 1984 incident involving the GSS known as the Bus 300 Affair, which subsequently led to the GSS leadership's involvement in criminal concealment of evidence and cover-ups to protect itself and its internal code of secrecy and loyalty. At issue was a conflict between the GSS's code of secrecy and the state's rule of law.

These scandals empowered the notion that in a democracy, the actions of secret state organizations also must be governed by the rule of law; they must not reside in a legal twilight zone. After almost two decades of hard legal labor, the GSS law was drafted, deliberated, amended, and finally legislated, and in 2002 it began regulating matters of domestic state security.[22]

Although the law does not deal with the sensitive subject of GSS interrogations, there was wide expectation that it would be a precedent for Israel's other secret organizations. The next in line should have been a law for the Mossad.[23] Some Israeli legal commentators, such as Professor Ze'ev Segal of Tel Aviv University and Moshe Negbi of the Hebrew University, raised the idea of a Mossad law in a number of editorials in which they detailed some of the components that such a law would require.[24]

But such a law is still not in sight. Following preliminary deliberations at the Justice Ministry, the Mossad headquarters, the Knesset, and elsewhere, it became apparent that there was no political will to overcome the traditional opposition to such a law. Opponents argued that the Mossad must act sometimes illegally, and indeed, the very business of intelligence and espionage is by nature based on deception and illegality. For the time being, therefore, the issue of a Mossad law is, at best, on hold.[25]

Unfortunately, public discussion about extending the rule of law has never included Israel's third secret organization, the IAEC. The special status of Israel's nuclear organization has made the notion of an IAEC law unthinkable. The paradox of drafting such a law is that one would need to know a great deal about the organization and its mission, but in the current culture of amimut, such knowledge is considered classified and hence unreachable. For this and other reasons, there has never been a public discussion—or even interest—regarding a law for the IAEC. Moreover, the current nuclear threat from Iran is likely to reinforce the public's reluctance to engage seriously in the issue.

Schiff and the Red Button Law

There was, however, one unusual exception to the interest in drafting a law for the IAEC. On March 13, 1998, in a provocatively phrased op-ed in *Ha'aretz* entitled "The Red Button Law," Ze'ev Schiff proposed legislating a law that would place checks on Israel's nuclear decision-making system.[26] Schiff revealed that in connection with the crisis two weeks earlier over Iraq's program of weapons of mass destruction, some Israelis were more worried about Israel's "extreme and unbalanced" possible action than about Iraq's President Saddam Hussein's possible first strike. Schiff made it clear that the source of the alarm was that Israel's response, according to the world press, might have been nuclear.[27]

> How could such a fateful decision be made? What would be the cause that would justify breaking the nuclear taboo that has been held since the United States destroyed Hiroshima on August 6, 1945? Who is eligible to make such a decision? What would be the legal standing of such a decision, and what actually made it legal? Who is authorized to decide? Can it be that under special circumstances it is only one person or maybe two, prime minister and minister of defense? And what happens if one person holds both portfolios?

Schiff warned that if such a decision were ever made,

> the entire world, not only the Middle East, would look different. . . . Israel itself would look different in a variety of fundamental ways, and so will be the place of the Jews in world history. There will be those who will ask if the new Israel is a safe place against nuclear revenge.

He noted that "moral and historical responsibility requires that the guardians of the red button should be wise and cautious professionals . . . those who know that wisdom requires to not act on nuclear matters out of panic." Schiff's proposal to legislate a law came at the end of the article:

> Maybe it is time to legislate a law to regulate this area and to determine answers to some of these questions. Such a law may not fit any situation and any scenario; there are scenarios that do not allow much time between an event and a decision. . . . It is inconceivable that such a decision would be left in the hands of one or two people, even those who are most senior in the cabinet.[28]

The questions Schiff raised are important to any nuclear democracy, but in Israel they carry extra meaning. Consider the legal-constitutional aspects of Schiff's questions: Who is constitutionally in charge of the Israeli bomb, let alone its use? Who is authorized to push the red button?

Details are lacking but logic suggests that Israel's nuclear command-and-control system must respond to two distinct and fundamental principles, each corresponding to a different executive layer that may be in great tension—if not in contradiction—with the other. The first principle is that Israel's prime minister must have exclusive ministerial responsibility over nuclear affairs. As noted, this principle must have been derived from the government's 1966 decision making the prime minister the chair of the IAEC and unofficially in full control of that body. The second principle is a fundamental feature of the Israeli command-and-control system: the system is designed so that no single person, including the prime minister, is in sole control of the nation's nuclear arsenal. Both principles may have some bearing on the legal issue of the residual power, but without detailed legal clarifications, confusion over who is legally in charge is inevitable.

For example, we also presume that under the Israeli arrangement, the IDF does not have custody of the nuclear assets (cores) in ordinary times, which are kept disassembled and separated from their means of delivery. To assemble the nuclear assets both keys must be turned on, at least metaphorically speaking; which means that both the prime minister and the minister of defense (and possibly others as well) must agree to the action. But what happens if they do not agree? (This arrangement may have changed in its procedural detail with the introduction of submarines as a delivery platform, but we should presume that the guiding dual-key concept remains intact.)

Whatever legal advice and clarifications, if any, that the attorney general may have given in classified form, those arrangements surely do not have the force of law. Rather, their legal-constitutional status is derived from the residual-power clause. Even if it resolves practical issues, this is not a satisfactory solution and has no explicit or adequate legal-constitutional status, which leaves the issue of who is constitutionally in charge of the bomb in a legal limbo.

In addition, the current legislation covering national security is alien to, and possibly incompatible with, scenarios of nuclear deterrence. For example, within Israel's jurisprudence framework, only the full government (cabinet) has the power to decide on matters of war and peace; the prime minister (even with the support of the minister of defense) cannot wage a war on his or her own. As noted, the Israeli government has far-reaching executive powers, but those powers are conferred on the government as a collective body. While the Basic Law: The Government recognizes the special role of the prime minister in heading the government, as the chief executive of the

state with the authority to appoint and fire ministers, it treats the prime minister as *primus inter pares*, first among equals.

The Israeli constitutional edifice in the area of national security is thin
and leaves a great deal of uncertainty as to how to manage national security affairs. Tradition, not law, determines practice.[29] Many of the jurisdictional boundaries between the main national security players within the
system—particularly between the prime minister, the minister of defense,
and the chief of staff—are loosely defined and regulated more by tradition
and practice than by law. Ultimately, the government's decisions are made in
the name of the cabinet as a whole, not in the name of the prime minister.
But in the nuclear age there might be times when the cabinet could not be
convened, maybe not even by phone. Who, then, would be authorized to
initiate a nuclear alert? What if Israel were under surprise attack, possibly
even a nuclear attack? What if the prime minister and the minister of defense
could not communicate?

Amimut and the Nuclear Decision-Making Process

What effect does amimut have on the integrity and quality of the highly classified decision-making process itself? Does amimut help or harm or make no
difference? Unfortunately, it is difficult to tell because we hardly know. Still,
despite the absence of empirical data—apart from knowing how firmly Israel
is committed to amimut itself—we can make some comments about Israel's
national security decision-making process, reflect theoretically on the sociology and culture of amimut, and finally make some educated guesses.

Over the years, we have learned much about Israel's decision-making system in the broader area of national security, in particular certain chronic and
systemic weaknesses. Israel's history offers evidence of a number of key national security decisions that were made in a haphazard manner incompatible
with the accepted norms and procedures of good governance.[30] Not only is it
unrealistic to expect that the nuclear field is free from such lapses, but in fact
there are reasons to suggest that the sociology and culture of amimut could
exacerbate them.[31]

Since the findings of the Agranat State Inquiry Commission in 1974 (regarding the 1973 war) and until the findings of the Vinograd Governmental Inquiry Commission in 2007 (regarding the 2006 war in Lebanon), through a list
of parliamentary, academic, and journalistic reports and case studies (on such
diverse issues as the Lavi aircraft episode, the Jewish settlement project in the

West Bank and Gaza, the First Lebanon War of 1981, the Pollard spy case, and more), Israelis have learned that their nation's national security decision-making process is deficient both constitutionally and organizationally. While these studies made various recommendations, two basic and related flaws were repeatedly pointed out in almost all of them.

First, the very constitutional basis of Israeli decision making, particularly the division of labor between the major decision-making players (prime minister, minister of defense, and the entire cabinet), is susceptible to flaws owing to an inherent weakness of the Israeli system of government. The weakness resides in part in the semiconstitutional structure, which makes the full cabinet the ultimate legal national security decision-making body but does not specify which national security decisions can be made by the prime minister and which require the full cabinet's approval. Furthermore, the Israeli framework does not define clearly the relations and processes among the three national security ministers (prime minister, minister of defense, and foreign minister). The system relies on both tradition and the ongoing power relations among the players.

Second, the Israeli cabinet lacks the tools of strategic policy research, evaluation, and oversight in the national security field. Consequently, the prime minister and the entire cabinet are not equipped to scrutinize the proposals that the minister of defense or the IDF brings up for decision. The result is that on matters of national security, the minister of defense (commonly backed up by the IDF) is in a stronger position to advance his or her position. While the law (Basic Law: The Government) makes the cabinet collectively the final decision maker on all matters of national security, the cabinet cannot truly perform its job, as the ministers do not have the time or the ability to deliberate thoroughly on issues they must decide.

These deficiencies have been debated ad nauseam since 1974, when the Agranat Commission proposed establishing a strong national security council (NSC) under the prime minister to serve the entire cabinet. Other studies offered similar ideas, such as giving the prime minister's office its own professional national security staff to help formulate, integrate, and oversee the nation's overall national security policies. Until recently, however, little has actually been done beyond giving lip service to their recommendations (such as situating an adviser on terror or intelligence in the prime minister's office).[32] Owing to strong opposition from the ministers of defense and all the IDF chiefs, supported by the heads of the secret organizations within the prime minister's office, most prime ministers felt that either they preferred to act on their own intuition or were too overwhelmed to overhaul the system.[33] In the wake of the Vinograd Commission report, and especially after Benjamin Netanyahu became Israel's prime minister for the second time in 2009, a fresh effort was made to address these pitfalls by strengthening the institution of the National Security Council.[34]

Although none of these public studies address the nuclear issue, some of the deficiencies identified in the Israeli national security decision-making process are probably relevant to the nuclear issue as well, especially the lack of independent professional capabilities (i.e., outside the executive agencies) to give the prime minister independent analysis, assessment, and oversight. Amimut could further exacerbate these shortcomings.

To begin with, one must evaluate the burden of culture of amimut and the secrecy rituals that go with it. In order to have access to prime nuclear secrets, one must hold a special security clearance for nuclear affairs (issued by the MALMAB's chief). Most national security officials with a regular security clearance are not permitted to deal with nuclear documents, which means that they cannot participate in nuclear forums. The membership in the nuclear group is small and segregated from the rest of the national security apparatus. In turn, the final decision makers—the prime minister, the minister of defense, and a few others—are able to discuss nuclear issues proper with only few officials with the appropriate nuclear clearance. The issue of having a clearance is deeply embedded in any nuclear establishment's organizational culture.[35]

This compartmentalized environment must affect the quality and nature of the discussions. The prime minister cannot talk about nuclear matters with most of his or her advisers or associates and thus presumably is denied the benefit of a wide range of opinions. In more mundane areas of policymaking, the prime minister may be comfortable discussing matters with close political allies in the cabinet and the Knesset, sometimes even with the public, and may receive feedback from the public in the form of editorials, but this is not the case for nuclear issues. This situation encourages certain tendencies and habits, six of which I describe next.

Conservatism: The Political Cost of Loneliness

Political leaders are likely to follow the advice they receive from authorized nuclear guardians, especially if that advice is delivered as the consensus recommendations of a classified expert committee. Consequently, under amimut there is less chance that the prime minister will be open to discussing bold or innovative initiatives before the authorized experts screen and approve them. For example, we would assume that an Israeli prime minister would be cautious in responding to any ideas involving a fissile materials cutoff or any other aspects of nuclear disarmament. If those ideas cannot pass the prime minister's guardians, there is little chance that they can reach the prime minister. Under amimut, a prime minister is unlikely to initiate a political initiative of his or her own in the nuclear field. The decision makers are safe by being conservative.

Conflicts of Interest

Under the organizational culture of amimut and in the absence of normal political feedback from the outside, prime ministers naturally tend to rely on the judgment of their closest and most familiar nuclear adviser, the director general of the nuclear agency. This was apparent in the special relationship between Gideon Frank, the IAEC's longest-serving director general, and Prime Ministers Ariel Sharon and Ehud Olmert. What is less obvious is that the prime minister's dependence on the head of the nuclear agency may involve a structural conflict of interest, such as the built-in tension between the role of the nuclear agency's chief and that of the prime minister's chief nuclear adviser.

Time Pressures

A third feature of the nuclear decision-making environment is the scarcity of time available to the ultimate decision maker, the prime minister. To properly oversee the country's nuclear affairs, a task as complex as overseeing the nation's intelligence services, the prime minister needs time, time that his busy schedule rarely affords. The technological complexity of this issue thus further strengthens the prime minister's dependence on the country's nuclear guardians.[36]

The Priesthood

Insulation and secrecy give rise to what is often referred to as the *nuclear priesthood*, the small group of senior current and former officials, all with the highest nuclear clearances. Members of that small elite group make up the classified committees that oversee the nuclear bureaucracy, and therefore they have direct access to the prime minister.

A powerful but largely invisible nuclear priesthood that maintains oversight of the country's nuclear policies is not unique to Israel, but under amimut, the priesthood has even more influence than in other nuclear democracies. The priesthood serves not only as the prime minister's source of nuclear knowledge and wisdom but also as a defensive wall against new ideas, thereby encouraging conservatism.

Groupthink

A fifth consequence of the organizational culture of amimut is groupthink. Secrecy enhances group bias and perpetuates conformity and consensus, which also encourage conservatism. Amimut creates a self-reinforcing sociological environment. An example is the former MALMAB chief, Yechiel Horev, and his influence on the quality and integrity of the nuclear decision-making process. As noted in chapter 4, Horev looked at the world from the perspective of a spymaster and was convinced that others looked at Israel from a similar perspective. Although this attitude is natural for a top security officer anywhere, it becomes a problem if that officer rises to become one of the country's most trusted nuclear guardians involved in nuclear decisions. Horev's prominent presence in the nuclear bureaucracy for two decades introduced yet more conservatism, even paranoia, into a social system that tended to be conservative in the first place. What the public was even less aware of was Horev's enormous influence over the years on the lower levels of the nuclear bureaucracy. With his extraordinary bureaucratic power, he also was able to influence many others.

No Experts Outside the Classified World

Sixth, because of amimut, Israel has been deprived of a core of qualified but independent political and technical nuclear experts to balance the government's view. Unlike the United States and the United Kingdom, amimut has effectively disallowed the creation of a knowledgeable but independent arms-control community capable of counterbalancing the nation's nuclear priesthood. In more recent years, the seeds of such a community may have been planted, but it is still too weak and ideologically too close to the establishment to serve as a counterweight to the nuclear elite.

Nuclear Weapons Decision Making Under Amimut

While we know very few facts about how Israel actually makes its nuclear decisions, we can still reflect about it based on the experience of others in a similar situation. It is fair to say that all mature nuclear-weapons states face a somewhat similar challenge: devising a review process that allows the country to periodically revisit its nuclear policies. In fact, the very existence of such a review process can be viewed as a measure of nuclear maturity: if new proliferators tend to have a more haphazard and piecemeal manner of making nuclear decisions, mature proliferators tend to have a more deliberative and process-oriented manner.

The periodic posture review is designed to look at all the relevant parameters—political, strategic, operational, economic, and doctrinal—of the nation's nuclear weapons. The review is a way to combine oversight with policymaking. Because nuclear-weapons policies are such an arcane subject and require consensus in the national security establishment, the deliberative process is a good way to reach agreement. A review also is a way to educate uninformed and newly elected policymakers about the nuclear priesthood's thinking.

In the United States, this highly bureaucratized policy process evolved from a series of piecemeal presidential directives during the cold war into what has been known since 1993 as the Nuclear Posture Review (NPR). The 1993 NPR was the effort by the Clinton administration to articulate its own outlook on the role of nuclear weapons in the post–cold war era. It was advertised as "the first DOD [Department of Defense] study of its kind to incorporate reviews of policy, doctrine, force structure, operations, safety and security, and arms control in one look." In reality, though, it turned into a bureaucratic battleground between the American nuclear priesthood's old and new guards. But it finally established the NPR as a congressionally mandated review process that every new administration is obliged to conduct within its first year under the responsibility of the Defense Department (DOD). On December 31, 2001, the Bush administration submitted its NPR to Congress.[37]

The NPR process is not without its democratic flaws, as critics have noted. For example, in the past, the entire NPR was classified, while an unclassified version was thin and insubstantial. The Bush administration's NPR, for example, left only the foreword unclassified, with essentially nothing of substance. In addition, the NPR process still abides by the traditional standards of secrecy that permit very limited democratic oversight. Classified DOD plans involving nuclear targeting and the roles of nuclear weapons in war fighting are not disclosed to members of Congress, even those who are regularly briefed on classified matters.[38]

The same tensions that have characterized past reviews persist as the United States conducts the 2009 NPR. The start of the latest review followed President Barack Obama's April 2009 speech in Prague, in which he held out the vision of "a world without nuclear weapons." Nonetheless, the 2009 NPR, which was delivered to Congress in early 2010, examined both the reductions in nuclear arsenals and the strengthening of nuclear deterrence, two objectives that may be difficult to reconcile.[39]

Britain has created its own nuclear review process, which results in a comprehensive white paper that the British government issues on nuclear policies. Although the formal product of these review processes is highly classified, both the United States and the United Kingdom issue a declassified version for the general public. The existence of such a public document is recognition that nuclear policies are legitimate matters for the public to debate in a mature nuclear liberal democracy, that citizens are entitled to know what its government thinks about nuclear weapons. Despite the shortcomings, therefore, at least there is a process of disclosure. These documents, then, reflect the accepted balance between the public's right to know and the guardianship's requirements about nuclear secrecy.

But such a balance does not exist in Israel where, under amimut, every bit of information related to nuclear weapons is prohibited. Nevertheless, we can assume that over the years, Israel developed its own bureaucratic procedures and mechanisms to conduct periodic reviews of its nuclear commitment. Whether such a review process is truly comprehensive or piecemeal is unknown, but it is apparent that the security requirements of amimut and the organizational culture of Israel's nuclear establishment must affect the process. We also can assume that these reviews are submitted to the prime minister, the minister of defense, the Knesset's Foreign and Defense Committee chair, the IEAC director general, and a handful of others who share responsibility for these strategic matters.

The periodic reviews should force the small and relatively insulated Israeli nuclear community to interact with the rest of the strategic community when revisiting and updating the nation's nuclear posture, particularly the operational aspects of deterrence. Since over the last decade Israel has built a sea-based strategic arm, this must have profoundly affected the basic parameters of the Israeli nuclear posture. Given the anticipated changes in Israel's security environment, especially the rise of a nuclear-capable Iran, it is plausible that Israel's decision-making system has been designed to respond quickly to emerging threats and unexpected changes in the strategic environment.

Who in the Israeli national security bureaucracy has direct responsibility for such reviews is unknown, but it is likely that under the current governance structure, the overall responsibility for the nation's nuclear policies review resides with the *minhal* (IAEC).

Democratic Oversight Under Amimut

The final consequence of amimut for governance pertains to oversight. Israel's state comptroller's office, the state's independent oversight agency, was formally established in May 1949, a year after the state had been founded, but it took the young state a long time to become accustomed to the idea of oversight, especially over security affairs. Israel's founding fathers, most prominently Prime Minister David Ben-Gurion, were busy building and defending a new state and had little patience or resources for oversight. Ben-Gurion himself was adamant about not letting auditors roam around and muddle through the secrets of his defense empire. *Kdushat habitachon* exempted Israel's security complex almost completely from external oversight.

Internal Oversight

The nuclear project, being the sanctum sanctorum of the empire, was sealed off from state oversight. The nuclear complex at Dimona came into being by violating all sorts of state laws, as funds were privately raised overseas and transferred outside state budgets and dispersed with no accountability. To this day, nobody knows how much it really cost to build the Dimona infrastructure. Today we would see this as an affront to the rule of law, but in those days it was just an unconventional aspect of a heroic enterprise designed to fulfill a sacred mission: Israel's survival. The idea of oversight was anathema to the creators of Dimona.

Functioning as a state within a state, the nuclear project's guardians had to devise their own system of internal oversight. Although they opposed external oversight, they recognized that internal oversight was necessary, so relatively early they established layers of semiautonomous oversight to serve as checks and balances for one another. This system was initiated while Dostrovsky was overhauling and rebuilding Israel's nuclear empire in the mid-1960s, and it was improved and upgraded significantly during Freier's tenure in the 1970s. The same Freier who wrote down amimut as a national strategy also designed the internal oversight code that had to be consistent with amimut. The idea was that each management level would have a layer of oversight reporting directly to the next higher level. Freier even arranged for his own senior subordinates to have direct access to the prime minister (Golda Meir and Yitzhak Rabin) without him, the director general, even being present.

To this day senior Israeli IAEC officials praise (off the record, of course) Freier's oversight system. They claim that the system's foundations are still in use today, and they are convinced that they provide the best possible oversight. The system's main architecture still consists of Freier's original idea of semi-independent institutionalized layers of internal oversight. Each layer reports to the level that appointed it: the first layer reports to the director of each of the research centers (Dimona [KAMAG] and Soreq [MAMAG]); the second reports to the IAEC's director general; and the third reports to the chair of the IAEC (or to someone whom the prime minister personally appoints). In recent years more layers have been added and strengthened, but the basic structure remains as Freier designed it in the 1970s: to provide maximum oversight with maximum amimut.

Oversight by the State Comptroller

Since the nuclear project began, Israel has grown up a great deal. It moved away from one national ethos to another. *Kdushat habitachon* is in decline, and the rule of law is in ascendance. Now that the state has been built, it needs to be maintained. Over time, Israel has learned that oversight is critical to maintaining proper governance and faith in the rule of law.

Israel's Basic Law: The State Comptroller, enacted in 1988, reflects these changes. This law gives the state comptroller's office a remarkably wide mandate and authority for oversight. According to article 2 of that law, the mission of the state comptroller is twofold: first, "to audit . . . the economy, the property, the finances, the obligations and the administration of any state organ, i.e. the government itself and any enterprise, institutions or corporations of the state or local authorities"; and, second, to "examine the legality, moral integrity, orderly management, efficiency and economy of the audited bodies, and any other matter which he deems necessary."[40]

The Knesset elects Israel's state comptroller by secret ballot for a single term of seven years. The incumbent is completely independent of the government and is responsible only to the Knesset. The state comptroller's budget is submitted directly to the Knesset's Finance Committee and is exempt from prior consideration by the Ministry of Finance. Aside from resigning or dying in office, the state comptroller can be fired only by the Knesset. Although lacking the authority to enforce compliance, the state comptroller has broad investigative powers and employs hundreds of staff members, including accountants, lawyers, and other relevant professionals.

Aviezer Yaari, a former army general who subsequently headed the defense division at the state comptroller's office from 1987 to 2000, observed that when he took office, the state comptroller had virtually no access to the country's secret organizations. Many quarters in the vast defense bureaucracy, including Israel's nuclear program and its most sensitive facilities, were outside the view of the oversight system. According to Yaari, before he took office he had informally asked the chiefs of the defense establishment whether they would cooperate with him and allow oversight of their sensitive affairs and had received "sympathetic" replies. But only later, in a special meeting in the fall of 1987 between the state comptroller, Yaari, and Prime Minister Yitzhak Shamir did the prime minister agree to give the state comptroller's office access to his own secret organizations, especially the Mossad, the GSS, and the IAEC:

> We worried that [our request] would not be welcomed, since all prime ministers had traditionally not considered it appropriate for state oversight to look into the state's deepest secrets; so state oversight, to the extent that it actually had existed, dealt merely with matters of administration and technical screening of budget management.

Yaari and the state comptroller were "surprised" to learn that Shamir was willing to accept the kind of oversight procedure they proposed and that he "even added certain subjects of his own."[41]

Shamir agreed to certain working principles regarding how to conduct oversight in his secret organizations. First, secrecy was paramount: the state comptroller had to conduct the oversight in a manner compatible with the maximum secrecy required to deal with such issues. Second, a special unit in the state comptroller's office was created, whose personnel had the appropriate security clearances to deal with these matters. Third, the oversight plan had to be coordinated and accepted by the heads of Israel's secret organizations. Fourth, disagreements that could not be resolved at the working level were to be resolved jointly by the state comptroller and the prime minister. Yaari pointed out that since this agreement had been made with the prime minister, only "a few" efforts were made to block state oversight in these organizations. Interestingly, it was a decision by the prime minister, not the enactment of the new Basic Law: State Comptroller, that led to the change. In a sense, the law only affirmed what the executive branch had already agreed to.

Since that agreement with the prime minister in 1987 and then the enactment of the Basic Law a year later, fundamental changes were made. The defense division at the state comptroller's office developed and introduced a rigorous system of auditing and oversight of the defense establishment. Yaari claims that he insisted that no area in the huge defense establishment was too sacred, or too classified, for thorough oversight. As a demonstration, the state comptroller's office has established a permanent presence at Dimona, as well as at a few other sensitive facilities.[42]

According to Yaari and others, the state comptroller's office normally issues two detailed reports a year on each of Israel's three main secret organizations. In addition to the annual report (issued in July), these special reports focus on well-defined subjects that the state comptroller's office finds worth investigating. The reports have the highest level of classification that exists at the state comptroller's office and is compatible with these organizations' security arrangement. Very few people have access to these reports. Unlike the more routine classified reports on the defense establishment that the state comptroller's office issues, which include a declassified summary, very few copies of the special reports are issued, and all are highly classified. Indeed, sometimes these reports have been considered so sensitive that they are not even shared with the Knesset. Yaari and others refused to provide examples or to be more concrete in their comments on the process.

Attitudes in the IAEC have changed as well. The IAEC's current leadership proudly insists (off the record) that the old culture of contempt and scorn toward state oversight is nearly extinct. While conceding that for decades, the IAEC had been governed by the culture of a state within a state, they maintain that this is no longer the case today. They maintain that the IAEC now is subjected to more scrupulous measures of outside oversight than ever before. Amimut as a policy, they claim, is not incompatible with democratic governance; it is not fundamentally different from other areas of national security that require secrecy. The IAEC's leader claims that the existence of state oversight, along with measures of parliamentary oversight (see next section), confirms that amimut is not antithetical to democratic governance.

Is this claim true? Notwithstanding the many improvements, state oversight under amimut is still problematic in at least two ways, one more procedural and the other more substantive. On the procedural side, amimut forces the state oversight process to be as invisible and as secretive as the agencies it oversees. There is a paradox here: no other state agency raises the democratic flag of openness and transparency higher than the state comptroller's office.[43] By definition, it is committed to releasing to the public as many of its findings as possible, and if open reports are impossible, it is committed to making a special effort to produce declassified summaries. But because of amimut and its absolutist requirements, the nuclear issue is exempt. Hence, the commitment to amimut defeats the idea of democratic oversight.

On the substantive side, the oversight process as defined by Israeli law focuses primarily on legality and "due process," but amimut forces these issues to be opaque and poorly defined. The whole point of amimut is to prevent Israel from acknowledging that it has nuclear weapons. It is designed to create a public discourse that avoids, ignores, or bypasses this fact. This policy effort leaves a legal and jurisdictional void. Issues of legality and due process must be measured and assessed in accordance with a set of laws. But there are no laws in this area at all, and all the existing rules and procedures are classified and some are probably opaque, which makes determining due process difficult.

Although my point is a bit abstract, it relates to concrete issues (but they are invisible to outsiders). Here is one example. The former MALMAB chief, Yechiel Horev, made it clear that the source of his extraordinary power regarding nuclear matters was directly derived from a secret cabinet decision that had appointed him the security czar of everything nuclear. Horev appeared to insist that his mandate went beyond facilities and organizations and covered amimut as a policy. In response to questions, Horev indicated that this authority was given to him in a secret document by a former minister of defense that related to an agreement between the prime minister and the minister of defense. Even if such a decision, or document, does exist, was the authority given to him by way of due process? Was such an authority legal? Has the state comptroller ever exercised effective oversight of the MALMAB's operations?

Ultimately, there remains the final question of the legal status of amimut itself. Has the state comptroller ever scrutinized the legality of amimut? Would any state comptroller dare to question such a key pillar of Israel's national security policy? Would any state comptroller ever dare to question such a national taboo?

Parliamentary Oversight

Finally, there is the Knesset, the Israeli parliament, which is the other body in the Israeli governance system with oversight authority. Despite being defined by law as "the representative body of the state," the Knesset is a rather weak parliament in terms of its power or influence over the executive branch. Israel's founding father, Prime Minister David Ben-Gurion, designed it that way. He saw the role of the Knesset largely as a symbol of national sovereignty, not a body that oversees the executive branch. Borrowing from the British constitutional system, Ben-Gurion did not view the Knesset as a true partner of the executive branch, a structural weakness that is most apparent in matters of national security. Israel's Basic Law: The Army does not even refer to the Knesset, and unlike other legislatures, the Knesset has no war power.

The Knesset's Defense and Foreign Affairs Committee (DFAC) reflects this basic weakness. The DFAC has always been the Knesset's most prestigious committee, but for decades it functioned as a House of Lords for respected politicians without an executive job: a mini-parliament whose members occasionally received privileged information and expressed their opinions but had no power to act. The phrase *parliamentary control* (or *oversight*) was understood in those days to be almost entirely symbolic, that is, passive access to information.[44] In a 1992 interview, Haim Zadok, chair of the DFAC in the early 1970s, described the committee's predicament:

> Unlike the Finance Committee, which has a well-defined statutory mandate of legislation, the DFAC has a very limited role in legislation, and most of it involves overseeing the executive branch. But the executive branch has no need for the DFAC in doing its job, unlike the need it has in the Finance Committee for making the budget possible. The DFAC is the most prestigious committee, but its ability to influence the government's action is highly limited. Parliamentary oversight is receiving information. . . . I am not sure if they tell us everything, but they tell us something.[45]

However, and without changing the fundamentals of Israel's constitutional framework, since the late 1970s the DFAC has become a more meaningful player in the realm of national security. Moshe Arens made the first move in that direction while serving as the DFAC chair after the 1977 election. The former aeronautics engineer, who until his election had been involved in classified national security research and development (he was almost appointed the IAEC's director general in 1971), realized that the way the DFAC functioned made it not much more than a debating society, not a forum where top defense officials could discuss serious and classified security matters. Arens decided to overhaul the DFAC by reorganizing its work into a few areas of parliamentary concern. Accordingly, he established five permanent small subcommittees, each in charge of a well-defined area of defense activities. Years later, reflecting on his reform, Arens proudly noted, "Without creating those subcommittees, the Knesset would have remained without any parliamentary oversight whatsoever."[46]

Since then, there has been a trend to strengthen the DFAC's parliamentary control. The committee now has more resources, more professional staff, and more part-time advisers and conducts more outside research, but the overall structure of Arens's overhaul has remained largely unchanged. By now, most of the DFAC's oversight work, primarily in the form of briefings, hearings, and reports on specific national security issues, takes place in those smaller subcommittees. There now are seven official subcommittees (instead of five at Arens's time), each with a handful of members.[47] The names of those subcommittees have changed over the years, but most of their functional boundaries remain the same.[48] According to a former chair of the committee, Yuval Steinitz, the DFAC chair is now privy to most of the classified documents that the Israeli defense bureaucracy produces at the national level.[49]

The further the DFAC has penetrated the defense bureaucracy, the more it has become concerned about its own secrecy. Hearings in most of the subcommittees are now designated "top secret."[50] Sometime in late 2004, chairman Steinitz issued new and elaborate secrecy regulations. Among them are requiring members to turn off and remove the batteries from their mobile phones during sessions. Members are allowed to review classified, sensitive material only in the DFAC secure room; members are not permitted to give interviews to the media next to the committee room while sessions are in progress. A veteran senior field security army officer was hired to oversee the security precautions.[51]

Finally there is the *sanctum sanctorum* of all, the tiny subcommittee without a public face that oversees those subjects that cannot even be stated. In 1992 during an interview, when I asked former chairman Arens what parliamentarian oversight had the DFAC exercised over the nuclear issue, he looked at me, grinned and replied, "This I will not discuss with you." Not much has changed since then. The little we know about this subcommittee, all off the record, is that at one time it was named Strategic Affairs Subcommittee, but it was also known as the Special Means Subcommittee. Evidently, here, too, the word *nuclear* is a taboo.

As it was in Arens's time, this mini-subcommittee is chaired by the chair of the DFAC, along with two or three members that he chooses. Not only that: the nuclear subcommittee is not even mentioned in the "founding document" concerning secrecy. When a *Ha'aretz* reporter asked Steinitz, then the chairman, why that committee was not mentioned in the document, he responded: "There are sensitive issues that we decided to include in another [classified] document, to be disclosed only to a limited staff. Some of the rules of secrecy will be included as part of this internal document." And in answer to a question whether the Knesset has any oversight over the Dimona reactor, Steinitz stated,

> Oversight of the reactor is carried out according to tradition, by the chairman of the committee. Since I entered office some two years ago, I have been overseeing this subject. I visited the reactor accompanied by experts, and I gained the impression that it is in good hands, in terms of safety.[52]

This quotation says it all. It highlights the democratic cost of amimut in parliamentary terms. Can anyone believe that one or even two visits by the tiny supersecret subcommittee to Dimona, even if accompanied by cleared experts, constitute adequate parliamentarian oversight of the nation's primary nuclear facility? Indeed, there is no better way to silence critical voices in the Knesset than to take the DFAC chair on a guided tour of Dimona.

Here is another example of the unique status of the nuclear issue: In September 2003 the speaker of the Knesset (Reuben Rivlin) and the DFAC chair (Yuval Steinitz) appointed a public commission, chaired by a former minister (and former parliamentarian) and constitutional scholar, Amnon Rubinstein, to examine the parliamentary oversight of the defense establishment and to propose ways of improving it. In December 2004, after thirteen sessions and a dozen witnesses, the commission issued its sixteen-page public report. After invoking the "politically correct" buzz phrases that praise both *kdushat habita-chon* and transparency as cherished democratic values, the document noted that current parliamentary oversight of Israel's defense establishment was "partial, flawed and arbitrary."[53] Still, one subject was totally missing from the report: the nuclear issue. In defining the scope of the parliamentary oversight of "the defense establishment," the commission named only the IDF and the intelligence secret services (Mossad, GSS).

In the United States, the Congress, as an elected institution, traditionally supports less secrecy and more openness on matters of national security. In the area of nuclear weapons, especially after the cold war, Congress made a detailed examination of virtually every major nuclear decision, and it periodically decides not to appropriate funds for certain nuclear projects. In Israel, in comparison, a much weaker Knesset is hardly a meaningful partner, and yet it is a bastion of nuclear secrecy. Without grasping the societal dimension of amimut, this cannot be understood.

Final Reflections

Some years ago, Dan Margalit, an influential Israeli journalist, described the profound changes he had witnessed in Israel over the years:

> The Israel in which I started my career as a journalist had built the atomic reactor in Dimona in ways that [today] would have resulted in the imprisonment of David Ben-Gurion and his lieutenants. In the 1990s, with current media exposure, investigative journalism, and criticism, the nuclear reactor would have never been built.[54]

In one sense, Margalit is correct. *Kdushat habitachon* is no longer above the law today in Israel. Ben-Gurion and his lieutenants were able to realize the Dimona project because they pursued it using a modus operandi that today would have been not just undemocratic but criminally unacceptable. In fact, in today's Israel such methods would also be bureaucratically impossible. The nuclear program is now under the rule of law.

The defenders of amimut argue that amimut is compatible with the rule of law and that the Israeli bargain with the atom is not undemocratic. Not only does the Israeli citizenry want amimut, they argue, but the current practice of amimut is compatible with democratic governance and the rule of law. If there were contradictions in the past, they now have been straightened out. Everything we do now, they say, we do under the rule of law. To illustrate their point, they contend that the nuclear program is subjected now to more rigorous external oversight and auditing, by both the state comptroller's office and the Knesset, than at any previous time. This oversight is consistent with the requirements of state secrecy, but it is not much different from the oversight that requires secrecy.

Others make the point in a more reformist slant. Although they are aware of the essential tension between amimut and the ideals of democratic control, they believe that the generic tension can be reduced to the minimum necessary. They believe that within the strictly defined parameters of amimut, there is still room for additional changes in the areas of oversight and accountability. From this reformist perspective, much has already been changed, and there is still room for even more democratic change.

I disagree with such claims. Putting aside the distant past, I argue that amimut continues to violate basic democratic values of governance, including due process and the rule of law. I contend, as I do in this chapter, that by its very insistence on total nonacknowledgment, amimut allows Israel to create areas of ambiguity and a lack of explicitness, both of which are inherently incompatible with due process. In contemporary liberal democracies, oversight is critical to democratic governance as both a symbol and a practice. As a symbol, oversight shows that the executive branch is under the democratic control of the people. As a practice, oversight is part of the democratic system of checks and balances. Much of the democratic value of the oversight process lies in its public nature. It is the transparency that makes oversight truly democratic.

But amimut is the enemy of democratic transparency. Whatever reforms have been made, almost all are classified and virtually nothing is visible. With no visibility, it is impossible to assess the level of change and reform. Moreover, from the tiny bit that is visible (e.g., from the IAEC's Web site), it is obvious how little the culture of supersecrecy has changed.

The absence of a law governing the IAEC in itself is inconsistent with contemporary ideas of the rule of law. More than half a century after Israel founded its national nuclear energy organization, its legality is not regulated by a real law but by the residual-power clause. This means that this organization's activities are lawful not because of a law but because they are government actions. It is primarily amimut that is responsible for this anachronistic and undemocratic arrangement. Only a new bargain would reform nuclear affairs in Israel and make them more democratic.

Chapter Eight
Domestic Reforms

Israel's bargain with the bomb comprises two conceptually distinct clusters of issues: strategic/international and domestic/democratic. These two clusters are not equal in their significance. The strategic/international issues are the driver, dominating and shaping the bargain. The domestic/democratic issues are the consequence, the unavoidable price that Israel pays for the bargain. Security has been the goal; everything else was secondary.

As pointed out in the last two chapters, the bargain with the bomb is at odds with Israel's commitment to democratic norms and practice (by Israel's commitment to democracy, I am referring to Israel within its pre-1967 borders) at home and even norms of international transparency abroad. Amimut undermines Israeli democracy, placing it at the far end of the spectrum of all nuclear democracies.

Can this domestic anomaly be repaired? Would it be possible to reform the bargain domestically, that is, to reduce its cost to democracy but without compromising amimut's strategic/international benefits? What might such a reform look like, and would it be possible or sufficient to "normalize" the bargain? In this chapter, I focus on two directions that could have a significant effect on the bargain at home: nuclear legislation and liberalization of the practice of the Censora. These reforms would reduce the tension between the requirements of amimut and the values of democracy, and they can be carried out incrementally and without entailing a premature and formal departure from the conduct of amimut. Because these reforms would not require a formal Israeli disclosure, they should be more readily acceptable internationally.

Road Map for a New Domestic Bargain

Nuclear Legislation

The most democratically symbolic way of indicating that Israel is seeking a new and more open bargain with its nuclear weapons would be through legislation. Only an act of legislation would place the nuclear issue under the rule of law.

To have a feel for how Israel is exceptional in lacking nuclear legislation, one should start with a comparison with the way other democracies govern their nuclear affairs. In the United States, the first democracy that developed nuclear weapons, the civilian leaders of the Manhattan Project were committed from the very beginning to the notion that after the war, the secret military project would be handed to civilian control through an act of legislation. It was apparent that the nature of nuclear affairs requires unprecedented governmental secrecy, but it was also understood that this secrecy—and the new civilian organization that would guard it—must be governed and regulated by law. Throughout the spring of 1946, even before political decisions were made in the international arena about the future of the atom (i.e., the Baruch Plan), Congress debated and passed the Atomic Energy Act of 1946 (known also as the McMahon Act).[1]

The Atomic Energy Act determined how the U.S. federal government should set up a new kind of governance, what was called in those days the "government of the atom," that would manage, control, guard and oversee the nuclear complex. Even if the "government of the atom" operated in some ways as a semiautonomous kingdom of secrecy, this governance was established by law. Most significantly, the act determined that the nuclear complex would be managed under a new civilian authority, not under the military. The act also established the terms of congressional oversight. The act was signed by President Harry S. Truman on August 1, 1946 (just about a year after the United States dropped atomic bombs on Japan), and went into effect on January 1, 1947.[2]

One year later, the United States reorganized its entire national security establishment through another landmark piece of legislation, the National Security Act of 1947, which also established the Central Intelligence Agency (CIA). These two key pieces of legislation reinforced the concept that America's most secret national security organizations must be subject to the rule of law.

Today, more than six decades after the United States pioneered the first piece of nuclear legislation, nearly every democratic nuclear state has crafted its own nuclear legislation. The Web site of the Organization for Economic Cooperation and Development (OECD) provides details of the nuclear legislation of some thirty liberal-democratic states (all are NPT signatories, including the three NPT declared-weapons states: France, the United Kingdom, and the United States).[3] Although the legislative differences among all these countries are significant, they all reflect the recognition that liberal democracies should manage their bargain with the atom under the rule of law: nuclear affairs should be handled in a transparent fashion; national nuclear activities must be governed and overseen by national laws; nuclear matters are important enough to require a national regulatory regime, and the law must govern such a regime.

Israeli Exceptionalism

Israel is an exception to this pattern. In chapters 4 and 7, I discussed the legal vacuum surrounding Israel's state nuclear organization. Briefly, Israel's primary nuclear organization, the Israel Atomic Energy Commission (IAEC), was founded by a secret order issued by Prime Minister David Ben-Gurion in 1952 and was reorganized into its current form in 1966 by a presumably similar set of executive orders. But the IAEC is not anchored in any act of legislation. Israel lacks a law that governs the management of its nuclear affairs; Israel does not even have any other *public*, semilegal, document determining the legality of issues such executive responsibility, jurisdiction, and authority at the IAEC.

The reasons for this Israeli exceptionalism are many and complex; some antedate and go deeper than the issue of amimut as a national code of nuclear conduct. As noted in the last chapter, their roots are grounded in an old Israeli tradition of how a state runs its secret national security organizations. For a long time the prevailing Israeli governance philosophy was that all secret national security organizations should be exempt from the scrutiny of the law, that by their nature and function these organizations reside outside the law. That is, in the most sensitive areas of national security the government should be free to act without well-defined legal constraints. Such activities belong to the twilight zone of the law.

This attitude typified Prime Minister Ben-Gurion's thinking, and it explains the tradition he founded, a tradition that has been upheld by his successors to this day: civilian organizations of national security fall under the direct ministerial responsibility of the prime minister. The legality of these secret organizations is derived directly from the legality of the state itself, the power of the government to act. These secret organizations embody the power of the state. As noted in the last chapter, this legitimacy is established constitutionally through the "residual power clause," clause 32 in the current version of Israel's Basic Law: The Government.[4] This clause gives the government far-reaching legal power: it provides the government with the authority to act on behalf of the state in any way it sees fit, as long as that authority is not conferred by existing law on any other entity and is not challenged by any supreme court ruling. It effectively grants legality to all governmental actions, as long as those actions are not in conflict with any other law. It is a legal device that precludes any legal vacuum in regard to government action.[5]

As noted in the last two chapters, this legal and societal outlook has been in retreat in the last two decades. There has been growing interest in Israel in bringing the security sector to the rule of law. The two landmark pieces of legislation in this area—the GSS Law (2002) and the National Security Council Law (2008)—are the prime products of this change. Public discussion about extending the rule of law, however, has never reached Israel's most secret organization, the IAEC. The special status of Israel's nuclear organization within the Israeli bureaucracy and the public, an agency whose secrecy is even more sanctified than that of the Mossad, has made the notion of an IAEC law unthinkable. In a way, there is a paradox in drafting such a law: to draft such a law one needs to know a great deal about the organization and its mission, but such knowledge, under amimut, is classified and hence unknowable.

For this and other reasons, there has never been public discussion about, or even interest in, drafting an IAEC law. The issue was apparently never raised for serious public debate in academia, the government, or the Knesset. Inside and outside government, there is no constituency that could promote such a law in the media. This is one more unfortunate consequence of the culture of amimut. Despite all the talk in the Israeli press in recent years about the "rule of law," nobody in the Israeli legal establishment has yet proposed such a law. This is the direct result of the dual nature of opacity: a consensus-based governmental policy, on the one hand, and a broad-based, taboolike societal prohibition against discussing nuclear matters, on the other.

Amimut and the Legal Reality

It is not merely that the IAEC and its activities are not anchored in the law. Rather, it is the very policy of amimut, in particular its insistence on not acknowledging Israel's possession of nuclear weapons, that exacerbates an already flawed legal situation. Under amimut the Israeli legal system is prohibited from dealing straightforwardly with the most defining aspect of the nation's nuclear reality. Accordingly, the Israeli legal system is incapable of addressing the serious implications of Israel's nuclear status. If the reality itself is unacknowledged and cannot even be stated directly, the legal system cannot address its legal consequences.

The result is a legal limbo. It appears that legal concerns critical to the executive control of the nation's nuclear complex cannot be dealt with adequately because they are not covered—indeed, they cannot even be stated—by the legal system. Presumably a variety of issues involving executive authority over custodianship of nuclear weapons are not covered directly by the legal system. The point I am making here is not that because the facts are classified, their legal discussion is also classified and must take place behind closed doors. Rather, it is that amimut makes it difficult to generate a legal discourse that would be adequate to these matters.

While we do not know this empirically, there are theoretical reasons to believe that amimut creates a strong bureaucratic tendency within the system to ignore complex *legal* issues such as responsibility and accountability regarding the nuclear complex and its products, and to address these issues primarily on the administrative level.

Serious public discussion of legislation on nuclear issues should no longer be postponed. It is time for Israel to end treating the nuclear issue as something whose legality is derived from the residual power of the government, which confers sweeping rights on the executive authority. The nuclear domain is just too important to be addressed by the government's residual power; it is a large and sensitive domain of governmental action that requires a legal standing of its own through legislation by the Knesset. The significance of such legislation is twofold: symbolism (demonstrating that the rule of law reaches even the most secretive organization in the Israeli government) and practicality (better governance and oversight).

What Should Nuclear Legislation Look Like?

Any law governing the IAEC would have great symbolic value, but its practical benefits would depend on how explicit and detailed it was. Specifically, much would depend on how clearly the law addressed the IAEC's mandate.

National security legislation in the past—the enactment of the GSS law in 2002 and the National Security Act in 2008—has demonstrated the feasibility of legislating on sensitive matters of national security.[6] At the least, nuclear legislation must address the legal status of the IAEC as the government's nuclear agency: its overall mission, authority, subordination, oversight, and so on. Such a law should also define the statutory authority of the prime minister over nuclear affairs; the working relationship between the prime minister and the IAEC; the system of executive oversight of policies and activities; supervision principles through the Knesset; issues of safety in the IAEC facilities; and more.[7] The greatest challenge of drafting such a law would be finding formulations that balanced the requirements of the Israeli government's nuclear policy with the need for regulation.

At present, the notion of an IAEC law is anathema to Israel's nuclear establishment, as they perceive it as incompatible with amimut. They fear that elevating the salience of Israel's doomsday weapons would damage both the country's national security interests and international and regional stability.

Initiating nuclear legislation would be a departure from the old bargain and would likely have some impact on the policy itself, but it would not necessarily bring a formal end to the current amimut policy. An IAEC law could be drafted in several formulations, with various degrees of vagueness or explicitness. In its minimal version such legislation could be drafted in a manner that would remain compatible with today's amimut discourse.

Three considerations are relevant to the opponents' concerns. First, by its very nature, legislative deliberation is slow, with many individuals and agencies involved. Fifteen years went by from the time the state commission of inquiry, headed by the former supreme court justice Moshe Landau, submitted its report on GSS interrogations (1987) until the law was passed and enacted in 2002.

Second, such legislation need not require a formal end to amimut. If the state of Israel were not politically ready to move beyond the current boundaries of amimut, no act of legislation could force it to do so. Accordingly, such legislation could substantially modify or redefine amimut or could be compatible with amimut as it now is. Most important is that such legislation provide some sort a legal standing for the nuclear organization.

Third, while legislation on such a sensitive matter with implications for Israel's international nuclear policy may require some consultation with outside parties, it is difficult to see how any foreign power could oppose the process for political reasons. Foreign countries do not normally interfere in domestic legislation, and if they have reservations, they presumably would be made discreetly.

Reforming the Censora

Domestic reform that altered the Israeli bargain with the bomb would mean also changing the Censora's practice. Here, too, the reform would have both symbolic and practical significance. Israel's Censora is the institution most directly involved in enforcing and perpetuating the special features of the bargain. The Censora is the embodiment of the country's nuclear taboo, that is, the enforcer of the prohibition of discussing Israel's possession of nuclear weapons in public.

Because I examined the Censora's role in guarding amimut in chapters 4 and 5, I will summarize it here in two observations. First, of the three institutional guardians of amimut, the Censora has probably been weakened the most. As an institution, its power and impact have steadily declined over the last two decades, from the supreme court ruling in the Schnitzer case in 1989 to the Second Lebanon War in the summer of 2006. Its decline is the result of domestic and global trends: Israel has become more of a civil society that no longer accepts *kdushat habitachon* as the ultimate societal maxim, and the world media now use new and easily accessible communication technologies (primarily Internet based) that make the world more transparent and also make the censor's work nearly impossible.

The other observation is that the task of protecting amimut stands out as the most striking exception to this general loss of power. On this single issue alone, the Censora is almost as powerful as it was in its heyday. Here, it still controls the Israeli national discourse by enforcing amimut as the proper way in which all Israelis must write about nuclear affairs. Guarding amimut is probably the Censora's most important activity and probably explains why Israel is still the only liberal democracy in the world that has an institutionalized military censor. I also suggested (in chapter 5) that the Censora's apparent strength on this issue is due mainly to the status of amimut itself. That is, the media on behalf of its public *want* to be censored on this matter.

Furthermore, few people in Israel know that the Censora's effectiveness has little to do with protecting true nuclear secrets. Rather than guarding nuclear secrets, the Censora mostly protects the rituals of the discourse of amimut. The Censora mainly enforces the discourse of amimut, making sure that banned phrases like *nuclear weapons* are changed to softer and more ambiguous phrases like *nuclear option, nuclear capability,* and the like; or, alternatively, attributing the banned phrases to "foreign sources."[8]

What about guarding real nuclear secrets, such as secret nuclear facilities, details of the command-and-control system, the size of the arsenal, the design of Israel's weapons, and the like? The truth is that such material is hardly ever submitted to the Censora because it is not available to journalists. Such classified information is so well guarded that Israeli journalists and analysts do not have access to it, and on those very rare occasions that outsiders gain access to it, the Israeli media would not dare to touch it.

I propose two possible ways of reforming the Censora. Both would result in reducing amimut and the amimut discourse but without requiring a full, official nuclear disclosure. They would not end amimut as a state policy but would be essentially a domestic liberalization of the Censora's practice; it would not be a political departure by the Israeli government from the amimut policy but a change in societal discourse. As such, these reforms would not leave much room for non-Israelis—Arab states, the nonproliferation orthodoxy, and so on—to oppose.

The first proposal is limited in that it calls only for amending the Censora's current practice regarding amimut. The proposal calls for treating Israeli writers in the same way as their overseas counterparts. The idea is to allow the Israeli media to refer to Israel factually as a nuclear-armed state just as their overseas colleagues do. At the same time, Israeli officials (and former officials) would continue to speak about the nuclear subject with the same caution that they do now, and the censor would continue to ensure that they do.

Such a reform would not be viewed as an official Israeli nuclear disclosure because it is not. It would be presented as no more than an internal reform that was aimed at free speech, but not as a change in the country's nuclear policy. Yet this change of practice would have a significant effect by normalizing Israel's nuclear discourse. Just as the foreign media assume that Israel is a nuclear-armed state, so, too, would the Israeli press.

Indeed, *Ha'aretz* also made this suggestion in an editorial that was published on September 6, 1998, for the occasion of the release of my book *Israel and the Bomb.* The editorial asserted that the Censora's practice of amimut was too restricted and too anachronistic, that it did not fit the values of Israeli democracy and should be modified. Although the editorial supported the official policy of amimut, it argued that the policy should be enforced only on those officially representing the state of Israel itself: "The nuclear ambiguity is based on policies and actions of the government, and not on censoring journalistic and academic publications."[9]

If this proposal sounds too restrictive and exclusive to the nuclear issue, the other proposal is democratically more promising, as it calls for Israel to abolish the office of the Censora in its present form. This proposal was made in 1993 by Hanoch Marmari, then *Ha'aretz*'s editor in chief.[10] Marmari suggested that Israel should abolish the institution of the Censora as we know it, that is, abolishing the principle of prepublication censorship review. Along with the abolition of the current Censora, Marmari proposed strengthening the national security secrecy aspects of Israeli criminal law. This could be done by adding a clause stating that whoever publishes information that, with near certainty would substantially harm national security, would be charged with a major national security offense.

In addition, Marmari proposed that the Censora's current bureaucratic apparatus be replaced by a smaller liaison office for information security affiliated with the entire defense establishment, which would provide guidance to the media and others on issues of information security but would not enforce a formal obligation to submit material for prepublication review. In other words, Marmari's proposal would transfer the Censora's responsibility to the publishers, guided by the belief that in a liberal democracy there is no room for a Censora and that it is time for Israel to join the rest of the Western world on this matter.[11]

Gradual elimination, or even abolition, of the Censora would not mean the end of secrecy regarding national security. Such secrecy would remain as it has in all other democracies that do not have military censorship. All the national security laws would stay intact, if not even reinforced, to prevent the leaking of classified information. From time to time, there undoubtedly would be leaks, but leaks are part of a democratic system. Official government spokespersons could always respond with no comment, neither confirming nor denying the leaked information.

Such a proposal would, however, end the anachronistic and undemocratic practice in which the government censors the Israeli discourse on nuclear affairs. If the Censora's function in protecting amimut is political and not related to security (i.e., demonstrating to the world via the Censora that Israel and the Israeli media have not changed their practice of amimut), abolishing the Censora's prepublication review would relieve Israel of needing to make such a demonstration. If there were no Censora, there would be no way to show that the Israeli discourse on nuclear matters is, well, censored.

The official policy of amimut might continue at the official government level, but Israeli discourse would be freed from the Censora's pronouncements on the official amimut discourse. It would not be the end of appropriate nuclear secrecy, which could be reinforced, but it would be the end of amimut discourse in regard to national security.

Final Reflections

Supporters of amimut in Israel (and elsewhere) tend to believe that any visible change in the bargain's domestic parameters would inevitably undermine amimut and thus would damage not only Israel's own existential security but even threaten international and regional security. Modifying amimut, they argue, could undermine the nonproliferation regime's ability to confront the Iranian nuclear issue, as Israel would be perceived as raising its nuclear profile, making it more difficult to demand that Iran abstain from developing its own nuclear weapons.

These are legitimate concerns that should be taken seriously. The first priority in dealing with amimut is akin to the Hippocratic Oath of "first, do no harm." If reforming the bargain would have harmful international consequences, it would be self-defeating. But these concerns should not prevent new thinking. The following are six heuristics for how to reform amimut in a manner that would do no harm, that would not have negative international repercussions.

1. Separate the domestic and the international sides of the bargain. Although both sides relate to and interact with each other, the two should be separated as much as possible. The more domestically driven the reform appears, the fewer and less likely the international risks would be. Since much of the motivation for reform is to correct democratic flaws in the bargain, domestic considerations should take priority. In general, the domestic front is more hospitable to reforms, as here Israel can move relatively freely with less need to consult international players.

2. Treat domestic reforms of amimut not as a radical departure from established policy but as a change in Israeli discourse. Although amimut functions as both policy and culture, it is better to introduce changes as cultural.

3. Make the reform process guarded and incremental. At the end of the process, a complete transition to a new, post-amimut bargain may look like a change in gestalt, but it should be introduced piecemeal.

4. Delay a formal political policy statement to the very end of the process. A move into a post-amimut environment should begin with measured domestic reforms within the bargain that in themselves do not necessarily require a political statement from the prime minister. At the end, there would be a political statement acknowledging Israel's nuclear status, but this would require special political timing. In any case, such an acknowledgment would be a political statement changing the entire bargain and thus would fall on the strategic/international side.

5. Recognize that Israel cannot change the entire bargain on its own, that it needs support from democratic friends outside the country, especially the United States. Changing the fundamentals of the bargain is not merely a domestic issue but a major political undertaking with international and strategic implications. Even relatively uncontroversial domestic changes would require some consultation with outside powers, especially the United States. Domestic moves need to be transparent so as to make it clear that Israel's intentions and motivations for change are peaceful.

6. *Be mindful of what the transition should* not *do*. India (and then Pakistan) ended their semi-amimut posture in 1998 by surprising the world with a series of nuclear tests, followed by a political statement asserting their right to possess nuclear weapons. Whatever Israel considers doing to come clean, it must not include a nuclear test, with the only possible exception being a response to an Iranian test of a nuclear device.

Finally, notwithstanding all the arguments presented in the last two chapters about the domestic shortcomings of Israel's bargain with the bomb and the moderate nature of the reforms proposed in this chapter, I know that the prospects of instituting such domestic/democratic reforms are not good. The bargain may be anachronistic and amimut may be flawed, but as long as Israelis still believe that the bargain is necessary for the nation's existential security and that amimut is indispensable to this bargain, there is little chance that it will change.

Amimut's great success reflects a societal state of mind. As long as Israelis continue to view themselves as living under a state of siege, they will not be interested in reforming a bargain that, they believe, gives them that existential security. Given Israelis' belief that Iran's nuclear program constitutes an existential threat to Israel, reforms for the sake of democracy are not likely. For such reforms to have any chance of succeeding, they must be seen as compatible with national security.

Chapter Nine
Iran, the Fissile Materials Cutoff Treaty (FMCT), and Beyond

The fate of Israel's bargain with the bomb, particularly the future of amimut, will not be decided by normative arguments about democracy or legislative reforms, but by arguments about national security and by the decisions of national leaders. The future of amimut hinges on some fundamental judgments. First, on its continued value to Israel: is amimut still beneficial to Israel's national security? Second, on its indispensability: are there any politically acceptable alternatives? Finally, on outside pressure: do other countries, especially the United States, want Israel to keep or end the practice of amimut?

At the present time, the answers to all these questions firmly support the continuation of amimut. As to the first question, Israelis believe that amimut best serves their national interest and provides them with existential security at the lowest price. On the second question, it is commonly believed by Israelis and others that at the present time there is no realistic alternative to amimut. Besides Israel, many countries favor amimut for the same reason it was seen as beneficial forty years ago: it gives Israel security while allowing the international community to look the other way at little cost. Thus as to the final question, there is currently no pressure on Israel to consider changing the bargain.

Underlying these judgments is the equivocation between amimut as a declaratory posture and Israel's ability to possess the bomb, which makes amimut so powerful. Because Israelis see amimut as a national security asset, they identify amimut with the nuclear arsenal itself, and this link between the nuclear arsenal and the policy and culture of amimut makes unmaking it so difficult.

This view has been strengthened as Israel carefully watches Iran approaching the nuclear threshold. As preparations for the eventuality of a nuclear Iran progress, (most) Israelis maintain that until Iran crosses the threshold Israel should adhere to its amimut. That is, as long as Iran does not move from what it describes as its peaceful nuclear activity to an overt nuclear military posture, Israel should keep amimut. Amimut keeps Israel's own nuclear profile low and makes linking Israel's nuclear situation to Iran's more difficult.

Still, given the volatility of the global nuclear situation, in particular the Iranian situation, the future of amimut is uncertain. It is conceivable, even plausible under some circumstances, that any resolution of the Iranian nuclear crisis could reverse the old fundamentals of the Israeli bargain. Those fundamentals are robust but not static. While one cannot predict the future, one ought to reflect about the future. Any major development on the Iranian nuclear scene is likely to shape the future of the Israeli bargain.

This chapter explores trends and issues related to the global and regional nuclear scene that are relevant to Israel's bargain with the bomb. While explaining why Israel would not be likely to consider in the near term any significant changes in its bargain with the bomb, especially not ending amimut, I also argue why in the middle and long terms it would be in Israel's best interest to consider such changes. In one way or another, developments in Iran are likely to shape the future of the Israeli bargain.

New Global Trends and Israel's Nuclear Bargain

More than six decades after the United States dropped nuclear bombs on Hiroshima and Nagasaki, the two aspects of the nuclear age, weapons and power, are being revisited.[1] Fundamentals are again being debated. The Baruch Plan was rejected in 1947, but its vision of a world without nuclear weapons is now seriously being rediscussed, and the cause of nuclear disarmament may now receive a second chance.[2] In January 2007 four members of the American national security establishment—former Secretaries of State George Schultz and Henry Kissinger, former Secretary of Defense William Perry, and former Senator Sam Nunn—invoked the old vision as a new realistic objective for America and the world.[3] The American "gang of four" was followed by other former prominent figures in the United Kingdom, Germany, India, and elsewhere.

Both President Barack Obama of the United States, along with his Republican presidential opponent, John McCain, adopted the vision as their own long-term goal as well. In his speech on nuclear nonproliferation in Prague on April 5, 2009, Obama declared, "America's commitment to seek the peace and security of a world without nuclear weapons." As the only nation ever to have used an atomic bomb, he proclaimed that the United States has a "moral responsibility" to remove the threat of mass destruction. "I'm not naïve. This goal will not be reached quickly—perhaps not in my lifetime. It will take patience and persistence. But now we . . . must ignore the voices who tell us that the world cannot change. We have to insist, 'Yes, we can.'"[4]

President Obama has committed to pursuing a nuclear weapons–free world, but his commitment is for the long term. At present, nobody in America or elsewhere has thought out how to free the world of nuclear weapons. Even the optimistic nuclear abolitionists admit that it would take decades, if ever, to achieve the goal of complete nuclear disarmament. Meanwhile, progress toward this goal could easily be thwarted before it has a chance to gain momentum.

If the challenge in the early days (1946/1947) was to devise a political scheme to delegitimize and ban the bomb, thereby moving control of atomic energy to a new, supranational body of global governance, today's challenge is to design a long-term international agenda that would lead to nuclear disarmament. Because horizontal and vertical forms of nuclear proliferation are linked, the best way to prevent the former is to reverse the latter. To persuade key nonnuclear-weapons states to strengthen the nonproliferation regime, particularly by restricting their own access to sensitive nuclear technologies, the nuclear-weapons states must live up to their commitment to nuclear disarmament, as stated in article VI of the Nuclear Non-Proliferation Treaty (NPT), which was subsequently reaffirmed when the NPT became permanent in 1995. An enhanced NPT should make access to these sensitive technologies more difficult, but nonnuclear-weapons states would resist new restrictions on their right to nuclear technology unless the nuclear-weapons states progressed toward disarmament.[5]

There is a twofold tension, if not conflict, between the logic of global nuclear disarmament and amimut. First, the movement toward global nuclear disarmament must include *all* nuclear-weapons states, both those under and outside the NPT, without exception. Israel must be included, whether or not it is a declared nuclear-armed state. Second, the logic of global nuclear disarmament assumes basic (minimal) transparency regarding nuclear status: all nuclear-weapons states must declare their nuclear possessions. Acknowledgment and declaration must precede verification. Nuclear weapons and nuclear energy are connected. Nuclear abolition is conditioned on tighter international safeguards on civilian nuclear energy to make it impossible to divert dual-use materials for bombs. Nuclear power carries the risk of nuclear proliferation, which is heightened by today's concerns about nuclear terrorism. As Robert Oppenheimer observed, "The close technical parallelism and interrelation of the peaceful and military applications of atomic energy" make nonproliferation difficult. Or as Hannes Alfvén, a Swedish physicist and Nobel laureate, pointed out, "Atoms for peace and atoms for war are Siamese twins."[6] This brings us to the trends of today. Along with the revival of nuclear disarmament, there has been a renewed and growing interest in nuclear power. After three decades of stagnation, nuclear energy is making a comeback. Industrial growth in developing countries, rising concerns about climate change, and wild fluctuations in oil prices all are driving this interest. In the Middle East, for example, at least thirteen countries have announced plans to develop civilian nuclear energy. They justify their plans by referring to the need for energy diversification and the economic and environmental benefits of nuclear power. Political factors also have helped renew the interest in nuclear energy, including the prestige and technological balancing of Iran's nuclear program.[7] The revived interest in nuclear energy must still contend with issues such as infrastructure cost, government support, waste, the safety of nuclear energy, and the risk of proliferation. In addition, a new regulative system for better transparency and oversight is needed in an industry known for its resistance to openness. The connection between nuclear energy and proliferation also goes the other way: if the revival of nuclear power leads to weapons proliferation, it will kill the drive toward their abolition. Whether progress toward a world free of nuclear weapons will be affected by the renewed interest in nuclear power is difficult to predict. In any event, how Iran's nuclear capability is handled will influence both issues. Success in preventing Iran from becoming a nuclear-armed state is necessary for any serious move toward global nuclear disarmament; failure would advance the opposite scenario. The outcome also will affect the future of nuclear energy. The Iranian nuclear case has taught the world lessons about the loopholes in the current NPT/IAEA safeguard system, allowing countries to master dual-use fuel-cycle technologies ostensibly for "peaceful purposes" while leaving them very close to the bomb threshold.

These trends could pose long-term challenges for the Israeli bargain, especially for the practice of amimut. One can conceive of two different, even opposite, long-term responses to these new trends. In one scenario, Israel is likely to view the abolition vision with great suspicion. It would be reluctant to make any visible commitment that goes beyond its past verbal commitment to a nuclear weapons–free zone. It is possible that Israel would even tighten its amimut policy to ensure that no external political pressure could force it to disarm prematurely. It is conceivable that Israel would formally link its commitment to amimut to the existence of the Arab-Israeli conflict.

Furthermore, for the sociological reasons discussed earlier, a public call for nuclear disarmament by distinguished Israelis is very unlikely. Thus without a dramatic social change, perhaps in response to radical changes on the Iranian front, Israel would remain without a significant domestic global nuclear-disarmament lobby.

But another scenario is also possible. If a nuclear renaissance becomes a reality in the Middle East, under certain political conditions Israel might be interested in cooperating in the establishment of a regional framework of nuclear control. Given the Israeli interest in preventing the diversion of nuclear material and expertise that could be used for weapons, one could conceive of an Israeli interest in cooperating with others on creating a new structure of mechanisms of nuclear control, in particular banning "sensitive technologies." Such cooperation could be seen as part of a road map toward a nuclear weapons–free zone in the region. Such a system of nuclear control might ultimately also apply to Israeli nuclear facilities. Such a movement would surely have an impact on the Israeli bargain, in particular on amimut. I will return at the end of this chapter to elaborate on these ideas.

In the short term, however, talk about a world without nuclear weapons will only strengthen the consensus behind amimut. Although Israelis may understand the long-term connection between horizontal and vertical proliferation, they do not regard it as applying to their own country. Israel would try to keep out of this discussion. Israelis view Obama's vision of a world without nuclear weapons in a similar fashion to the way they treat their own government's vision of a nuclear weapons–free zone in the Middle East. Both efforts are, for Israelis, not much more than wishful thinking. For Israelis, the nation's nuclear conversation starts and ends with one subject only, Iran.

Israel and the Iranian Nuclear Challenge

Of all the international nuclear-related challenges facing Israel, the most urgent and important is the possibility of a nuclear Iran.[8] Israel's intense response to Iran tells us much about Israel's own existential predicament. The consensus in Israel is that the advent of a nuclear Iran, albeit depending on what this would mean exactly, would pose an unprecedented threat to Israel. For the first time, Israel would confront a hostile state in the region that possesses nuclear weapons.

Is nuclear Iran an existential threat? Often the phrase used to characterize the gravity of nuclear Iran to Israel is "existential threat." But there is no consensus or clarity among Israelis on this term. Until his election in early 2009, Prime Minister Benjamin Netanyahu commonly used this phrase, implying that Israel should be committed to prevent the rise of a nuclear Iran, preferably with cooperation with others but, if necessary, on its own. (Since his election, however, Netanyahu appears to be minimizing the use of this phrase in his public speeches.)[9] Uzi Arad, Netanyahu's national security adviser, continues to use this phrase, however, when he refers to preventing Iran from manufacturing nuclear weapons as an "existential imperative."[10] More recently, Mossad's head, General Meir Dagan, whose organization has the overall responsibility of the Israeli effort to prevent Iran from acquiring such weapons, claimed that if and when Iran developed such weapons, it would pose "a significant existential threat to the state of Israel."[11] Some American civilian and military leaders reiterate this language. For example, Admiral Michael Mullen, chairman of the Joint Chiefs of Staff, declared in November 2009 that it is clear to him "a nuclear weapon in Iran is an existential threat to Israel."[12]

But other Israeli national leaders have reservations about using the term *existential threat* in public. Ehud Barak, the Israeli minister of defense, was cited as declaring, "I am not among those who believe Iran is an existential issue for Israel. Israel is strong, I don't see anyone who could pose an existential threat," although he did note that Iran was a challenge to the whole world.[13] Others, among them the current opposition leader and former foreign minister Tzipi Livni, former Mossad chief Efraim Halevy, and President Shimon Peres, have also expressed misgivings about this term, making the point that they refuse to legitimize statements to the effect that "Israel cannot live" with a nuclear Iran. They all insisted that Israel is a strong state and it could protect itself under any circumstances.[14]

In any way, the Israeli reference to Iran as an existential threat is based on the connection Israelis make between the Iranian regime and its determined pursuit of a nuclear-weapons capability and the regime's extreme open hostility toward Israel, particularly its rejection of its legitimacy as a state.[15] The Israeli-based assessment sees Iran's strategic intentions and capabilities as well formed, homogenous, and well defined, even as it sees Iran as occasionally amorphous and hesitant on matters of political tactics. That is, Israel views Iran as pursuing a full nuclear-weapons capability but also as flexible in the way it manages its strategic pursuit.[16] Furthermore, Israelis' assessments of Iran tend to be more alarmist than those of other countries. The U.S. National Intelligence Estimate (NIE) on Iran in November 2007, which concluded that Iran had halted its overt nuclear weaponization work in 2003, did not alter Israel's basic assessment.[17]

In regard to the second issue, there is an abundance of evidence of the Iranian government's extreme hostility toward Israel. This has been true since the Islamic revolution, but it became more pronounced after the 2005 election of Mahmoud Ahmadinejad as president of Iran. From a historical perspective, Ahmadinejad's statements are a return to the old Arab discourse about the destruction of the Zionist entity, although this discourse is hardly ever found anymore in the Sunni Arab world (some would argue that this is partly due to the existence of the Israeli bomb). The difference between the anti-Israeli rhetoric in Ben-Gurion's era and today's is that now, for the first time, such threats are voiced by a president of a state that is seriously pursuing a nuclear-weapons capability. Moreover, Ahmadinejad's rhetoric is combined with Iran's increasing involvement in other parts of the Middle East, most visibly though Hezbollah in Lebanon and Hamas in the Palestinian territories.[18]

To Israelis, the Iranian nuclear threat is not that Iran may one day drop the bomb on Israel. Most Israeli strategists agree that it is extremely unlikely that Iran, unprovoked, would attack Israel with nuclear weapons because Iranians are aware of the catastrophic consequences of such an act.[19] Rather, a nuclear confrontation between Israel and Iran might arise from misperceptions and miscalculations during a conventional crisis. Israel must also consider the possibility (however low) of an accidental or unauthorized nuclear launch by Iran and the risk of terrorist organizations' acquiring nuclear weapons from Iran.

In the Israeli view, Iran's acquiring a nuclear capability could profoundly change the region's political dynamics. As Uzi Arad pointed out, "We cannot live with a nuclear Iran because a nuclear Middle East would not be the same as the cold war nuclear stalemate. A nuclear Middle East would become a multi-nuclear Middle East, with all that entails." Specifically, the first area of concern is that nuclear weapons could exacerbate concerns about other aspects of Iran's foreign and defense policies by giving rise to more risk-prone and aggressive strategies. A nuclear Iran would pressure the Palestinians and possibly other Arabs (e.g., Syria) to take more extreme positions that would encourage terrorism and make peace negotiations with Israel even more difficult. Under the shadow of its bomb, Iran could become a source of political and military adventurism in the region. Furthermore, a mutual assured destruction (MAD) deterrent situation between Israel and Iran could be destabilizing owing to the differences in size and population of Iran and Israel. Mutual hostility and the lack of communication between the two states would further increase the danger.[20]

The second concern is that if Iran becomes a recognized nuclear state, even opaquely recognized, this could lead to a spiraling nuclear-arms race in the Middle East.[21] Israelis believe that a nuclear Iran would be dangerous because it would undermine the subtle nuclear order currently existing in the Middle East under the facade of Israeli nuclear opacity, possibly even unraveling it. A nuclear Iran would be the end of Israel's nuclear monopoly in the region. Israel would have to declare its capability.[22]

The third concern is the social and psychological impact that a mutual assured destruction–like balance of terror with Iran might have on the Israeli public and its psyche.[23] Some Israeli public figures who push the politics of Iranian scare (such as former Deputy Minister of Defense Ephraim Sneh, journalist Ari Shavit, and academic historian Benny Morris) assert that Iran might be able to "wipe the Zionist state off the map" without actually dropping the bomb.[24] That is, the mere existence of the Iranian bomb or the fear that Iran has the bomb, they argue, might lead Israelis to leave Israel for a friendlier place where their existence is not threatened. After the Holocaust, Sneh argues, Jews would have no desire to live in the shadow of an Iranian bomb, waiting for another Holocaust. Those who have the means to leave would leave. Likud Party leader and Israel's current prime minister, Benjamin Netanyahu, has pushed this line of reasoning to its ultimate limit by comparing President Ahmadinejad with Hitler.[25]

The Iranian Challenge

From an Israeli perspective, perhaps the most fundamental feature of dealing with the Iranian nuclear issue is understanding the nature of the problem and internalizing Israeli political and military limitations of acting alone. One may call it the choice between going alone versus forming an alliance. The Israeli government realizes that the challenge the Iranian nuclear issue poses to Israel will force it to think in a way very different from the familiar old way Israel used to think about its national security. Israel has very limited room to act truly alone on this issue. Israel must act on this issue with others, mostly the United States. While Israel is a major stakeholder on the Iranian issue, major decisions are ultimately made by others. Its power of dissent is limited, and Israel must be very cautious about using its limited freedom of action on the Iranian issue. Making mistakes on this matter could even be catastrophic.

To illustrate this point, one should compare the situation today with the situation in 1981 when Israel decided unilaterally to strike the Iraqi Osiraq reactor. An examination of the two cases shows that the difference is more striking than the resemblance. In 1981 Israel found itself virtually alone in dealing with the Iraqi nuclear issue. The international community did not consider the Iraqi nuclear issue to be an international problem. Furthermore, in 1981 the nature of the Iraqi nuclear program vis-à-vis Israel's military capabilities left Israel with sufficient latitude to confront its dilemmas on its own. Prime Minister Menachem Begin consulted no one but his own cabinet. While the risks and uncertainties Israel was facing in 1981 were significant, Israel was in a position to take action on its own. A success or failure would have been Israel's own.

The fundamentals of the situation with Iran today are radically different at least in four major respects. First, while Israel may see itself as being at the forefront of the Iranian nuclear threat, possibly the only country that may be existentially threatened by Iran, Israel is surely not alone in confronting the problem. In contrast with the situation in 1981, the Iranian issue has been dealt with as a collective global issue almost from the start. Second, the Iranian nuclear program is built geographically and organizationally in a way that makes it extremely difficult to be addressed by a country such as Israel. Third, the intensity of the expected Iranian retaliation if it were attacked would be much different. Fourth, due to distance and geography, it would be extremely difficult, if not impossible, for Israel to take action unilaterally against Iran. Due to these reasons (and more), Israel's military option of acting alone is limited and difficult. The incentive for Israel to form a coalition with others is unprecedented.

With this in mind, one could sketch the basic dilemmas Israel has to confront. The closer that Iran is perceived to acquiring nuclear weapons, the more urgent it will be for Israel to draw its red lines, including amimut. As Iran has been crossing one technological milestone after another and as its enrichment program becomes almost a *fait accompli*, these policy challenges for Israel become more acute. The challenges I outline here are not ordered in chronological order but in a conceptual or logical order. In reality, decision makers could deal simultaneously with all these challenges. Stripped to their conceptual essentials, these challenges are as follows.[26]

The first challenge is organizing the Israeli decision-making process itself and the bilateral and multilateral politics surrounding it. Given the fundamental realization that Israel's ability to act alone is limited and that it must act primarily with others on this issue, the first challenge is organizing the national decision-making system in a manner that is adequate to the problem. One aspect of the problem, for example, is dealing with the nation's so-called lines in the sand: how to articulate, introduce, and convey them to its own people and to others. Israel's leaders would also have to decide how much they are willing to compromise their own perspective and freedom of action in favor of keeping a coalition with others; how much they are willing to discuss with others the limits to their tolerance and the relevant intelligence, especially with the United States as well as other key allies. Moreover, since any diplomatic deal with Iran would entail a compromise, Israel would have to find channels to consult and convey to its close allies, especially the United States, what kind of compromise it could and could not accept.[27]

While Israeli assessments have determined that Iran is involved with various aspects of nuclear weaponization, the overall Israeli concern with the Iranian nuclear program has focused on its fissile material (currently uranium enrichment) capability.[28] In the past, when Israeli officials used the phrase "point of no return," it generally meant the point at which Iran would have mastered centrifuge technology. The implication was that once Iran mastered in full the enrichment technology, it would become a nuclear weapons–capable state, which would be a point of no return. But after criticism from both inside and outside the intelligence community that the term was conceptually and politically flawed, it was dropped.[29] Israel now uses the phrase "technological threshold." In July 2009 Arad referred specifically to this terminological/definitional issue:

> The point of nuclear no-return was defined as the point at which Iran has the ability to complete the cycle of nuclear fuel production on its own; the point at which it has all the elements to produce fissionable material without depending on outsiders. Iran is now there. I don't know if it has mastered all the technologies, but it is more or less there. However, the term "no-return" is misleading. Even if Iran has fissionable material

for one bomb, it is still at a low grade of enrichment. And if it wants to conduct a test, it will not have even one bomb. It follows that Iran is not yet nuclear and not yet operational. Serious obstacles still lie in the way. The international community still has enough time to make it stop of its own volition.[30]

Israelis insist that even though a technological threshold is not equivalent to weapons capability, politically and strategically the conceptual difference between the two is misleading. Once the technological threshold has been reached and mastered, it would be much more difficult for intelligence agencies to ascertain the precise status of the Iranian nuclear program. Accordingly, the Israeli intelligence community rejected the implicit definition in the November 2007 NIE that weaponization is the defining feature of a nuclear-weapons program.[31] One wonders to what extent might Israel assess Iran's nuclear program by drawing on its own nuclear history.

At the time of this writing it appears that Iran has crossed that threshold and has made enrichment a *fait accompli*. Mastery of enrichment no longer appears to be a feasible line in the sand, even if it remains a formal demand of the United Nations Security Council. Even if a deal with Iran had been possible, Iran would have used it to legitimize its domestic enrichment activities.

The second challenge Israel may face is whether and how to act unilaterally if Iran reaches Israel's point of no return. So far Iran continues to defy the will of the Security Council on the matter of enrichment, having mastered enrichment technology to the industrial level. If the international community either proves powerless to enforce those Security Council resolutions or reaches a deal with Iran that places it too close to manufacturing a bomb, Israel would face a difficult decision either to follow the lead of the international community and accept a nuclear Iran (by Israeli definition) or to take independent action and forestall the Iran nuclear program. That decision would amount to a strategic choice between prevention and deterrence. It would test Israel's commitment to the 1981 Begin Doctrine: the commitment to take preventive action, including military action, against any hostile neighbor close to acquiring nuclear weapons.[32]

This obviously is a very sensitive issue, and little of the behind-the-scenes deliberations has been leaked. Israeli leaders have tended to keep silent on this subject, and when Minister Shaul Mofaz warned in June 2008 that Israel could not accept a nuclear Iran—implying that military action would be necessary—he was criticized.[33] Against this official policy of silence, then, it was surprising that in his final interview before departing from office on the eve of the Jewish New Year (late September 2008), Prime Minister Ehud Olmert dismissed openly as "megalomania" any thought that Israel should or would attack Iran on its own to halt its nuclear program: "Part of our megalomania and our loss of proportion is the things that are said here about Iran. We are a country that has lost a sense of proportion about itself." It is the international community, and not Israel, that should deal with Iran's nuclear issue.[34]

Of course, if Iran openly acquired nuclear weapons and clearly signaled its intent by withdrawing from the NPT, it would simplify Israel's choices by posing a more clear-cut casus belli and creating more international support for preemption. In addition to deciding whether to take military action, Israel would have to decide whether to change its own bargain with the bomb, that is, whether to adopt an overt deterrence policy and to dispense with amimut. There were some indications that Prime Minister Netanyahu entertained this seriously at one time. Notwithstanding the common wisdom in Israel that if Iran tested a weapon, Israel would have to follow suit in some fashion, Israeli policymakers might still see more benefit in not testing and letting Iran bear the brunt of international opprobrium if it declared its nuclear capability. In any case, Israel's reaction to Iran's departure from the NPT or even testing a device would not be automatic.

Apart from the need to overcome a domestic impulse to trade an eye for an eye, an overt weapons posture by Iran would simplify Israel's options for deterrence and containment. At a minimum, Israel would make sure that the Iranians had no doubt about their ability to devastate Iran in retaliation, including using its sea-based assets. Israel also would strengthen its missile defense and pursue civil defense measures as a means of deterrence by denial. On the diplomatic front, it would amplify its efforts to sanction Iran and to deny it all trade that could assist its weapons capability.

Another, longer-term challenge pertains to deterrence, arms control, and containment. If prevention ultimately fails and a new kind of nuclear regime takes shape in the Middle East, how should Israel respond? During the height of the cold war, as the world learned to live under the balance of mutual assured destruction, the theory and practice of arms control were developed to provide a modicum of stability. But those dialogues took place against the declared presence of nuclear weapons. Would it be possible to have such a dialogue in a context of amimut on both sides? How would a conversation about nuclear weapons be possible when neither side acknowledged having them?

Apart from the political costs of diplomatically engaging Iran—for which there currently is almost no support in Israel—diplomatic engagement presents other difficulties, as it would be perceived as accepting, and thereby legitimizing, Iran's nuclear capability. On the surface, as long as Ahmadinejad remains in power in Tehran, the issue of engagement is moot, since anti-Zionism is central to his and other hard-liners' worldview.

If prevention fails, it currently is unlikely that Israelis would propose arms control as a solution. In the face of a nuclear-capable and hostile Iran, the feasibility of changes in amimut would be unlikely. In theory, Israelis may prefer having no nuclear-weapons states in the Middle East, compared with there being two. But given Iran's record and its anti-Israel posture, Israelis would not trust Iran to comply with disarmament measures. This distrust would be difficult to overcome, particularly because the traditional view of nuclear disarmament in the Middle East is based solely on the vision of a nuclear weapons–free zone (NWFZ). The problem is that the NWFZ vision is only a vision and thus is not anchored in the current political reality of the Middle East. As elaborated in chapter 2, for Israel, a NWFZ is conditioned on peaceful relations among all the members of the region, which does not appear possible under the current regime in Tehran.

Still, under different political circumstances in Iran, with a different governing group, a new regional grand deal might be possible. If leaders think creatively, other conceivable versions of arms control, disarmament, and nonproliferation might be compatible with the region as it is.

The Irony of Amimut

On May 30, 1961, at the Waldorf-Astoria Hotel in New York, the Israeli prime minister, David Ben-Gurion, and the new U.S. president, John F. Kennedy, met to discuss the future of the Dimona project, the secret Israeli nuclear project that had been discovered by U.S. intelligence only a few months earlier and that Kennedy opposed.[35] Ben-Gurion had repeatedly pledged to Kennedy, both publicly and privately, that the Dimona project was for peaceful purposes only, but Kennedy was not convinced.

The minutes of the meeting were classified for some thirty years on both sides of the Atlantic, and not until the mid-1990s were they released for publication.[36] The two leaders spent only the first fifteen minutes of the meeting on the nuclear issue. Kennedy emphasized the importance of the Israeli pledge that the atomic initiative was for peaceful purposes only and also the importance of this commitment being not only stated but also seen by visitors. In response, Ben-Gurion told Kennedy about Israel's future energy problems, repeated his pledge that Dimona was for peaceful purposes, added a caveat, and concluded in a somewhat vague manner:

> We are asked whether it is for peace. For the time being the only purposes are for peace. Not now but after three or four years we shall have a pilot plant for separation, which is needed anyway for a power reactor. There is no such intention now, not for four or five years. But we will see what happens in the Middle East. It does not depend on us. Maybe Russia won't give bombs to China or Egypt, but maybe Egypt will develop them herself.[37]

I recalled Ben-Gurion's statement in February 2007 when I heard Ali Larijani (then the secretary-general of Iran's Supreme National Security Council and the head of its nuclear negotiating team) declare in public that Iran's nuclear program is currently for peaceful purposes only, but as far as the future is concerned, he continued, nobody knows what is in store. If Iran is threatened, everything is open. It was not difficult not to see the historical resemblance between Iran's nuclear situation today and Israel's nuclear situation in the early 1960s: both countries with an ambitious national nuclear initiative designed to create a nuclear-weapons option, but without a good idea yet of how far it could go. As was the case in Israel in the early to mid-1960s, the Iranians today seems to be committed to obtaining some sort of nuclear-weapons capability, but despite their determination, they still have no idea how far they will be able to push.

Important historical differences in the two countries' nuclear situation make the Iranian pursuit easier in one way and more difficult in another. Technologically, today it is far easier to acquire nuclear weapons than it was in the early to mid-1960s, when only four countries had such weapons. Politically, however, now we have the Nuclear Non-Proliferation Treaty. Apart from its political pledges to the United States, Israel is sovereign in terms of law and international norms and thus is free to pursue its nuclear ambitions, albeit secretly. Dimona has never been controlled by anything like the safeguards of the International Atomic Energy Agency (IAEA). All Israel has had to deal with are the United States' visits to Dimona, whose ground rules it controlled and which ended with the Nixon-Meir amimut deal in 1969. There was nothing illegal, or even improper, about having an opaque nuclear capability.

This is not the case with Iran today. Iran is a signatory to the NPT; that is, it has a legal obligation not to develop nuclear weapons. Iran also is under both the IAEA's safeguards and today's verification technology. With today's technology, it is exceedingly difficult to disguise highly enriched uranium (HEU) production, even in small amounts, particularly because on-site environmental sampling (e.g., swipe samples) is now part of the IAEA's accepted procedures. Thus, Iran will have difficulty hiding its production of HEU. But if Iran has undeclared secret enrichment facilities—a severe violation of its obligation under the NPT—the IAEA's technology would be incapable of detecting this activity.

All signs indicate that, at the least, Iran wants to come very close to the nuclear-weapons threshold by maintaining a large-scale enrichment capability (while keeping enrichment at a low level) and keeping its weaponization activities secret. The Iranian political leadership may look at a nuclear Israel today and hope that they could follow the same course. But in reality, even apart from the Nixon-Meir political deal that relieved Israel from any doubts about going nuclear, Iran will have more difficulty doing likewise. Only by massive deception—say, by building large-scale undeclared enrichment facilities—could Iran develop nuclear weapons while still subscribing to the NPT. In sum, it would be difficult and politically dangerous for Iran to mimic Israel.

The worry about Iran's enrichment at an industrial-scale capacity, what Israeli intelligence refers to as the *technological threshold*, is not that it can lead to secret nuclear weapons but that large-scale, low-enriched uranium (LEU) enrichment capabilities can quickly be reconfigured into a HEU mode of production, thereby giving little lead time to the international community. If Iran withdraws from the NPT, that would clearly be a sign of nonpeaceful intent. It thus is a breakout that is the main worry. In contrast, Israel has never been under safeguards, so nuclear weapons under amimut always have been an option. Iran may create its own nuclear opacity, and the political differences between an actual bomb and industrial production are not significant for a country that chooses a strategy of opacity.

Again the question that dominates the Israeli discourse about Iran: How should Israel react to the emergence of an opaquely nuclear Iran? This depends on what is meant by a "nuclear Iran." According to my analysis, as long as Iran remains within the NPT's boundaries, there probably would never be a nuclear Iran, insofar as that means an Iran with actual nuclear weapons, even if they were not declared. In this respect, much of the Israeli discourse on a nuclear Iran is a scare campaign, which says more about the Israeli psyche than about Iran.

We are likely to face a nuclear Iran that develops a nuclear-weapons capability opaquely, under the guise of its peaceful program within the NPT, thereby blurring the difference between possession and nonpossession. All signs are that Iran already has that capability. This type of opacity, call it *latent opacity*, would be politically convenient for Iran precisely because it is a signatory to the NPT. Such opacity also is flexible, politically and technologically, because it rests on true ambiguity about Iran's intentions and capabilities. Any explicit weaponization activities may remain concealed, disguised, or even put on hold.

Iran would gain a political advantage by having an advanced nuclear-weapons capability that brought it both deterrence and prestige. At the same time, it would allow Iran to maintain tension with the world within the parameters of its legal claims under the NPT. This means that Iran would continue to claim that its nuclear program was for peaceful purposes and that it had a right under the NPT to have access to the entire nuclear fuel cycle. At the same time, too, Iran would spread rumors that it was on the verge of acquiring nuclear weapons (or maybe already had) and therefore should be considered a de facto nuclear state, just as Israel is an undeclared nuclear state.

Iran's choice of nuclear opacity would be a political challenge for the international nuclear system but even a far greater challenge to Israel, which was the first and only country to use amimut as a nuclear posture. The difference is that Israel's amimut has succeeded because the world, particularly the United States, decided to accept its maintaining such a policy. Iran's choice of latent opacity, however, would come after the world had explicitly expressed its opposition to anything resembling a nuclear program in Iran.

When should Israel and the international community remove the mask of amimut? When should the world start calling the Iranian capability a virtual bomb? Is it preferable to remove the mask from Iranian ambiguity, or is an opaque Iran preferable to an openly nuclear Iran? At what point should we insist on international nuclear accountability? And what will be the future of Israeli ambiguity in such a world? Until now, these questions have seldom been asked, but they demand a great deal of thinking, both worldwide and in Israel.

The complexity of the Iranian nuclear situation is another incentive for Israel to maintain its current bargain using amimut. Israel would have little to gain by ending its own opacity, and it would have much to lose, including possibly sparking regional nuclearization and an unraveling of the NPT. This possibility became closer to reality with the Arab League's announcement on March 6, 2008, that if Israel acknowledged it had nuclear weapons, the Arab states would collectively withdraw from the treaty.[38]

Israel presumably has prepared for the possibility that Iran one day may become an openly nuclear state, but Israelis agree that these preparations should be done under the cover of amimut. The strategic consensus in Israel is that it should preserve amimut as long as it can, that is, as long as Iran sticks to its declaration of peaceful nuclear activity. Amimut is not only the safest public posture, especially during times of strategic uncertainty; it is also a firewall against changes.

The Fissile Materials Cutoff Treaty (FMCT)

The second item on today's international nuclear agenda that is relevant to Israel's bargain is a global treaty to cap or end the production of fissile materials for nuclear weapons, or what is known as the Fissile Materials Cutoff Treaty (FMCT).[39] The basic purpose of the FMCT idea is to create a legal mechanism to address a key aspect of nuclear proliferation that is missing from the NPT, namely, the nuclear-weapons states' production of fissile material for nuclear weapons, principally highly enriched uranium (HEU) and plutonium. A treaty of this kind would presumably address not only the five declared weapons states under the NPT but also the four de facto weapons states outside the NPT (India, Israel, North Korea, and Pakistan). Because the United States, United Kingdom, Russia, and France have officially declared an end to their production of fissile material for weapons, and China has unofficially halted its production, the FMCT would effectively target the four states outside the NPT, including Israel.

From an Israeli perspective, the FMCT is a challenge. Israel, unlike the other weapons states, must consider and decide whether (and how far) the FMCT is compatible with its long-standing commitment to amimut and whether the benefits of an FMCT would outweigh the costs of compromising or even partially abandoning amimut.

A Brief History

The idea of capping stockpiles of fissile material is almost as old as the nuclear age itself. The early efforts to control the production of fissile material for weapons began with the early initiatives to internationalize atomic energy in 1946/1947. A version of it appeared in the 1946 Baruch Plan, which called for the "complete managerial control of the production of fissionable materials."[40] Then in December 1946, the United Nations Atomic Energy Commission recommended establishing an international nuclear agency whose task would be verifying the prohibition of the manufacture of nuclear weapons.[41] As cold war enmities solidified, however, attempts to control fissile material production for weapons were abandoned.

After the end of the cold war, the idea resurfaced in June 1991, initially in the context of the Middle East, as part of a new arms-control initiative that the (first) Bush administration proposed following the (first) Gulf War.[42] Although the proposal did not mention a specific country, its focus was clearly on Israel, presumably the only Middle Eastern state that produced fissile material. Since the 1969 Nixon-Meir nuclear accord, the Israeli nuclear program had not been on the United States' political agenda. Not having been consulted in advance on the matter, Israel took a wait-and-see attitude, neither accepting nor rejecting the proposal. Technically, Israel refers to it as "under study."

Internally, however, Bush's proposal led to a heated debate within Israeli national security officialdom. While some people thought that the Bush initiative could offer interesting and creative opportunities for Israel (e.g., providing the seeds of openly accepting Israel as a nuclear weapons–capable state), the majority felt that the proposal could erode the benefits of amimut and could lead to a dangerous slippery slope toward premature disarmament. This conservative position prevailed, along with its interpretation of amimut, and became the consensus within the national security establishment. But Israel also concluded that it would not be wise to formally reject the U.S. proposal. Conveniently, the Arab states were not endorsing it either, and the (first) Bush administration had no desire for a showdown with Israel on the nuclear issue. This was an important lesson for Israel: it may not need to reject nuclear proposals that it does not like; let others do it or let it die naturally.

In any case, the U.S. Middle East Arms Control Initiative was short lived. A few months later, after the 1991 Madrid Peace Conference, the United States decided to take a different approach and let the parties negotiate their differences. Five working groups were established, including a working group on arms control and regional security known as ACRS, cochaired by the United States and Russia (see chapter 2). Three years later, the ACRS process reached a final impasse over how to deal with the Israeli nuclear issue and collapsed, but the FMCT issue was never seriously discussed at the ACRS level.[43] Neither side, each for its own reasons, had any interest in doing so.

Nevertheless, the FMCT remained a global arms-control issue that Israel could not avoid. In September 1993, in a speech to the United Nations, President Bill Clinton proposed a "multilateral convention banning the production of fissile materials for nuclear explosives or material outside international safeguards."[44] Two months later the UN General Assembly adopted resolution 48/75L calling for the negotiation of a "non-discriminatory, multilateral and international effectively verifiable treaty banning the production of fissile material for nuclear weapons or other nuclear explosive devices."[45] In March 1995, the Geneva-based Conference on Disarmament (CD) established an ad hoc committee to carry out this mandate.

Despite its reservations, Israel decided both to join the General Assembly consensus resolution and to participate in the negotiations in the CD. Despite the high stakes in these negotiations, Israel kept a low profile, calculating that it would be wiser to let others impede the negotiating process, which indeed soon stalled. This strategy proved correct until the summer of 1998 when Israel's joining the consensus became imperative.

By early August 1998 (shortly after the series of nuclear-weapons tests by India and Pakistan), China, India, and Pakistan joined the consensus. Israel was left as the last holdout in the CD, and its position became critical to the entire process in the sixty-one-nation body that makes decisions only by consensus. For the first time in its history, Israel found itself in the unique position of being able to derail a global issue. It was in those days in mid-August 1998 that the otherwise friendly Clinton administration exerted the harshest pressure the United States had used against Israel for decades (perhaps comparable to the pressure the Kennedy administration had exerted against Israel in the summer of 1963, demanding annual American inspection visits to Dimona).

Even though no draft cutoff treaty was imminent, Israeli Prime Minister Benjamin Netanyahu recognized that any FMCT might have serious long-term implications for the future of Israel's nuclear policy, particularly on the issue of amimut. Under intense pressure from Washington, however, he announced that Israel would join the consensus on the negotiation mandate at the CD but also that Israel opposed the treaty. In a letter on this issue Prime Minister Netanyahu wrote President Clinton, "We will never sign the treaty, and do not delude yourselves—no pressure will help. We will not sign the treaty because we will not commit suicide."[46]

This rough confrontation between Netanyahu and Clinton over the FMCT stirred concerns in Netanyahu's circle, especially his national security adviser, Uzi Arad. They feared that Clinton's strong commitment to the FMCT could undermine or erode the old American commitment to amimut, the Nixon-Meir understandings. So two months later, during the Wye River negotiations over Hebron, Netanyahu asked for and received an appendix to the agreement in the form of a signed secret letter from President Clinton in which the United States was committed to being sympathetic to Israel's preservation of its "strategic deterrence capabilities" and its ability to defend itself by itself against any threat. This "sympathy" was understood as a reaffirmation of the 1969 Nixon-Meir accord. The presidential letter also assured Israel that the United States would consult Israel in advance of global arms-control initiatives relevant to Israel, an implicit and partial assurance that the United States would be sympathetic in the future to Israeli concerns about the FMCT.[47]

Netanyahu's concerns were premature. During George W. Bush's administration, disagreements over the scope and purpose of the FMCT and over connections to other arms-control issues stalled the negotiations for nearly a decade. Although the Bush administration claimed to remain loyal to the FMCT idea, it dropped the demand that the treaty be verifiable. In July 2004, the United States made it official when it expressed "serious concerns" about whether realistic and effective verification of an FMCT was possible. Ambassador Jackie Sanders, the U.S. ambassador to the CD, explained that "the objective of an FMCT is not its verification, but the creation of an observed norm against the production of fissile material intended for weapons." This change testified in part to the Bush administration's ideological outlook on arms-control and international treaties. In May 2006, the Bush administration tabled an FMCT draft at the CD that would not contain any verification provisions. Instead, it would ban new production of plutonium and highly enriched uranium for use in nuclear weapons for fifteen years and would apply to only the five established nuclear-weapons states. In 2008, as the Bush administration finished its term, the CD was still unable to agree on an FMCT and consequently was unable to begin negotiations.[48]

Amimut and the FMCT

Throughout the 1990s, during the Clinton administration, Israel was reticent about explaining its reservations and concerns about the FMCT. After the showdown in August 1998, particularly following the letters that Netanyahu and Defense Minister Moshe Arens sent to their American counterparts, the Clinton administration suggested convening a quiet strategic dialogue between the two states on the cutoff issue in order for the United States to better understand Israel's reservations. This suggestion set off an intense debate in Israel about whether such a dialogue would be in Israel's best interests. In the end, once again, the conservative view prevailed, and Israel decided not to discuss its specific reservations beyond stating obliquely that the cutoff would be detrimental to Israel's security.[49]

The underlying reasons for Israel's opposition to the FMCT seemed to be both political and technical, especially a perceived conflict between the FMCT and amimut. Israel's main political concern was that an FMCT would be the first step toward Israel's premature nuclear disarmament. Israel feared that without an explicit agreement, the Arab states would argue that an FMCT must not be a substitute for the establishment of a nuclear weapons–free zone in the Middle East and should not legitimize Israel's nuclear monopoly, something the Arab states could never accept. Hence, the Israelis believed that the Arab states would regard Israel's agreement to an FMCT as the first step toward establishing a nuclear weapons–free zone in the Middle East. Indeed, as I stated earlier, the Arab countries' foreign ministers declared that if Israel admitted to having nuclear weapons but did not commit to destroying them, the Arab states would withdraw from the NPT.[50]

Technically, Israel would have difficulty maintaining its amimut under an FMCT, especially if the treaty contained provisions for credible verification. While the shutdown of Israel's Dimona reactor, which presumably is used to produce plutonium for its weapons program, could theoretically be verified remotely, the reactor also is used to produce tritium by means of neutron irradiation of lithium-6 targets.[51] Because tritium has a relatively short half-life (12.3 years), shutting down the reactor would eventually lead to a degradation of the tritium-boosted weapons in Israel's arsenal. Although as a party to the

FMCT, Israel could continue to produce tritium, it would have to agree to verification to ensure that the reactor was not also being used to produce plutonium.[52] This might be able to be accomplished without intrusive on-site inspections that would compromise amimut.[53]

In recent years, Israel has become more assertive in its objections to the FMCT by linking them to the Iranian nuclear issue. On November 11, 2004, the day when the FMCT resolution was voted on at the UN First Committee, Israel provided an official explanation for its decision to abstain.[54] The Iranian nuclear issue created a new context that reinforced Israel's initial objections to the FMCT. First, the nuclear issue must be negotiated in a regional framework and in close connection to the political situation; second, the FMCT does not address Israel's grave concerns about the deficiencies of the NPT.[55] From these general principles, we can articulate Israel's two specific objections to the FMCT:

• The FMCT would allow the operation of both uranium enrichment and reprocessing facilities as long as the enriched uranium and plutonium were used for ostensibly peaceful purposes, not weapons. Furthermore, even if the safeguards to detect possible diversion of these fissile materials to weapons were reliable, they could not prevent a breakout.

• Israel insisted that the only avenue for nuclear disarmament in the Middle East was through a regional nuclear weapons–free zone, not the FMCT, and that such a zone could be created only through a comprehensive peace process in which peace was the primary driver, not the nuclear issue.

The Israeli bottom line is simple: Israelis see a great deal of damage to their amimut without any benefits. From an Israeli perspective, the FMCT adds nothing constructive to the Iranian nuclear problem: it would restrict only Israel while not strengthening the current safeguards on Iran. Israel has always looked at the FMCT with a great deal of suspicion, as a "slippery slope" toward the erosion of amimut, and now the Iranian nuclear situation only has magnified Israel's objections. The combination of the ideological bent of the second Bush administration and the rise of the Iranian nuclear issue explains the strength of Israel's opposition to an FMCT. Furthermore, Israel views any international attention to its own nuclear program as a dangerous distraction from the urgent need to focus on the threat of Iranian nuclearization.

The result was that the FMCT issue hardly challenged Israel's fundamental's thinking about its own bargain. Even though the FMCT had the potential to force Israel to rethink amimut, it was never real enough to do so.

But this thinking may change. The Obama administration is committed to reverse the Bush administration's nuclear status quo. The FMCT is an item, and a rather early one, on President Obama's nuclear agenda. In his speech in Prague in April 2009, he referred to this issue explicitly when he declared the need for a treaty that "verifiably ends the production of fissile materials intended for use in state nuclear weapons."[56] Obama's Republican opponent, Senator John McCain, also endorsed a vision of a world without nuclear weapons, in which the FMCT has an important role.[57]

Weeks later, on May 29, 2009, that commitment became more real as the CD, for the first time since 1996, unanimously agreed on an agenda to resume arms-control talks. It agreed to create a working group to negotiate "an international ban on the production of new nuclear bomb–making material."[58] The FMCT issue now may become an important platform that could force Israel to rethink its bargain.

Between Natanz and Dimona

Although an FMCT in the Middle East is not a viable near-term prospect, we might still ask whether Israel could do anything else, apart from military action against Iran, to lessen the dangers of nuclearization in the region and possibly to contribute to a satisfactory diplomatic deal with Iran. (In regard to the military option, one should recall that in the long run, even successful military action could not prevent a willing advanced state from acquiring nuclear weapons.) The question is important especially if there were a change of regime in Iran in the future. After all, the Iranian nuclear problem will not disappear even if President Ahmadinejad disappears.

Israel's semiofficial answer is firmly in the negative. Israel refuses to see any connection—legal, political, or otherwise—between the two countries' nuclear programs. These are totally two different issues; there is no connection between Natanz and Dimona.[59] It is Iran that defies the will of the international community; it is Iran that rejects the UN Security Council's resolutions; it is Iran that refers to Israel as an illegitimate political entity to be "wiped off the map." Furthermore, Israel maintains that the old Nixon-Meir accord and subsequent American presidential understandings are tantamount to an American commitment to keep Israel's nuclear issue away from regional discussion. Indeed, according to reliable Israeli and American sources, President Obama gave Prime Minister Netanyahu a classified document that reaffirms American-Israeli understandings on the nuclear issues, even though it is somewhat unclear whether and to what extent Obama explicitly committed to this nonlinkage.[60] Iran has formally never linked Natanz and Dimona, even though informally Iranians commonly invoke the "double standard" charge.

Israel is legally correct that there is no formal justification for linking Natanz and Dimona. In reality, however, for many people, such a connection is not only commonsensical and inescapable but desirable.[61] Some analysts regard as deceptive the dichotomy that Israel seems to advance, "either accept nuclear Iran or bomb Iran before."[62] Bombing Iran would most likely guarantee that Iran would withdraw from the NPT and would declare its right to nuclear weapons. The only way that could prevent a nuclear Iran is for Iran to make the strategic decision that not having nuclear weapons was in its own interest. At this point, Israel would have to decide about its own strategic preference: Would Israel prefer an open nuclear deterrence to accepting the connection between Natanz and Dimona in order to establish a regional arms-control scheme? The answer to this question is not a simple one but it is worth debating. This issue, largely due to the grip of amimut, has hardly been discussed in Israel.

In a paper that I wrote with Marvin Miller in 2008, we suggested that there are, at least theoretically, modalities of engaging Israel in a regional nonproliferation/denuclearization effort but that it would require a great deal of creative thinking and acting, by both Israel and all other states with an interest in promoting nonproliferation and security in the Middle East. For Israel, such thinking would necessitate departing from amimut (at least from its current interpretation).[63]

Our argument was twofold. First, we noted the intrinsic connection between the problem of nuclear weapons in the region and the enduring conflict between Israel and its Arab neighbors. It was the perception that Israel faced an existential threat that motivated David Ben-Gurion to pursue the nuclear option in the 1950s. Although today the military balance in the region is significantly different from what it was when Israel initiated its nuclear project, Israel still faces an existential threat, first and foremost from Iran (and possibly from others). As long as Israel sees itself as facing existential threats, or even the possibility of existential threats, it will not abandon its national insurance policy, that is, its nuclear deterrent. Israel will never move toward nuclear disarmament unless a just and durable peace in the region is achieved. At the moment, peace and the end of the conflict still seems a distant prospect, which in the Israeli mind justifies the retention and upgrading of Israel's nuclear deterrent.[64] A just and durable peace in the region is a necessary condition for a nuclear-free Middle East. This is one important aspect of Israel's bargain with the bomb.

Second, we also argued that short of a just and durable peace in the Middle East, there should be efforts to introduce arms-control initiatives that place some constraints on Israel's nuclear deterrent while simultaneously reducing the risk of proliferation elsewhere in the region, with a special focus on Iran. As we have argued in the past, arms control and progress toward a just and durable peace are mutually reinforcing if pursued incrementally and cooperatively.

Specifically, given Israel's opposition to an FMCT, it might consider establishing a regional zone free of all proliferation-sensitive nuclear facilities, that is, uranium enrichment and fuel-reprocessing plants as well as large research reactors fueled with either natural or weapons-grade uranium.[65] While Israel would retain its nuclear arsenal in such a zone, it would have to verify shutting down the Dimona reactor and its associated reprocessing plant.[66]

However, unlike the situation under an FMCT, there would be a significant *quid pro quo* between Israel and Iran. The establishment of such a zone would eliminate the risk that, for example, Iran could obtain weapons-usable nuclear materials via the misuse of declared and safeguarded enrichment or reprocessing plants. In addition, credible means would have to verify that such plants had not been constructed clandestinely, and strong measures would have to ensure that if such plants were found, they would be destroyed. These are complex issues that will require a great deal of thinking and the support of the principal actors as well as the international community.[67]

Like the FMCT itself, this arms-control proposal also is incompatible with amimut. Like the FMCT, this proposal would require verification that the facilities had been shut down and were no longer producing. When we noted that our proposed initiatives would require a sea change in nuclear thinking in both Israel and the United States, we meant that both countries would have to reexamine amimut, particularly whether amimut is a wasting asset in that it makes arms-control measures—essential to thwarting the Iranian threat—difficult if not impossible to implement.[68] As long as Israel adheres to amimut, such proposals would not work because they erode amimut.

To make this proposal more attractive to Israel, it could be coupled with a reexamination by both the Nuclear Suppliers Group as a whole as well as its individual members (especially the United States) of the current laws and guidelines that prohibit the transfer to Israel of civilian nuclear materials and reactors, particularly natural uranium and power reactors. Although Israel has proved in the past that it would not jeopardize its national security to gain fuller access to the benefits of nuclear energy, a "package deal" combining both arms control and peaceful use could be attractive.[69]

Final Reflections

At present, the focus of the international community, and Israel itself, is on the Iranian nuclear impasse. The delicate battle of wills between Iran and the international community is ongoing, and it is impossible to tell what the result of this battle will be. But it is almost certain that the outcome of this impasse will determine a great deal of the future of the Israeli bargain as well.

For now, Israel (with tacit support of many in the international community) is anxious to contain the Iranian problem without allowing any outside links, regional or global. This means that as long as the Iranian nuclear impasse remains unresolved, Israel will be reluctant to change its own bargain, especially on the issue of amimut, and also will object to others doing so. But once the impasse will reach its moment of truth and is shattered by a major diplomatic breakthrough, regime change, military action or a combination of all of them, it is quite conceivable, even likely, that the international community would pressure both Iran and Israel to reach a long-term regional arrangement.

A more tolerant and open Iran may be Netanyahu's nightmare. If Iran is willing to negotiate seriously, it might agree to substantial concessions only on a regional basis, as a step toward establishing a Middle Eastern nuclear weapons–free zone. In such a case, Israel could be pressed to make its own nuclear contribution, possibly even to shut down the Dimona reactor as part of the price for halting Iran's enrichment activities at Natanz.

At present, then, Israel is not willing to tolerate an international deal with Iran that would be linked to Israel's own nuclear deterrent. Accordingly, momentum for a change in amimut is unlikely. Yet Israel's insistence on the exceptionalism of amimut is not only parochial and anachronistic; it is wrong for both Israel and the world. This attitude may ultimately compromise Israel's interests, domestic democratic values, and security and stability. When

Iran has a new government and its anti-Israeli rhetoric disappears, it will be more difficult for Israel to refuse to cooperate in a regional resolution of the nuclear issue.

Israel wants to stick to its own benign monopoly, with amimut at its core, as long as possible, which means probably until Iran itself openly declares itself as a nuclear-weapons state, by test or declaration. Given Israel's own amimut, it appears that Israel would be cautious in officially recognizing Iran as an actual nuclear-weapons state. Israel may be reluctant to do so but may not have full control over the events.

Israelis tend to see two ways of addressing the conflict with Iran—either Israel takes action against Iran, perhaps by imposing sanctions that would topple the regime or some sort of air strike backed up by a naval blockade, or it accepts a nuclear Iran. Israelis tend to see no way out of this either/or choice. But the reality is that in order to be lasting, virtually any outcome must be backed up by some political deal. This is true even for military action: a successful military action against Iran would be lasting only if it could be translated into a political arrangement.

The irony is that a successful military action could generate pressure on Israel to change its own deal with the bomb in favor of some regional settlement.

Chapter Ten
Toward a New Bargain

Today, as the Nixon-Meir 1969 nuclear accord enters its fifth decade, its force and impact appear as robust as ever. The commitment of the Israeli government to amimut is absolute and unyielding. From the Israeli perspective, amimut has been a great strategic and diplomatic success. As I indicated in the last chapter, Israel's commitment to amimut appears to be strengthening while the Iranian nuclear issue remains unresolved.

The rationale that led to the accord forty years ago still prevails today, and since 1969 it has been reaffirmed by all seven American presidents and all eight Israeli prime ministers. Most recently, this strategic rationale was reaffirmed in writing in May 2009 in the first meeting between President Barack Obama and Prime Minister Benjamin Netanyahu, as new Israeli and American leaders have become accustomed to doing in their first meeting.[1] Other international players continue to tacitly support the bargain because they see no alternative.

Below the surface, however, there is a growing sentiment that the old bargain, centered on amimut, has become anachronistic and awkward. It is anachronistic because Israel's nuclear status is no longer ambiguous. Both deliberate and inadvertent leaks over the years leave no doubt that Israel has a sophisticated nuclear arsenal. Israel's bargain is awkward because amimut has become a political fiction empty of content. It may have outlived its political usefulness because it is incompatible with emerging new norms and challenges to the global nuclear order. Above all, amimut prevents Israel from being included as a major stakeholder in today's nuclear community.

While Israelis still regard amimut as the best possible solution to their nuclear dilemma, many others view it as parochial, a manifestation of local groupthink. Indeed, most Israelis are not even aware that their philosophy of amimut appears strange, even inexplicable, to others.

My aim in this final chapter is first to articulate the flaws of amimut as an international posture and, second, to start outlining a new international bargain for Israel, that is, what a new bargain might contain, how it can come into being, how and under what political circumstances Israel would depart from amimut, and how Israel should disclose the existence of its nuclear weapons.

The Anachronism of Amimut

On February 7, 2004, at a security conference in Munich, Germany, Secretary of Defense Donald Rumsfeld was asked an unexpected question by a Palestinian official about the American "double standard" regarding Israeli nuclear weapons:

> Question: Mr. Secretary, you talked about countries that were trying to produce weapons of mass destruction. You talked about Iraq and you talked about Iran and North Korea. I have a question, a direct question to you. What are you doing with Israel? As far as Israel is concerned, Israel has more atomic weapons in the region than any other country. Why do you remain silent in regard to Israel? I think it's important to answer this question because this has to do with the world, the strategy that we are pursuing today. I think that if the position towards Israel were different, then the situation would be different in the Near East, and this is a great problem.
>
> Rumsfeld: You know the answer before I give it, I'm sure. The world knows the answer. We take the world like you find it; and Israel is a small state with a small population. It's a democracy and it exists in a neighborhood that in many—over a period of time has opined from time to time that they'd prefer it not be there and they'd like it to be put in the sea. And Israel has opined that it would prefer not to get put in the sea, and as a result, over a period of decades, it has arranged itself so it hasn't been put in the sea.[2]

This brief exchange captures the essence of the problem of amimut, in both practice and concept. Amimut means in America a restrictive protocol on what American officials (and former officials) are allowed to say in public regarding the Israeli nuclear issue. As is the case in Israel, they are forbidden to disclose any facts about the subject, not even to acknowledge unequivocally that the U.S. government *knows* that Israel has the bomb. Instead, Israel's nuclear status must be left ambiguous, or at least assumed.[3] Rumsfeld's linguistic acrobatics allowed him to confirm implicitly something that he otherwise could not have stated. Instead of refuting the charge of a double standard, his rhetorically and politically awkward reply seems only to confirm it.

Then, four days later, British Prime Minister Tony Blair was placed in a position similar to Rumsfeld's when asked a similar question in the British House of Commons:

> Sir Peter Tapsell (Louth and Horncastle): What steps are being taken to persuade Israel to give up her weapons of mass destruction?
>
> The Prime Minister: I would like to see the whole of the Middle East free from the threat of weapons of mass destruction, but I hope that the hon. Gentleman will recognise the particular worries that Israel has about security, given that it is surrounded by many countries, some of whose stated objective is still to get rid of the state of Israel altogether. I have my criticisms of Israeli policy, but I would remind the hon. Gentleman that it is a democracy, whose Governments are elected by its people. At the same time as we try to strive for a region free of weapons of mass destruction, in whatever country, we must recognise that it is important to respect the security of Israel.

Blair's reply was similar to Rumsfeld's in its substance, if not its style. As was the case with Rumsfeld, Blair neither acknowledged Israel's possession of nuclear weapons nor denied it. But in doing so, he revealed that Britain also is committed to the Nixon-Meir accord.[4] Rumsfeld's and Blair's nearly identical responses underline the problem of amimut today: it prevents the world from dealing with the reality of a nuclear Israel.

The Gang of Three's Attack on Amimut

In the early 1990s, McGeorge Bundy, William Crowe, and Sidney Drell, distinguished statesmen involved in national and international security, were the first to openly argue against the "hypocritical pretense" of amimut. They wrote their book before India and Pakistan conducted tests and declared themselves openly as nuclear-weapons states. At that time, the authors considered it "certain that Israel has a significant stock of warheads" and that India "has the skills and the materials to have warheads as quickly as it wants and it is highly probable that Pakistan is in a similar situation on a somewhat smaller scale."[5] Although Israel already was viewed as the most certain and advanced case of the three countries, India (which actually did not have complete nuclear weapons) and Pakistan (which had very few unassembled weapons) went ahead to develop a full capability, which they then tested. India and Pakistan had no deep normative attachment to opacity, so they operated on the basis of realistic political needs.

Bundy, Crowe, and Drell's argument for nuclear openness can be read as both realistic and normative. Their neighbors, indeed the whole world, consider Israel, India, and Pakistan as nuclear capable and believe that they should find a way to acknowledge this. The reason for this call for nuclear openness, the three writers contend, is to some extent normative, "the destructive political impact of the pretense they are not what they are."[6]

In regard to Israel, the only one of the three states that turned amimut into an ideology of national security, the writers' argument for openness appears more normative because Israel is a different, and more difficult, case. Israel (and its ally in this hypocrisy of pretense, the United States) "suffers for what look to other countries in the region as hypocritical deception," but Israelis have a difficult time in facing reality. Here the authors make the normative argument that the possession of nuclear weapons is a very serious matter for the state involved, its neighbors, and the entire world, and therefore basic transparency should be required of all nuclear-weapons states.

Furthermore, Bundy, Crowe, and Drell seem to think that this "pretense" is so perverse (they use the words *offensive* and *absurd*) that it prevents Israelis from realizing their own best interests; that is, amimut does not allow Israel to justify openly, on legal and moral grounds, their possession of nuclear weapons. "The pretense [of amimut] prevents any public defense of the Israeli program by the Israeli government and any effective argument that no state or group need fear an Israeli bomb unless it attempts the destruction of Israel."[7]

Whether the authors knew in 1993 much about the Nixon-Meir secret accord—and I tend to doubt it—is not clear. In any case, they are proposing that the American government end its own participation in the game of amimut and state in public that it considers Israel a nuclear-weapons state.

"Such a statement would clarify an important reality, would follow the guidelines of openness, and help the Israelis themselves to tell the truth." Still, they concede, the trouble with this action is that on nuclear matters, "countries do not like their secrets to be told by others." Ultimately, "the best way out of this cul-de-sac is Israeli openness by Israeli decision."[8] Bundy, Crowe, and Drell's instrumentalist/realist argument about the utility of truth telling in nuclear affairs thus turns into a normative argument about states' obligation to acknowledge their nuclear status:

> The advantage of recognizing India, Israel and Pakistan for what they are is not merely a matter of dealing with reality, important though that is. It is also a matter of *not* dealing with these countries as they are *not*. One cannot make much sense in talking about nuclear restraint in the Middle East if one omits the existence of Israeli warheads.[9]

The Normative Argument Against Amimut

The argument that Bundy, Drell, and Crowe developed in the early 1990s was embryonic in form. It incorporates both political and normative issues and leaves the connection somewhat vague and implicit. Furthermore, the situation itself changed as both India and Pakistan tested weapons and openly went nuclear while Israel remained stuck to its amimut ideology.

In the following I offer a more current version of the argument made by the three writers, proposing that amimut is incompatible with today's global nuclear agenda in both its challenges and norms. Amimut, I argue, is also incompatible with Israel's own vital interests. In agreement with the three authors I posit that it is in Israel's interests to be recognized for what it is, a nuclear-weapons state.

In today's political context, especially given the centrality of the cases of Iran and North Korea, the emphasis on acknowledgment and truth telling in nuclear matters seems even more important than it was in the early 1990s. As discussed in earlier chapters, there is a built-in tension between amimut and the ability to address the reality of a nuclear Israel as a political and strategic fact. The original purpose of amimut was to keep a nuclear Israel outside the global nuclear order as long as disclosing Israel's nuclear capabilities would have complicated the international situation, both regionally and globally. Over time, however, amimut has only complicated the situation, even for Israel. It is nearly impossible to engage Israel on nuclear issues because of the requirements of amimut, as, for example, with the Fissile Materials Cutoff Treaty (FMCT) in the past, and it is apparent in Israel's reluctance to accept a regional approach to the Iranian nuclear problem.

Such a denial of reality is not in the interests of the international community. A nuclear Israel is too important a player, both regionally and globally, to be left out of the arms-control dialogue. What seemed politically necessary in 1969 is unacceptable today. When we deal with nuclear-weapons issues, some basic normative measures of transparency and accountability are required from all; at the minimum, all nuclear states should acknowledge their status as such.

Some analysts suggest, however, that formal acknowledgment is largely symbolic and its importance should not be overstated. To recognize Israel formally as a nuclear-weapons state, especially against its own will, is neither necessary nor desired. Given Israel's reluctance to acknowledge its nuclear status, even under amimut Israel could participate in matters of arms control and disarmament in the context of both regional and global initiatives. For example, George Perkovich of the Carnegie Endowment suggests that the Israeli case could be handled in terms of "unsafeguarded fissile material," without saying anything explicit about weapons. Such a terminology, he argues, would be consistent with amimut but would still allow Israel to participate in almost all current issues of arms control and disarmament.[10]

I disagree. There is a significant political and technical difference between a true nuclear-weapons state (as Israel is) and a state with a nuclear option, such as the possession of unsafeguarded fissile material. These are two distinct categories, each creating its own political and technical issues for arms control (let alone disarmament). Furthermore, in reducing the Israeli case to mere "unsafeguarded fissile material," one is deliberately blurring the reality of nuclear weapons, making it opaque and undefined. This would be a wrong precedent for the regime in future cases.

Moreover, Perkovich and others imply that the issue is primarily a semantic or terminological issue, namely, how to refer to Israel's status, given its lack of acknowledgment. But the problem is deeper than that. Under amimut, Israel refuses not only to acknowledge its status but also to provide any physical access to its nuclear facilities.

I agree with Bundy, Crowe, and Drell that the issue of the future of amimut is both political and normative. In chapter 5 I argued that the nuclear issue is too important for a liberal democracy not to acknowledge it, that the spirit of liberal democracy entails the moral obligation to acknowledge such truth. Conversely, amimut is unacceptable as a norm of conduct in a democracy. Even if the public were ignored initially, once a nation possesses nuclear weapons, its citizens must know it.

A similar international norm should exist as a code of conduct within the community of nations over the issue of nuclear possession. The reason is similar: the possession of nuclear weapons is the type of issue that nations must acknowledge among themselves. One could argue that this norm is already entailed implicitly in the Nuclear Non-Proliferation Treaty (NPT), a two-tiered treaty whose premise is the act of status declaration. Of all nine countries that possess nuclear weapons, Israel is the only one that refuses to acknowledge its nuclear status.

Ultimately, amimut is incompatible with vital Israeli interests. Amimut implies that Israel's case for possessing the bomb is weaker than the cases of other declared nuclear states, either politically or legally. It treats Israel not only as a nuclear "untouchable" but also as a country that resides outside the global nuclear regime. This exceptionalism is unfair to Israel's own interests today.

There is a historical irony here. In the early days of its nuclear program Israel had no concerns about legitimacy, recognition, status, and the like. All it cared about then was acquiring the capabilities. The virtue of the Nixon-Meir accord was that it left Israel alone to build its nuclear capabilities: no more American visits to Dimona, no NPT constraints, no arms-control obligations, and no transparency.

Today the situation is different. The virtue has turned into a liability. Israel is now a mature nuclear-weapons state but lacks the recognition of the international community, something it has never sought or received. Instead of being part of the responsible establishment, a member of the club, Israel still operates in the shadows, sometimes as an exemption and other times as a nuclear pariah.

This dilemma became more apparent in the wake of the U.S.-India nuclear deal, which, by default, had an impact on the Israeli bargain. Israel was viewed as the ranking member in the second-tier nuclear club made up of India, Israel, and Pakistan until the U.S.-India deal dissolved the group, giving status and prestige to India while leaving Israel alone in the cold.

The D-3 Approach

At home, Israel may have some flexibility to make democratic reforms on its own, but the international arena is more complex and more resistant to policy changes. One reason for the complexity is the symbiotic nature of the current bargain: amimut is, for all practical purposes, a secret bilateral nuclear arrangement. Thus Israel cannot change this policy on its own. The other reason is that amimut's target audience is multilateral, the nonproliferation regime. Indeed, one reason that Israel and the United States chose amimut was their desire not to undermine the nonproliferation regime. This was true in 1969 and is still true today.

There is some support, in the United States and elsewhere, for Bundy's suggestion that nuclear reality must be recognized for what it is and that Israel should be openly treated and engaged as a nuclear-weapons state, but there also is serious concern that recognition or acceptance of Israel (or India and Pakistan) as a recognized nuclear state would weaken the nonproliferation regime by being interpreted as legitimizing nuclear proliferation. In fact, from the perspective of many nonnuclear-weapons states under the NPT, all existing nuclear weapons should be disarmed, and none deserves legitimacy in the first place. Finally, the Arab states would, of course, oppose any proposal to recognize Israel as a nuclear-weapons state.

Until the U.S.-India nuclear agreement (and also the weakening of the central government in Pakistan), a number of scholars and practitioners believed that the challenge of recognizing the reality of a nuclear Israel without legitimizing it was worth exploring as a generic problem for all three de facto nuclear-armed states: India, Israel, and Pakistan. Rebecca Johnson, founder of the journal *Disarmament Diplomacy*, coined the abbreviation D-3 in reference to these three de facto nuclear states outside the NPT.[11] In 2004 Tom Graham and I referred to this problem as "the three-state problem."[12]

In June 2006, the then director general of the International Atomic Energy Agency (IAEA), Mohammed ElBaradei, highlighted the need for a "creative approach" for dealing with the D-3, indicating that "our traditional strategy"—treating the three as outsiders or outliers—"no longer had a chance of bringing these three last few countries into the fold."[13] The IAEA head's view of the importance of engaging the D-3 in arms-control initiatives is shared by many other scholars and analysts.[14]

The specific issue of ending amimut is viewed as a broader, NPT-related issue. The benefit of bringing the D-3 into the NPT fold is that once the regime is universally recognized and complete, all problems of nonproliferation will "come from inside the regime" rather than from outside where the regime has no legal authority. That would make nearly all disputes and disagreements issues of compliance within the regime.[15]

Analyst Jenny Nielson wrote a detailed comparative study of the D-3 problem, counting as many as ten different proposals regarding this subject.[16] Some of the proposals overlap. A number of them advocate high-level talks with the D-3, possibly along with the NPT review process or with the IAEA, resulting in some form of nonproliferation code of conduct for the D-3; other approaches would advance the idea of a nuclear weapons–free zone (NWFZ) or even a weapons of mass destruction–free zone (WMDFZ) as a way to approach the D-3 problem; still other proposals suggest a new protocol that would grant the D-3 associate membership in the NPT or would treat the D-3 as if they were nuclear-weapons states under the NPT in return for accepting disarmament clauses.

These are interesting proposals. They highlight the importance of the need to engage the D-3 for what they are, just as Bundy and his colleagues urged. Yet none of these proposals has been considered or adopted by governments. The 3-D approach has at least two, related, flaws. First is viewing the nuclear ambitions of these three very different states as if their common denominator was sufficient for treating them as if they were generically similar. But vast geostrategic and political differences distinguish these countries' attitudes toward nuclear weapons. Second is presuming that these states' nuclear issue is separate from the larger security issues that led them to acquire nuclear weapons in the first place.

In any case, the 3-D approach faded in July 2005 when President George W. Bush and Prime Minister Manmohan Singh jointly announced the bilateral U.S.-India agreement on peaceful nuclear cooperation. A new Indian bargain with nuclear weapons was in the making, and the other two de facto nuclear-weapons states, Pakistan the declared one and Israel the undeclared one, were left out.

The Indian Precedent

The United States helped India rewrite its bargain with nuclear weapons to reflect the current international reality. It was a difficult process that lasted more than three years, but in the end, India transformed itself from a nuclear pariah—a state that was subjected to international sanctions for its nuclear tests—to a global nuclear power recognized by the United States as a "responsible state with advanced nuclear technology." Although India still remains outside the NPT, it has been granted a formal "exemption" from the Nuclear Suppliers Group (NSG), which makes India, for all practical purposes, one of the declared members of the nuclear club under the NPT. Could the Indian precedent apply to the Israeli case, in full or in part?

Despite the differences in India's and Israel's geography and population, their nuclear pursuits started along similar lines and around the same time. In both cases, their early nuclear history was shaped by a special alliance between the national leaders (Jawaharlal Nehru in India and David Ben-Gurion in Israel) and visionary scientists (Homi Bhabha in India and Ernst David Bergman in Israel). By 1954 India had begun building its primary nuclear research center, the Atomic Energy Establishment at Trombay (outside Mumbai), and months later India's Department of Atomic Energy was created with Bhabha as its head, reporting to Nehru. A small British reactor, followed by a larger 40-MWt (CIRUS) reactor—supplied by Canada and by U.S. heavy water—were the initial elements. For the Israelis, India's CIRUS project was a model of how it too could acquire extensive dual-use nuclear technology.

Despite this initial resemblance, the purpose of the two projects was different from the start. The Israeli program was secretly launched and narrowly focused, whereas the Indian program was publicly launched and broadly focused. Over the years, besides nuclear reactors, India developed a wide array of dual-use nuclear facilities to mine uranium, manufacture fuel and heavy water, reprocess spent fuel to extract plutonium, and, more recently, enrich uranium. Despite the fast buildup of the infrastructure, Nehru's opposition to nuclear weapons ensured that India would not follow a direct path to weapons.

Within a decade or so, Israel and India had settled on two different national styles of nuclear development. Israel created a dedicated, narrowly focused, secretive nuclear infrastructure aimed directly at manufacturing weapons, with nuclear power as only a long-term bonus. Israel had almost no public debate on the bomb. Although the country secretly crossed the weapons threshold in 1967, it did not conduct a test. In 1969 this modus operandi was sealed as a bargain with the United States.

India took a different path. Indian politicians endlessly and publicly debated nuclear weapons in parliament, and the country moved slowly. Although Prime Minister Lal Bahadur Shastri authorized Bhabha to work on a nuclear explosive as early as in 1964, it took another decade for Indian scientists to conduct their first test. In this way, India remained on the weapons threshold without crossing it; instead its large infrastructure supported nuclear power. In 1974 India exploded a nuclear device mostly to demonstrate its capability, called it "peaceful," but was condemned worldwide, even though it truly lacked a dedicated weapons program.[17]

India took another quarter century to decide that as an awakened economic global giant, it should declare itself as a nuclear-weapons state, and in 1998, a new nationalist government decided that India should become a member of the nuclear club.[18] After India tested its weapons, Pakistan followed suit, and South Asia became nuclearized. The United States sanctioned both countries for defying the NPT regime.

The U.S.-India nuclear pact thus transformed relations that for three decades had been strained over the nuclear issue. This is not only a watershed in U.S.-India bilateral relations, but it also introduces a precedent to the nonproliferation regime. The deal is remarkable in at least three respects that may have some relevance to the Israeli case. First, it shows that in special political circumstances, the United States may be willing to amend the rigid nonproliferation regime to accommodate the needs of an ally that the administration wants to reward. Indeed, the pact is a recognition of India's rising economic role in today's world and the growing strategic importance of the U.S.-India partnership, especially vis-à-vis China. Second, the deal gives India access to nuclear technology and expertise, something it has never had for the last three decades. It also gives India access to nuclear energy cooperation with other countries, which will be vital for India to meet its developmental goals. Third, the deal signifies the end of the "nuclear apartheid attitude."

The United States and the Nuclear Suppliers Group (NSG) have stated that the Indian case is unique and that it would be improper to use it to decide on other cases.[19] The United States' main public argument in favor of the deal is that India is now an emerging economic giant thirsty for energy and that it is in the United States' interest that it receive clean nuclear energy. These economic and strategic arguments do not apply to Israel, however.

Israel would like to receive similar treatment, albeit tailored to its particular circumstances, from the United States. Israelis believe that they deserve it not less than India and perhaps even more, based on their good record of nuclear constraint and caution. Israel cannot duplicate India for many reasons, political, strategic, and technological, but they would like a special new bargain. One major obstacle—but, from another perspective, an advantage—to any new bargain is amimut itself. Within the current framework, it would be difficult for Israel to seek a new bargain and for others to offer one. Any new bargain would have to chip away at amimut.

Nonetheless, not by accident Israel has tried to project a new image, using phrases resembling those the United States now uses to refer to India. Representing Israel at the 2007 IAEA annual meeting, for example, Ambassador Gideon Frank (then the Israel Atomic Energy Commission director general and today its vice chair) referred to "Israel's long standing commitment to norms of security, responsibility, accountability and restraint in the nuclear domain."[20] This new language allows Israel to hint at—but not explicitly acknowledge—its nuclear-weapons status while promoting its new image as a supporter of the international nonproliferation regime. While still consistent with amimut's core bargain, this new image presents a tacit but significant departure from Israel's past nuclear policy.

Furthermore, in a direct response to the U.S.-India deal, Israel lobbied the NSG throughout 2007 to change the organization's export control policies so that Israel, too, will have the same access to the materials and technology that the United States agreed to give India in the U.S.-India nuclear agreement. Unlike the U.S. effort to treat India as exempt from U.S. laws and NSG guidelines, however, the Israeli initiative was based on meeting a set of "nuclear responsibility criteria" rather than a specific exemption. The U.S. government nevertheless rebuffed the Israeli initiative. Despite the widespread bipartisan support in Washington for stronger ties with India, the United States wants to avoid dealing simultaneously with Israel (and Pakistan) on the sensitive issue of nuclear technology transfer. The response to Israel's low-profile initiative runs along the lines of "this is not the time."[21]

A Formal Statement of Acknowledgment

Only an official statement of disclosure issued by the Israeli government would constitute the true end of amimut. This would be the ultimate act of acknowledgment, an act that logically entails the Israeli government's taking responsibility for and granting legitimacy to Israel's activities in the nuclear field. A formal statement would most appropriately be made by the prime minister, in coordination with the head of the opposition, and with all living Israeli prime ministers attending. Such a statement would be significant both at home and around the world and would unite both aspects of the bargain into one whole.

What should be the political parameters of such a disclosure statement? First and foremost, such a statement should be made only after a great deal of preparatory work with all the international players involved, especially the

United States, the major Arab states, and key elements of the nonproliferation regime (short of dramatic circumstances that may not allow time for
that, such as an Iranian nuclear test). Ideally, such a statement should be part
of or in conjunction with the outcome of a negotiated political deal, either
regional or global.

This deal could be, for example, an agreement on a regional peace plan
between Israel and the Arab states (perhaps based on a modified version of
the Arab League's peace plan derived from the Saudi plan). Or it could be
Israel's full participation in a global effort to reduce nuclear weapons worldwide, as a step toward their abolition. There are other scenarios as well. The
general point is that the specific content of Israel's statement on its nuclear
program would be part of a broader political deal.

What would be the contents of such a disclosure statement? At the minimum, it should include a short official history and a short chronology of
the Israeli nuclear project. Some historical dates are important to understand
the intensity of the Israeli commitment to its nuclear project and its origins.
The history should start by explaining why Israel in its first decade, under the
leadership of Prime Minister Ben-Gurion, when the memory of the Holocaust was still fresh and against the background of the Arab world's vow to
destroy Israel, decided to develop a nuclear-weapons capability as an existential insurance policy.

This history also should reveal that Israel reached the nuclear technological threshold around 1966, two years before the Nuclear Non-Proliferation
Treaty (NPT), and could have tested its first device even before the NPT's
deadline of January 1, 1967, had it chosen to do so. But Israel was not interested in introducing nuclear weapons to the region, so it did not follow that
path. The history probably also should note that on the eve of the 1967 war,
Israel improvised a rudimentary but operational nuclear capability but that
its leaders decided not to demonstrate it. During the 1973 war, Israel's leaders
again decided not to demonstrate the existence of its nuclear option. These
milestones would show that Israel has treated its nuclear capability as sacred
and has not tried to gain any political or military benefit from it.

This statement of acknowledgment should describe the basic tenets of
Israel's nuclear policy, stressing the aspects of caution and restraint. Indeed,
Israel has never issued a direct nuclear threat to any of its enemies, not even
during war when Israel's security was in danger. Just as no countries in Europe see British or French nuclear weapons as a threat, Israel should ask its
neighbors to view Israel's capability similarly. The historical reference to the

Holocaust should be only a way to justify Israel's decision to seek this national insurance policy.

Although this statement should emphasize that Israel views its nuclear capability as an insurance policy as long as its existence and its legitimacy are questioned by others, this capability does not contradict Israel's commitment to its vision of the region—indeed, of the whole world—as free of nuclear weapons. Such statement should highlight the fact that Israel views its own commitment to nuclear disarmament as similar to the commitment by the five nuclear-weapons states. These states, under the NPT's article VI, are committed to the "to cessation of the nuclear arms race at an early date and to global nuclear disarmament."[22]

Final Reflections

In the end, Israel alone will have to decide whether it is ready to consider a new, more transparent and more honest bargain. Currently Israel, as the impasse over Iran's nuclear program continues, anxiously keeps what it has. American support is important, even essential, but it is Israel that has to make the move.

While for Bundy, Crowe, and Drell (or even myself), the act of coming clean would be an act that ultimately grants Israel the rights and obligations of a stakeholder in the global nuclear order, most Israelis see things differently. For them, the idea of coming clean on the nuclear issue is a mistaken, if not dangerous, first step on a risky road that would deprive Israel of its ultimate insurance policy. This reasoning resonated in the past, when Israel was in the early period of its nuclear pursuit, but it no longer suitable for today's realities.

For forty years the world, including the Arab states, has lived with and accepted a nuclear Israel. During most of that period, particularly in the 1973 war, Israel proved to be a cautious and responsible nuclear state. Even if amimut helped weaken the desire of many countries in the region to acquire nuclear weapons, it did not, and could not, prevent efforts by some states in the region—Iraq, Iran, Syria, and even Libya—to acquire a nuclear capability.[23]

Israeli fears about the future of amimut are genuine, but they stem from a mind-set and ethos that is engraved in amimut itself. There is a circular connection between these fears and amimut. At its core, the issue of amimut is an issue of identity. Amimut reflects a conservative defensive Israeli mind-set—"the world is against us"—that has changed little over the years.[24]

Israelis assume that Israel is politically too weak to acknowledge its possession of nuclear weapons; that Israel has no political standing to justify its nuclear status in the international arena; that "the world" would be less tolerant of Israel's nuclear weapons than of other states'; that the Arab world would vehemently oppose Israel's open nuclear monopoly, as indeed the Arab League declared in 2009; and that the Arab countries would withdraw from the NPT and acquire nuclear weapons.[25] Finally, the Israeli passion for amimut goes deeper than reasons of national security. Only under amimut can bureaucrats and politicians enjoy complete freedom to govern with no interference from the outside world, domestic or foreign.

In early May 2009, soon before the first meeting between President Barack Obama and Prime Minister Benjamin Netanyahu, two events took place almost simultaneously to highlight the sensitivity of this matter. The first was the opening statement by the new U.S. Assistant Secretary of State, Rose Goettemoeller, at the NPT Preparatory Committee meeting on May 5 at the United Nations. One sentence in that statement brought anxiety to Israel: "Universal adherence to the NPT itself—including by India, Israel, Pakistan and North Korea—also remains a fundamental objective of the United States."[26]

Within hours, Goettemoeller's statement made the headlines all over the Israeli media. Reporting soon turned into commentary, which then stirred a week-long national discussion about whether her statement signaled a new U.S. policy toward Israel's nuclear program, which could force Israel to abandon amimut and ultimately shut down Dimona. In a television interview a few days later, even Defense Minister Ehud Barak appeared to give credence to the view that the speech might be a sign of a new U.S. policy. In the words of one leading Israeli commentator, Amir Oren, the controversy was "a tsunami in a test tube."[27]

The Israeli media were not alone in producing such pandemonium, which brings us to the second event. Hours after Goettemoeller's speech at the UN, the *Washington Times* published a lengthy news story under the headline "Secret U.S.-Israel Accord Is in Jeopardy."[28] Its opening paragraph claimed that President Obama's nonproliferation efforts "threaten to expose and derail a 40-year-old secret U.S. agreement to shield Israel's nuclear weapons from international scrutiny." The story added that the nuclear issue will "come to a head when Israeli Prime Minister Benjamin Netanyahu meets with Mr. Obama on May 18" and that Netanyahu would seek assurances to uphold the Nixon-Meir accord.[29]

The *Washington Times* news story was accompanied by an editorial criticizing the Obama administration for withdrawing its support of Israel's ultimate insurance policy. Under the headline "Breaking Faith with Israel: Not a Time to Change a Policy That Produced Four Decades of Stability," the *Times* issued a statement supporting Israel's amimut along with criticism of the administration for its willingness to consider abandoning the Nixon-Meir accord. As is so common in Israel, the editorial saw the end of amimut as the end of Israel's nuclear deterrent, equating the policy of amimut and the weapons themselves. The *Washington Times* expressed a fear of linking negotiations with Iran to Israel's nuclear arsenal. The editorial contended that Israel was indeed a mature liberal democracy and a dependable U.S. ally geographically close to Iran, which should be considered an enemy.[30]

There was no factual basis for any of these claims except, at best, that single sentence in Goettemoeller's speech at the UN (and her subsequent refusal to say whether the United States would pressure Israel to sign the NPT), perhaps implying that this speech could signal a radical departure from the Nixon-Meir accord. Still, the *Washington Times* story and editorial reflect apprehension, even anxiety, about the future of the old bargain.

What are the sources of this anxiety? One explanation, close to the surface, invokes issue of processes and political linkages. Both Obama's and Netanyahu's administrations had just taken office and had not had a chance to conduct briefings and reviews before the leaders were scheduled to reaffirm old understandings on nuclear matters. Netanyahu was rightly worried that the "special relationship" between the two countries (viewed in Israel as a strategic asset) could be jeopardized by differences over the two-state solution and Israel's nonaction on the Palestinian issue. Israeli leaders feared that Israel's nuclear exceptionality could be compromised if the U.S.-Israel relationship were damaged. By raising questions in the American media and Jewish community over the Obama administration's attitude toward Israel's nuclear deterrent, Israeli sources might have been seeking to mobilize counterpressure on the United States more broadly.

Another, more structural explanation pertains to Israel's long-term concerns about the compatibility between amimut and Obama's nuclear agenda, in regard to both Obama's policy on Iran and the United States' overall vision of a world without nuclear weapons. In both areas Israelis worry that given Obama's long-term vision of a postnuclear world (and region), his commitment to amimut is, at best, partial. In fact, under some circumstances Obama might want to revisit, and possibly end, amimut.

Finally, it is impossible to address the Israeli nuclear bargain independently of the core political issues that gave rise to that special bargain. That would mean acknowledging the connection between Israel's bargain with the bomb and the enduring political conflict in the Middle East. The basic premise of Israel's bargain has always been that as long as its environment is hostile, as long as Israel is not accorded political legitimacy by its neighbors, it must maintain this insurance shield in the form of the bomb. The other persistent premise in the bargain has been shaped by a sense of caution: Israel is a small country, not a world power, so it must be very cautious and secretive in the way it pursues the bomb. Not only would the external world, including the United States, not be happy if Israel brandished its nuclear capabilities, but Israel also must be careful not to push its neighbors to a similar pursuit.

At the moment, a regional peace seems a distant prospect, which in the minds of the Israeli government justifies the retention and possible upgrade of Israel's nuclear deterrent. But it makes more sense to accept the premise that a just and durable peace in the region is a necessary precondition for a nuclear-free Middle East and also to intensify efforts to achieve such a peace, particularly with regard to settling the long-standing dispute between Israel and the Palestinian people.

The current focus of Israel and the international community is on the Iranian nuclear issue. It is impossible to tell how the confrontation between Iran and the international community will be resolved. For now, Israel, along with most of the other countries, is anxious to contain the Iranian problem without allowing it to be connected to Israel's nuclear weapons. At the end of the last chapter, I suggested how such a linkage could open the door to a denuclearization of the entire region. Although this has no chance today with the current regime in Tehran, it may have more success under another regime.

To make this proposal more attractive, it could be coupled with a reexamination, by both the NSG as a whole and its individual members, of the current laws and guidelines prohibiting the transfer to Israel of civilian nuclear materials and reactors, particularly natural uranium and power reactors. Although none of these states would jeopardize its national security to gain more access to the benefits of nuclear energy, a package deal with arms-control and peaceful-use components should be attractive to both Israel and other states in the Middle East.

Perhaps the Saudi peace plan could be linked to the vision of a fuel cycle–free zone in the Middle East; that is, a region free of enrichment and reprocessing plants. Unlike the FMCT, this would eliminate the risk that Iran or another Middle Eastern country could obtain weapons-grade nuclear materials through the misuse of declared and safeguarded enrichment or reprocessing plants. The goals of a nuclear weapons–free world and a nuclear weapons–free Middle East would require a major change in nuclear policy in both Israel and its partner in amimut, the United States.

Epilogue

In an interview on the eve of Israel's sixtieth anniversary in 2008, author David Grossman reflected on his country's condition: "Our army is big, we have this atom bomb, but the inner feeling is of absolute fragility, that all the time we are at the edge of the abyss."[1] Grossman is not the first Israeli to refer to the angst hovering over Israel, but he is one of few who link it, by contrasting it, with the bomb.

Today, Israel is the Middle East's military powerhouse, the region's only state with nuclear weapons, but this has not alleviated Israelis' sense of insecurity. They still are surrounded by enemies who publicly proclaim their desire to see the destruction of Israel. Thus, sixty years after their country was created, Israelis still face existential threats. Despite all the remarkable achievements of Israel as a state and a society, the Israeli identity is still infused with the collective experience of being under siege, and the Israeli collective psyche cannot be understood without considering the centrality of this sense of siege, the old Jewish "the-world-is-against-us" outlook.

This mentality or, better, "disposition" stems from the Israeli condition of having to grapple with the very legitimacy of Israel as a state. Israel's existence is still not formally recognized by most of its regional neighbors, especially its most immediate neighbors, the Palestinians. Israel seeks normalcy, and Zionism as its national ethos means normalizing the condition of the Jewish people. But after sixty years this normalcy is still elusive.

When Iranian President Mahmoud Ahmadinejad declared that Israel was an abnormal, illegitimate, and illegal political entity that was bound to disappear from the pages of history, Israelis interpreted his statement as openly expressing the desire to have Israel obliterated by the bomb. When he denied that interpretation and claimed that Iran had no intention of dropping nuclear weapons on Israel—in fact, that Iran has no intention of developing them and all he meant was that Israel itself, as a matter of historical force, would cease to exist as a Jewish state, he touched an Israeli nerve.

When Palestinian mainstream intellectuals and politicians lose faith in the two-state solution to the Israeli-Palestinian conflict and proclaim support for a one-state binational solution, they also touch an Israeli nerve.[2] Those who support this view argue that left to demography—the Palestinian birthrate is much higher than the Israelis'—that over time Israel would cease to be a Jewish-Zionist state. This also is Hamas's historical outlook on the conflict.

Israel's conflict with its next-door neighbors (the Palestinians) and its more distant neighbors (the Iranians) concerns recognition and legitimacy. As long as the core of the conflict, the Palestinian issue, remains unresolved, the rest of the conflict will also remain unresolved. Notwithstanding Israel's peace treaties with Egypt and Jordan, Israel still has not been recognized by the majority of its Arab neighbors and the majority of Muslim countries around the rest of the world (the United Nations has 192 member nations, of which fifty-two are Muslim countries, most of which do not recognize Israel).

Just as Israel lacks legitimacy from its neighbors with regard to its identity as a Jewish-Zionist state with recognized and defined borders, it also suffers problems with legitimacy at home. Six decades after independence, Israel still does not have a constitution, the fundamental document by which a citizenry defines the contract that links it with its state.[3]

The absence of a constitution means that none of the issues concerning Israel's identity as a Jewish-Zionist state has been determined and resolved: the nature of Israel as a Jewish-Zionist state, the relation between the Jewish state and its non-Jewish communities, the relations between Israel and the rest of the world's Jewry, and the like. One consequence of governing without a constitution is that it reinforces the old Jewish idea of governance as a communal arrangement built on consensus (such as the Censora).

At home and outside, Israel is defined by its problems with legitimacy. The lack of recognized borders and the absence of a constitution are two faces of the unresolved, undefined, and even opaque nature of the Israeli condition. If normalcy is the goal of classical Zionism, if the driving idea of Israel is creating a homeland for the Jewish people and thereby normalizing the Jewish condition, this normalcy has not been attained and is still far away.

Amimut, indeed, is the proper Hebrew term to describe the Israeli condition more broadly.

Israel's special bargain with the bomb, centered on amimut, is a microcosm of the larger Israeli predicament. The close relationship between the two, the Israeli condition and the bomb, can be seen in the metaphor that Israeli essayist Ari Shavit suggested, seeing the Israeli bomb as a "glass greenhouse shield" encapsulating and shielding Israel's existence.[4] As long as Israel exists in a hostile, conflict-ridden environment, it needs a shield. But this shield—this greenhouse—is not a substitute for normalcy. The bomb is not a substitute for peace with and recognition by neighbors. In fact, the bomb is a manifestation of this abnormal situation.

Israel's bargain with the bomb reflects one of the great achievements of the Zionist enterprise. David Ben-Gurion thought of that greenhouse shield from the very start, soon after the United States dropped atomic bombs on Hiroshima and Nagasaki. He took action to initiate the nuclear project by the end of Israel's first decade, and the outcome became available on the eve of the 1967 Six-Day War. Realizing this hope took less than a decade.

The bomb has made two contributions to the Zionist enterprise. It gave Israel that "greenhouse glass," a deterrence shield that allowed Israel to grow and flourish in a hostile environment. The bomb may also have helped lower the intensity of the conflict and even may have contributed to the recognition of Israel by Egypt and Jordan. But it has not transformed the core of the conflict. It has not been able to persuade Israelis and Palestinians to reach a realistic compromise; it has not even led them to a cold coexistence with Israel. In fact, the presence of the bomb may have even strengthened Israeli intransigence.

Furthermore, as long as Israel can maintain a regional nuclear monopoly, the bomb gives it existential comfort, what Shalheveth Freier referred to as "assurances in times of gloom." But once that monopoly is no longer assured, the old Jewish angst will resurface. Israelis are more anxious today about an Iranian bomb that does not (yet) exist than Iranians are about the sizable Israeli arsenal of atomic destruction, which they believe does exist. The bomb has not liberated Israelis from that feeling of being "at the edge of [an] abyss."[5]

Israel's bargain with the bomb is a microcosm of the Israeli condition in another sense. The bargain with the bomb suffers from the same basic flaws that characterize the Israeli predicament more generally. Just as the Israeli condition is typified by problems with legitimacy, the Israeli bomb lacks recognition, legitimacy, and acknowledgment. Israel is the world's sixth nuclear-weapons state, and yet it has never been recognized as such by others or even its own people. Unlike all the other nuclear-weapons states, including India, Pakistan, and even North Korea, Israel has yet to find a way to acknowledge its nuclear status.

If amimut reflects a fundamental feature of Israel's national predicament, it also is the ultimate mark of Israel's nuclear condition. Taboo and nonacknowledgment at home and exceptionalism and lack of recognition abroad are two sides of the same legitimacy problem. If I am correct, the problem of amimut is more than an issue of politics and strategy; it is an issue of Israeli identity.

In conclusion, I want to suggest some abstract and philosophical ideas that capture and connect some of this book's themes. First, a few words about the historicity of Israel's bargain, specifically about its growth from infancy into maturity. In his *Knowledge and Human Interests*, Jürgen Habermas offered a variant of the Hegelian-Marxist project of historicizing the human enterprise. Habermas argued that human societies are defined by their interest in physical control and in intersubjective understanding, and how they respond to each.

The interest in physical control is the interest in controlling nature, which leads to the creation of agriculture and architecture, technology and engineering. The interest in intersubjective understanding is the ability to communicate and reflect through language and ultimately to transform personal wonder into intellectual products. This interest gives rise to language and culture, religion and folklore, literature and art, philosophy and science.

Habermas argues that beyond a certain point in pursuing these interests, these human practices may become counterproductive, even detrimental, to our existence. Continuing to pursue physical control after it already has been achieved can lead to the wasteful consumption of material goods, the waste and spoilage of resources, and pollution and ecological disasters. Likewise, pursuing an intersubjective understanding beyond a certain point may lead to xenophobia, nationalism, racism, and belligerence.

This leads, then, to a need for a third interest to be addressed, what Habermas refers to as the interest in authentication. By "authentication" Habermas means being tuned to the historicity of the human endeavor, the need to address the authentic needs of today, rather than to ritualize interests that were met long ago. This outlook could acquire a Freudian flavor. That is, as children grow up, vulnerable and exposed, they develop various defense and denial mechanisms and the behavioral practices associated with them that allow them to cope with certain difficulties and challenges of childhood. But ritualizing these very practices when they are adults may be counterproductive and damage their perspective of reality. The mark of a healthy and well-integrated adult is the ability to modify, even abandon, those behavioral responses that used to be beneficial in the past and instead to adopt modes of behavior that address today's needs and interests.

I believe that the same is true with amimut. From its very beginning, amimut was a unique Israeli defensive (at times, even a denial) strategy designed to allow Israel to handle its early pursuit of nuclear capabilities. At that time, Israel was unsure about its ability to seek legitimacy for its nuclear pursuit and certainly was not ready to announce it. Israel had good reasons to be concerned about the risks of "introducing" nuclear weapons to the region. So amimut, with the United States' blessing, allowed Israel to possess nuclear weapons without really "introducing" them.

Amimut served Israel well in the early days of its nuclear pursuit. But today, both Israel and the world are radically different. Israel's original interests on the nuclear front have already been met, and amimut helped make it possible. Therefore, exhibiting the same defensive behavior regarding nuclear issues as if these interests have not yet been met may now be, or soon will be, counterproductive. Amimut forces Israel to maintain total nuclear secrecy, which is incompatible with the values of contemporary Israel. Israel thus needs to authenticate its nuclear conduct, at home and abroad, to make it compatible with today's and tomorrow's interests and norms, not with yesterday's interests.

This leads me to my other conclusion. Israelis are mistaken in continuing to believe that there is a direct connection between amimut, on the one hand, and their possession of nuclear weapons, on the other hand. This equivocation may have been acceptable at a certain time, but by now it has outlived its usefulness. The belief that the two are inextricably linked is by now not only a myth but also an obstacle to seeing things differently, to moving beyond amimut.

In his annual report to Congress in 1862, Abraham Lincoln observed:

The dogmas of the quiet past are inadequate to the stormy present. The occasion is piled high with difficulty, and we must rise with the occasion. As our case is new, so we must think anew, and act anew. We must disenthrall ourselves, and then we shall save our country.

Israel's past was not that quiet, but Lincoln's assertion that the dogmas of the past are no longer adequate to the stormy present also applies to a nuclear Israel. The growing interest in a world free of nuclear weapons and in the production of nuclear energy, as well as Iran's progress toward nuclear weapons, force new choices and outlooks on Israel. The most important step toward this new thinking and new action is for Israel to begin divorcing itself from amimut. The notion that doing so is too perilous to contemplate also is a myth. Israel must disenthrall itself. Israel now must find a way to live more openly, honestly, and maturely with the nuclear issue. If Israel believes that it has the right to have the bomb as long as others have the bomb, it should find a way to say so. Israel does not have fewer rights than other states do, and among these rights is the right to self-defense, especially when Israel's very existence is being threatened.

But Israel does not have fewer obligations, either. There are obligations to the international community and the norms of nonproliferation that this community adopted four decades ago, and there are domestic obligations to the rule of law and the values of democracy.

After sixty years, Israel should be less worried or defensive about proclaiming its rights, and it should also be more forthright and honest about accepting the obligations that civilized states have accepted.

Such an open and honest acceptance of rights and obligations would not, in itself, normalize the Israeli condition, but it would be a step in the right direction. It is time for Israel to take this step.

Notes

Preface

1. Nuclear-armed states are usually considered to be those states that, following a test, openly possess nuclear arms without violating any international obligations. The seven nations that have nuclear weapons on these terms are the United States, Russia, Great Britain, France, China, India, and Pakistan. North Korea is a special case, and it probably does not belong to this category. Note, however, that even North Korea made a point to test and to announce its nuclear capability, even if its first test, in 2006, seemed to fail. North Korea's most recent test, in May 2009, seemed to be more successful technically, which presses the point even further.

2. Ari Shavit, "Dimona," *Ha'aretz Weekly magazine*, December 12, 1999.

3. Historically, Israel was not the only state with a policy of nuclear opacity. India, Pakistan, and South Africa also followed the Israeli precedent and developed their own versions of nuclear opacity. Since its initial nuclear explosion in 1974, India has kept itself near the nuclear threshold, whereas since the mid- to late 1980s, Pakistan has crossed the threshold and maintained a version of a "bomb in the basement" posture. South Africa developed its own version of nuclear opacity when it possessed (but did not deploy) a small arsenal of fission weapons throughout the 1980s. Nevertheless, the official policy of all three states was not associated with a social taboo against disclosure or discussion of the kind that has existed in Israel since the 1960s. Unlike Israel, India stockpiled weapons-grade plutonium, but until 1998 it did not produce or deploy an actual arsenal. Unlike India, Pakistan produced and stockpiled a small arsenal of nuclear weapons, considering opacity primarily as a matter of political convenience. Pakistan was never committed to the Israeli policy of

constraints, nor was its policy grounded on a bilateral understanding with the United States. South Africa was probably the state that adhered most closely to the Israeli model, but it lacked bilateral understandings with the United States. See also Avner Cohen and Benjamin Frankel, "Opaque Nuclear Proliferation," in *Opaque Nuclear Proliferation*, ed. Benjamin Frankel (London: Routledge, 1989).

4. Gerald Steinberg, "Middle East Peace and the NPT Extension Decision," *Non-Proliferation Review*, fall 1996; see also Gerald Steinberg, "Deterrence and Middle East Stability: An Israeli Perspective" *Security Dialogue*, March 1997, 49–56; Gerald Steinberg, "Examining Israel's NPT Exceptionality: 1998–2005," *Nonproliferation Review*, March 2006.

Introduction: Amimut as a National Bargain

1. Yossi Klein, "Six Hairs Stretched Across the Scalp," *Ha'aretz*, May 2, 2006.

2. A small but revealing illustration of this anxiety as a national state of mind can be found in the efforts of so many Israelis to prove legal entitlement to hold a foreign passport in addition to their Israeli passport. Israelis view a foreign passport issued by virtually any European country, including the most obscure post-Communist emergent democracies, as a sort of insurance policy. The scope of this not widely reported social trend is remarkable, and I believe it indicates a great deal about the Israeli state of mind, particularly the need to ensure against an uncertain future.

3. "Is Israel Finished?" is the title of Jeffrey Goldberg's cover story for the May 2008 issue of *Atlantic Monthly*. Timed for publication for Israel's sixtieth anniversary, Goldberg's article raises fundamental questions about the success and failure of the Zionist enterprise and about Israel's future. *Will Israel Survive?* is the title of Mitchell G. Bard's book (New York: Palgrave Macmillan, 2007). Bard, too, raises a number of basic issues, from Iran's nuclear quest to demography and to internal tensions in Israel itself, all of which pose long-term questions about Israel's future and survival. There are many more. Benjamin Schwarz's article "Will Israel Live to 100?" in the May 2005 *Atlantic Monthly* explores the demographic aspect of the Palestinian-Israeli conflict, and *Newsweek*'s April 1, 2002, cover story was entitled "How Will Israel Survive?" by Christopher Dickey and Daniel Klaidman.

4. Quoted in Goldberg, "Is Israel Finished?" 37.

5. Amos Oz, *The Slopes of the Volcano* (Jerusalem: Keter Publishing, 2006), 45–47.

6. Shlomo Ben Ami, *Scars of War, Wounds of Peace* (New York: Oxford University Press, 2005), introduction.

7. Herman Kahn, *Thinking About the Unthinkable in the 1980s* (New York: Touchstone, 1984). See also Joseph Margolis, "The Peculiarities of Nuclear Think-

ing," in *Nuclear Weapons and the Future of Humanity*, ed. Avner Cohen and Steven Lee (Totowa, N.J.: Rowman & Allanheld, 1986), 153–68.

8. A series of polls on national security matters conducted by Asher Arian since the early 1990s show that the Israeli public perceives the acquisition of nonconventional weapons by Arab states as the "most serious" threat to their country. Between 1991 and 1998 the percentage of Israelis who ranked the issue at the top of their concerns was usually between 70 and 80 percent. See Asher Arian, *Security Threatened: Surveying Israeli Opinion on Peace and War* (New York: Cambridge University Press, 1995), 200.

9. When it was recently leaked that the government of Israel has been secretly digging a huge underground atomic command-and-control shelter in an undisclosed location in the Judea hills to protect its leadership against nuclear attack, hundreds of Israelis angrily responded on Internet sites on the eeriness of this Holocaust-driven contingency project.

10. Cam Simpson, "Israeli Citizens Struggle amid Iran's Nuclear Vow," *Wall Street Journal*, December 22, 2006.

11. For the full CIA report on the Syrian nuclear reactor, see http://www.washingtonpost.com/wp-dyn/content/video/2008/04/24/VI2008042403257.html?sid = ST2008042501916; Randall Mikkelsen, "Syrian Reactor Capacity Was 1–2 Weapons/Year: CIA," Reuters, April 29, 2008, available at http://www.washingtonpost.com/wp-dyn/content/article/2008/04/28/AR2008042802145.html; Pamela Hess, "Hayden: Syrian Site Could Have Produced Fuel for 2 Weapons," *Washington Post*, April 28, 2008, available at http://www.washingtonpost.com/wp-dyn/content/article/2008/04/28/AR2008042802122.html; and Robin Wright, "Syrian Nuclear Plant," *Washington Post*, April 25, 2008, available at http://www.washingtonpost.com/wp-dyn/content/discussion/2008/04/25/DI2008042501853.html.

12. Akbar Hashemi Rafsanjani, "Voice of the Islamic Republic of Iran" (in Farsi), Jerusalem Day speech, trans. BBC Worldwide Monitoring, December 14, 2001, GlobalSecurity.Org, available at http://www.globalsecurity.org/wmd/library/news/iran/2001/011214-text.html (accessed April 29, 2008).

13. Dr. Anthony H. Cordesman, Center of Strategic and International Affairs (CSIS), issued in November 2007 a report entitled "Iran, Israel and Nuclear War: An Illustrative Scenario Analysis," which supports this gloomy outlook. While the report acknowledges from the outset that "there is no way to predict the forces each side will have in the future, or how they might target those forces and use them in war," it makes the point that

> both sides would probably be forced to target the other's population centers in any scenario that escalated beyond an initial demonstrative strike. . . . It also seems likely that such a conflict would quickly

become existential in the sense that both sides would seek to inflict the maximum possible casualties on its opponent, and to destroy its ability to recover as a nation. . . . The outcome would be so costly to both sides, however, any such advantage would [have] little or no practical value. It is unclear that either nation could reconstitute itself on anything like a prewar basis, if at all. (Available at http://www.csis .org/media/csis/pubs/071119_iran.is&nuclearwar.pdf)

14. Tom Segev, *The Seventh Million: The Israelis and the Holocaust* (New York: Hill & Wang, 1993).

15. Avner Cohen, *Israel and the Bomb* (New York: Columbia University Press, 1998), 42–43.

16. Itamar Rabinovich, *Waging Peace* (New York: Farrar, Straus & Giroux, 1999), 4.

17. Soon after taking office in August 2005, President Ahmadinejad started to issue statements in which he voiced both themes. In October 2005 he began propagating the theme of "wiping Israel off the map," and on December 14, 2005, he started to refer to the Holocaust as "a myth" and suggested that Israel be moved to Europe, the United States, Canada, or Alaska; available at (http://www.cnn.com/2005/WORLD/meast/12/14/iran.israel). A year later, in December 2006, President Ahmadinejad organized and hosted in Tehran an "international" conference of Holocaust deniers. In his keynote speech he stated that "just as the Soviet Union was wiped out and today does not exist, so will the Zionist regime soon will be wiped out"; available at http://www.haaretz .com/hasen/spages/800098.html. Ahmadinejad's assertion was a slogan used often by the father of the 1979 revolution, Ayatollah Ruhollah Khomeini. Although "wiped off the map" was the translation provided by the Iranian official news agency, the Farsi phrase is more accurately rendered as calling for the regime to vanish from the pages of time. Ahmadinejad's meaning is that as an "illegal occupier," the state of Israel is doomed to disappear. But just as when he predicted the imminent demise of the United States, he did not use the slogan as a call for slaughter. See, for example, Ali Ansari, "Iran Under Ahmadinejad: The Politics of Confrontation," Adelphi papers no. 393, International Institute for Strategic Studies (2007):51–52. For background information on Ahmadinejad's Holocaust denial, see George Michael, "Deciphering Ahmadinejad's Holocaust Revisionism," *Middle East Quarterly* 14, no. 3 (2007), available at http://www.meforum.org/article/1704.

18. Charles Krauthammer, "Never Again?" *Washington Post*, May 5, 2006.

19. Commonly, Israeli political and military leaders and columnists refer to the Iranian bomb as an "existential threat." Recently, in a lecture before the senior Israeli military leadership, Minister of Defense Ehud Barak used this phrase in reference to the Iranian bomb. See Amos Harel, "Barak: Iranian

Nuclear Weapons Would Be an Existential Threat on Israel," *Ha'aretz*, February 17, 2009.

20. Ari Shavit, "Unity Before Calamity," *Ha'aretz*, February 26, 2009, available at http://www.haaretz.com/hasen/spages/1067054.html.

21. Simpson, "Israeli Citizens Struggle amid Iran's Nuclear Vow."

22. Yossi Melman, "Peres: Israel Has No Intention of Attacking Iran," *Ha'aretz*, October 21, 2006, available at http://www.haaretz.com/hasen/spages/777440. html.

23. Naomi Darom, "What Would You Do If Ahmadinejad Drops a Bomb Here Within Two Months?" *Ha'aretz Friday Magazine*, October 27, 2006, available at http://www.haaretz.co.il/hasite/spages/779307.html.

24. "Sneh: If Iran Gets the Bomb, Many Will Leave," *Ha'aretz*, November 12, 2006.

25. Avner Cohen, "Crossing the Threshold: The Untold Nuclear Dimension of the 1967 Arab-Israeli War and Its Contemporary Lessons," *Arms Control Today* 37, no. 5 (2007):12–16.

26. International Institute for Strategic Studies (IISS), *Nuclear Programmes in the Middle East: In the Shadow of Tehran* (London: IISS, 2008).

27. Jimmy Carter estimated around 150 nuclear weapons. See "Israel Has '150 Nuclear Weapons,'" *BBC News*, May 26, 2008, available at http://news.bbc. co.uk/2/hi/middle_east/7420573.stm?.

28. For example, the Stockholm International Peace Research Institute, *SIPRI Yearbook 2004: Armaments, Disarmament and International Security* (New York: Oxford University Press, 2004) ranks Israel as the fourth nuclear nation in the world in its deployed weapons in active service, just below France but above the United Kingdom and China. The two more recently declared nuclear-weapons states, India and Pakistan, are lagging significantly behind Israel in the SIPRI tables.

29. This is evident in the official Web site of the Israel Atomic Energy Commission, which was launched after big internal debates in 2005. The Web site says virtually nothing about what the IAEC actually does and what its real responsibilities are. The IAEC states only that "the IAEC operates two research centers: the Soreq Nuclear Research Center and the Nuclear Research Center Negev." The Web site provides the same nominal power capacities that were given decades ago but fails to cite even the minimal amount of information about the functional activities of these two facilities. See http://www.iaec.gov.il/pages_e/card_e.asp.

30. Hutton Webster, *Taboo: A Sociological Study* (Stanford, Calif.: Stanford University Press, 1942), 2, 13.

31. Memorandum of discussion at the 165th NSC Meeting, October 7, 1953, in *Foreign Relations of the United States, 1952–54*, vol. 2:532–33. See also McGeorge Bundy, *Danger and Survival* (New York: Random House, 1988), 249.

32. Robert McNamara, "The Military Role of Nuclear Weapons: Perceptions and Misperceptions," *Foreign Affairs* 62 (fall 1983):58–80; Bundy, *Danger and Survival*;

Thomas Schelling, "An Astonishing Sixty Years: The Legacy of Hiroshima," Prize lecture, Beijersalen, Royal Swedish Academy of Sciences, Stockholm, December 8, 2005; Nina Tannenwald, *The Nuclear Taboo: The United States and the Non-Use of Nuclear Weapons Since 1945* (New York: Cambridge University Press, 2007); Harald Müller, David Fischer, and Wolfgang Kotter, *Nuclear Nonproliferation and Global Order* (New York: Oxford University Press, 1994); T. V. Paul, "Nuclear Taboo and War Initiation: Nuclear Weapons in Regional Conflicts," *Journal of Conflict Resolution* 39, no. 4 (1995):696–717.

33. George Ball, "The Cosmic Bluff," *New York Review of Books*, July 1983, 37.

34. Avner Cohen, "The Last Nuclear Moment," *New York Times*, October 6, 2008.

35. Klein, "Six Hairs Stretched Across the Scalp."

36. Avner Cohen and Benjamin Frankel, "Why the Israeli Spy Was Imprisoned," *New York Times*, April 15, 1988, A35.

37. Robert Dahl, *Controlling Nuclear Weapons: Democracy Versus Guardianship* (Syracuse, N.Y.: Syracuse University Press, 1985), 5.

38. Richard Falk, "Nuclear Weapons and the Renewal of Democracy," in *Nuclear Weapons and the Future of Humanity*, ed. Avner Cohen and Steven Lee (Totowa, N.J.: Rowman and Allanheld, 1986).

39. Japan is perhaps the first case of nonproliferation exceptionalism that comes to mind. Without a bilateral understanding between Japan and the United States defining what kinds of activities Japan was permitted under the NPT, it is doubtful whether it could join the NPT. The United States was rumored to know about Japan's involvement in weapons physics work, but it did not report this to the IAEA. Japan is not the only NPT state that has made secret bilateral understandings with the United States regarding its obligations under the NPT. The United States is believed to have made exceptions for Brazil, Germany, and other countries as well. Then, of course, the recent U.S.-Indian nuclear pact is about officially making India a nuclear exception. In addition, before India, during the mid- to late 1980s, Pakistan was treated as an exception, when year after year, the Reagan White House issued national security presidential waivers for the application of the Pressler amendment.

40. Seymour Hersh, *The Samson Option: Israel's Nuclear Arsenal and American Foreign Policy* (New York: Random House, 1991).

41. I try to minimize my use of adjectives here, but the late Ze'ev Schiff was universally recognized as truly one of a kind, the dean of all Israeli commentators on matters of national security. For an excellent obituary that highlights Schiff's uniqueness, see Lawrence Joffre, "Ze'ev Schiff: Israeli Author, Military Analyst and Journalist Who Said Things Others Did Not Dare," *The Guardian*, July 23, 2007, available at http://www.guardian.co.uk:80/israel/comment/0,,2132490,00.html.

42. In his comments Schiff actually acknowledges that he does not really know much about the historical intricacies of how *amimut* as a national concept came into being and the who-did-what of the stories. Instead, his main point is a general one.

43. One of the major historical claims in my book *Israel and the Bomb* is that Israel stumbled into opacity in a piecemeal fashion. See Avner Cohen, *Israel and the Bomb* (New York: Columbia University Press, 1999), 196.

44. The first Israel academic to explicitly invoke the notion of "nuclear ambiguity" as a strategic concept and to analyze how Israel's nuclear program used ambiguity for political and strategic purposes was Yair Evron, "Israel and the Atom: The Uses and Misuses of Ambiguity," *Orbis* 17 (1973):1326–43. Around the same time, other Israeli academics also argued, all based on the open literature, that Israel's mode of nuclear proliferation used nuclear ambiguity. Prominent among those scholars were Alan Dowty, "Israeli Perspectives on Nuclear Proliferation," in *Security, Order, and the Bomb: The Role of Nuclear Weapons in the Politics and Defense Planning of Non-Nuclear Weapon States*, ed. Johan J. Holst (Oslo: Oslo University Press, 1972), 142–51; Alan Dowty, "Israel's Nuclear Policy," in *M'dina, Mimshal, V'yahasim Benleumiim* 7 (in Hebrew), reprinted in *Diplomatia b'tsel eimut* (Diplomacy in the Shadow of Confrontation), ed. Binyamin Neuberger (Tel Aviv: Open University Press, 1984):160–88; and Avigdor Haselkorn, "Israel: From an Option to a Bomb in the Basement?" in *Nuclear Proliferation: Phase II*, ed. Robert M. Lawrence and Joel Larus (Wichita: University Press of Kansas, 1974), 149.

45. Rodney Jones, Cesare Merlini, Joseph Pilat, and William Potter, eds., *The Nuclear Suppliers and Non-Proliferation: International Policy Choices* (Lanham, Md.: Lexington Books, 1985); William Potter, ed., *International Nuclear Trade and Nonproliferation: The Challenge of Emerging Suppliers* (Lanham, Md.: Lexington Books, 1990); Harold A. Feiveson and Theodore B. Taylor, "Alternative Strategies for International Control of Nuclear Power," in *Nuclear Proliferation-Motivations, Capabilities, and Strategies for Control*, ed. Ted Greenwood, Harold A. Feiveson, and Theodore B. Taylor (New York: McGraw-Hill, 1977), 125–90.

46. Cited in Avner Cohen, "The Bomb That Never Is," *Bulletin of the Atomic Scientists* 56, no. 3 (2000):22–23. Also see Avner Cohen, "The Bomb That Never Is," *The Economist*, October 19, 1991.

47. Gideon Frank, "Statement to the 51st General Conference of the International Atomic Energy Agency," Vienna, September 2007, available at http://www.iaec.gov.il/docs/statementGC51.pdf, 5.

48. White House, "White House Fact Sheet on the United States–India Peaceful Atomic Energy Cooperation Act," December 18, 2006, available at http://www.whitehouse.gov/news/releases/2006/12/20061218-2.html.

1. The Birth of Amimut

1.   William Burr and Avner Cohen, "Israel Crosses the Threshold," *Bulletin of the Atomic Scientists* 62, no. 3 (2006):23.

2.   National Intelligence Estimate 4–3-61, "Nuclear Weapons and Delivery Capabilities of Free World Countries Other Than the U.S. and UK," September 21, 1961, available at www.gwu.edu/~nsarchiv/NSAEBB/NSAEBB155/index.htm.

3.   Special National Intelligence Estimate (SNIE) 30-2-63, "The Advanced Weapons Programs of the UAR and Israel," May 8, 1963, available at http://www.gwu.edu/~nsarchiv/NSAEBB/NSAEBB155/prolif-7.pdf.

4.   Avner Cohen, *Israel and the Bomb* (New York: Columbia University Press, 1998), 154.

5.   Ibid., 175–94.

6.   Ibid., 231–35.

7.   "Israel: The Nuclear Issue and Sophisticated Weapons," December 31, 1967, State Department Records, Record Group 59 [RG 59], Subject–Numeric Files, 1967–1969 [SN 67–69], DEF 12. Some in the intelligence field believed, however, that such views were politically biased and that Israel was well under way to getting the bomb. Interview with Thomas L. Hughes, March 14, 2006, Chevy Chase, Md.

8.   Ibid.

9.   For the details of the Rabin-Warnke negotiations, see Cohen, *Israel and the Bomb*, 311–18.

10. Cohen, *Israel and the Bomb*, 316–19.

11. Cohen, *Israel and the Bomb*, 319; interview with Paul Warnke, May 21, 1996, Washington, D.C.

12. Yitzhak Rabin, *Pinkas Sherut* (Tel Aviv: Ma'ariv, 1979), 222.

13. Ibid.

14. Rabin, *Pinkas Sherut*; interview with Morton Halperin, January 20, 2006, Washington, D.C.

15. National Security Decision Memorandum 6, "Presidential Decision to Ratify Nuclear Non-Proliferation Treaty," February 5, 1969.

16. Seymour M. Hersh, *The Samson Option: Israel's Nuclear Arsenal and American Foreign Policy* (New York: Random House, 1991), 210. Hersh cites Morton Halperin in reference to Kissinger: "I heard him say that if he were the Israelis he would get nuclear weapons. He did not believe that the United States should try and talk them out of it."

17. Henry Owen to Secretary of State William Rogers, "Impact on U.S. Policies of an Israeli Nuclear Weapons Capability," February 7, 1969, Record Group 59 (RG 59), Subject-Numeric Files, 1967–69 (SN 67–69), DEF 12 Isr.

18. Melvin Laird to William Rogers, et al., "Stopping the Introduction of Nuclear Weapons into the Middle East," March 17, 1969, NPMP, NSCF, box 604, Israel vol. I. Awareness of the trend is evident in documents prepared for the Rabin-Warnke talks in October 1968. See Parker T. Hart to Dean Rusk, "Issues to Be Considered in Connection with Negotiations with Israel for F-4 Phantom Aircraft," briefing memorandum, October 15, 1968, SN 67–69, Def 12-5 Isr.

19. Joseph Sisco to William Rogers, "Israel's Nuclear Policy and Implications for the United States," April 3, 1969, SN 67–69, DEF 12 Isr.

20. For discussion of Plumbat affair and the alleged NUMEC diversion, see Seymour Hersh, *The Samson Option* (New York: Random House, 1991); Glenn Seaborg, *Adventures in the Atomic Age: From Watts to Washington* (New York: Farrar, Strauss & Giroux, 2001), 218–22; Elaine Davenport, Paul Eddy, and Peter Gillman, *The Plumbat Affair* (Philadelphia: Lippincott, 1978).

21. Cohen, *Israel and the Bomb*, 273–76; William Burr, telephone conversation with Melvin Laird, January 23, 2006.

22. Laird to Rogers et al., "Stopping the Introduction of Nuclear Weapons," March 17, 1969.

23. Joseph Sisco to William Rogers, "Israel's Nuclear Policy and Implications for the United States," April 3, 1969, SN 67–69, DEF 12 Isr.

24. Ibid.

25. Robert Dallek, *Nixon and Kissinger: Partners in Power* (New York: HarperCollins, 2007), 79. Also see Henry Kissinger, "Domestic Structure and Foreign Policy," in his *American Foreign Policy*, expanded ed. (New York: Norton, 1969), 11–50.

26. For the role of Halperin and Saunders, see Hal Saunders to Henry Kissinger, April 4, 1969, NPMP, NSCF, box 604, Israel vol. I.

27. "Nodis" or "No distribution" without the permission of authorized officials.

28. Nixon had consigned Seaborg to dealing with "technical" matters only, keeping him completely out of high policy issues. See Seaborg, *Adventures in the Atomic Age*, 213–17.

29. For the claim that NSSM 40 is still fully classified, see http://nixon.archives .gov/virtuallibrary/documents/nationalsecuritystudymemoranda.php. Evidently, this is not the case. While technically NSSM 40 is said to be fully classified, the NSSM 40 folder (mostly administrative documents) can be found at the U.S. National Archives in College Park, Md., and some of its substantive documents were declassified and can be found in various other files.

30. Interview with Morton Halperin, January 20, 2006.

31. Rodger Davies to Mr. Austin et al., "Review Group Consideration of Response to NSSM-40 June 26, 1969," June 30, 1969, RG 59, Top Secret Subject-Numeric Files 1970–73, box 11, Pol Isr.

32. Ibid.

33. Ibid.

34. Kissinger's memo of July 19 was declassified (almost entirely) and publicly released following a mandatory review by the Nixon Presidential Library on November 28, 2007. NPMP, NSCF, Box 0612 Israeli Nuclear Program. This particular memo is available on the Nixon Library Web site, http://nixon.archives .gov/virtuallibrary/documents/mr/071969_israel.pdf.

35. One of the attachments, entitled "Summary of the Situation and Issues," may provide a further hint to how the U.S. intelligence community viewed the facts regarding the Israeli nuclear program in the summer of 1969. While the general intelligence judgment about the facts is sanitized in that document, it does state that while there is a general consensus on the general judgment, "the issue dividing it [the intelligence community] is the more specific question of whether Israel has already produced completed nuclear weapons." Then, after another sanitized sentence, the paper observes that

> although views in State differ, the institutional position emphasizes that concrete proof is lacking and that Israel is concerned enough about its relations with us . . . to think twice about putting nuclear weapons openly in its arsenal. This difference of assessment raises the choice between recording a judgment that Israel may have nuclear weapons and recording only a general judgment as to Israel's capability.

The U.S. intelligence community clearly recognized that Israel had reached the nuclear threshold, but it had difficulty characterizing its precise status, whether Israel was merely "nuclear weapons capable" or actually "nuclear weapons armed." NPMP, NSCF, box 612, Israeli Nuclear Program.

36. "Summary of the Situation and Issues." Kissinger's paper (tab A) that was attached to his memo adds the following about the missile issue: "Israel has set up a production line and plans by the end of 1970 to have a total force of 24–30, ten of which are programmed for nuclear warheads. The first domestically produced missile is expected to be completed this summer [1969]. Preparation of launch facilities is under way."

37. "Summary of the Situation and Issues."

38. Ibid.

39. Ibid.

40. Ibid.

41. Ibid.

42. "The Issues for Decision," n.d. (early July 1969), NPMP, NSCF, box 604, Israel vol. II. The document stands alone without cover memos, annotations, or other indications that Nixon actually saw it or that Kissinger actually used it.

43. Telcon, Elliot Richardson and Henry Kissinger, July 16, 1969, 5:55 p.m., NPMP, Henry A. Kissinger Telephone Conversation Transcripts, box 2; Richardson to

Nixon, "Israel's Nuclear Program," with memorandum of conversation attached, August 1, 1969, NPMP, NSCF, box 604, Israel vol. II.

44. For the talks with Rabin, see Elliot Richardson to Richard Nixon, "Israel's Nuclear Program," with seven-page memorandum of conversation attached, August 1, 1969, NPMP, NSCF, box 604, Israel vol. II. All references and citations from that meeting are based on these documents.

45. Richardson to Nixon, "Israel's Nuclear Program."

46. Ibid.

47. Memorandum of conversation, "1969 Dimona Visit," August 13, 1969, SN 67–69, AE 11–2 Isr.

48. Ibid.

49. State Department cable 127273 to Tel Aviv, July 31, 1969, SN 67–69, Def 12–5 Isr.

50. Richardson to Nixon, "Israel's Nuclear Program."

51. Ibid.

52. Elliot Richardson and David Packard, July 16, 1969, Elliot Richardson Papers, Library of Congress, box 104, Telcons-July-August 1969.

53. Elliot Richardson to Richard Nixon, "Israel's Nuclear Program," August 28, 1969, SN 67–69, DEF 12–1 Isr.

54. Rodger Davies to Elliot Richardson, "Call on You by Israeli Ambassador Rabin, Thursday, August 28, 1969 at 11 a.m.," August 28, 1969, SN 67–69, DEF 12–1 Isr.

55. Dallek, *Nixon and Kissinger*, 535.

56. Harold Saunders to Henry Kissinger, December 8, 1969; and Walworth Barbour to Joseph Sisco, November 19, 1969, Nixon Presidential Materials Project (hereafter NPMP), NSC Files (hereafter NSCF), box 605, Israel vol. III.

57. My own inquiry on the American side, particularly with Dr. Timothy Naftali, director of the Nixon Presidential Library, revealed that the original memo of the conversation dictated by President Nixon apparently is not in the library's collection. See my e-mails, correspondence, and phone conversations with Dr. Naftali, May 2009. An inquiry in late 2008 to Israel's state archivist, Dr. Yehoshua Freundlich, also indicates that the minutes of the conversation known to be prepared by Golda Meir cannot be found in Israel's state archives. This mysterious absence from the official archives of any original documentation of the conversation underscores the issue's huge sensitivity and suggests that the ambiguity and uncertainty about that conversation are likely to continue. See Avner Cohen, "Between Natanz and Dimona," *Ha'aretz*, May 17, 2009 (English ed.), available at http://haaretz.com/hasen/spages/1085633.html.

58. William Rogers to Richard Nixon, "Suggested Position for You to Take with Israeli Prime Minister Meir During Her Forthcoming Visit," September 18, 1969; and Theodore L. Eliot to Henry Kissinger, "Briefing Book—Visit of Mrs. Golda Meir," September 19, 1969, enclosing "Background—Israel's Nuclear Weapon and Missile Programs," SN 67–69, Pol 7 Isr.

59. Ibid.

60. Rogers to Nixon, "Suggested Position."

61. Avner Cohen and William Burr, "Israel Crosses the Threshold," *Bulletin of the Atomic Scientists*, May/June 2006.

62. This could be deduced from a memo Kissinger wrote to Nixon two weeks later in which he referred to these "private understandings," implying that he was not privy to all of them. See Henry Kissinger to Richard Nixon, "Rabin's Proposed Assurances on Israel Nuclear Policy," October 8, 1969, NPMP, NSCF, box 605, Israel vol. III. But for historians studying the Nixon-Kissinger relationship, this sounds unlikely. They point out that just because the subsequent memo shows Kissinger's lack of familiarity with the details of what Nixon discussed with foreign leaders does not indicate that Nixon reached understanding with Meir that had not been coordinated with Kissinger before the meeting or had been kept from Kissinger after the meeting. Rather, some scholars have suggested that the apparent lack of familiarity might have been a clever attempt by Kissinger to commit to only some things on paper.

63. Strikingly also in October 1969, Nixon ordered a secret nuclear alert, whose purposes were known only to a few officials at the White House and the Pentagon. See William Burr and Jeffrey Kimball, "Nixon's Nuclear Policy," *Bulletin of the Atomic Scientists* 59, no. 1 (2003):28–73. Nixon also kept this order closely held at the White House and at the Pentagon.

64. Yitzhak Rabin, *The Rabin Memoir* (Boston: Little, Brown, 1979), 155.

65. James Adams, *The Unnatural Alliance* (New York: Quartet Books, 1984), 162.

66. Aluf Benn, "Even After Vanunu's Stories," *Ha'aretz*, November 29, 1991: "For more than 20 years there is an understanding between Israel and the US on the nuclear weapons. The Nixon administration agreed to accept an Israeli formula, upon which Israel will not test a nuclear weapon and will not declare its existence."

67. "An Evening with Former President Richard Nixon," *Larry King Live*, CNN, January 8, 1992.

68. Avner Cohen and George Perkovich, "The Obama-Netanyahu Meeting: Nuclear Issues," *Proliferation Analysis*, May 14, 2009, Carnegie Endowment for International Peace, available at http://www.carnegieendowment.org/publications/index.cfm?fa=view&id=23124&prog=zgp&proj=znpp.

69. Henry Kissinger to Richard Nixon, "Discussions with the Israelis on Nuclear Matters," October 7, 1969; and Henry Kissinger to Richard Nixon, "Israel's Nuclear Program," November 6, 1969, NPMP, NSCF, box 605, Israel vol. III.

70. Hersh, *The Samson Option*, 209.

71. Dallek, *Nixon and Kissinger*, 144.

72. Henry Kissinger to Richard Nixon, "Discussions with the Israelis on Nuclear Matters," October 7, 1969.

73. Henry Kissinger to Richard Nixon, "Rabin's Proposed Assurances on Israel Nuclear Policy," October 8, 1969, NPMP, NSCF, box 605, Israel vol. III.

74. This interpretation should be taken with caution. Some scholars insist that Kissinger's memos cannot be read as if they reflected all his knowledge and thinking at the time. Indeed, Kissinger was known to have used memos to create a paper record that would, in effect, conceal the real record of the actions being taken.

75. Once again, we should be careful when interpreting this assertion. Kissinger's remarks may well mean that he did not want to commit on paper some explicit statements made by Meir to Nixon, of which Kissinger was well aware.

76. Henry Kissinger to Richard Nixon, "Israel's Nuclear Program," November 6, 1969, with the memorandum of conversation attached.

77. Ibid.

78. Minutes, "Meeting of Special NSC Review Group on Israeli Assistance Requests," January 26, 1970, NPMP, NSC Institutional Files, Box H-111, SRG Minutes Originals 1970 (5 of 5); memorandum of conversation, Henry Kissinger and Yitzhak Rabin, February 23, 1970, NPMP, Henry A. Kissinger Office Files, box 134, Rabin/Kissinger 1969–1970 vol. I.

79. For "defensible record" and "record," see "The Issues for Decision," n.d. (early July 1969), NPMP, NSCF, box 604, Israel vol. II; and Kissinger to Nixon, "Israel's Nuclear Program," November 6, 1969, with memorandum of conversation attached.

80. Robert Munn to Joseph Sisco, "Scheduling of Visit to Dimona Reactor," June 12, 1970, RG 59, Records Relating to Israel and Arab-Israeli Affairs, 1951–1976, box 26, NSSM-40; telephone interview with Melvin Laird, January 23, 2006.

81. Alfred Atherton and Myron Kratzer to Joseph Sisco, "Response to Congressional Questions on Israel's Nuclear Capabilities," October 15, 1975, RG 59, Records of Joseph Sisco, box 40.

82. Aluf Benn, "Israel Asks Bush to Explain Its 'Special Relationship' with U.S. to Obama," Ha'aretz, November 26, 2008.

83. Aluf Benn, "In That Oval Office Where Netanyahu and Obama Meet," Ha'aretz, May 15, 2009, available at http://www.haaretz.co.il/hasite/spages/1085577 .html; Eli Lake, "Obama Agrees to Keep Israel's Nukes Secret," Washington Times, October 2, 2009.

84. Aluf Benn, "Obama Will Not Close Dimona," Ha'aretz, May 7, 2009; see also Cohen and Perkovich, "The Obama-Netanyahu Meeting"; Lake, "Obama Agrees to Keep Israel's Nukes Secret."

85. Benn, "Obama Will Not Close Dimona."

86. Aluf Benn, "Israel Asks Bush to Explain Its "Special Relations" with U.S. to Obama," Ha'aretz, November 26, 2008.

2. The Case for Amimut

1. Scott Sagan and Kenneth Waltz, *The Spread of Nuclear Weapons: A Debate* (New York: Norton, 1995); David R. Steven, Brahma Chellaney, Shai Feldman, Brad Roberts, Kenneth N. Waltz, and Scott Sagan, "The Kenneth Waltz–Scott Sagan Debate: The Spread of Nuclear Weapons—Good or Bad?" *Security Studies* 4, no. 4 (1995):149–70.

2. The phrase *nuclear resolve* is used in this context merely to indicate Ben-Gurion's deep commitment to the Israeli nuclear project and does not address his willingness to deploy, let alone to use, nuclear weapons. Nuclear resolve has otherwise been used in the academic literature by many cold-war theorists in reference to the willingness of nuclear powers to back up the deterrence posture with the actual use of nuclear weapons. For example, questions were raised about the efficacy of the United States' extended deterrence to NATO members because it was not obvious that the United States would have the resolve to use nuclear weapons against the Soviet Union in the case of Soviet attack on western Europe if the cost of such a U.S. attack would be a devastating Soviet retaliation against American cities. It was precisely in order to shore up the credibility of extended deterrence that Secretary of Defense Robert McNamara initiated in May 1962 the "city avoidance" strategy. The belief was that the U.S. reputation for resolve would be enhanced if its strategy called for attacking Soviet military targets first, avoiding cities and inviting the Soviets to avoid American cities. See Jonathan Mercer, *Reputation and International Politics* (Ithaca: Cornell University Press, 1996); and Theodore Hopf, *Peripheral Visions: Deterrence Theory and American Foreign Policy in the Third World* (Ann Arbor: University of Michigan Press, 1995).

3. *David Ben-Gurion Diaries*, April 26, 1949, and October 23, 1950. For a detailed analysis of Ben-Gurion's views, see Zaki Shalom, *David Ben-Gurion: The State of Israel and the Arab World, 1949–1956* [in Hebrew] (Sdeh Boker: Ben-Gurion University of the Negev Press, 1995).

4. Avner Cohen, *Israel and the Bomb* (New York: Columbia University Press, 1998), 10–12.

5. Ben-Gurion was particularly fearful of the scenario in which by way of pan-Arabic political unity, a huge Arab army would suddenly materialize on the Israeli border. The closest instance to such a scenario took place during the crisis in May 1967 that led to the Six-Day War. Ben-Gurion's conduct during that crisis, including his fateful conversation with Chief of Staff Yitzhak Rabin (which led to Rabin's temporary mental breakdown) is the result of this worldview.

6. Shimon Peres, *Battling for Peace: A Memoir* (London: Weidenfeld & Nicolson, 1995), 132.

7. Since the late 1980s, the links between the Holocaust and Israel's nuclear thinking became more apparent as younger generations of Israelis established a tradition of pilgrimage to the primary Holocaust site. A few years ago the government of Poland allowed Israel to fly a few F-15s over Auschwitz as a symbolic gesture to the memory of the Holocaust. The official Israel Defense Force (IDF) Web site refers to the "never again" speech that IDF Chief of Staff Lieutenant General Gabi Ashkenazi made to his general staff at the Hall of Names at Yad Vashem in Jerusalem in the 2007 Holocaust Memorial Day ceremony. "We are gathered here," said Ashkenazi, "the members of the general staff and I, in order to declare that this will never happen again. Almost every soldier in the IDF visited and was involved in programs in museums such as Yad Veshem in order to remember and learn from the Holocaust." Quoted in Dor Blech, "Never Again," Israel Defense Forces, April 15, 2007, available at http://dover.idf.il/IDF/English/News/holiday/2007/april/1501.htm.

8. On October 21, 2006, Iranian President Mahmoud Ahmadinejad talked again about the Holocaust, saying, "Even if we assume that six million Jews were killed in World War II, how come you don't have sympathy for the other 54 million who were killed, too? It is not even clear who counted those you have sympathy for." He maintained that Israel had effectively held European countries hostage for what happened during World War II. Quoted in Nazila Fathi, "Iran's Leader Warns West on Support for Israel," *New York Times*, October 21, 2006. Further discussion of this quotation and President Ahmadinejad can be found in the introduction.

9. In a nonscientific survey conducted in 2000 by the leading Israeli newspaper *Yediot Achronot*, most respondents ranked Ben-Gurion's decision to initiate the nuclear project as the "best" decision that any Israel leader has ever made.

10. Reuven Pedatzur and Yatza Yaacov, "250,000 Deaths and Half a Million Wounded," *Ha'aretz*, May 23, 2008, available at http://www.haaretz.co.il/hasite/spages/845241.html.

11. It now seems parochial to think that countering Israel was the only reason that the Arab nations and Iran sought their own nuclear weapons. A state has many possible domestic and international reasons to develop a nuclear capability. However, during much of Israel's early nuclear program, it seemed plausible and colored much of Israelis' thinking regarding proliferation and the introduction of nuclear weapons to the region.

12. To be sure, from a conceptual point of view, the Israeli predicament is not that different from that of all the other NPT nuclear-weapons states: they lecture nonproliferation to others but are reluctant to disarm themselves (as article VI of the NPT stipulates). But the Israeli situation is more complicated because Israel is not recognized by the NPT as a nuclear-weapons state and it lacks the legitimacy of the NPT.

13. See the discussion in chapter 1 about the meeting between Kissinger and Carter.

14. The most prominent among those voices was that of former Minister of Defense Moshe Dayan, who in 1976/1977 openly argued that it was time for Israel to change its ambiguous policy in favor of an open policy of nuclear deterrence. Prime Minister Rabin publicly ridiculed those who believed in "mystical weapons," but he quietly funded new advanced projects.

15. Initially, Israel was busy constructing its own nuclear resolve—building its own nuclear capabilities—in a manner that would not violate the United States' nonproliferation policy. Then the Nixon-Meir deal relieved Israel from American pressure to sign the NPT. But after the NPT regime was established, Israel had to develop a nonproliferation policy despite its specific reservations about the NPT.

16. Aluf Benn, "Seven Stages in a Long Corridor," *Ha'aretz*, February 7, 1995.

17. Gideon Frank, "Shalheveth Freier Legacy at the IAEC," in his *Shalheveth Freier* (Tel Aviv: The IAEC, 1995), 31–43.

18. This was an "excuse" of sorts for why Israel had to stay away from the NPT. The real issue was not that the NPT was deficient but that it was inconsistent with Israel's own nuclear-weapons program. Signing the NPT would mean that Israel would have to give up a great deal of its nuclear program or begin a scheme of deception and concealment. In any case, Israel's nuclear deterrence capability would have been substantially reduced. Any way you look at it, the NPT is inconsistent with the fundamentals of Israel's nuclear resolve. Israel did not want to be recognized as a nonnuclear-weapons state. Even if the NPT/IAEA system had been much stronger, Israel still would not have signed it. But Israel was proved correct in pointing out the dangerous weaknesses of the safeguard system. As the Iraqi case proved twice and as the Iranian case is believed to demonstrate now, the NPT safeguard system, even after being reformed, cannot provide real assurance to states facing an existential threat.

19. Personal knowledge; the former director general of the Israeli Ministry of Defense, David Ivri, referred to this review in some of his lectures.

20. David Ivry, "Nuclear Friction Between Egypt and Israel," paper no. 21, February 2004, Fisher Brothers Institute for Air and Space Strategic Studies, available at http://www.fisherinstitute.org.il/Eng/_Articles/Article.asp?ArticleID=60& CategoryID=25&Page=2.

21. Ze'ev Schiff, "The Meridor's Report," *Ha'aretz*, April 24, 2006.

22. Nonacknowledgment is what allowed Israel to respond so successfully to the Vanunu revelations in 1986, as it meant that Vanunu's claims were merely allegations.

23. It is ironic that none other than Shimon Peres, Israel's most senior statesman, the sitting president of Israel, and the nuclear project's chief executive in its

formative years, has repeatedly violated the strict protocol of amimut. Peres claims that he is the father of the amimut formula, that the formula was born in his accidental conversation with President John Kennedy in April 1963. In his autobiography, *Battling for Peace*, Peres includes passages about his actions on behalf of the nuclear project that barely, if at all, could be dismissed as compliance with a "nonacknowledgment" policy. In his biography of Shimon Peres, Michael Bar-Zohar states that as early as 1957, Peres signed agreements with the French to produce nuclear weapons cooperatively. Then in 1995, while serving as foreign minister under Yitzhak Rabin, Peres caused a major public incident in which he was blamed for violating the amimut policy when he appeared to suggest that for full and lasting peace, Israel would give up its nuclear weapons. See Michael Bar-Zohar, *Shimon Peres: The Biography* (New York: Random House, 2007).

24. Judith Miller, "Veteran: Israel's New President on Iran's Nuclear Program, and His Own," Weekend Interview, *Wall Street Journal*, July 21, 2007. At one point in the interview, in response to a question comparing Iran's and Israel's nuclear quests, Peres noted that "Pakistan did it before us and India" (apparently in reference to a nuclear test). The interviewer immediately noticed Peres's off-protocol comment and pointed out, "His comment would seem to be a departure, by the way, from Israel's steadfast refusal to publicly confirm or deny its possession of what analysts estimate is a nuclear arsenal of some 300 weapons." Incidentally, Prime Minster Ehud Olmert's slip on German TV, a few months earlier, also was made in answer to a question comparing the nuclear ambitions of Iran and Israel.

25. While it is difficult to discern the specific effects of nuclear deterrence—in part, because Israel has not faced (at least since the 1973 war) any real existential threats—it is widely believed that Israel's nuclear deterrence helped persuade Saddam Hussein in 1991 to limit his missile attacks against Israel to conventional weapons. I should also note that the case is far from being empirically or methodologically clear. Not only is it difficult to "observe" the specific effects of nuclear deterrence under opacity. But also, in this particular case, the epistemic difficulties are compounded by the difficulty of distinguishing between the effects of U.S. and Israeli deterrence; both countries threatened Saddam with horrific consequences if he used unconventional weaponry.

26. One could even argue that Israel has enjoyed more freedom of action and less interference in its nuclear affairs than have the official members of the nuclear club (probably all of them, with the possible exception of China). Since their nuclear-weapons programs became public, those states have had to deal with some pressure at home (in the case of the democratic nuclear states) or with international treaties and norms. Israel, in contrast, not only avoided making

any formal obligations regarding its nuclear program but also was "allowed" to keep its nuclear activities virtually off-limits to any diplomatic discussion with any other state or international body.

27. Michael R. Gordon, "Norway Says More Heavy Water May Be Missing," *New York Times*, May 25, 1988.

28. For details, see chapter 9. In brief, in August 1998, after China, India, and Pakistan joined the consensus in the Conference on Disarmament (CD) on the mandate to negotiate a treaty, Israel became the last holdout. For the first time in its history, Israel found itself able to derail a global arms-control agreement. It was then that the otherwise friendly Clinton administration exerted the harshest pressure that an American administration has ever used against Israel on the nuclear issue since the Kennedy administration. See Aluf Benn, "The Struggle to Keep Nuclear Capabilities Secret," *Ha'aretz*, September 14, 1998. For a broader discussion of Israel and the FMCT, see Avner Cohen and Marvin Miller, "Israel," in *Country Perspectives on the Challenges to a Fissile Material Cutoff Treaty*, a companion volume to the *Global Fissile Material Report* 2008 (Princeton, N.J.: Princeton University, International Panel of Fissile Material (IPFM), Program on Science and Global Security, 2008), 27–36.

29. Kurt Campbell, Robert Einhorn, and Mitchell Reiss, eds., *The Nuclear Tipping Point: Why States Reconsider Their Nuclear Choices* (Washington, D.C.: Brookings Institution Press, 2004), 48.

30. Emily Landau, *Arms Control in the Middle East* (Portland, Ore.: Sussex Academic Press, 2006), 83; Ezer Weizman, *On Eagles' Wings* (New York: Macmillan, 1976); Peter Jones, "Arms Control in the Middle East: Some Reflections on ACRS," *Security Dialogue* 28, no. 1 (1997):57–70; Peter Jones, "Negotiating Regional Security and Arms Control in the Middle East: The ACRS Experience and Beyond," *Journal of Strategic Studies* 26, no. 3 (2003):137–54; Dalia Dassa Kaye, *Beyond the Handshake* (New York: Columbia University Press, 2001).

31. Initially, Egypt insisted that the peace treaty had to include a clause requiring Israel to join the NPT, but when Israel (and the United States) made it clear that this would be a nonstarter for Israel, Egypt agreed to look the other way regarding the Israeli nuclear issue. See Campbell et al., *Nuclear Tipping Point*, 48.

32. There are multiple instances of Middle Eastern states seeking to develop nuclear programs only to be stopped through force or international pressure. The Israeli air force attacked and destroyed nuclear reactors in Iraq in 1981 and Syria in 2007, forcefully maintaining Israel's regional nuclear monopoly. Both Egypt in 1981 and Libya in 2003 halted their nuclear efforts amid intensive diplomatic efforts and changing global dynamics.

33. On Israel and the issue of the FMCT, see Cohen and Miller, "Israel," 27–36.

34. I noted in the introduction that the history of American nonproliferation policy is littered with exceptions: Japan, German, Brazil, not to mention India and

Pakistan. One could still maintain, however, that the Israeli case has its own qualitative differences that are missing from the others. I contend that the exceptionalism I discuss in this section is unique to the Israeli case.

35. Without written discussions of the subject, it is difficult to substantiate this view by referring to specific authors. Nonetheless, this is a point of view I often heard in conversations with former senior officials who were involved in the nuclear program.

36. This insight appeared in the early sociological literature about Israel under the concept of the "garrison state" phenomenon. See Harold Laswell, "The Garrison State," *American Journal of Sociology* 46, no. 4 (1941):455–68; Dan Horowitz, "Is Israel a Garrison State?" *Jerusalem Quarterly* 4 (1977):58–75.

37. There may exist some internal studies on this issue, and some insiders claim that the spin-offs were significant, but such studies were never published and they may be biased.

38. Ze'ev Schiff, "Preferring Political Ambiguity," *Ha'aretz*, January 23, 1992; Ze'ev Schiff, "A Fortified Nuclear Wall," *Ha'aretz*, January 27, 1995; Ze'ev Schiff, "Six Difficult Nuclear Questions," *Ha'aretz*, February 24, 1995; Shai Feldman, *Nuclear Weapons and Arms Control in the Middle East* (Cambridge, Mass.: MIT Press, 1997), 113; Dan Margalit, "Ambiguity Is Preferable," *Ha'aretz*, September 10, 1998; Janine Zachariah, "'Exiled' Israeli Academic Seeks Knesset Hearing on Book About Nuclear History," *Jerusalem Post*, June 13, 2000.

39. George Perkovich, "The Samson Option," *Washington Post Book World*, February 19, 2006.

40. Patrick Morgan, informal comments made in the second workshop on "Nuclear Weapons and Security in 21st Century Asia," Singapore, November 2006.

3. Israel's Nuclear Path: The Key Decisions

1. Avner Cohen, "On the Historiography of the Israeli Nuclear Project," *Israel* 9 (2006):245–54. I spent nearly a decade researching this history, but the result, my book *Israel and the Bomb* (New York: Columbia University Press, 1998), captured mostly the external political and diplomatic layers of the story, leaving the tale of those decisions almost untouched.

2. Cohen, *Israel and the Bomb*, 41–42. This may have been one of the considerations that persuaded him to end his retirement.

3. Cohen, *Israel and the Bomb*, 44–47. Documents that were inadvertently released in the mid-1990s by the Israel State Archives indicate unequivocally how dedicated Israel was in its search for a foreign supplier. These documents indicate clearly that access to plutonium extraction technologies was a key consideration in Israel's decision to join the U.S. Atoms for Peace program in 1955. The guiding force in the Israeli probes was whether and to what extent the new

American initiative could be used as a platform to start up a secret Israeli nuclear project. See http://www.gwu.edu/~nsarchiv/israel/documents/before/03-01.htm and http://www.gwu.edu/~nsarchiv/israel/documents/before/02-01.htm.

4. Cohen, *Israel and the Bomb*, 57–78.

5. Cohen, *Israel and the Bomb*, 52–55. When Ben-Gurion instructed the deputy chief of military intelligence, Colonel Yuval Ne'eman, who also was the officer in charge of the special intelligence liaisons with France, in July 1956 to share with the French every piece of intelligence information that he might have, he explained this to him by saying, "I want the bomb." Ne'eman first told me about this in 1994, but he repeated it in our last conversation in March 2006, just two weeks before his death, saying that he never forgot the impact that Ben-Gurion's powerful words had on him. Cf. Cohen, *Israel and the Bomb*, 362, n. 45. When a new generation of science recruits were selected for the project in 1955/1956, they were solemnly informed that their mission was to prepare for the Jewish people the means that a holocaust could never happen again. They all understood that the project's ultimate vision was building the bomb. Conversations with Professor Dror Sadeh, 1994/1995.

6. The best account of the French side of the Dimona deal is still Pierre Pean's *Les Deux bombes* (Paris: Fayard, 1981). In one memorandum of understanding that Peres signed with French Defense Minister Maurice Bourges-Maunoury on August 23, 1957, the parties agreed to cooperate in the research and production of nuclear weapons. This was probably an improper, if not illegal, document, since neither man was authorized to commit their countries to such objectives, but it surely tells us something about Israel's nuclear resolve. See Michael Bar-Zohar, *Shimon Peres: The Biography* (New York: Random House, 2007), 211–12. This memorandum of understanding was most likely signed without the knowledge of the French cabinet, which at that point had not yet made a formal decision on the bomb. See also "Author [Bar-Zohar] Says Shimon Peres Persuaded France to Backdate Nuclear Deal with Israel in 1957," *International Herald Tribune*, March 20, 2007. This memorandum was frozen shortly after it was signed and subsequently annulled, but no one could be mistaken about Israel's long-term intentions that it reflects.

7. From the outset, the initiation vision was setting up the organizational structure for the two aspects required for a nuclear-weapons complex: the plutonium-based production facility at Dimona and a central weapons lab to be part of a newly organized defense R&D authority (RAFAEL) to be located in northern Israel. Both organizations were established in 1958, with both reporting to the project chief, Shimon Peres. The driving idea behind this organizational structure of a "house divided" was security and control. Each side

in the divided project was to focus on its job with as little direct contact as possible until such contact became imminent and necessary. Over time, this organizational structure became increasingly inefficient and costly, to the point of becoming almost a threat to the mission itself, but initially it provided a way to ensure security even in the case of premature disclosure.

8.   Cohen, *Israel and the Bomb*, 12. Oddly enough, even today, more than forty years after Pratt was forced to retire from Dimona, Israel has not yet given him full credit for his role in making Israel's nuclear resolve so strong.

9.   Cohen, *Israel and the Bomb*, 63–67. During the initiation stage, Israel became highly dependent on the goodwill of its foreign supplier, France, to carry out its commitment. Had France pulled out at an earlier stage without reaching a compromise, the entire project could have collapsed. An early discovery of the project by the United States also could have killed the project.

10.   As a matter of speculation, it is doubtful whether Ben-Gurion told even his closest ministerial colleagues about the underground reprocessing plant under construction: the core of the project.

11.   Cohen, *Israel and the Bomb*, 76–78.

12.   Shimon Peres, "About Shalheveth," in his *Shalheveth Freier, 1920–1994* (Tel Aviv: Israel Atomic Energy Commission, 1995), 9.

13.   The fact that Ben-Gurion was both prime minister and minister of defense, along with the fact that the prime minister's office was small and without resources, made it natural that the project should be run in a way similar to projects in the other defense industries.

14.   Bar-Zohar, *Shimon Peres*, 228.

15.   Ibid., 231.

16.   Ibid., 231–34.

17.   Interestingly, this detail appears only in the Hebrew edition of Bar-Zohar's biography (Tel Aviv: Yediot Achronot, 2006), 326.

18.   Ibid., 234.

19.   On practical issues, however, Ben-Gurion was more cautious. He evaded the question of ownership of the plutonium and rejected formal international inspection of Dimona. He accepted a visit by American scientists but made it clear that it would be carried out under Israeli control.

20.   Cohen, *Israel and the Bomb*, 95.

21.   The real rationale and purpose of the Dimona complex has nothing to do with peaceful scientific research but all to do with the purpose of producing plutonium.

22.   Apparently for this reason, Ben-Gurion postponed his resignation for two months. In December 1960 he had been in the midst of a domestic crisis over

the Lavon affair, and he was determined not to resign from the government under these circumstances.

23. Cohen, *Israel and the Bomb*, 132.

24. Bar-Zohar, *Shimon Peres*, 256–58.

25. Shimon Peres had serious reservations about the specifics of the Mossad's alarmist assessments, but he viewed the Egyptian missile project as a new trend toward "deterrent weapons" that he considered historically inevitable. During the second half of 1962, Peres was a vocal advocate for the "new deterrence" school. Without explicitly advocating the bomb—the bomb issue was already a taboo—he argued that Israel must develop new and powerful "deterrent weapons," not to win the war, but to persuade the Arabs not to arrive at the "wrong conclusions." These discussions were so intense that they caused the U.S. embassy in Tel Aviv to issue a seven-page report on the strategic debate in Israel. See Cohen, *Israel and the Bomb*, 144–45.

26. Cohen, *Israel and the Bomb*, 148.

27. Some senior ministers from MAPAI (Land of Israel Workers Party) knew of and even discussed the nuclear project—Treasury Minister Levi Eshkol, Foreign Minister Golda Meir, Trade Minister Pinchas Sapir, and others—but they lacked security credentials, and for largely strategic reasons, they did not discuss the nuclear issue.

28. I discussed this meeting in a long interview with Arnan Azaryahu (Sini) at his home in Kibbutz Yiron on August 22, 1992. I took extensive notes from that taped interview. But I hardly used them when I wrote *Israel and the Bomb*, and this is the first time that I have returned to them. I interviewed Azarayahu one more time in January 2008 (that interview was videotaped).

29. Interviews with Arnan Azaryahu, summer 1992 and January 2008. According to another account, the meeting took place under the auspices of the Ministerial Committee on Defense, which Ben-Gurion chaired. Notably, in 1962 Galili and Allon were the leaders of the Achdut Ha'avodah Party, but they were not ministers in Ben-Gurion's cabinet, so this may have taken place in more than one meeting. See Moshe A. Gilboa, *Six Years, Six Days: Origins and History of the Six Day War* (in Hebrew) (Tel Aviv: Am Oved, 1968), 29–30; Yigal Allon, *Contriving Warfare* (in Hebrew) (Tel Aviv: Ha'kibbutz Ha'meuchad, 1990), 200, 205, 207, 305; Yair Evron, *Israel's Nuclear Dilemma* (Ithaca, N.Y.: Cornell University Press, 1994), 6–7.

30. Scott D. Sagan and Kenneth N. Waltz, *The Spread of Nuclear Weapons: A Debate Renewed* (New York: Norton, 1995). Peres and Dayan were surely influenced by the thoughts of the French strategist, Pierre Gallois.

31. Gilboa, *Six Years, Six Days*, 30.

32. I also should note that in the late 1950s and early 1960s, both Dayan and Peres advocated what was called a "European orientation." Both promoted the

idea of common interests between key European states—especially France and Germany—and Israel, whereas the interests of the United States, under Presidents Dwight D. Eisenhower and Kennedy, and those of Israel diverged. The French were fighting a bitter colonial war in Algeria, and they saw Egypt's Nasser as an important supporter of the Algerian independence movement. Moreover, Nasser's radical pan-Arab ideology threatened French interests in its African Muslim colonies beyond Algeria and complicated France's relations with conservative, monarchical Arab regimes. Following an approach used by President Franklin D. Roosevelt in the 1940s, both the Eisenhower and Kennedy administrations disapproved of Britain's and France's colonial holdings. Moreover, both the Republican Eisenhower and the Democrat Kennedy believed that one way to undercut the Soviet Union's growing appeal in the emerging Third World was for the United States to take a firm anticolonial stance.

Furthermore, after de Gaulle returned to power in 1958, France saw the acquisition of nuclear weapons as essential if France were to maintain its great-power status. Because of its history, West Germany was more disposed to help Israel economically and militarily, sometimes in the open but often secretly. Ben-Gurion repeatedly referred to West Germany as "another Germany" (i.e., different from Hitler's Germany).

Until he left office in 1969, de Gaulle staunchly resisted the bipolar structure of the post–World War II world, believing that in a bipolar arrangement France's role would be diminished. Instead, the way for France to revive its glory and influence was to help bring about a multipolar global structure. De Gaulle pursued the idea of a united Europe (although this "Europe of states," as he called it, is not today's more intimate European Union) serving as a third, balancing, power between the Soviet Union and the United States, and he also supported the rise of China as an additional "pole" balancing the Soviet Union and the United States. De Gaulle believed that France's military might and a rehabilitated West Germany's growing economic prowess would enable Europe to play this role.

Peres and Dayan believed that France's opposition to pan-Arabism and its desire to check the United States' growing power and reach would benefit Israel. Despite de Gaulle's initial discomfort with France's nuclear cooperation with Israel, France became Israel's major weapon supplier.

33. Yigal Allon, *Curtain of Sand* (in Hebrew) (Tel Aviv: Ha'kibbutz Ha'meuchad, 1968), 400–402. See also Allon, *Contriving Warfare,* 195–209.

34. Interviews with Azaryahu.

35. Interview with Azaryahu, January 2008.

36. Allon, *Contriving Warfare,* 305; Gilboa, *Six Years, Six Days,* 29–30.

37. To this day, Israel has not officially acknowledged the history of its ballistic missile program, but references to the missile contract appeared in U.S.

documents as early as in mid-1963. In 1996 Marcel Dassault published its own history of the MD-620 project, according to which Israel commissioned its request for development of the tactical missile on September 7, 1962, from Dassault Aviation. The original Israeli specification was for a surface-to-surface ballistic missile system capable of delivering a 750-kg warhead with a range of 235 km to 500 km, with a CEP (circular error probability) of less than 1 km. Israel's initial request also specifies a missile system that could launch between four and eight missiles per hour in all weather from either a fixed or a mobile launcher. The request specifies a preparation time of two hours and a success rate of 90 percent. The Jericho I design is revolutionary in that it was the first French missile to use an onboard computer. The Jericho I (originally designated MD-620) was secretly developed by Dassault in cooperation with the French Ministerial Armaments Committee (DMA), but without financial support from the French government. See Pierre Langereux, "Dassault lève le voile sur le missile Jericho" [Dassault Lifts the Lid on the Jericho Missile Story], *Air and Cosmos / Aviation International*, December 6, 1996, 36. See also http://www .aeronautics.ru/archive/wmd/ballistic/ballistic/jericho_1–01.htm.

38. Allon, *Contriving Warfare*, 305.

39. Moshe Dayan kept alive a veiled variant of this view in some of his writings and speeches before the 1977 elections, but subsequently he abandoned his open nuclear advocacy.

40. According to French sources, plutonium was being separated at Dimona by 1966; the theoretical and experimental design of the first Israeli nuclear device was at an advanced stage; and the French-Israeli missile under contract with Marcel Dassault in France (designated MD-620) was in its first testing stage.

41. Interviews with Professor Yuval Ne'eman, 1996 and March 2006.

42. Cohen, *Israel and the Bomb*, 223–24.

43. The French-Israeli missile project was leaked to the public by U.S. intelligence services as early as 1966. See John W. Finney, "Israel Said to Buy French Missiles," *New York Times*, January 7, 1966. As early as 1970 the CIA cited "Jericho" as the name of the Israeli missile (its original French version was known as MD-620 or MD-660), claiming that France had tested eleven such missiles for Israel. See Hedrick Smith, "U.S. Assumes the Israelis Have A-Bomb or Its Parts," *New York Times*, July 18, 1970.

44. The quotation is from an interview with Zvi Dinstein, Eshkol's trusted aide and the deputy minister of defense in 1966/1967. Later, a site was chosen and certain preparations were made to enable Israel to conduct a test, following a political decision, on relatively short notice.

45. Indeed, in his speech in the Knesset in May 1966, Eshkol confirmed that interpretation when he stated plainly that Israel had no nuclear weapons. See Cohen, *Israel and the Bomb*, 233–34.

46. This paragraph is based on long discussion with various people who were intimately involved with the nuclear project during that time.

47. Cohen, *Israel and the Bomb*, 207–15.

48. Ibid., 231–35.

49. Specifically, the concern was that Dimona's lack of international "legitimacy" could tempt Egypt to attack it while making it difficult for Israel to respond. In a top-level meeting in 1965, Rabin expressed this very concern: "If Egypt bombs Dimona and we want to wage a war, we could be issued an ultimatum from the entire world." See Ami Gluska, *Eshkol, Give the Order!* (in Hebrew) (Tel Aviv: Ministry of Defense, 2004), 71.

50. There was even some vague concern about the possible Soviet reaction to the discovery that Israel was approaching the nuclear threshold. In retrospect, it appears that Israel should have been even more concerned about the Soviet reaction to Dimona. In *Foxbats over Dimona*, Israeli researchers Isabella Ginor and Gideon Remez make a circumstantial case that the Soviets instigated the false reports that led to the Six-Day War as part of a larger plot aimed at Israel's nuclear program. See Isabella Ginor and Gideon Remez, *Foxbats over Dimona* (New Haven, Conn.: Yale University Press, 2007).

51. Gluska, *Eshkol, Give the Order!* 71.

52. Meir Amit, *Head to Head: A Personal View of Great Events and Clandestine Operations* (in Hebrew) (Or Yehuda: Hadi Artzi, 2000); Ronen Bergmann, "Peace, Try After: How Peace Was Missed on the Eve of the Six Day War," *Yediot Achronot*, June 6, 2005.

53. Personal information from various individuals who were involved in the matter.

54. Ambassador Walworth Barbour to Rodger Davies, March 9, 1967, *Foreign Relations of the United States*, 1964–68, vol. 18, p. 391, n. 2.

55. Interview with Floyd Culler, May/June 1996. Culler declined in 1996 to give the details of De-Shalit's message but suggested that I talk to him again a few years later. Culler died in late 2004.

56. Avner Cohen, "Crossing the Threshold: The Untold Nuclear Dimension of the 1967 Arab-Israeli War and Its Contemporary Lessons," *Arms Control Today* 37, no. 5 (2007):12–16. This article, as well as this paragraph, is based on the testimony of key individuals who were personally involved in the drama. They asked me to keep their identities anonymous.

57. Cohen, "Crossing the Threshold."

58. Cohen, "Crossing the Threshold." During that intense crisis, Shimon Peres, the former leader of the nuclear project and then an opposition RAFI party leader, privately suggested testing the devices as a deterrent move designed to avert war. Peres, like Ben-Gurion, was looking for any opportunity to avert war, fearing that it would be disastrous for Israel. In his 1995 *Memoirs*, Peres hinted at this episode. "My contribution during that dramatic period was

something that I still cannot write about openly for reasons of state security. After Dayan was appointed defense minister I submitted to him a certain proposal which . . . would have deterred the Arabs and prevented the war." It is impossible, of course, to predict what would have been the political, military, and psychological effects of such a spectacular move and whether it would have actually helped "resolve" the crisis peacefully. Surely a nuclear test would have introduced a dramatic new issue into a complex political environment that already was highly explosive. Clearly, Peres considered the crisis situation as Israel's best opportunity to obtain international legitimacy and sympathy for the bomb, but it also could be argued that given the intense crisis situation, including concerns about the Soviet Union's reaction, the big powers would have forcefully demanded that Egypt withdraw its forces from the Sinai and open the Strait of Tiran and that Israel give up the bomb and accept international safeguards on its nuclear program. Despite the great risks involved, Peres's idea made some sense. After all, what else had the bomb been built for if it were not to avert calamity in a war of survival? You would expect the IAF to win the air battles, but you couldn't know in advance that there would be a complete surprise and total victory in an air war with so few casualties. If the war had started and gone badly—say, the Egyptians had attacked early and wiped out much of the Israeli air force on the ground, followed by a sweep into the south—any test would have looked like, and in effect would have been, "use-in-war." It might have led to a second Cuban missile crisis with the Soviet Union and the United States building up nuclear forces in the area, but that would have been a small price to pay for Israel. Of course, Peres had a vested interest in making the nuclear-weapons program public because it would have made him look like the man whose project saved the nation. As it turned out, winning the war and keeping the bomb quiet was the best of all possible worlds for Israel, but I'm not sure it would have looked that way in May 1967.

59. One of them recalled, as he told me decades later, that he proposed after the war to seize the moment and to conduct a test with one of those cores. His proposal was never seriously considered. "It was a total taboo to them," he remembered. It shows the strength of nuclear caution at the political level, but we can only speculate how cautious Israel would have been had that proposal been accepted. (My source insisted on anonymity.)

60. With the appointment of Dayan as minister of defense, Prime Minister Eshkol asked former Chief of Staff Yigal Yadin to write a document, referred to as the "constitution," defining the division of labor between the prime minister and the minister of defense. Theoretically, the formal executive authority over nuclear matters remained in the hands of the prime minister, but in practice much of the budgetary responsibility was with the minister of defense. See

Yehuda Ben-Meir, *Civil-Military Relations in Israel* (New York: Columbia University Press, 1995), 101.

61. The cabinet was divided between Minister of Defense Moshe Dayan, a strong advocate of nuclear resolve, and the security-oriented ministers of the Achdut Ha'avodah Party, Deputy Prime Minister Yigal Allon and Minister Without Portfolio Israel Galili. Prime Minister Eshkol, who since mid-1968 had become increasingly troubled by medical issues, did not have the charisma and authority that Ben-Gurion had on this issue.

62. There are hints that sometime in the second half of 1968 Eshkol transferred the issue of the NPT to a small ad hoc ministerial committee.

63. Not many people realize today how important the Israeli case was to the evolution of the NPT. I elaborated on this issue in chapter 2, but here I remind readers that from an American perspective, Israel was hovering between the irreversible proliferation of the past and the new nonproliferation prohibition movement of the future. It is on that divide where the nonproliferation norm enforced a new global order. Since the mid-1960s, it was hoped that the NPT would be able seal Israel's nuclear status on the nonnuclear side, even if Israel were not allowed to cross the threshold. See Avner Cohen, "Before the Non-Proliferation Norm: Israel's Nuclear History," *Current History* 104, no. 681 (2005):169–75.

64. Possibly seven bureaucracies were involved, at one level or another, in some aspects of strategic thinking about the nuclear project's future. Their thinking was not coordinated, as often each body treated its own thinking as highly classified and not to be shared with the other bodies, and often there were major disconnects between those bureaucracies. The following is a short list of those bureaucratic bodies: Prime Minister's Office (reporting to Yaakov Herzog), Israel Atomic Energy Commission (reporting to Professor Dostrovsky), Ministry of Defense (reporting until May 1967 to Zvi Dinstein and afterward to Zvi Zur), Foreign Ministry (reporting to Foreign Minister Abba Eban), the IDF (reporting to Chief of Staff Rabin), Israeli air force (reporting to Commander of the Air Force General Hod and Brigadier General Peled), and Mossad (reporting to Chief of Mossad Meir Amit).

65. Cohen, *Israel and the Bomb*, 299–300.

66. I discuss this issue in *Israel and the Bomb*. Briefly, in May 1968 it was reported that the Israeli cabinet "had decided finally that it is useful for Israel to join those states favoring the treaty" and that Israel was close "to announcing its intention to join the NPT at the U.N., despite its concerns that the extent of its nuclear development would become an 'open secret.'" See "Israel: We Will Join the Nuclear Treaty," *Ha'aretz*, May 28, 1968.

67. This was exactly the argument that Deputy Secretary Paul Warnke used in linking the NPT with the Phantoms sale during his tough negotiations with Ambassador Rabin. See Cohen, *Israel and the Bomb*, 311–19.

68. If this analysis is true, it highlights the problematic way in which Israel dealt with its own nuclear situation. Owing to a combination of secrecy, ambiguity, and inhibition, senior Israeli officials—surely those at the foreign ministry and possibly even Prime Minister Eshkol himself—did not realize that the NPT was inconsistent with Israel's nuclear capability, that if Israel had signed the treaty, it would have been legally required to roll back that capability. Those Israeli officials who believed that Israel would likely sign the NPT had little understanding of the NPT and its far-reaching legal and political implications. At that point there still seems to have been little coordination among the various aspects of the Israeli bureaucracy that was dealing with the nuclear issue.

69. Israeli sources still maintained that Israel would soon sign the NPT. See "Israel Conducts Consultations of the Nuclear Treaty," *Ha'aretz*, July 2, 1968.

70. "Israel Will Set Its Policy After the Non-Nuclear State Conference," *Ha'aretz*, August 30, 1968. By 1978 all three co-custodians of the NPT made statements that pledged negative security assurances. See Thomas Graham and Leonor Tomero, "Obligations for Us All: NATO and Negative Security Assurances," *Disarmament Diplomacy* 49 (2000).

71. Cohen, *Israel and the Bomb*, 311–19.

72. Interview with Professor Yuval Ne'eman, 1994 and March 2006.

73. Cohen, *Israel and the Bomb*, chap. 12.

74. Yuval Ne'eman, "Israel and Nuclear Deterrence," *Ma'archot* 308 (1986):19–21.

75. Cohen, "Crossing the Threshold"; Cohen, *Israel and the Bomb*, 273–76.

76. The academic literature refers to three different possible uses of nuclear weapons:

    1. *As a deterrent*: Knowledge of the existence of the weapons would persuade the other side not to attack, or to attack only in a limited fashion. Accordingly, to enhance deterrence, a nation conducts a test or a demonstration of its nuclear capabilities.

    2. *As a war-fighting weapon*: During the cold war, military planners used to talk about three sets of targets in this category: *Bravo* targets (for "blunting") that used tactical nuclear weapons to destroy enemy units; *Delta* targets (for "denial") that used nuclear weapons to destroy the other side's own nuclear weapons and missiles, thus denying it these capabilities; and *Romeo* targets (for "retardation") that used nuclear weapons to destroy the enemy's industrial base.

    3. *As punishment*: Even if nuclear weapons are not effective as deterrence or war-fighting weapons, they can be used to inflict punishment on the other side in return for what it did.

    We have no evidence that would allow us to say whether or not the higher echelons of the Israeli military establishment discussed using nuclear weapons for war fighting. (Seymour Hersh argues that after 1973, they did discuss whether or not Israel should develop nuclear land mines and nuclear artillery for the purpose of stopping large Arab tank formations, such as those attacking Israel during the 1973 war.) To the best of my knowledge, Israel's approach to nuclear weapons emphasizes only deterrence and punishment.

77. See Dan Margalit, *I Saw Them* (in Hebrew) (Tel Aviv: Zamora-Bitan, 1997); Tom Segev, *1967: Israel, the War and the Year That Transformed the Middle East* (New York: Metropolitan Books, 2007); and Bar Zohar, *Shimon Peres.*

78. Avner Cohen, "Nuclear Arms in Crisis Under Secrecy: Israel and the Lessons of the 1967 and 1973 Wars," in *Planning the Unthinkable: How New Powers Will Use Nuclear, Biological and Chemical Weapons,* ed. Peter Lavoy and Scott Sagan (Ithaca, N.Y.: Cornell University Press, 2000), 104–24.

79. Ibid.

80. This anecdote was told to me by the late Arnan Azaryahu ("Sini"), who also was waiting outside the cabinet room for his own boss, Minister Israel Galili. Interview, January 2008, Kibbutz Yiron, Israel

81. Interview with Professor Yuval Ne'eman, Zahala, March 2006.

82. We should note, though, that it would be inaccurate to say that Meir stared into the "abyss" in the way that Kennedy did in 1962 during the Cuban missile crisis. Meir's situation was completely different from Kennedy's. Kennedy had to consider not only using nuclear weapons against the Soviet Union but also how it would retaliate. Defense Secretary Robert McNamara estimated that around 20 million people in the United States would be killed if the Soviets retaliated with nuclear weapons. Egypt and Syria, however, could not have done that. So Meir may have had moral qualms about using nuclear weapons, but there was no abyss. Her decision not to resort to nuclear weapons even during the darkest hour of the 1973 war tells much about Israel's nuclear caution: Unlike the United States during the Cuban missile crisis, Israel did not have to take into account a devastating nuclear retaliation by the other side. Meir demonstrated that Israel was a responsible and cautious nuclear custodian. Her actions recognized that nuclear weapons were not like other weapons and that under almost no circumstances must they be used.

83. Nuclear weapons may not have a military use during a war between Israel and its neighbors, but they likely have shaped Egypt's and Syria's war strategies. Owing to the effects of amimut, the issue has never been rigidly researched in the Arab side, but speculations persist that among the reasons the two countries had chosen in 1973 limited war aims and did not plan to exploit the success of their initial surprise beyond the battlefield is their belief that if they crossed certain Israeli red lines and went beyond inflicting localized military setbacks on the front and tried to inflict serious destruction on Israel's society and economy, then Israel might resort to using its nuclear weapons.

I personally heard various distinguished Egyptians, including even former senior military officers, suggest this. It was never clear to me whether their claims were based on actual factual knowledge or on their own theoretical presumptions.

Not surprisingly, in Israel itself, the proponents of nuclear weapons adopted this perspective and argue that Israel's nuclear capabilities despite amimut already have played a useful role. The presumed presence of these capabilities was sufficient to convince Egyptian and Syrian leaders that they could not regain by military means the territories they had lost in the 1967 war, let alone destroy the state of Israel. Sadat may have concluded that a limited war was necessary to force Israel to negotiate the future of these territories but that it was only through negotiations, not war, that they stood a chance of attaining their goals. The counterargument, however, asserted that neither the Egyptians nor the Syrians needed even to consider the nuclear issue because they did not see themselves as militarily capable to sustain their onslaught beyond its limited geographical aims. In fact, since the very purpose of the 1973 war was to shatter the political status quo, Egypt had no need to move beyond the limited scope of its war plans. In the early 1980s Israeli academics Shlomo Aronson and Yair Evron debated the issue, but the debate was largely theoretical because both sides lacked conclusive empirical evidence. See Shlomo Aronson, "The Nuclear Dimension of the Arab-Israeli Conflict: The Case of the Yom Kippur War," and Yair Evron, "The Relevance and Irrelevance of Nuclear Options in Conventional Wars: The 1973 October War," both in *Jerusalem Journal of International Relations* 7, no. 1/2 (1984).

84. Jeffrey T. Richelson, *Spying on the Bomb* (New York: Norton, 2006). See also David Albright, "The Flash in the Atlantic." *Bulletin of Atomic Scientists*, July 1994.

85. See table 1 in the introduction.

86. Seymour Hersh, *The Samson Option: Israel's Nuclear Arsenal and American Foreign Policy* (New York: Random House, 1991).

87. International Institute for Strategic Studies (IISS), *Nuclear Programmes in the Middle East: In the Shadow of Iran* (London: IISS, 2008), 133; "Revealed: The Secrets of Israel's Nuclear Arsenals," *Sunday Times*, October 5, 1986; Frank Barnaby, *The Invisible Bomb: The Nuclear Arms Race in the Middle East* (London: I. B. Tauris, 1989), 24; Hersh, *The Samson Option*, 291, 312, 319; Anthony Cordesman, *Perilous Prospects: The Peace Process and the Arab-Israeli Military Balance* (Boulder, Colo.: Westview Press, 1996), 234; Wisconsin Project on Nuclear Arms Control, "Israel's Plutonium Production," *Risk Report* 2, no. 4 (1996); DIA estimate published in Rowan Scarborough, *Rumsfeld's War: The Untold Story of America's Anti-Terrorist Commander* (Washington, D.C.: Regnery, 2004), 194–223; Kenneth Bower, "A Propensity for Conflict: Potential Scenarios and

Outcomes of War in the Middle East," *Jane's Intelligence Review*, special report no. 14 (1997):14–15; Stockholm International Peace Research Institute (SIPRI), *SIPRI Yearbook 2007: Armaments, Disarmament and International Security* (Stockholm: SIPRI, 2007), 548.

88. Joseph Cirincione, Jon Wolfsthal, and Miriam Rajkumar, *Deadly Arsenals: Nuclear, Biological and Chemical Threats* (Washington, D.C.: Carnegie International Press, 2005).

89. A case in point is Iran, a state that for some three decades has been establishing its nuclear infrastructure.

90. I believe that every historical narrative is based to some extent on reconstruction. This is so even if we don't have the problems with the historical evidence that we do in this case. It always is true that in the real world such dilemmas never occur in isolation and insulation from other aspects of the big picture. Furthermore, in the real world, those dilemmas are tied to budgetary constraints, as well as other policy options and personnel considerations. It is those internal and external connections that make the actual decision-making process much messier than any historian's narrative. The very historian's act of creating narratives inevitably involves some reconstruction as well.

4. The Infrastructure of Amimut

1. Here is one example. In Israel, former heads of the intelligence services (Mossad and GSS) usually maintain a certain public profile on matters of national security after retirement, but this is not the case with the former heads of the IAEC. Although there are no legal formal prohibitions, in accordance with a self-imposed code of conduct, Israel's nuclear priesthood tends to maintain silence on these matters. They do not write books; they hardly ever deliver public speeches; and they do not write memoirs.

2. The Institute for Intelligence and Special Operations, otherwise known as the Mossad, was charged by the state of Israel to "collect information, analyze intelligence, and perform special covert operations beyond its borders." See Mossad, "About Us," available at http://www.mossad.gov.il/Eng/AboutUs.aspx. After this mission statement is a description of the specific missions falling under the Mossad mandate:

   • Covert intelligence gathering beyond Israel's borders.
   • Preventing the development and procurement of non-conventional weapons by hostile countries.
   • Preventing terrorist acts against Israeli targets abroad.
   • Developing and maintaining special diplomatic and other covert relations.

- Bringing Jews home from countries where official Aliya agencies are not allowed to operate.
- Producing strategic, political and operational intelligence.

3. Israel Security Agency, "Core Values of the Israel Security Agency," available at http://www.shabak.gov.il/English/about/Pages/valuseEn.aspx.

4. There are some differences as well. The IAEC's mandate is broader because it also includes that of the U.S. Nuclear Regulatory Commission (NRC). The IAEC, like the original American Atomic Energy Commission (AEC), is responsible for all national nuclear energy activities, both civilian and military.

5. National Nuclear Security Agency, "About NNSA," available at http://nnsa.energy.gov/about/index.htm. See also Congressional Research Service, "Nuclear Weapons R&D Organizations in Nine Nations," March 16, 2009, available at http://www.fas.org/sgp/crs/nuke/R40439.pdf.

6. Israel Atomic Energy Commission, "About Us," available http://www.iaec.gov.il/pages_e/card_e.asp.

7. Israel Atomic Energy Commission, "About Us." Its existence did not become known to the citizens of Israel for two more years. Almost by chance, during a radio interview, Professor Ernst David Bergmann, the agency's founding chair, accidentally revealed that Israel had formed its own atomic energy commission.

8. Avner Cohen, *Israel and the Bomb* (New York: Columbia University Press, 1998), 31.

9. On July 15, 1951, the day that Bergmann was fired from his position as scientific director of the Weizmann Institute, Ben-Gurion offered him two new hats: scientific adviser to the prime minister and head of R&D in the Ministry of Defense (MOD). Bergmann also was a professor of organic chemistry at the Hebrew University in Jerusalem.

10. Cohen, *Israel and the Bomb*, chap. 2.

11. For a brief comparative study of how all nine nuclear states manage their nuclear affairs, see Congressional Research Service, "Nuclear Weapons R&D Organizations in Nine Nations," March 16, 2009, available at http://www.fas.org/sgp/crs/nuke/R40439.pdf.

12. On classification issues, the U.S. Department of Defense (DOD) opposed several important declassification actions that the U.S. Department of Energy (DOE) recommended. For example, the DOE recommended declassifying the number of warheads in the U.S. stockpile, but the DOD opposed this. See U.S. Department of Energy, "Fact Sheet: Proposed Declassification of the Number of Nuclear Warheads in the U.S. Stockpile," available at http://www.fas.org/sgp/othergov/doe/fs_stockpile.html. Likewise, the DOE recommended declassifying former nuclear-weapons storage sites outside the United States,

and the DOD opposed it. See U.S. Department of Energy, "Fact Sheet: Proposed Declassification of the Locations of the Former Nuclear Weapons Storage Sites," available at http://www.fas.org/sgp/othergov/doe/fs_sites.html. Since concurrence by both DOE and DOD was required to declassify such information, it remained classified.

13. I learned about this document from a conversation with Azaryahu Arnan (Sini), Minister Galili's senior aide who made references to its existence. Interviews with Arnan, Kibbutz Yiron, summer 1992 and January 26, 2008. See also Yehuda Ben Meir, *Civil-Military Relations in Israel* (New York: Columbia University Press, 1995), 101; Tom Segev, *1967: Israel, the War and the Year That Transformed the Middle East* (New York: Metropolitan Books, 2007).

14. Interviews and conversations with Azaryahu Arnan, Kibbutz Yiron, summer 1992 and January 26, 2008. See also Ben Meir, *Civil-Military Relations in Israel*, 101; Tom Segev, *1967*.

15. Ben Meir, *Civil Military Relations in Israel*, 102; see also Yoram Peri, *Between Battle and Ballots: Israeli Military in Politics* (Cambridge: Cambridge University Press, 1983), 137–38.

16. Seymour Hersh, *The Samson Option: Israel's Nuclear Arsenal and American Foreign Policy* (New York: Random House, 1991), 217.

17. Ruud Van Dijk, "Defense Condition (DEFCON) Alert System," *Encyclopedia of the Cold War* (London: Taylor & Francis, 2008), 237.

18. Douglas Frantz, "Israel's Arsenal Is Point of Contention: Officials Confirm That the Nation Can Now Launch Atomic Weapons from Land, Sea and Air," *Los Angeles Times*, October 12, 2003.

19. We can speculate that here the analogy between the Israeli and the American nuclear arrangement breaks down. Earlier I compared some of the IAEC's functions with those of the American NNSA. Both are the national bureaucracies in charge of the nuclear-weapons complex. But in Israel the prime minister is in charge of the entire nuclear system overall, and the minister of defense has certain responsibilities for some of the system's nonnuclear components. In regard to command and control, no single decision maker can independently use Israel's nuclear arsenal.

20. Amir Oren, "Where Did the 300 Million Go?" *Ha'aretz*, March 27, 2006; Amir Oren, "Nuclear Deterrence, with a Grain of Salt," *Ha'aretz*, June 10, 2008.

21. One historical anecdote illustrates my point. When the first IAEC director general, Professor Israel Dostrovsky, was nearing retirement in 1971, the entire defense establishment leadership believed that the most qualified man to be the new head the IAEC was Moshe Arens, at that time a distinguished aeronautics engineer and professor (and subsequently twice the minister of defense). Arens was one of the founding fathers of Israel's missile program, and

given the challenges facing the IAEC in 1971, he was probably the best-qualified man for the job. But even though Arens was formally removed from party politics, he was nevertheless known to have hawkish political views and to be personally close to the Herut (later Likud) Party's leaders. Although we do not know exactly why, Prime Minister Golda Meir was not comfortable with having Arens as her atom chief, so she rejected the bureaucracy's candidate and offered the job to another professional, Shalheveth Freier, who was truly apolitical. Meir had known Freier well when he was the science attaché in Paris in the late 1950s, as the man who handled the Dimona deal. As foreign minister at the time, Golda Meir had fought hard with Freier's boss, Shimon Peres, but she had learned to respect his man in Paris. A decade later, as prime minister, Meir now preferred the apolitical and quiet Freier to the hawkish Arens. Two years later the Yom Kippur War erupted and Freier was her right-hand man on the bomb. With Freier at her side, Meir resisted Dayan's proposals to demonstrate Israel's nuclear capability. She kept her promise to President Nixon and amimut was saved. We can only speculate about what might have happened if Arens had been appointed in 1971, as the leaders of the defense establishment originally proposed.

22. Conversations with Shalheveth Freier, 1991 to 1994.

23. Aluf Benn, "The Official," *Ha'aretz*, September 17, 2001.

24. Ibid.

25. There was at least one previous case in which the prime minister delegated some of his authority over the IAEC to another minister. Professor Yuval Ne'eman, who served as minister of science under Prime Minister Menachem Begin from July 1982 until October 1983, was asked by Begin to serve as the acting chair of the IAEC for part of that period. Since early 2009, under Prime Minister Benjamin Netanyahu, Dan Meridor has been serving as the deputy prime minister and the minister in charge of intelligence and nuclear energy in the prime minister's office. Yet it remains unclear what formal executive authorities, if any, actually were given to Mr. Meridor or whether he simply acts on behalf of the prime minister. See also chapter 8.

26. Benn, "The Official."

27. Ran Edelist, "The Man Who Rides the Tamnun," *Ma'ariv*, February 25, 2000, available at http://www.nrg.co.il/online/archive/ART37/265.html.

28. Horev's name was disclosed in 2000 by an Arab member of the Knesset who used his parliamentary immunity to name Horev in a speech. Once released, the censor could no longer forbid its publication. His picture was disclosed a few months later by the BBC.

29. On Benjamin Blumberg, see Yossi Melman, "Discrete," *Ha'aretz Friday Magazine*, April 23, 2005. As a man of secrecy, Blumberg ran each of his three port-

folios (the third was as the LEKEM's chief) from a different physical base, supported by a different set of assistants.

30. Perhaps the best testimony to Blumberg's great success in guarding the secrets of Dimona lies in the following anecdote: Sometime in the mid-1990s, as part of my research on *Israel and the Bomb*, I interviewed Edward Kitner, a member of a number of the AEC teams that had "visited" the Dimona facility in the 1960s. Kitner has the reputation among the Israelis as the toughest of all the American inspectors. In our conversation, I made a passing reference to Vanunu's disclosure, specifically to the underground reprocessing plant, which Vanunu revealed. Kitner, who apparently was not aware of the Vanunu affair, stunned me when he noted that he would be very suspicious of Vanunu's information. As far as he was concerned, he could not believe that an underground reprocessing plant could have been hidden and undetected in the Dimona facility during the time that he had inspected it. See telephone interview with Edward Kitner, June 1996.

31. Yossi Melman, "The First MALMAB," *Ha'aretz*, March 16, 2004. According to other sources, the MALMAB had been created years before that, probably in the 1960s when it was a small cell in the LEKEM. According to the investigative journalist Ronen Bergman, however, the MALMAB was created in the 1960s as a supersecret subunit of the LEKEM. Even the acronym was so secret that it was impossible even to record it. Decades later, when Yechiel Horev became the MALMAB's chief, he accepted the interpretation that the acronym MALMAB referred to the chief of security in the defense establishment. General David Ivry, the MOD's director general, accepted Horev's interpretation. See Ronen Bergman and Gil Meltzer, "The Silencer," *Yediot Achronot Weekly Magazine*, August 6, 2004.

32. The Bus 300 affair refers to the hijacking of Egged Bus 300 on April 12, 1984, by four armed Palestinians. After a twelve-hour standoff, elite Israeli antiterrorist forces stormed the passenger bus, killing two of the hijackers and capturing the remaining terrorists alive. While in GSS custody, both surviving hijackers were beaten to death, and the media were told that all four hijackers had died during the operation. Before their deaths, though, photographers had taken pictures of the two detainees alive in GSS custody, and a scandal erupted during the later investigation. These revelations led to the resignation of the senior GSS (Shin Bet) leadership and Israelis' erosion of trust in the security service. The investigations exposed the GSS's widespread abuses of power and misinformation. See Glenn Frankel, "Israel's Security Service Has Found New Enemy: Itself," *Washington Post*, July 2, 1987; and Ian Black and Benny Morris, *Israel's Secret Wars* (New York: Grove Press, 1991), 401.

33. Yossi Melman, "Who's Afraid of Vanunu?" *Ha'aretz*, March 16, 2004.

34. Ibid.

35. Once the MALMAB as a security organization within the MOD and Yechiel Horev as its chief became public, much was written about the two in the Israeli press. Until his retirement in 2007, Horev insisted on not being interviewed, even though he gave many off-the-record briefings to a few selected journalists. For journalistic accounts of Horev's ascent, see Edelist, "The Man Who Rides the Tamnun"; Galit Yemini and Guy Leshem, "The Private Spies of the Ministry of Defense," *Yediot Achronot*, December 19, 1997; Yossi Melman, "The Chief: 2000 Edition," *Ha'aretz*, February 18, 2000; Amnon Barzilai and Yossi Melman, "The Strong Man of the Defense Establishment Decided to Start an Investigation," *Ha'aretz*, April 23, 2000; and Bergman and Meltzer, "The Silencer."

36. Edelist, "Man Who Rides the Tamnun"; Yossi Melman, "The Secret Chief Does Not Want a Minister," *Ha'aretz*, June 29, 2000; Yossi Melman, "Why Are They Afraid of Yechiel Horev?" *Ha'aretz*, April 30, 2001; Bergman and Meltzer, "The Silencer."

37. Yossi Melman, "MALMAB Will Not Be Israel's Fourth Intelligence Organization," *Ha'aretz*, June 30, 2000.

38. Bergman and Meltzer, "The Silencer."

39. For the legislative prohibition of satellite high-resolution photography of Israeli sites, see "Conference Report on H.R. 3230, National Defense Authorization Act for Fiscal Year 1997" (1996), *Congressional Record*, available at http://www.fas.org/irp/congress/1996_cr/h960730r.htm. Interestingly, one Republican Congressman, Robert Walker, objected to the provision, though without effect. See "Conference Report on H.R. 3230, National Defense Authorization Act for Fiscal Year 1997: Honorable Robert S. Walker," August 1, 1996, *Congressional Record*, available at http://www.fas.org/irp/congress/1996_cr/h960801r.htm.

40. Yossi Melman, "Defense Ministry Security Chief Yehiel Horev Set to Retire This Summer," *Ha'aretz*, April 30, 2007.

41. As of 2006, Israel had only twenty-eight full-time military censors, according to the chief censor, Colonel Sima Vaknin (Vaknin, Testimony to Vinograd Commission, November 2006, at http://www.vaadatwino.org.il/pdf/תמליל%20ואקנין%20סימה20.pdf).

42. Ze'ev Segal, *Freedom of the Press: Between Myth and Reality* (Tel Aviv: Papyrus Publishing, 1996).

43. For more on the early days, see Shalom Rosenfeld, "The Press Between Basel and Schenkin" (in Hebrew), available at http://www.amalnet.k12.il/sites/commun/library/newspaper/comi2713.htm. See also Dina Goren, *Secrecy and the Right to Know* (in Hebrew) (Tel Aviv: Turtledove, 1979); and Dina Goren, *Secrecy, Security, and Freedom of the Press* (in Hebrew) (Jerusalem: Magnes, 1976).

On the Zionist ethos of the Hebrew press in the Yishuv period, see Menachem Hofnung, *Israel: Security Needs Versus the Rule of Law, 1948–1991* (in Hebrew) (Jerusalem: Nevo, 1991).

44. Hofnung, *Israel*. See also Moshe Zack, "The *Censora* and the Press in Five Wars," *Kesher* 13 (1993):5–20, available at http://www.amalnet.k12.il/sites/commun/law/comio157.htm.

45. Hofnung, *Israel*. See also Rosenfeld, "The Press Between Basel and Schenkin."

46. In 1990, a subcommittee headed by Member of the Knesset Yossi Sarid was appointed to look into the unsatisfactory legal status of the Censora, and they concluded against recommending "at this time" passing a Censora law. The argument was that all the press representatives who testified firmly opposed such a law because it would grant quasi permanence to the Censora's existence. The committee recommended keeping the 1945 Emergency Regulations as the Censora's sole legal source and only updating the agreement between the IDF and the chief editors.

47. For the details of this account, see Zack, "The *Censora* and the Press in Five Wars."

48. The ethos was manifested in a dictum familiar to generations of Israeli recruits: "hand on mouth, the enemy listens" (*yad la'peh, ha'oyev ma'azin*). Posters with this dictum could be found hanging on the walls in every military office.

49. For a good historical and legal background of the 1966 agreement, see Segal, *Freedom of the Press*, 77–81.

50. "The Reactor: Open Secret in Beer Sheba," *Ha'aretz*, December 22, 1960.

51. One occasion when Peres used the Censora to suppress nuclear dissent was the case of Eliezer Livneh, a former MAPAI parliamentarian who formed an antinuclear lobby group, named the Committee for Denuclearization of the Middle East (see a full discussion of this episode in chapter 6).

52. In early August 1963, amid the Eshkol government's response to President Kennedy's demands, *Ha'aretz* reported that a total blackout had been imposed on the diplomatic exchanges with the United States. The paper reported on important meetings between the American ambassador and the prime minister, noting that the issue was "the main conversations" among political circles, hinting that there was division within Eshkol's government but not providing any details. Even the headline itself was censored, and it appears that two words were blacked out. I believe the headline was meant to be "The United States Exerted Heavy Diplomatic Pressure on Israel," *Ha'aretz*, August 2, 1963.

53. *Ha'olam Ha'zeh*, Israel's nonestablishment weekly of the time, was apparently the only Israeli newspaper that exposed the use of the daily editors' committee

to conceal information from the public. See "The Prime Minister: Ten Minutes Against Four Years," *Ha'olam Hazeh*, July 17, 1963.

54. I know about this personally. My late father, who at that time was a journalist covering the Middle East in the daily paper *Lamerhav*, was very interested in the subject, but the Censora did not allow him to write about it. Years later, Ze'ev Schiff confirmed to me that he had faced similar difficulties. Israel's policy was to minimize the possible danger involved in the Dimona issue, and the censor was the vehicle to control the press and suppress this concern.

55. Both the Bus 300 affair (1984 to 1986) and the Vanunu affair (1986) may have been the tipping points.

56. This point has been made by many Israeli scholars who examined the censor in Israel: Segal, *Freedom of the Press*, 59–91; Moshe Negbi, *A Paper Tiger* (in Hebrew) (Tel Aviv, Sifriyat Hapoalim, 1985); Hillel Nosek and Yechiel Limor, "Military Censorship in Israel: Temporary Compromise Between Conflicting Values," in *Democracy and National Security in Israel*, ed. Binyamin Noyberger and Ilan Ben-Ami (in Hebrew) (Tel Aviv: Open University Press, 1996), 415–448. In November 2006, in testimony before the Vinograd Commission (the legal body that examined the war with Lebanon a few months earlier), the chief military censor, Colonel Sima Vaknin-Gil, candidly acknowledged the weakness of the Censora in its current form.

57. In the summer of 1988, a journalist named Aluf Benn, who then was a not well-known young reporter for *Ha'ir*, a Tel Aviv local weekly independent paper, submitted for a censorship review an investigative article that examined critically the Mossad and its chief. The entire original article was initially banned and was subsequently resubmitted three more times to the censor's review. Its fourth version was cleared, but with some thirty-two items that were deleted or rewritten. Those items included critical information that could have shed light on the identity of the Mossad chief (at that time the identity of the Mossad chief was confidential), criticism of his professional performance, and reference to his retirement. The censor claimed that the publication of those thirty-two items was sufficient to cause substantial harm to Israeli national security. In response to this decision, Meir Schnitzer, the editor of *Ha'ir*, decided to petition for a judicial review of the case before the Supreme Court. Since *Ha'ir* was not a member of the editors' committee, which meant that it was not a party to the 1966 Censora agreement, the road to the Supreme Court was open. This was the first time in Israel's history that a ruling by the Censora had been submitted for judicial review.

58. Segal, *Freedom of the Press*, 59–91.

59. Vaknin-Gil, testimony, November 2006.

60. Vaknin-Gil, testimony, November 2006. See also Yuval Azoulay, "Censor: IDF Revealed Classified Data During the Lebanon War," *Ha'aretz*, December 10, 2007.

61. Matti Friedman, "Stop the Press," *Jerusalem Report*, April 4, 2005, 17.

62. Quoted in Vaknin-Gil, testimony, November 2006.

63. Friedman, "Stop the Press," 16.

5. The Citizenry: The Taboo Keepers

1. Livneh became very bitter toward MAPAI, so much so that in 1958 he joined Uri Avneri, Shmuel Tamir, and Elyakim Ha'etzni to create a new party, the Hamishtar Hachadash, to run for the Knesset.

2. Eliezer Livneh, "Warning in the Last Moment," *Ha'aretz*, January 12, 1962.

3. "Professors Against Nuclear Armament in the Middle East," *Ha'aretz*, March 13, 1962.

4. Shortly after the petition was submitted, "senior officials" from the Ministry of Defense (apparently Shimon Peres himself) exerted pressure on the Israeli press association to cancel a briefing by Livneh on "nuclear weapons in the Middle East" because of considerations of national security. Although the briefing was canceled, the episode was critically discussed in the press and was brought to the attention of the Knesset's Foreign Affairs and Defense Committee. See "Unacceptable Intervention," *Ha'aretz*, March 27, 1962; "Peculiar Decision," *Ha'aretz*, April 5, 1962. See also Eliezer Livneh, "Nuclear Interim Review," *Ha'aretz*, October 12, 1962.

5. Shimon Peres, interview with *Davar*, August 24, 1962; Shimon Peres, interview with *Ma'ariv*, July 27, 1962. Among the unofficial spokesmen, see Elkana Gali, "How Israel Would Respond to Nasser's Missiles," *Yediot Achronot*, August 10, 1962; Poles, "Defense Outlook in the Missile Age," *Ha'aretz*, September 28, 1962.

6. Peres, interview with *Ma'ariv*.

7. Peres, interview with *Davar*; Peres, interview with *Ma'ariv*.

8. "Shimon Peres Criticizes Public Figures and Scientists Who Demanded Denuclearization," *Kol Ha'am*, September 17, 1962; *Davar*, September 16, 1962.

9. Peres, interview with *Ma'ariv*.

10. Twenty-five years later, in the wake of the Vanunu affair, the secretary of the committee published his memoirs about the group's activities: see Yehuda Ben-Moshe, "25 Years Before Vanunu," *Koteret Rashit*, November 26, 1986.

11. "Scientists Call for Regional Denuclearization," *Ha'aretz*, July 25, 1962.

12. Ben-Moshe, "25 Years Before Vanunu"; interview with professor Amos Korchin (Korchin was a member of the committee), Tel Aviv, August 18, 1992;

interview with Yoram Nimrod (Nimrod was a member of the committee), Ein Hahoresh, September 4, 1992.

13.   The views of the members of the committee were published in late 1963 after lengthy bickering with the military censor: see Committee for Denucleariza- tion of the Middle East, *Israel-Arab: Nuclearization or Denuclearization* (in He- brew) (Tel Aviv: Amikam, 1963).

14.   It is unclear how much factual information Livneh had on the nuclear project. His archive shows clearly that he consulted a number of times in that period with Professor Amos de-Shalit, one of Israel's leading physicists who knew something about the project. Surely Livneh had direct access to prominent people in the political arena. One should keep in mind that in those days the consensus among Israelis was that the Dimona project was all about security, not about science. While Israelis did not know any details about Dimona, the basic presumption was that Dimona was all about the bomb: either having the bomb as a physical reality or about the bomb as an option for the future.

15.   Interview with Korchin; interview with Nimrod.

16.   In 1961 the Ministry of Defense asked the daily newspapers not to publish Livneh's articles on the subject for reasons of national security. See Gavriel Zi- forni (editor of *Haboker*) to Eliezer Livneh, letter dated January 5, 1961 (Livneh Archive, box 29, Efal).

17.   Sometime in 1963 or 1964 the committee's secretary, Yehuda Ben-Moshe, had a meeting with an official of the American embassy. The Shin Bet detained him after the meeting, and he was interrogated for hours about the exact informa- tion that he passed on to the American official. Following the incident Livneh was summoned to the Shin Bet headquarters and was severely warned that such a meeting "with a foreign agent" was against the law and, should it oc- cur again, would have grave consequences for the committee. That incident had a traumatic impact on the group. See Yehuda Ben-Moshe, "25 Years Before Vanunu" (in Hebrew), *Koteret Rashit*, November 26, 1986. Also my interviews with Nimrod and Korchin.

18.   Interview with Korchin; interview with Shlomo Zalman Abramov, August 26, 1992; interview with Nimrod.

19.   Committee for Denuclearization of the Middle East, *Israel-Arab: Nuclearization or Denuclearization*.

20.   In mid-November 1968, days after Nixon's electoral victory and soon after the Warnke-Rabin exchange on the NPT and the Phantoms, Israel informed the State Department of its specific objections. Israel still maintained formally that it was studying the treaty, but it told the United States—and the press—of its substantial reservations about the NPT. The unstated implication was that as long as these security issues remained outstanding, Israel would not sign the treaty. The Israeli reservations were leaked to the press with great accuracy. See

John W. Finney, "Israelis Reported to Be Reluctant at This Time to Sign Treaty Barring Spread of Nuclear Arms," *New York Times*, November 20 1968; Elyahu Salpeter, "The Nuclear Treaty Vis-à-vis Israel's Security: Conventional and Nuclear Guarantees Are Needed Prior to Signature," *Ha'aretz*, November 24, 1968.

21. In early January 1969, the Israeli nuclear program was back in the headlines. *NBC News* reported that Israel either had a nuclear weapon or would soon have one. According to the report, this was the result of a decision that had been made two years earlier "to embark on a crash program to produce a nuclear weapon." See "TV Report of an Israeli A-bomb Draws a Denial in Washington," *New York Times*, January 9, 1969. A follow-up story reported:

> It is generally agreed in the United States intelligence community that Israel now stands on the threshold of becoming a nuclear power and needs only a political decision to move in that direction. If such a decision is made, it is estimated that Israel could build in a year or so a crude atomic bomb. Some officials believe that the period might be measured in months. (Finney, "Israelis Reported to Be Reluctant")

    For more on the context, see Avner Cohen, *Israel and the Bomb* (New York: Columbia University Press, 1998).

22. The following is a partial list of this huge bibliography. The Vanunu's original 1986 revelations to the *Sunday Times* are available online: "Mordechai Vanunu: The Sunday Times Archives," *Sunday Times*, available at http://www .timesonline.co.uk/tol/news/article830147.ece; Yoel Cohen, *The Whistleblower of Dimona: Israel, Dimona and the Bomb* (New York: Holmes & Meier, 2003); Peter Hounam, *The Woman from Mossad: The Torment of Mordechai Vanunu* (London: Vision, 1998); Louis Toscano, *Triple Cross: Israel, the Atomic Bomb and the Man Who Spilled the Secrets* (New York: Carol Publishing, 1990); Frank Barnaby, *The Invisible Bomb: The Nuclear Arms Race in the Middle East* (London: I. B. Tauris, 1989).

23. Ariel E. Levite and Emily B. Landau, *Israel's Nuclear Image: Arab Perceptions of Israel's Nuclear Posture* (Tel Aviv: Papyrus, 1994), 52–57.

24. Avner Cohen and Benjamin Frankel, "Israel's Nuclear Ambiguity," *Bulletin of the Atomic Scientists* 43, no. 2 (1967):15–19.

25. Yossi Melman, "Who's Afraid of Mordechai Vanunu?" *Ha'aretz*, April 25, 2004.

26. Tomer Zarchin, "High Court Extends Vanunu's Travel Ban by 6 Months," *Ha'aretz*, July 7, 2009.

27. "Court Reduces Vanunu's Prison Time from 6 to 3 Months Due to Health," *Jerusalem Post*, September 23, 2008; "Jerusalem Court Reduces Vanunu Sentence," *Yedi'ot Aharonot*, September 23, 2008; Nir Hasson, "Vanunu to Return to Prison for Violating the Terms of His Parole," *Ha'aretz*, March 1, 2008; Nir

Hasson, "Vanunu to Return to Prison for Violating the Terms of His Parole," *Ha'aretz*, July 2, 2007; Conal Urqhart, "Vanunu Jailed Again After Talks with Foreigners," *The Guardian*, July 3, 2007.

28. Yossi Melman, "It Is Time to Free Vanunu," *Ha'aretz*, April 16, 2008.

29. Ibid.

30. Many of the facts mentioned in this section I know personally, as I was involved in this affair: I connected Yatza to Ronen Bergman, and in 2003 I wrote a long "for the record" memo in which I gave my own account of the affair. See also chapter 1 in this volume. All the factual material here that is not backed up by reference to published material is based on personal memory and that 2003 memo (Avner Cohen, "Memo on the Yatza Affair," unpublished, 2003).

31. Cohen, "Memo on the Yatza Affair."

32. Available at http://www.ynet.co.il/articles/1,7340,L-691929,00.html.

33 I met Yatza in New York City for the first time in mid-1999. I saw a man infatuated with that unique memory, often not sure himself of all the facts but eager to retrieve them. I also got the impression that while living in New York City for the previous two decades, Yatza had "forgotten" how entrenched that taboo had become in the domestic Israeli psyche. It was at that time that I introduced him to journalist Ronen Bergman, a fateful connection that ultimately led to this affair after Yatza spelled out to Bergman his recollections of his role in the 1967 war.

34. Eyal Gonen, "Without Censora," *Yediot Achronot* (*Shivah Yamim*), November 3, 2005, 22–28. Some background is needed. There used to be a gentleman's understanding between the Censora and the media that materials submitted for the Censora's review would never be shared with other security agencies and would never be used for a law enforcement investigation against journalists or their sources. Brigadier General Shani, the second chief censor (1978–1999), proudly referred to this understanding in his departure interview as an example of the Censora's ethics code. Dolev violated that code. Had she not reported the banned interview to Horev, the affair would never have been revealed. Evidently, she did it because the interview was such an affront to amimut. See Ronen Bergman, "His Lost Honor," *Yediot Achronot*, April 16, 2003.

35. Ronen Bergman, "Inside They Celebrated, Outside They Watched" (in Hebrew), *Yediot Achronot*, April 23, 2001; Amir Oren, "An Old General's Manhattan Project," *Ha'aretz*, May 4, 2001; *Ha'aretz*, "They Still Haven't Learned a Thing," April 27, 2001; Yossi Melman, "Why Are They Afraid of Yechiel Horev?" *Ha'aretz*, April 30, 2001; Ronen Bergman, "His Lost Honor," *Yediot Achronot*, April 16, 2003.

36. Tony Allen Mills, "Israel Holds Bomb Scientist in Spy Scare," *Sunday Times*, April 22, 2001. I can admit now, for the first time in public, that I deserve a

small credit as well for the disclosure of the Yatza arrest. In order to bypass the Israeli Censora, the Washington correspondent Tony Mills was asked by his editors to give his own byline to the story that the *Times* correspondent Uzi Machanaymi first wrote. Mills was unsure whether or not he should publish the story under his byline. Since he knew nothing about the story, he asked me whether I could verify the major elements of story. The problem was that the story that he received from Machanaymi was highly inaccurate. It indicated, for example, that there was a connection between Yatza's arrest and Soviet espionage. I knew that the main elements of the story were inaccurate, but I could not reveal this to Mills. Yet I thought that regardless of those inaccuracies, the *Sunday Times* should publicize the secret arrest anyway. I told him that the story contained all sorts of inaccuracies but that they did not matter much. The most important thing was that the world should know about this secret arrest. I was able to persuade Mills to do it, and the rest is history.

37. Sharon Sadeh, "Israel Said Holding Nuclear Scientist," *Ha'aretz*, April 22, 2001.

38. Zvi Harel and Amnon Barzilai, "Gag Order Partially Lifted in Ya'akov Espionage Case" (in Hebrew), *Ha'aretz*, April 23, 2001.

39. Deborah Sontag, "Israel Arrests Ex-General as Spy for Spilling Old Secrets, *New York Times*, May 2, 2001.

40. Ze'ev Segal, "The Courts Should Not Be the Censor" (in Hebrew), *Ha'aretz*, April 24, 2001.

41. This paragraph represents my own construction of the case and goes beyond what has been published on the affair. It is based not only on my own personal understanding of the affair but also on subsequent conversations with many of the other players. I should note that I have never discussed the matter with Horev himself, but I believe that I have a good sense of his thinking. See also Bergman, "Inside They Celebrated, Outside They Watched"; Oren, "An Old General's Manhattan Project"; *Ha'aretz*, "They Still Haven't Learned a Thing"; Melman, "Why Are They Afraid of Yechiel Horev?"; Ronen Bergman, "His Lost Honor," *Yediot Achronot*, April 16, 2003.

42. Zvi Harel, "Ya'akov Charged with Revealing State Secrets," *Ha'aretz*, May 9, 2001.

43. When Chen retired in 2004 she revealed that early on during the Yatza trial, she agreed with Yatza's lawyers on a plea bargain under which the state would drop the main count and Yatza would admit to the lighter count, which was similar to the actual outcome of the trial. But Horev vehemently refused to accept it, threatening to complain to the prime minister, so Arbel ruled it out. In her extensive interview on her departure in 2004, Chen acknowledged that she had reservations about Horev's conduct in the Yatza case (but not the actual decision to prosecute Yatza). See Ronen Bergman and Tova Zimuki, "The Speech of the Prosecutor," *Yediot Achronot*, November 5, 2004.

44. Even former Chief Censor General Rachel Dolev agreed that at the time, Horev conducted himself like the Israeli version of J. Edgar Hoover. See Eyal Gonen, "Without Censora," *Yediot Achronot Weekly Magazine*, November 3, 2005, 26.

45. "They Still Haven't Learned a Thing"; Aluf Benn, "Israel: Censoring the Past," *Bulletin of the Atomic Scientists* 57, no. 4 (2001):17–19; Reuven Pedatzur, "A Brave Judge Stands Up to Security Bullies," *Ha'aretz*, November 28, 2001.

46. Aviv Lavi, "Disinformation," *Ha'aretz*, April 27, 2001; "They Still Haven't Learned a Thing."

47. The Yatza affair led the Knesset's Constitution, Law and Justice Committee to undertake a sweeping revision of Israel's espionage law. Knesset Member Yossef (Tommy) Lapid defined the problem: "Today there is an absurd situation that Vanunu who wanted the destruction of Israel and Yatza who wanted to show off are indicted on the very same article." The committee was convinced that the law defining the transfer of classified information as "severe espionage" is both misleading and draconian. Quoted in Gideon Alon, "Justice Committee: The Espionage Law Is Too Sweeping," *Ha'aretz*, May 14, 2001; Yossi Melman, "MKs Want to Change the Scope of Severe Espionage," *Ha'aretz*, May 21, 2001. For legal background of the issue, see http://www .knesset.gov.il/MMM/doc.asp?doc=m01346&type=pdf (in Hebrew).

48. In addition to the party papers, three privately owned independent papers— *Ha'aretz*, *Ma'ariv*, and *Yediot Achronot*—were affiliated with Israel society's urban and bourgeois segments.

49. This trend came to its peak during the 2006 war with Hezbollah when the media reported in real time almost every development in the battlefield. This, in return, created a strong backlash against the media, in an outcry that both the media and the Censora had become too "promiscuous." This sentiment shaped the sections in the Vinograd report dealing with the media and the Censora. For the full Vinograd report, see http://www.haaretz.co.il/hasite/ images/printed/P300108/vino.pdf.

50. An example is the media's coverage of Israel's intelligence organizations. The Mossad and the GSS are under the public eye much more than they were at any time before this. In the wake of the botched Mossad operation to assassinate Haled Mashaal in Amman, Jordan, in 1996, a lot of information, some of it apparently classified, was leaked and published. The entire decision-making process that led to the operation was reported in the media. The Censora proved unable to shield sensitive information. Israeli journalists had access to sensitive information from within, and they were able to publish much of it. This was a sea change. After the 1989 Schnitzer case Israeli journalists have indisputably become more aggressive in their journalistic pursuits and in their dealings with the Censora.

51. Chaim Rivlin, broadcast on Israeli Channel 2, January 18, 2002.

52. Aluf Benn, "Clinton Committed to Netanyahu: Israel's Nuclear Capability Will Be Preserved," *Ha'aretz*, March 14, 2000.

53. The only possible exception to the rule is Israeli national security analyst Reuven Pedatzur, who raised the issue through questions in some of his articles.

54. For example, Ze'ev Schiff, "Nuclear Opacity: For How Long?" *Ha'aretz*, August 24, 2000; Ze'ev Schiff, "Why Nobody Debates the Nuclear Issue," *Ha'aretz*, March 29, 2000; Ze'ev Schiff, "Comments on the Balance of National Strength and Security," in *The Balance of National Strength and Security*, ed. Uzi Arad (in Hebrew) (Tel Aviv: Yediot Achronot Press, 2001).

55. At one time, the Israeli daily newspaper *Yediot Achronot* made a legal effort to force the government to release the protocols of the Vanunu trial. That effort, which resulted in the submission of a petition to the supreme court, was directed not at the censorship policy but at the Justice Department for keeping sealed all of the trial's testimony. The court never ruled on the petition because the government, in its effort to avoid a losing battle in court, decided to release voluntarily some 40 percent of the testimony. The government appears to have released the material that it believed it could not defend in court, given the 1998 ruling on the Schnitzer petition. To the best of my knowledge, other than in this case, the mainstream Israeli press has never tried to test the Censora's policies in court.

56. While acknowledging that my factual description is correct, Aluf Benn noted that "media organizations don't challenge the censor in Bagatz [the Israeli High Court of Justice], since we are afraid to get an about-face of Schnitzer" (Aluf Benn, personal correspondence, May 2008). I think this response is fair, and I agree that it is not a trivial decision for an editor in chief to go to court. Many cases of such petitions ended with the justices advising the petitioners to withdraw the petition, something close to what had actually happened in my own case in Bagatz in 1994.

57. One example may illustrate this point. In September 1986, as the Israeli government learned that the *Sunday Times* was about to publish the Vanunu revelations, Prime Minister Shimon Peres convened the nation's council of editors, informed them about the imminent disclosure, and asked them— independently of any censorship requirements—to avoid editorializing on the story. He requested voluntary cooperation on what he referred to as the nation's vital interest. The editors understood, appreciated, and fully complied with the prime minister's request, tacitly agreeing that a nuclear debate, a democratic debate, would be a disaster for Israel's national security. Ultimately, the Israeli press did cover the human aspect of the Vanunu affair, but to this day it has ignored almost entirely the policy issues involved in Vanunu's disclosure, including the question of democratic control.

58. To be more precise, even if an individual member wanted to raise the nuclear issue, the speaker or his or her deputies would not allow placing the nuclear issue on the agenda for an open session. But the truth is that Knesset members were not willing to challenge the informal prohibition.

59. Interview with Azaryahu Arnan, Kibbutz Yiron, January 26, 2008.

60. Dalia Shori, "The Knesset Discussed Israel's Nuclear Policy for the First Time," *Ha'aretz*, February 3, 2000.

61. "In the Appropriate Caution," *Ha'aretz*, February 4, 2000.

6. The Democratic Cost of Amimut: The Impact on the Citizenry

1.   Richard G. Hewlett and Oscar E. Anderson Jr., *The New World: A History of the United States Atomic Energy Commission*, vol. 1, 1939–1946 (University Park: Pennsylvania State University Press, 1962), 408–9.

2.   Ibid., 530.

3.   A. Devolpi, G. E. Marsh, T. A. Postol, G. S. Stanford, and S. H. Unger, *Born Secret: The H-bomb, the Progressive Case, and National Security* (New York: Pergamon, 1981).

4.   Hewlett and Anderson, *The New World*, 608–10, 617–19.

5.   Harold Green and Alan Rosenthal, *Government of the Atom* (New York, Atherton, 1963); Hugh Gusterson, *Nuclear Rites: A Weapons Laboratory at the End of the Cold War* (Berkeley: University of California Press, 1996); Peter Katzenstein, ed., *The Culture of National Security* (New York: Columbia University Press, 1997); Daniel Patrick Moynihan, *Secrecy: The American Experience* (New Haven, Conn.: Yale University Press, 1998).

6.   Marc Trachtenberg, *A Constructed Peace* (Princeton, N.J.: Princeton University Press, 1999), 96–97.

7.   Richard Halloran, "Protracted Nuclear War," *Air Force Magazine*, March 2008, 56–59.

8.   The public seems to have been reasonably comfortable with the MAD-inspired deterrence, the only role assigned to nuclear weapons for nearly two decades (1964 to 1981), but when Reagan began to talk about (a) fighting and winning a nuclear war, (b) arming space vehicles to fight in and from space, and (c) replacing deterrence with ballistic missile defense (itself an indication that he did not believe deterrence would prevent a nuclear war), the public got scared.

9.   Robert Dahl, *Controlling Nuclear Weapons: Democracy Versus Guardianship* (Syracuse, N.Y.: Syracuse University Press, 1985), 5.

10. Richard Falk, "Nuclear Weapons and the Renewal of Democracy," in *Nuclear Weapons and the Future of Humanity*, ed. Avner Cohen and Steven Lee (Totowa, N.J.: Rowman & Allanheld, 1986).

11. Hugh Miall, *Nuclear Weapons: Who's in Charge?* (London: Macmillan, 1987).

12. George Perkovich, *India's Nuclear Bomb: The Impact on Global Proliferation* (Berkeley: University of California Press, 1999), 459–64.

13. Dahl, *Controlling Nuclear Weapons*, 3.

14. Perkovich, *India's Nuclear Bomb*, 459–64.

15. An English translation of Ben-Gurion's statement appeared in the *Jerusalem Post*, December 22, 1960, and was cited in a Department of State compilation. See U.S. Department of State, "Political Statements Concerning the Israeli Reactor," January 17, 1961, 3207, National Security Archives, Washington, D.C. For a summary, see "Ben Gurion Explains Project," *New York Times*, December 22, 1960.

16. Richard G. Hewlett and Francis Duncan, *Atomic Shield: A History of the United States Atomic Energy Commission*, vol. 2, 1947–1952 (University Park: Pennsylvania State University Press, 1962).

17. Ze'ev Schiff, "Why Nobody Debates the Nuclear Issue," *Ha'aretz*, March 29, 2000.

18. In his published writings, Schiff was much more conservative and cautious on the matter of amimut than he sometimes appeared in one-on-one conversations. In his writings over the years, Schiff praised the political wisdom of amimut virtually without reservation, arguing that it was a sacred national security asset that Israel must cling to as long as it could politically, thereby minimizing its democratic flaws. See, for example, Ze'ev Schiff, "Preferring Political Ambiguity," *Ha'aretz*, January 23, 1992; Ze'ev Schiff, "Six Difficult Nuclear Questions," *Ha'aretz*, February 24, 1995; Ze'ev Schiff, "No Change in Nuclear Policy," *Ha'aretz*, September 11, 1998; Schiff, "Why Nobody Debates the Nuclear Issue"; and Ze'ev Schiff, "Nuclear Opacity for How Long?" *Ha'aretz*, August 24, 2000. At the same time, in personal conversations Schiff expressed concerns about the overbearing impact of amimut on Israelis' ability to discuss the nuclear issue intelligently. He appeared to concede that under the current practice of amimut, too much information that the Israeli public should know is actually repressed and that the Israeli press was obligated to try its best to educate the Israeli public on the nuclear issue.

19. Schiff was proudest of his critical editorial column concerning the need to have a more formal and legal system of controlling nuclear weapons. In that column, Schiff said nothing explicitly factual, only "opinions," but the piece is extraordinary in what it implies. See Ze'ev Schiff, "The Law of the Red Button," *Ha'aretz*, March 13, 1998. When I first read it, I was amazed that the censor allowed such a piece to be published.

20. Schiff, "Why Nobody Debates the Nuclear Issue." Some other Israeli defense intellectuals argue in a similar way. But some Israelis question whether Iran's current religious leadership could be deterred at all by other nuclear weapons,

given their views on Israel, Shiite religious beliefs, and Israeli concerns that such beliefs could affect the Iranian leaders' sense of rationality.

21. Schiff, "Law of the Red Button."

22. Personal correspondence with Uzi Arad, July 2008.

23. John Stuart Mill, *On Liberty* (London: Longman, Roberts, and Green, 1869).

24. A striking example of this trend is the tale of the CIA's torture documents that were released by the Obama administration on April 16, 2009, in response to a Freedom of Information Act request by the American Civil Liberties Union that led a judge order to release these documents. See http://www.aclu.org/safefree/torture/torturefoia.html.

25. Leonard S. Spector and Avner Cohen, "Israel's Airstrike on Syria's Reactor: Implications for the Nonproliferation Regime," *Arms Control Today* 38, no. 6 (2008):15–21.

26. This was the first of two workshops that our project organized for American and Israeli audiences in the spring of 1992. Unfortunately, no transcript of Bundy's keynote speech is available.

27. Petition 10379/06 to the Supreme Court (2007).

28. Avner Cohen, "Crossing the Threshold: The Untold Nuclear Dimension of the 1967 Arab-Israeli War," *Arms Control Today*, June 2007.

29. This account was mentioned a number of times in my conversation with Professor Israel Dostrovsky.

30. Interviews with Shalheveth Freier, 1991–1994.

31. Israeli attorney Avigdor Feldman (Vanunu's chief lawyer) once noted that secrets are contagious: "If something is secret, and something else touches it, it too becomes a secret. Secrecy becomes a disease. Everything around the secret issue becomes secret, so the trial became a secret, so I became a secret." See Avigdor Feldman, "Vanunu, Secrecy and the Law," in *Voices for Vanunu*, ed. Peter Hounam (London: Campaign to Free Vanunu, 1997), 118.

32. William Burr, Thomas Blanton, and Stephen Schwartz, "The Costs and Consequences of Nuclear Secrecy," in *Atomic Audit: The Costs and Consequences of U.S. Nuclear Weapons Since 1940*, ed. Stephen Schwartz (Washington, D.C.: Brookings Institution Press, 1998), 433.

33. Yossi Melman, "MALMAB Will Not Be Israel's Fourth Intelligence Organization," *Ha'aretz*, June 30, 2000.

34. It was none other than Prime Minister Yitzhak Rabin who half-jokingly warned his minister of environment, Yossi Sarid, when he appointed Sarid to be the environmental czar over Dimona, that the IAEC people are good "in concealing evidence." I heard that anecdote in an interview with Mr. Sarid in 2003. Much has been said about the ways in which the chief of MALMAB abused his power in the case of Yitzhak Yaakov (Yatza), as well as in other cases that came to the public attention. For more on the Yatza affair, see chapter 5.

35. Dahl, *Controlling Nuclear Weapons*, 5.

36. I thank my research assistant Christopher Neu, who pressed me to see the "false" trade-off in the common conceptualization of democracy and national security.

37. Fareed Zakaria, *The Future of Freedom: Illiberal Democracy at Home and Abroad* (New York: Norton, 2009).

38. Kai Bird, *American Prometheus: The Triumph and Tragedy of J. Robert Oppenheimer* (New York: Knopf, 2005).

39. My thanks again to Christopher Neu.

40. Green and Rosenthal, *Government of the Atom*; Gusterson, *Nuclear Rites*; Katzenstein, *The Culture of National Security*; Moynihan, *Secrecy*.

41. The NPT's definition of a nuclear-weapons state is the actual explosion of a nuclear device before January 1, 1966. Israel could have conducted a nuclear test, which would have qualified it as a nuclear-weapons state.

42. A case in point: the U.S. Freedom of Information Act (FOIA) was conceived in the late 1950s, debated in the 1960s, and enacted in 1966. But since the 1980s, other democratic nations (including Israel) have adopted their own versions of FOIA. By now, the idea of freedom of information is understood as a human right. The political culture of the freedom of information idea, of which this project is a part, is a new phenomenon. See Ann Florini, "The End of Secrecy," *Foreign Policy* 111 (1998); Athan Theoharis, *A Culture of Secrecy: The Government Versus the People's Right to Know* (Lawrence: University Press of Kansas, 1998); Steven Aftergood, ed., "Special Issue on Government Secrecy," *Bulletin of the Atomic Scientists* 56, no. 6 (2000).

43. Peter Feaver, *Guarding the Guardians: Civilian Control of Nuclear Weapons in the United States* (Ithaca, N.Y.: Cornell University Press, 1992); Bruce Blair, *Strategic Command and Control: Redefining the Nuclear Threat* (Washington, D.C.: Brookings Institution Press, 1985).

7. The Democratic Cost of Amimut: Governance

1. Robert Dahl, *Controlling Nuclear Weapons: Democracy Versus Guardianship* (Syracuse, N.Y.: Syracuse University Press, 1985).

2. Avner Cohen, *Israel and the Bomb* (New York: Columbia University Press, 1998), 34.

3. Yehuda Ben-Meir, *Civil-Military Relations in Israel* (New York: Columbia University Press, 1995), 101.

4. On Ben-Gurion's fondness of using "constructive ambiguity," see Ben-Meir, *Civil-Military Relations in Israel*, 100.

5. For a historical background of that organizational overhaul, see Cohen, *Israel and the Bomb*, chap. 12.

6.   I learned about this document from a conversation with Azaryahu Arnan (Sini), Galili's senior aide, who referred to the existence of this document. See my interviews with Azaryahu Arnan, Kibbutz Yiron, summer 1992 and January 26, 2008. Very few actually saw the document, however, which apparently was drafted by Minister Israel Galili, Prime Minister Eshkol's close political ally, in consultation with the IAEC's new director general, Israel Dostrovsky; the deputy minister of defense, Zvi Dinstein; the MOD's director general, Moshe Kashti; and a few others.

7.   Yoram Peri, *Between Battles and Ballots: Israeli Military in Politics* (Cambridge: Cambridge University Press, 136–367; and Ben-Meir, *Civil-Military Relations in Israel*, 101. See also Tom Segev, 1967: *Israel, the War and the Year That Transformed the Middle East* (New York: Metropolitan Books, 2007), 320. The reference to the prohibition on using unconventional weapons appears in the Hebrew edition of Segev's book, which was banned by the Censora.

8.   Peri, *Between Battles and Bullets*, 137; Ben-Meir, *Civil-Military Relations in Israel*, 102.

9.   Ben-Meir, *Civil-Military Relations in Israel*, 101.

10. Peri, *Between Battles and Bullets*, 139.

11. Segev, 1967, 549.

12. Freier referred to this matter in various conversations with me between 1991 and 1994.

13. Quoted in Avner Cohen, *The Last Taboo* (in Hebrew) (Tel Aviv: Zamora-Bitan, 2005), 84–85.

14. Another example of the jurisdictional ambiguity surrounding the nuclear issue pertains to security. As usual, details are vague and not public, but the same shared arrangement of controlling the nuclear complex seems to apply also to security. The MALMAB, the security arm of the Ministry of Defense, provides security services for Israel's nuclear project (the MALMAB is discussed more fully in chapter 4). Because of amimut's special security requirements, MALMAB's head is involved in all major nuclear decisions, from matters of personnel and their security clearances to matters of operations. All those decisions have security implications that give the MALMAB chief veto power over most top-level nuclear decisions (and, in case of an unresolved disagreement, to bring the issue to the prime minister for a decision). The MALMAB's chief is a senior civil servant at the MOD, appointed by the MOD's director general and the minister of defense, but on nuclear matters he is subordinate to the prime minister (or his ministerial representative). This shared arrangement also opens the door to similar jurisdictional ambiguities.

15. Interviews with Avraham Hermony, 1992 to 1996.

16. According to an old story, General Benny Peled, commander of the Israeli air force in the early 1970s, was frustrated about having to make complex and

fateful decisions in this area without political guidance. He reportedly felt that the political leadership used amimut as an excuse to escape from its own responsibility. Years later Peled argued that the system's main deficiency was the absence of constitutional clarity: the absence of boundaries.

17. Sometime in the 1970s, in a private conversation with Ezer Weitzman (who was chief of military operations in the general staff from 1966 to 1970 and later a minister in Golda Meir's cabinet and minister of defense in Menachem Begin's cabinet), he expressed a sense of dread that one day, people might look at the process under which Israel became a nuclear power and would find a total mess. My sense of what he said—and my understanding of the subject in those days was poor, and I did not dare to probe him on this—was that he thought that Israel became a nuclear power through a process for which nobody was authorized and nobody was really accountable. Maybe I misunderstood his comments, but I recall that I was struck by their intensity.

18. "The Government is authorized to perform in the name of the State and subject to any law, all actions which are not legally incumbent on another authority." For the law in its current form, see Israeli Knesset, "Basic Law: The Government (2001)," available at http://www.knesset.gov.il/laws/special/eng/basic14_eng.htm. This is now clause 32, but in the original version of the law from 1968 it was clause 28, and much of the literature refers to that number. See Israeli Knesset, "Basic Law: The Government—1968" (original version), available at http://www.knesset.gov.il/laws/special/eng/basic1_eng .htm). For a brief discussion of how the Israeli constitutional system applies to national security, including the residual-power clause, see Ben-Meir, *Civil-Military Relations in Israel*, chap. 3.

19. In May 1948, in response to the predicament of a legal void, the newly established state of Israel found itself in a state of war, with no legal code and with a government that had to act. Since then, the residual-power clause has become a mainstay of Israel's constitution.

20. Ben-Meir, *Civil-Military Relations in Israel*, 203, no. 8.

21. Dina Goren, *Secrecy, Security and Freedom of the Press* (in Hebrew) (Jerusalem: Magnes, 1976); Dina Goren, *Secrecy and the Right to Know* (Tel Aviv: Turtledove, 1979); Menachem Hofnung, *Israel: Security Needs Versus the Rule of Law, 1948–1991* (in Hebrew) (Jerusalem: Nevo, 1991); Avner Yaniv, ed., *National Security and Democracy in Israel* (in Hebrew) (Boulder, Colo.: Lynne Rienner, 1992).

22. Gideon Alon, "The GSS Law Was Approved in the Knesset by Great Majority," *Ha'aretz*, February 12, 2002.

23. Gideon Alon, "The Mossad the Next in Line," *Ha'aretz*, December 20, 2001.

24. Ze'ev Segal, "Grounding the Mossad in Law," *Ha'aretz*, February 22, 1998; "The Mossad Under Law," *Ha'aretz*, September 20, 2002.

25. Amir Oren, "Amateur Hour," *Ha'aretz*, April 25, 2008.

26. Ze'ev Schiff, "The Law of the Red Button," *Ha'aretz*, March 13, 1998.

27. Schiff was not the only prominent Israeli journalist who was alarmed at what took place in Israel in February 1998 in response to the crisis with Iraq. Israeli journalists Nachum Barnea and Shimon Shipper, among the most knowledgeable Israeli journalists, wrote that "previous Israeli governments had treated their potential destruction capability as for deterrence purposes only, this time the nonconventional war was already on the table." See Nachum Barnea and Shimon Shipper, "The Button and the Finger," *Yediot Achronot*, February 27, 1998.

28. This and the preceding quotations are from Schiff, "The Law of the Red Button."

29. Ben-Meir, *Civil-Military Relations in Israel*.

30. Yehuda Ben-Meir, *National Security Decision-Making: The Israeli Case* (in Hebrew) (Tel Aviv: Jaffe Center for Strategic Studies, 1980).

31. To be clear, there are no direct correlations between procedure and substance in regard to decision making; that is, a proper decision-making process does not guarantee producing good decisions, just as improper decision making does not necessarily mean that the decision will be bad. Still, since democracy believes in the fallibility of human decisions, autocratic decisions increase the likelihood of poor decision making.

32. Among the well-recognized Israelis who wrote and spoke on these issues are the following: General Avraham Tamir (one of the fathers of national security planning), Professor Yekhezkel Dror (the "grand strategy" academic), Dan Meridor (the chair of the 1987 and 2007 "Meridor Committees," on Israel's national security doctrine), Yehuda Ben-Meir (organizational psychologist who turned into a politician and deputy minister who studies Israel's governance and decision-making system), and Reuven Pedatzur (a defense commentator who wrote tens of editorials on the economic oversight of the defense budget and Israel's decision-making system).

33. An exception was the newly elected prime minister, Benjamin Netanyahu, in his first term in office, who, soon after his election victory in 1996, announced the establishment of a National Security Council (NSC) in his office. Within weeks, however, he had to drop the idea because his defense minister, Yitzhak Mordechai, threatened not to cooperate with the new body. It took three more years, until Mordechai was ousted in March 1999, for Netanyahu (now with the support of his new minister of defense, Moshe Arens) to establish the NSC as the prime minister's central body responsible for coordination, integration, analysis, and monitoring policy in the area of national security. This time Netanyahu did it through a formal cabinet resolution (no. 4889, March 7, 1999). It then took another two years until the NSC was formally established through an act of legislation, an amendment to the Basic Law: The Government. But

the amendment only vaguely defined the NSC role in advisory terms, as article 7 in the amended law states that "the Government will have a staff, established by the Prime Minister, to provide professional consulting in the fields of national security; the Prime Minister is authorized to entrust the staff with additional consulting fields." When Ehud Barak became prime minister and minister of defense in 2000, he once again had no need for the system. The NSC was pushed aside into a small long-term planning role.

By the time Benjamin Netanyahu became prime minister for the second time, in the spring of 2009, the Israeli NSC has been in existence for nearly a decade, under five prime ministers and six national security advisers, but its formal bureaucratic existence (even after it became anchored in the 2008 National Security Council Law) still hardly addresses the real issues that led to its establishment. At that time, most insiders considered the NSC a toothless bureaucratic entity. Even though the office of the NSC head moved in late 2006 to the prime minister's main office in Jerusalem (most of the NSC staff is still located in an isolated facility in the Tel Aviv area), this has not changed the fundamental situation. The same old concerns over turf that led past ministers of defense and heads of the secret organizations to oppose the establishment of a strong NSC still prevailed. Thus, it is not surprising that until the current national security adviser, Dr. Uzi Arad, all six previous NSC heads resigned from their position out of frustration.

34. In 2007, the Vinograd Inquiry Commission, which looked into the hasty and faulty decision-making process that led Israel into the Second Lebanon War in July 2006, urged in its interim and final report that the prime minister must be served by a strong NSC that could stand up to the IDF. The commission called for substantial improvements in the NSC's structure and function, including establishing a national assessment team and creating a center for crisis management at the prime minister's office. Olmert accepted these recommendations and appointed a committee to implement them. In 2008 the Knesset passed new legislation, called the NSC law, which aimed at expanding the NSC chief's powers. According to the legislation, the NSC chief would have the power to summon for deliberation any person in the defense establishment, including the chiefs of the secret organizations. The NSC's chief would be the central adviser to the prime minister on all matters of national security and, as such, would be invited to every cabinet meeting involving foreign and defense affairs, would receive information from all state bodies, and would be the prime minister's representative at all meetings of the heads of secret organizations. See Ilan Shachar, "Knesset Approves Expanding Powers of National Security Chief," Ha'aretz, July 29, 2008; Barak Ravid, "Ten Years On, National Security Council Comes into Its Own," Ha'aretz, July 12, 2009. It is too early to tell to what extent the NSC will be a real participant in national security decisions.

35.   Hugh Gusterson, *Nuclear Rites: A Weapons Laboratory at the End of the Cold War* (Berkeley: University of California Press, 1996), 68.

36.   U.S. Department of Defense, "Findings of the Nuclear Posture Review," January 9, 2002, available at http://www.defenselink.mil/dodcmsshare/briefing slide/120/020109-D-6570C-001.pdf.

37.   E-mail correspondence with Steven Aftergood, September 14, 2008; Hon. Bob Kerrey, letter to Hon. William Cohen, October 11, 2000, available at http://www.fas.org/sgp/congress/2000/kerrey2.html; David Smalley, "Kerrey Rebuffed, Frustrated in Attempt to See Nuclear Targets Plan," *Inside the Air Force*, December 22, 2000, available at http://www.fas.org/sgp/news/2000/12/iaf122200.html; "Strategic Nuclear Weapons Policy," *Congressional Record*, June 30, 2000, at http://www.fas.org/sgp/congress/2000/kerrey.html.

38.   Pentagon briefing, April 23, 2009, available at http://www.defenselink.mil/transcripts/transcript.aspx?transcriptid=4408.

39.   Concerns about the prime minister's inability to devote adequate time to oversee the nation's secret organizations have been openly recognized by past prime ministers, from Ariel Sharon to Benjamin Netanyahu. In 2001 Prime Minister Sharon appointed Dan Meridor as minister without portfolio in the prime minister's office, effectively making him the minister in charge of liaison and oversight over the secret organizations under the prime minister's responsibility. One of Meridor's prime tasks reportedly was to take the ministerial lead in following up on the state comptroller's top-secret oversight reports on these organizations, which until then had not been handled at the ministerial level. In early 2003, Uzi Landau, a former Likud chair of the Knesset's Foreign Affairs and Defense Committee, replaced Meridor. For political and personal reasons, though, Sharon gave Landau a more limited mandate than Meridor had. Landau was not authorized to be part of the decision-making process involving special operations and projects, and he was not a member of the smaller and prestigious ministerial body known as the security cabinet.

Still, Landau tried to study the legal and bureaucratic issues involved in maintaining effective ministerial oversight over the secret organizations. The outcome was a classified report that Landau submitted in the fall of 2004 to Prime Minister Sharon, just weeks before he, Landau, resigned from the government (over an issue unrelated to his report). In the report Landau proposed a comprehensive overhaul of the system of ministerial control over the prime minister's secret organizations. He acknowledged that the prime minister's executive oversight was deficient and proposed creating a professional body in the prime minister's office to monitor and oversee these secret organizations. Landau recommended that the oversight body be run and managed by a group of senior professionals with expertise in the areas of each organization's operation, who would report to a special minister in the prime minister's office. Sharon reportedly accepted most of Landau's recommendations, but Landau resigned weeks later, and the report, as was the case with others before it, was buried in one of the safes in the prime minister's office.

Olmert continued with this tradition, and during his three years in office, two ministers, Tzachi Hanegbi and Meir Sheetret, helped him oversee the nuclear bureaucracy. In April 2009 Prime Minister Benjamin Netanyahu appointed Dan Meridor as the deputy prime minister and the minister responsible for overseeing the intelligence and nuclear energy organizations in the prime minister's office, his old job under Sharon. Reports suggest that the appointment of Minister Meridor will not alter the existing arrangement in which the three organizations are administratively and functionally subject to the prime minister. The minister's authority stems from the authority of the prime minister but is not grounded in any legislation or protocol. As such, the status of Minister Meridor's authority appears problematic from a legal point of view. See Mazal Mualem, "Dan Meridor and Benny Begin Are Sharing a Secretary, but Lack a Clear Job," *Ha'aretz*, April 23, 2009.

40. Israeli State Comptroller and Ombudsman, "Basic Law: State Comptroller," available at http://www.mevaker.gov.il/serve/site/english/eyesod.asp.

41: Aviezer Yaari, *The Road from Merhavia* (in Hebrew) (Or Yehuda: Kinneret, 2003), 221–53. The quotation is from p. 230.

42. Yaari, *The Road from Merhavia*.

43. The reference to publicity and transparency as the trademarks of the state comptroller's office is apparent on its Web site. The first paragraph devoted to the principles of state audit says:

> State audit is one of the foundation of democracy. The state auditor is part of the system of checks and balances in a democratic state. His status within the system of government is one of the measures of its strength as a democracy. Audit of the executive authority has its expression in the principle that public officials in a democratic state are the trustees and servants of the public and not its masters. It is a central factor in increasing the accountability and transparency of the public administration. (http://www.mevaker.gov.il/serve/site/english/eintro.asp)

44. Ben-Meir, *Civil-Military Relations in Israel*, 44–51.

45. Interview with Haim Zadok, Tel Aviv, December 23, 1992.

46. Interview with Moshe Arens, Savion, September 7, 1992.

47. Currently, the seven official subcommittees are the Subcommittee for Intelligence and Secret Services, Subcommittee for Foreign Affairs and Public Diplomacy, Subcommittee for Personnel in the IDF, Subcommittee for National Security and Force Structure, Subcommittee for the Home-Front Security, Subcommittee for Readiness and Field Security, and Subcommittee for Judea and Samaria. See Israeli Knesset, "Foreign Affairs and Defense Committee, "available at   http://www.knesset.gov.il/committees/eng/committee_eng.asp?c_id=4 and http://www.knesset.gov.il/committees/heb/docs/defense16-1.htm. For the most updated Hebrew official document see http://portal.knesset.gov.il/ NR/rdonlyres/FE91D3EB-41A1-4D4A-B8EE-6A1E9472BB20/437/yesod.doc.

48. For a detailed (and most updated) account of the mission, structure, and organization of the DFAC, see its official "founding document," updated to the Eighteenth Knesset (2009), available at http://portal.knesset.gov.il/NR/ rdonlyres/FE91D3EB-41A1-4D4A-B8EE-6A1E9472BB20/437/yesod.doc.

49. Yuval Steinitz, "The Civilian Control on the IDF and the Defense Establishment," in *An Army That Has a State: A New View on Israel's Security and Security Sector*," ed. Gabi Shefer (in Hebrew) (Jerusalem: Van Leer, 2007), 71–76.

50. Under the chair, Steinitz, the DFAC has created an unprecedented elaborated protocol of secrecy, involving both procedures and technology. Even the subcommittees' schedules are now classified. See Gideon Alon, "The Foreign Affairs and Defense Committee Is Pushing for an Overhaul of Knesset Confidentiality Measures," *Ha'aretz*, December 28, 2004.

51. But this is not all. According to Alon, the document also details some specific secrecy regulations: a security inspection will be conducted every morning in the committee chambers by the Knesset Guard; items such as computers, furnishings, and air-conditioning units will not be installed without permission from the Knesset security officer; an annual "bug inspection" of the premises will be carried out by the GSS; no classified material can be left in the committee chambers without the direct supervision of one of its employees; the alarm system will be activated every night; all staffs of committee members and stenographers will have an adequate security clearance; all classified material slated for destruction will be shredded; classified documents will be distributed only through a courier or by means of a "red fax"; and classified material will not leave the Knesset grounds. See Alon, "The Foreign Affairs and Defense Committee."

52. Quoted in Alon, "The Foreign Affairs and Defense Committee."

53. Available at http://www.knesset.gov.il/committees/heb/docs/defense16-1 .htm, p. 8. See also Gideon Alon, "Panel: Monitoring the Defense System Is Flawed," *Ha'aretz*, December 26, 2004.

54. Dan Margalit, *I Saw Them* (in Hebrew) (Tel Aviv: Zamora-Bitan, 1997), 7.

8. Domestic Reforms

1.   U.S. Atomic Energy Commission, *Atomic Energy Act of* 1946. Public Law 585, 79th Cong. Washington, D.C.: U.S. Government Printing Office, 1965.

2.   "Atomic Energy Control Now in Civilian Hands." *Los Angeles Times*, August 2, 1946.

3.   Organization for Economic Co-operation and Development, "Nuclear Legislation in OECD Countries," available at http://www.nea.fr/html/law/legislation/welcome.html (accessed September 29, 2008).

4.   "The Government is authorized to perform in the name of the State and subject to any law, all actions which are not legally incumbent on another authority." For the law in its present form, see Israeli Knesset, Basic Law: The Government (2001), available at http://www.knesset.gov.il/laws/special/eng/basic14_eng.htm. It is now clause 32, but in the original version of the 1968 law, it was clause 28, and much of the literature refers to that number. See Israeli Knesset, Basic Law: The Government—1968 (original version), available at http://www.knesset.gov.il/laws/special/eng/basic1_eng.htm. For a brief discussion of how the Israeli constitutional system applies to national security, including the residual power clause, see Yehuda Ben-Meir, *Civil-Military Relations in Israel* (New York: Columbia University Press, 1995), chap. 3.

5.   Historically, it was a response to the predicament of a legal void that the newly born Israel found itself in May 1948: in a state of war, with no legal code and with a government that had to act. Since then, the residual power clause has become a pillar in the Israeli constitutional system.

6.   Israel National Security Council, *The National Security Council Act,* 2008, Government Resolution no. 4889, Jerusalem, Israel, 2008, available at http://www.nsc.gov.il/NSCWeb/Docs/The_National_Security_council_Act.pdf.

7.   The need for constitutional clarity in this area became apparent recently when Dan Meridor was appointed in March 2009 as the minister in charge of the three secret organizations under the responsibility of the prime minister: the GSS, the Mossad, and the Atomic Energy Commission. Only the GSS is by law under the prime minister; the two others are by tradition backed up by governmental decisions and classified executive orders. Reports suggest that the appointment of Minister Meridor will not alter the existing arrangement by the three organizations that are administratively and functionally subject to the prime minister. The minister's authority stems from the authority of the prime minister but is not grounded in any legislation or protocol. As such, the status of the authority of Minister Meridor appears problematic from a legal point of view. See Mazal Mualem, "Dan Meridor and Benny Begin Are Sharing a Secretary, but Lack a Clear Job," *Ha'aretz*, April 23, 2009.

8. The anachronism of the amimut discourse sometimes looks so silly that only satirists and writers who never submit their columns to the Censora can make fun of this practice. For example, see Meir Shalev, "Brain Amimut," *Yediot Achronot*, August 23, 2002; and Aluf Benn, "The Price of Amimut," *Ha'aretz*, May 4, 2001.

9. "Knowledge and Discussion on the Nuclear Issue," *Ha'aretz*, September 6, 1998. See also Benn, "The Price of Amimut"; and Aluf Benn, "Israel: Censoring the Past," *Bulletin of the Atomic Scientists* 57, no. 4 (2001):17–19.

10. Hanoch Marmari, "A Practical Proposal to Abolish the Censora," *Ha'aretz*, October 31, 1993; Hanoch Marmari, "Life After the Censora," *Ha'aretz*, November 2, 1993.

11. The text of article VI in the NPT states: "Each of the Parties to the Treaty undertakes to pursue negotiations in good faith on effective measures relating to cessation of the nuclear arms race at an early date and to nuclear disarmament, and on a Treaty on general and complete disarmament under strict and effective international control."

9. Iran, the Fissile Materials Cutoff Treaty (FMCT), and Beyond

1. There already is a growing academic and policy literature on the issue of the future of the nuclear order, for example, Joseph Circione, *Bomb Scare: The History and Future of Nuclear Weapons* (New York: Columbia University Press, 2007); Kurt Campbell, Robert Einhorn, and Mitchell Reiss, eds., *The Nuclear Tipping Point: Why States Reconsider Their Nuclear Choices* (Washington, D.C.: Brookings Institution Press, 2004); George Perkovich, Jessica Tuchman Mathews, Joseph Cirincione, Rose Gottemoeller, and Jon Wolfsthal, *Universal Compliance: A Strategy for Nuclear Security* (Washington, D.C.: Carnegie Endowment, 2005); and Harald Müller, "The Future of Nuclear Weapons in an Interdependent World," *Washington Quarterly* 31, no. 2 (2008):63–75.

2. George Perkovich and James M. Acton, *Abolishing Nuclear Weapons*, Adelphi Paper no. 396 (London: International Institute for Strategic Studies, 2008); Hans Blix, *Why Nuclear Disarmament Matters*; Richard Rhodes, *The Twilight of the Bombs* (Boston: MIT Press, 2008).

3. George P. Shultz, William J. Perry, Henry A. Kissinger, and Sam Nunn, "A World Free of Nuclear Weapons," *Wall Street Journal*, January 4, 2007, A15; and, George P. Shultz, William J. Perry, Henry A. Kissinger, and Sam Nunn, "Toward a Nuclear-Free World." *Wall Street Journal*, January 15, 2008.

4. White House, "Remarks by President Barack Obama in Prague," April 5, 2009, available at http://www.whitehouse.gov/the_press_office/Remarks-By-President-Barack-Obama-In-Prague-As-Delivered/.

5. Article VI in the NPT states: "Each of the parties of the Treaty undertakes to pursue negotiations in good faith on effective measures relating to cessation of the nuclear arms race at an early date and to nuclear disarmament, and on a treaty on general and complete disarmament under strict and effective international control."

6. Steven L. Spiegel, Jennifer D. Kibber, and Elizabeth D. Matthews, *The Dynamics of Middle East Nuclear Proliferation* (New York: Mellen Press, 2002), 67.

7. International Institute for Strategic Studies, *Nuclear Programmes in the Middle East: In the Shadow of Iran* (London: IISS, 2008), 136–38.

8. This section is based in part on my "Israel: Nuclear Monopoly in Jeopardy," in International Institute for Strategic Studies, *Nuclear Programmes in the Middle East: In the Shadow of Iran* (London: IISS, 2008).

9. This phrase was used by Benjamin Netanyahu when he was the opposition leader before his election in 2009. Others who used the phrase are the former chief of staff and former minister of defense Shaul Mofaz, as well as columnists like Ari Shavit and Benny Morris. On Netanyahu's extreme views on the gravity of the "Iranian threat," see Ronen Bergman, *The Secret War with Iran* (New York: Free Press, 2008), 343–44; and International Institute for Strategic Studies, *Nuclear Programmes in the Middle East*, 136–38.

10. Ari Shavit, "There Is No Palestinian Sadat, No Palestinian Mandela: An Interview with Uzi Arad," *Ha'aretz*, July 16, 2009, available at http://www.haaretz.com/hasen/spages/1099064.html.

11. "Mossad: Iran Will Have Nuclear Bomb by 2014," *Ha'aretz*, June 16, 2009.

12. Jason Ditz, "Mullen: 'Nuclear Iran' an Existential Threat to Israel," Global Research, November 9, 2009, available at http://www.globalresearch.ca/index.php?context=va&aid=16000.

13. Reuters, "Israel Defense Chief: Iran Is Not a Nuclear Threat," Jerusalem, September 17, 2009, available at http://www.reuters.com/article/idUSTRE58G0ZF20090917.

14. Gidi Weitz and Na'ama Lanski, "Livni Behind Closed Doors: Iran Nukes Posed Little Threat to Israel," Ha'aretz, October 25, 2007. Efraim Halevy, the former Mossad chief (1998–2003), was perhaps the most explicit in his criticism of the term. In an interview with David Ignatius, he suggested that official Israel should end using the claim that a nuclear Iran could pose an "existential threat" to Israel. The rhetoric is wrong, he argued, and it gets in the way of the diplomatic effort. "I believe that Israel is indestructible," Halevy insisted. He also noted that Iranian President Mahmoud Ahmadinejad may tout his desire to wipe Israel off the map, but Iran's ability to consummate this threat is "minimal." "Israel has a whole arsenal of capabilities to make sure the Iranians don't achieve their result." Even if the Iranians did obtain a nuclear

weapon, says Halevy, "they are deterrable," because for the mullahs, survival and perpetuation of the regime is a holy obligation. See David Ignatius, "The Spy Who Wants Israel to Talk," *Washington Post*, November 11, 2007.

15. For a mainstream Israeli analysis of these concerns, see Ephraim Kam, "A Nuclear Iran: What Does It Mean, and What Can Be Done," memorandum no. 88 (Tel Aviv: Institute for National Strategic Studies, 2007), available at http://www.tau.ac.il/jcss/memoranda/memo88.pdf.

16. Former Prime Minister Ehud Olmert highlighted this outlook in a public policy speech in Herzelya in early January 2007: "For many long years, we have followed Iran's efforts to acquire nuclear weapons, in the guise of a civilian nuclear program. They are working through secret channels in a number of sites spread out across Iran."

17. National Intelligence Council, "Iran: Nuclear Intentions and Capabilities," National Intelligence Estimate, November 2007, available at http://www.dni .gov/press_releases/20071203_release.pdf. For a dissenting Israeli view of the November NIE, see Bergman, *The Secret War with Iran*, esp. 338–40, 346–49.

18. Matthew Clark, "Egypt Slams Iran's Hamas, Hezbollah Connection," *Christian Science Monitor*, January 28, 2009.

19. Yet some Israelis question whether the current religious leadership of Iran could be deterred at all by other nuclear weapons, given their views on Israel and Shiite religious beliefs and Israeli concerns that such beliefs could have an impact on Iranian leaders' sense of rationality.

20. Shavit, "There Is No Palestinian Sadat."

21. This point was central to Prime Minister Ehud Olmert's Herzliya speech in January 2007:

> The Iran of today, whose leadership is motivated by religious fanaticism and ideological extremism, has chosen a policy of confrontation with us and threatens to wipe Israel off the map of nations. It supports terror and undermines stability in the region. The Iranian regime, in its aspiration to regional hegemony, bears responsibility for the riots perpetrated by the Hezbollah today to bring down the Lebanese government. (Olmert, "Prime Minister Ehud Olmert's Address," translation available at http://www.pmo.gov.il/NR/exeres/C672BEFF-A736–42A0–83F5–6907958ADCBA,frameless.htm?NRMODE = Published)

22. But some Israeli leaders, such as Benjamin Netanyahu (before he took office), believe that Israel's deterrence must be explicit and crystal clear. In Netanyahu's words, "Against lunatics, deterrence must be absolute, perfect, including a second strike capability. The crazies have to understand that if they raise their

hands against us, we'll put them back in the Stone Age" (quoted in Bergman, *The Secret War with Iran*, 344).

23. Cam Simpson, "Israeli Citizens Struggle amid Iran's Nuclear Vow," *Wall Street Journal*, December 22, 2006.

24. Benny Morris, "Using Bombs to Stave Off War," *New York Times*, July 18, 2008.

25. In a speech in late 2006, Netanyahu declared, "It's 1938 and Iran is Germany. And Iran is racing to arm itself with atomic bombs. Believe him and stop him." See "Netanyahu: It's 1938 and Iran Is Germany," *Ha'aretz*, November 14, 2006.

26. Chuck Freilich, "Speaking About the Unspeakable: U.S.-Israeli Dialogue on Iran's Nuclear Program," Policy Brief no. 77 (Washington, D.C.: Washington Institute for Near East Policy, 2007), available at http://www.washingtoninstitute.org/templateC04.php?CID=284.

27. The substance of this section is taken from my "Israel: Nuclear Monopoly in Jeopardy."

28. Ehud Olmert, "Prime Minister Ehud Olmert's Address at the 2007 Herzliya Conference," Prime Minister's Office, January 24, 2007, available at http://www.pmo.gov.il/PMOEng/Archive/Speeches/2007/01/speechher240107.htm.

29. I was one of the critics of this phrase. See Avner Cohen, "Point of No Return?" *Ha'aretz*, May 17, 2005.

30. Shavit, "There Is No Palestinian Sadat."

31. National Intelligence Council, "Iran: Nuclear Intentions and Capabilities," National Intelligence Estimate, November 2007.

32. Shlomo Nakdimon, *First Strike: The Exclusive Story of How Israel Foiled Iraq's Attempt to Get the Bomb* (New York: Summit Books, 1987).

33. "Mofaz Criticised over Iran Threat," *BBC News*, June 8, 2008.

34. Ethan Bronner, "Olmert Says Israel Should Pull Out of the West Bank," *New York Times*, September 29, 2008.

35. This section is based in part on my op-ed "The Nuclear Opacity Route," *Ha'aretz*, February 12, 2007.

36. Avner Cohen, "Most Favored Nation," *Bulletin of the Atomic Scientists* 51, no. 1 (1995):44–53; Avner Cohen, *Israel and the Bomb* (New York: Columbia University Press, 1998), 108–9.

37. Ibid.

38. "Arab League Vows to Drop Out of NPT If Israel Admits It Has Nuclear Weapons," *Ha'aretz*, May 3, 2008, available at http://www.haaretz.com/hasen/spages/961275.html.

39. This section is based on Avner Cohen and Marvin Miller, "Israel," in *Country Perspectives on the Challenges to a Fissile Material Cutoff Treaty*, a companion

volume to *Global Fissile Material Report* 2008 (Princeton, N.J.: Program on Science and Global Security, International Panel of Fissile Material (IPFM), Princeton University, 2008), 27–36.

40. U.S. Department of State, "Acheson-Lilienthal and Baruch Plans, 1946," available at http://www.state.gov/r/pa/ho/time/cwr/88100.htm (accessed August 18, 2009).

41. United Nations General Assembly, 1st session, resolution 41, "Principles Governing the General Regulation and Reduction of Armaments," December 13, 1946, available at http://daccessdds.un.org/doc/RESOLUTION/GEN/NR0/032/92/IMG/NR003292.pdf?OpenElement.

42. White House, "White House Fact Sheet on the Middle East Arms Control Initiative," May 29, 1991.

43. Emily B. Landau, *Arms Control in the Middle East: Cooperative Security Dialogue and Regional Constraints* (Portland, Ore.: Sussex Academic Press, 2006); Peter Jones, *Towards a Regional Security Regime for the Middle East: Issues and Options* (Stockholm: Stockholm International Peace Research Institute, 1998); Peter Jones, "Negotiating Regional Security and Arms Control in the Middle East: The ACRS Experience and Beyond," *Journal of Strategic Studies* 26, no. 3 (2003):137–54.

44. United Nations General Assembly, President William Jefferson Clinton, "First Address to United Nations," September 23, 1993.

45. United Nations General Assembly, 48th session, resolution 75, "General and Complete Disarmament," December 16, 1993, available at http://www.un.org/documents/ga/res/48/a48r075.htm.

46. Aluf Benn, "The Struggle to Keep Nuclear Capabilities Secret" (in Hebrew). *Ha'aretz*, September 14, 1999.

47. Ibid. See also Avner Cohen and George Perkovich, "The Obama-Netanyahu Meeting: Nuclear Issues," Carnegie Endowment for International Peace, May 14, 2009, available at http://www.carnegieendowment.org/publications/index.cfm?fa=view&id=23124. Also see Eli Lake, "Secret U.S.-Israel Nuclear Accord in Jeopardy," *Washington Times*, May 6, 2009, available at http://www.washingtontimes.com/news/2009/may/06/us-weighs-forcing-israel-to-disclose-nukes/print/.

48. "Fissile Materials Cutoff Treaty," *Reaching Critical Will*, available at http://www.reachingcriticalwill.org/legal/fmct.html (accessed August 18, 2009).

49. Such a dialogue would almost certainly necessitate openly treating Israeli nuclear weapons as a given; it would be nearly impossible to avoid it. For the guardians of amimut, a "normalized" open dialogue on this with the United States would mean breaking a taboo.

50. "Arab League Will Call for Leaving Nuclear Treaty If Israel Admits to Nuclear Weapons," Associated Press, March 5, 2008; Arab League Vows to Drop Out

of NPT If Israel Admits It Has Nuclear Weapons," *Ha'aretz*, May 3, 2008, available at http://www.haaretz.com/hasen/spages/961275.html.

51. See, e.g., Frank Barnaby, *The Invisible Bomb* (London: I. B. Tauris, 1989), 38–40.

52. One possible nonintrusive way of verifying that plutonium wasn't being extracted from spent fuel would be to remotely monitor the noble gas fission products, specifically krypton-85, that are released during the reprocessing of spent nuclear fuel. However, it's technically possible to prevent the release of these gases, so that the Arab states might demand on-site inspections to verify that plutonium wasn't being produced. If Israel didn't want to shut down the Dimona reactor, it could insist that such inspections be conducted according to the principle of "managed access," but it is very doubtful that the process would work without compromising amimut. If Israel would be willing to shut down the Dimona reactor and produce tritium at a new reactor or an accelerator specifically designed for this purpose, it might be easier to achieve credible verification of the nonproduction of plutonium without seriously compromising opacity.

53. Maybe these issues are one reason why the IAEC decided to shut down the reactor in Soreq and to produce isotopes by purchasing a new accelerator. See Yael Ivri-Darel, "Soreq Nuclear Research Center's Reactor to Shut Down in 8 Years," *Ynet News*, March 4, 2008, available at http://www.ynet.co.il/english/articles/0,7340,L-3514334,00.html.

54. "FMCT: Explanation of Vote by Mr. Alon Bar," UN First Committee, November 4, 2004, available at http://www.ipfmlibrary.org/bar04b/pdf.

55. Here is the language of the Israeli statement: "Israel views the FMCT in both regional and global contexts, and its policy is governed by these two considerations:

> In the regional context of the Middle East, issues related to nuclear disarmament can be dealt with only after achieving lasting relations of peace and reconciliation, and within the context of the overall regional security and stability. Israel's approach on the way to move forward on these issues, inspired by the experience of other regions, is anchored in Israel's long-term vision, and is elaborated in our delegation's explanation of vote on the draft resolution entitled "The Establishment of a NWFZ in the region of the Middle East."
>
> In the global context, recent developments highlight the fact that, non-compliance of states with their international obligations, as well as the misuse and un-checked dissemination of nuclear fuel cycle capabilities, have become among the most pressing challenges in the nuclear non-proliferation field. The FMCT does not address these challenges and can further complicate them. We therefore, believe that an

overall priority in non-proliferation should be assigned to developing a
new effective non-proliferation arrangement pertaining to the nuclear
fuel cycle.

56. White House, "Remarks by President Barack Obama in Prague."
57. Still, strong Republican opposition to President Obama's nuclear-weapons
     agenda persists, with Senators John Kyl (R-AZ) and Jeff Sessions (R-AL) lead-
     ing the charge against the Comprehensive Test Ban Treaty (CTBT). Whether
     enough Republicans will support a verifiable FMCT to ensure ratification re-
     mains to be seen. See John Isaacs, "A Strategy for Achieving Senate Approval
     of the CTBT," *Bulletin of the Atomic Scientists*, April 15, 2009.
58. United Nations Office at Geneva, Conference on Disarmament, "Seven States
     Join Growing Consensus Around Conference on Disarmament Draft Pro-
     gramme of Work," May 28, 2009, available at http://www.unog.ch/unog/
     website/news_media.nsf/(httpNewsByYear_en)/C1DAB4F8EECDEB56C1257
     5C40037C344?OpenDocument.
59. For one academic articulation of the Israeli position why there should be no
     link between Iran's and Israel's nuclear programs, see Emily Landau, "If Iran
     Then Israel? Competing Nuclear Norms in the Middle East," *Strategic Assess-
     ment* 12, no. 3 (November 2009):97–107.
60. Aluf Benn, "Obama Warns Netanyahu: Don't Surprise Me with Iran Strike,"
     Ha'aretz, May 14, 2009. See also Aluf Benn and Barak Ravid, "Obama-
     Netanyahu Meet, Iran Thought to Top Agenda," *Ha'aretz*, May 18, 2009,
     available at http://www.haaretz.com/hasen/spages/1086366.html; Eli Lake,
     "Secret U.S.-Israel Nuclear Accord in Jeopardy," *Washington Times*, May 6,
     2009. For background, see also Avner Cohen and George Perkovich, "The
     Obama-Netanyahu Meeting: Nuclear Issues," Carnegie Endowment for Inter-
     national Peace, Proliferation Analyses, May 14, 2009, available at http://www
     .carnegieendowment.org/publications/index.cfm?fa=view&id=23124.
61. Bruce Riedel, a former CIA and U.S. National Security Council official and a
     senior fellow at the Brookings Institution's Saban Center, expresses this per-
     spective in the following way: "If you're really serious about a deal with Iran,
     Israel has to come out of the closet. A policy based on fiction and double stan-
     dards is bound to fail sooner or later. What's remarkable is that it's lasted so
     long." In Lake, "Secret US-Israel Nuclear Accord in Jeopardy."
62. Mark Fitzpatrick, "The Iranian Nuclear Crisis: Avoiding Worst-Case Scenar-
     ios," *Adelphi Paper* 398, International Institute for Strategic Studies, November
     2008.
63. See Avner Cohen and Marvin Miller, "Israel," in *Country Perspectives on the Chal-
     lenges to a Fissile Material Cutoff Treaty*, a companion volume to *Global Fissile
     Material Report* 2008 (Princeton, N.J.: Program on Science and Global Security,

International Panel of Fissile Material (IPFM), Princeton University, 2008), 27–36. See also Avner Cohen, "Between Natanz and Dimona," *Ha'aretz*, May 17, 2009, available at http://www.haaretz.com/hasen/spages/1085633.html.

64. See the replies by Uzi Arad to Shavit's questions on the nuclear issue. Shavit, "There Is no Palestinian Sadat." See also Gideon Frank, "Statement to the 51st General Conference of the International Atomic Energy Agency," Vienna, September 2007, available at http://www.iaec.gov.il/docs/statementGC51.pdf.

65. Such a zone was suggested by Marvin Miller and Lawrence Scheinman, "Israel and a Nuclear Weapons Free Zone in the Middle East," in *Nuclear Proliferation and International Security*, ed. Morton Bremer Maerli and Sverre Lodgaard (London: Routledge, 2007), 143.

66. Thus, other means of producing tritium would be required.

67. Verification means should go beyond implementation of the additional protocol to include the establishment of a wide-area environmental sampling network in the region.

68. This view received strong support from McGeorge Bundy, William J. Crowe Jr., and Sidney D. Drell in their *Reducing the Nuclear Danger* (New York: Council on Foreign Relations, 1993), 62–72.

69. Glenn Kessler, "Israel Submits Nuclear Trade Plan," *Washington Post*, September 30, 2007. On the Israeli "criteria-based" document, see also Arms Control Association, available at http://www.armscontrol.org/pressroom/2007/20070927_IsraelNSG. Israel recently reiterated its interest in building nuclear reactors in its country in response to the need to meet its growing energy demands in a manner consistent with global concerns about climate change. See Gideon Frank, "Statement to the 51st General Conference of the International Atomic Energy Agency," Vienna, September 2007, available at http://www.iaec.gov.il/docs/statementGC51.pdf.

10. Toward a New Bargain

1. See Aluf Benn and Barak Ravid, "Obama-Netanyahu Meet, Iran Thought to Top Agenda," *Ha'aretz* May 18, 2009, available at http://www.haaretz.com/hasen/spages/1086366.html. Also see Avner Cohen and George Perkovich, "The Obama-Netanyahu Meeting: Nuclear Issues," Carnegie Endowment for International Peace, May 14, 2009.

2. Also see Donald Rumsfeld, "Munich Conference on European Security Policy" (transcript), Office of the Secretary of Defense, February 7, 2004, available at www.defenselink.mil/speeches/speech.aspx?speechid=96.

3. Based on my own experience with U.S. classified documents about Israel's nuclear issues, I have noticed that American classification censors draw a thin line

between factual statements and statements of belief: only the latter are declassified. In the very few declassified U.S. documents that seem to acknowledge or imply U.S. knowledge about Israeli nuclear weapons, those assertions are made under the "we believe" mode rather than the "we know" mode. This includes the commonly cited 1974 Special National Intelligence Estimate (SNIE) about nuclear proliferation that states, "We believe that Israel already has produced and stockpiled a small number of fission weapons" (National Intelligence Estimate, "Special National Intelligence Estimate: Prospects for Future Proliferation of Nuclear Weapons," 1974, http://www.gwu.edu/~nsarchiv/NSAEBB/NSAEBB240/snie.pdf). According to one former U.S. senior official, the only sentence that U.S. government censors deleted from his book-length manuscript referred to Israeli nuclear weapons.

4. *Parliamentary Debates,* Commons, vol. 417, part 539 (2004), col. 1408.
5. McGeorge Bundy, William J. Crowe Jr., and Sidney D. Drell, *Reducing the Nuclear Danger* (New York: Council on Foreign Relations, 1993), 67.
6. Ibid., 69.
7. Ibid.
8. Ibid.
9. Ibid., 70.
10. George Perkovich and James M. Acton, *Abolishing Nuclear Weapons*, Adelphi Paper no. 396 (London: International Institute for Strategic Studies, 2008).
11. Rebecca Johnson, "The NPT in 2004: Testing the Limits," *Disarmament Diplomacy* 76 (March/April 2004):3–6.
12. Avner Cohen and Thomas Graham Jr., "An NPT for Non-Members," *Bulletin of the Atomic Scientists* 60, no. 3 (2004):40–44. In response, see George Perkovich, "Strengthening Non-Proliferation Rules and Norms: The Three-State Problem," *Disarmament Forum* 2004, no. 4 (2004):21–32, available at http://www.unidir.org/pdf/articles/pdf-art2187.pdf.
13. Mohamed ElBaradei, "Rethinking Nuclear Safeguards." *Washington Post,* June 14, 2006, A23.
14. Rebecca Johnson, "Politics and Protection: Why the 2005 NPT Review Conference Failed," *Disarmament Diplomacy* 80 (autumn 2005):3–32.
15. Sverre Lodgaard, "Making the Non-Proliferation Regime Universal: Asking Non-Parties to Behave 'As If' They Were Members," WMDC paper no. 7 (2004):11.
16. Jenny Nielson, "Engaging India, Israel, and Pakistan in Non-Proliferation," *Disarmament Diplomacy* 86 (August 2007):15.Nielson, "Engaging India, Israel, and Pakistan in Non-Proliferation."
17. Joseph Cirincione, John B. Wolfsthal, and Miriam Rajkumar, "Deadly Arsenals," Carnegie Endowment for International Peace, June 2002, 191–206.

18. George Perkovich, *India's Nuclear Bomb* (Berkeley: University of California Press, 1999).

19. Sarah Squassoni, "Missed Opportunity: Nuclear Suppliers Group," Carnegie Endowment for International Peace, September 10, 2008, available at http://www.carnegieendowment.org/publications/index.cfm?fa=view&id=20448.

20. Gideon Frank, "Statement to the 51st General Conference of the International Atomic Energy Agency," Vienna, September 2007, available at http://www.iaec.gov.il/docs/statementGC51.pdf.

21. Glenn Kessler, "Israel Submits Nuclear Trade Plan," *Washington Post*, September 30, 2007. On the Israeli "criteria-based" document, see also Arms Control Association, available at http://www.armscontrol.org/pressroom/2007/20070927_IsraelNSG.

22. The text of article VI in the NPT states: "Each of the Parties to the Treaty undertakes to pursue negotiations in good faith on effective measures relating to cessation of the nuclear arms race at an early date and to nuclear disarmament, and on a Treaty on general and complete disarmament under strict and effective international control."

23. Ashley Tellis, "American Giver," *Forbes*, September 29, 2008.

24. Daniel Bar Tal, *Shared Beliefs in a Society* (London: Sage, 2000).

25. "Arab League Will Call for Leaving Nuclear Treaty If Israel Admits to Atomic Weapons," Associated Press, March 5, 2008.

26. Regardless of naming Israel, this sentence was not unusual. As a matter of policy, the United States has sought universal adherence from the very beginning of the treaty's enforcement in 1970 and, on occasion, has named the states outside the NPT. For example, the Bush administration's assistant secretary of state for nonproliferation, John Wolf, mentioned Israel by name in his speech at the NPT conference in 2004. Goettemoeller's speech thus reflects a bipartisan and long-standing U.S. position on the NPT, even if that position has not been articulated as frequently and loudly as others. See Rose Goettemoeller, U.S. Assistant Secretary of State, UN NPT Preparatory Meeting, May 5, 2009, available at http://www.unmultimedia.org/tv/unifeed/d/12805.html.

27. Amir Oren, "Tsunami in a Test Tube," *Ha'aretz*, May 11, 2009, available at http://www.haaretz.com/hasen/pages/ShArtStEngPE.jhtml?itemNo=1084586&contrassID=2&subContrassID=4&title=%27Tsunami%20in%20a%20test%20tube%20%27&dyn_server=172.20.5.5.

28. An earlier headline posted on the *Washington Times* Web site, but removed within an hour, was even more stunning: "U.S. Weighs Forcing Israel to Disclose Nukes."

29. Eli Lake, "Secret U.S.-Israel Nuclear Accord in Jeopardy," *Washington Times*, May 6, 2009, available at http://www.washingtontimes.com/news/2009/may/06/us-weighs-forcing-israel-to-disclose-nukes/.

30. "Breaking Faith with Israel," *Washington Times*, May 6, 2009, available at http://www.washingtontimes.com/news/2009/may/06/breaking-faith-with-israel/.

Epilogue

1.   Quoted in Jeffrey Goldberg, "Is Israel Finished?" *Atlantic Monthly*, May 2008, 37.

2.   Noted in Isabel Kershner, "Support for 2-State Plan Erodes," *New York Times*, September 4, 2008.

3.   In 1948, because Ben-Gurion realized that producing a constitution would be extremely difficult politically and could even tear apart the tiny Jewish enclave, he decided to leave the issue for another time, so that the many newcomers could participate in the process.

4.   Ari Shavit, "Dimona: Thought at the End of the Zionist Century," *Ha'aretz*, December 31, 1999.

5.   Shalheveth Freier, "A Nuclear-Weapons Free Zone (NWFZ) in the Middle East and Its Ambience," unpublished ms., 1992.

Bibliography

Books

Adams, James. *The Unnatural Alliance*. New York: Quartet Books, 1984.

Arian, Asher. *Security Threatened: Surveying Israeli Opinion on Peace and War*. New York: Cambridge University Press, 1995.

Bard, Mitchell G. *Will Israel Survive?* New York: Palgrave Macmillan, 2007.

Barnaby, Frank. *The Invisible Bomb: The Nuclear Arms Race in the Middle East*. London: I. B. Tauris, 1989.

Bar Tal, Daniel. *Shared Beliefs in a Society*. London: Sage, 2000.

Bar Zohar, Michael. *Shimon Peres: The Biography*. New York: Random House, 2007.

Bass, Warren. *Support Any Friend: Kennedy's Middle East and the Making of the U.S.-Israel Alliance*. Oxford: Oxford University Press, 2003.

Ben-Ami, Shlomo. *Scars of War, Wounds of Peace*. New York: Oxford University Press, 2005.

Ben-Meir, Yehuda. *Civil-Military Relations in Israel*. New York: Columbia University Press, 1995.

———. *National Security Decision-Making: The Israeli Case* (in Hebrew). Tel Aviv: Jaffe Center for Strategic Studies, 1980.

Ben-Tzvi, Abraham. *Decade of Transition: Eisenhower, Kennedy, and the Origins of the American-Israeli Alliance*. New York: Columbia University Press, 1998.

Bergman, Ronen. *The Secret War with Iran*. New York: Free Press, 2008.

Bird, Kai, and Martin J. Sherwin. *American Prometheus*. New York: Random House, 2006.

Black, Ian, and Benny Morris. *Israel's Secret Wars*. New York: Grove Press, 1991.

Blair, Bruce. *Strategic Command and Control: Redefining the Nuclear Threat*. Washington, D.C.: Brookings Institution Press, 1985.

Bundy, McGeorge. *Danger and Survival*. New York: Random House, 1988.

Bundy, McGeorge, William J. Crowe Jr., and Sidney D. Drell. *Reducing the Nuclear Danger*. New York: Council on Foreign Relations, 1993.

Campbell, Kurt, Robert Einhorn, and Mitchell Reiss, eds. *The Nuclear Tipping Point: Why States Reconsider Their Nuclear Choices*. Washington, D.C.: Brookings Institution Press, 2004.

Cirincione, Joseph. *Bomb Scare: The History and Future of Nuclear Weapons*. New York: Columbia University Press, 2007.

Cohen, Avner. *Israel and the Bomb*. New York: Columbia University Press, 1998.

———. *The Last Taboo* (in Hebrew). Tel Aviv: Zamora-Bitan, 2005.

Cohen, Yoel. *The Whistleblower of Dimona: Israel, Vanunu and the Bomb*. New York: Holmes & Meier, 2003.

Committee for Denuclearization of the Middle East. *Israel-Arab: Nuclearization or Denuclearization* (in Hebrew). Tel Aviv: Amikam Press, 1963.

Dahl, Robert. *Controlling Nuclear Weapons: Democracy Versus Guardianship*. Syracuse, N.Y.: Syracuse University Press, 1985.

Dallek, Robert. *Nixon and Kissinger: Partners in Power*. New York: HarperCollins, 2007.

Davenport, Elaine, Paul Eddy, and Peter Gillman. *The Plumbat Affair*. Philadelphia: Lippincott, 1978.

DeVolpi, Alexander, G. E. Marsh, T. A. Postol, G. S. Stanford, and Stephen H. Unger. *Born Secret: The H-Bomb, the Progressive Case, and National Security*. New York: Pergamon Press, 1981.

Feaver, Peter. *Guarding the Guardians: Civilian Control of Nuclear Weapons in the United States*. Ithaca, N.Y.: Cornell University Press, 1992.

Feldman, Shai. *Israeli Nuclear Deterrence: A Strategy for the 1980s*. New York: Columbia University Press, 1982.

———. *Nuclear Weapons and Arms Control in the Middle East*. Cambridge, Mass.: MIT Press, 1997.

Ginor, Isabella, and Gideon Remez. *Foxbats over Dimona*. New Haven, Conn.: Yale University Press, 2007.

Goren, Dina. *Secrecy and the Right to Know* (in Hebrew). Tel Aviv: Turtledove, 1979.

———. *Secrecy, Security, and Freedom of the Press* (in Hebrew). Jerusalem: Magnes, 1976.

Green, Harold, and Alan Rosenthal. *Government of the Atom*. New York: Atherton, 1963.

Gusterson, Hugh. *Nuclear Rites: A Weapons Laboratory at the End of the Cold War*. Berkeley: University of California Press, 1996.

Hersh, Seymour. *The Samson Option: Israel's Nuclear Arsenal and American Foreign Policy*. New York: Random House, 1991.

Hewlett, Richard, and Oscar Anderson Jr. *The New World: A History of the United States Atomic Energy Commission.* Vol. 1, 1939–1946. University Park: Pennsylvania State University Press, 1962.

Hewlett, Richard, and Francis Duncan. *Atomic Shield: A History of the United States Atomic Energy Commission.* Vol. 2, 1947–1952. University Park: Pennsylvania State University Press, 1962.

Hofnung, Menachem. *Israel: Security Needs vs. the Rule of Law, 1948–1991* (in Hebrew). Jerusalem: Nevo, 1991.

Hopf, Theodore. *Peripheral Visions: Deterrence Theory and American Foreign Policy in the Third World.* Ann Arbor: University of Michigan Press, 1995.

Hounam, Peter. *The Woman from Mossad: The Torment of Mordechai Vanunu.* London: Vision Paperbacks, 1998.

Jones, Rodney, Cesare Merlini, Joseph Pilat, and William Potter, eds. *The Nuclear Suppliers and Non-Proliferation: International Policy Choices.* Lanham, Md.: Lexington Books, 1985.

Kahn, Herman. *Thinking About the Unthinkable in the 1980s.* New York: Touchstone, 1984.

Karpin, Michael. *The Bomb in the Basement: How Israel Went Nuclear and What That Means for the World.* New York: Simon & Schuster, 2006.

Katzenstein, Peter, ed. *The Culture of National Security.* New York: Columbia University Press, 1997.

Kaye, Dalia Dassa. *Beyond the Handshake.* New York: Columbia University Press, 2001.

Landau, Emily. *Arms Control in the Middle East.* Portland, Ore.: Sussex Academic Press, 2006.

Levite, Ariel E., and Emily B. Landau. *Israel's Nuclear Image: Arab Perceptions of Israel's Nuclear Posture.* Tel Aviv: Papyrus, 1994.

Margalit, Dan. *I Saw Them* (in Hebrew). Tel Aviv: Zamora-Bitan, 1997.

Mercer, Jonathan. *Reputation and International Politics.* Ithaca, N.Y.: Cornell University Press, 1996.

Miall, Hugh. *Nuclear Weapons: Who's in Charge?* London: Macmillan, 1987.

Mill, John Stuart. *On Liberty.* London: Longman, Roberts, and Green, 1869.

Moynihan, Daniel Patrick. *Secrecy: The American Experience.* New Haven, Conn.: Yale University Press, 1998.

Müller, Harald, David Fischer, and Wolfgang Kotter. *Nuclear Non-Proliferation and Global Order.* New York: Oxford University Press, 1994.

Nakdimon, Shlomo. *First Strike: The Exclusive Story of How Israel Foiled Iraq's Attempt to Get the Bomb.* New York: Summit Books, 1987.

Negbi, Moshe. *A Paper Tiger* (in Hebrew). Tel Aviv: Sifriyat Hapoalim, 1985.

Oren, Michael. *Six Days of War.* New York: Presidio Press, 2003.

Organski, Kenneth. *The $36 Billion Bargain: Strategy and Politics in U.S. Assistance to Israel.* New York: Columbia University Press, 1990.

Oz, Amos. *The Slopes of the Volcano.* Jerusalem: Keter Publishing, 2006.

Parsi, Trita. *Treacherous Alliance: The Secret Dealings of Israel, Iran and the U.S.* New Haven, Conn.: Yale University Press, 2007.

Paul, T. V. *Power Versus Prudence: Why Nations Forgo Nuclear Weapons.* Montreal: McGill-Queen's University Press, 2000.

————. *The Tradition of Non-Use of Nuclear Weapons.* Stanford, Calif.: Stanford University Press, 2009.

Peres, Shimon. *Battling for Peace: A Memoir.* London: Weidenfeld & Nicolson, 1995.

Perkovich, George. *India's Nuclear Bomb: The Impact on Global Proliferation.* Berkeley: University of California Press, 1999.

Perkovich, George, Jessica Tuchman Mathews, Joseph Cirincione, Rose Gottemoeller, and Jon Wolfsthal. *Universal Compliance: A Strategy for Nuclear Security.* Washington, D.C.: Carnegie Endowment, 2005.

Potter, William, ed. *International Nuclear Trade and Nonproliferation: The Challenge of Emerging Suppliers.* Lanham, Md.: Lexington Books, 1990.

Quandt, William. *Camp David: Peace Making and Politics.* Washington, D.C.: Brookings Institution Press, 1996.

Rabin, Yitzhak. *Pinkas Sherut* (in Hebrew). Tel Aviv: Ma'ariv, 1979.

————. *The Rabin Memoir.* Boston: Little, Brown, 1979.

Rabinovich, Itamar. *Waging Peace.* New York: Farrar, Straus & Giroux, 1999.

Reiss, Mitchell. *Bridled Ambitions: Why Countries Constrain Their Nuclear Capabilities.* Washington, D.C.: Woodrow Wilson Center Press, 1995.

Rhodes, Richard. *The Twilight of the Bombs.* Boston: MIT Press, 2008.

Sagan, Scott, and Kenneth Waltz. *The Spread of Nuclear Weapons: A Debate.* New York: Norton, 1995.

Schell, Jonathan. *The Abolition.* New York: Knopf, 1984.

Seaborg, Glenn. *Adventures in the Atomic Age: From Watts to Washington.* New York: Farrar, Strauss & Giroux, 2001.

Segal, Ze'ev. *Freedom of the Press: Between Myth and Reality* (in Hebrew). Tel Aviv: Papyrus Publishing, 1996.

Segev, Tom. *1967: Israel, the War and the Year That Transformed the Middle East.* New York: Metropolitan Books, 2007.

————. *The Seventh Million: The Israelis and the Holocaust.* New York: Hill & Wang, 1993.

Shalom, Zaki. *David Ben-Gurion: The State of Israel and the Arab World, 1949–1956* (in Hebrew). Sdeh Boker: Negev Press of Ben-Gurion University, 1995.

Spiegel, Steven L. *The Other Arab-Israel Conflict: Making America's Middle East Policy from Truman to Reagan.* Chicago: University of Chicago Press, 1985.

Stockholm International Peace Research Institute. *SIPRI Yearbook 2004: Armaments, Disarmament and International Security*. New York: Oxford University Press, 2004.

Tannenwald, Nina. *The Nuclear Taboo: The United States and the Non-Use of Nuclear Weapons Since 1945*. New York: Cambridge University Press, 2007.

Theoharis, Athan. *A Culture of Secrecy: The Government Versus the People's Right to Know*. Lawrence: University Press of Kansas, 1998.

Toscano, Louis. *Triple Cross: Israel, the Atomic Bomb and the Man Who Spilled the Secrets*. New York: Carol Publishing, 1990.

Trachtenberg, Marc. *A Constructed Peace*. Princeton, N.J.: Princeton University Press, 1999.

Webster, Hutton. *Taboo: A Sociological Study*. Stanford, Calif.: Stanford University Press, 1942.

Weizman, Ezer. *On Eagles' Wings*. New York: Macmillan, 1976.

Yaari, Aviezer. *The Road from Merhavia* (in Hebrew). Or Yehuda: Kinneret Publishing, 2003.

Yaniv, Avner, ed. *National Security and Democracy in Israel* (in Hebrew). Boulder, Colo.: Lynne Rienner, 1992.

Zakaria, Fareed. *The Future of Freedom*. New York: Norton, 2004.

Zohar, Michael Bar. *Shimon Peres: The Biography*. New York: Random House, 2007.

Book Chapters, Unpublished Essays, and Journal Articles

Aftergood, Steven, ed. "Special Issue on Government Secrecy." *Bulletin of the Atomic Scientists* 56, no. 6 (2000):24–30.

Amnesty International. "Israel: Mordechai Vanunu Sentence Clear Violation of Human Rights." July 2, 2007. Available at http://www.amnesty.org/en/library/asset/MDE15/044/2007/en/dom-MDE150442007en.html.

Ansari, Ali. "Iran Under Ahmadinejad: The Politics of Confrontation." Adelphi Papers no. 393. International Institute for Strategic Studies, 2007.

"Arms Control and Regional Security—A Chronology." *Foundation for Middle East Peace*. November 1996. Available at http://www.fmep.org/reports/special-reports/arms-control-proliferation-in-the-middle-east/PDF.

Ball, George. "The Cosmic Bluff." *New York Review of Books*, July 21, 1983.

Benn, Aluf. "Israel: Censoring the Past." *Bulletin of the Atomic Scientists* 57, no. 4 (2001):17–19.

Blech, Dor. "Never Again." Israeli Defense Forces. April 15, 2007. Available at http://dover.idf.il/IDF/English/News/holiday/2007/april/1501.htm.

Burr, William, Thomas Blanton, and Stephen Schwartz. "The Costs and Consequences of Nuclear Secrecy." In *Atomic Audit: The Costs and Consequences of U.S.*

Nuclear Weapons Since 1940, ed. Stephen Schwartz, 433–85. Washington, D.C.: Brookings Institution Press, 1998.

Burr, William, and Avner Cohen. "Israel Crosses the Threshold." *Bulletin of the Atomic Scientists* 62, no. 3 (2006):23.

Burr, William, and Jeffrey Kimball. "Nixon's Nuclear Ploy." *Bulletin of the Atomic Scientists* 59, no. 1 (2003):28–73.

Cohen, Avner. "The Bomb That Never Is." *Bulletin of the Atomic Scientists* 56, no. 3 (2000):22–23.

———. "Crossing the Threshold: The Untold Nuclear Dimension of the 1967 Arab-Israeli War and Its Contemporary Lessons." *Arms Control Today* 37, no. 5 (2007):12–16.

———. "Iraq and the Rules of the Nuclear Game." *Bulletin of the Atomic Scientists* 47, no. 6 (1991):10–11, 43.

———. "Israel's Nuclear Ambiguity." *Bulletin of the Atomic Scientists* 43, no. 2 (1987):15–19.

———. "Memo on the Yatza Affair." Unpublished manuscript, 2003.

———. "Most Favored Nation." *Bulletin of the Atomic Scientists* 51, no. 1 (1995):44–53.

———. "Nuclear Arms in Crisis Under Secrecy: Israel and the Lessons of the 1967 and 1973 Wars." In *Planning the Unthinkable: How New Powers Will Use Nuclear, Biological and Chemical Weapons*, ed. Peter Lavoy and Scott Sagan, 104–24. Ithaca, N.Y.: Cornell University Press, 2000.

———. "Opaque Nuclear Proliferation." *Journal of Strategic Studies* 13, no. 3 (1990):14–44.

Cohen, Avner, and Thomas Graham Jr. "An NPT for Non-Members." *Bulletin of the Atomic Scientists* 60, no. 3 (2004):40–44.

Cohen, Avner, and Marvin Miller. "Israel." In *Country Perspectives on the Challenges to a Fissile Material Cutoff Treaty*, a companion volume to *Global Fissile Material Report* 2008, published by the International Panel of Fissile Material (IPFM), Program on Science and Global Security, Princeton University, 2008.

Cohen, Avner, and George Perkovich. "The Obama-Netanyahu Meeting: Nuclear Issues." Carnegie Endowment for International Peace, May 14, 2009. Available at http://www.carnegieendowment.org/publications/index.cfm?fa=view&id=23124.

Congressional Research Service. "Nuclear Weapons R&D Organizations in Nine Nations." March 16, 2009. Available at http://www.fas.org/sgp/crs/nuke/R40439.pdf.

Cordesman, Anthony H. "Iran, Israel and Nuclear War: An Illustrative Scenario Analysis." Center for Strategic and International Studies, November 2007. Available at http://www.csis.org/media/csis/pubs/071119_iran.is&nuclearwar.pdf.

Dowty, Alan. "Israeli Perspectives on Nuclear Proliferation." In *Security, Order, and the Bomb: The Role of Nuclear Weapons in the Politics and Defense Planning of Non-*

Nuclear Weapon States, ed. Johan J. Holst, 69–86. Oslo: Oslo University Press, 1972.

———. "Israel's Nuclear Policy." In *M'dina, Mimshal, V'yahasim Benleumiim* 7 (in Hebrew). Reprint, *Diplomatia b'tsel eimut* (*Diplomacy in the Shadow of Confrontation*), ed. Binyamin Neuberger. Tel Aviv: Open University Press, 1984.

Evron, Yair. 1974. "Israel and the Atom: The Uses and Misuses of Ambiguity." *Orbis* 17 (1973):1326–43.

Falk, Richard. "Nuclear Weapons and the Renewal of Democracy." In *Nuclear Weapons and the Future of Humanity*, ed. Avner Cohen and Steven Lee, 115–30. Totowa, N.J.: Rowman & Allanheld, 1986.

Feiveson, Harold A., and Theodore B. Taylor. "Alternative Strategies for International Control of Nuclear Power." In *Nuclear Proliferation: Motivations, Capabilities, and Strategies for Control*, ed. Ted Greenwood, Harold A. Feiveson, and Theodore B. Taylor, 125–90. New York: McGraw-Hill, 1977.

Feldman, Avigdor. "Vanunu, Secrecy and the Law." In *Voices for Vanunu*. London: Campaign to Free Vanunu, 1997.

Feldman, Shai, "President Mubarak's Visit and the Middle East Nuclear Debate." *Washington Institute for Near East Policy*, April 5, 1995. Available at https://www.washingtoninstitute.org/templateC05.php?CID=2867.

Ferguson, Charles. "Nuclear Energy: Balancing Benefits and Risks." *Council on Foreign Relations Special Report* 28 (2007).

Fissile Materials Cutoff Treaty." *Reaching Critical Will.* Available at http://www.reachingcriticalwill.org/legal/fmct.html.

Florini, Ann. "The End of Secrecy." *Foreign Policy* 111 (1998):50–63.

Frank, Gideon. "Statement to the 51st General Conference of the International Atomic Energy Agency." Vienna, September 2007. Available at http://www.iaec.gov.il/docs/statementGC51.pdf.

Freier, Shalheveth. "A Nuclear-Weapons Free Zone (NWFZ) in the Middle East and Its Ambience." Unpublished manuscript, 1992.

Freilich, Chuck. "Speaking About the Unspeakable: U.S.-Israeli Dialogue on Iran's Nuclear Program." *Policy Brief 77.* Washington Institute for Near East Policy. December 2007. Available at http://www.washingtoninstitute.org/templateC04.php?CID=284.

Friedman, Matti. "Stop the Press" (in Hebrew). *Jerusalem Report*, April 4, 2005.

Gazit, Mordechai. "The Genesis of the U.S.-Israeli Military-Strategic Relationship and the Dimona Issue." *Journal of Contemporary History* 35, no. 3 (2000):413–22.

Gideon, Frank. "Shalheveth Freier Legacy at the IAEC." In *Shalheveth Freier.* Tel Aviv: Israel Atomic Energy Commission, 1995.

Goldberg, Jeffrey. "Unforgiven." *Atlantic Monthly*, May 2008. Available at http://www.theatlantic.com/doc/200805/israel.

Halloran, Richard. "Protracted Nuclear War." *Air Force Magazine*, March 2008, 56–59.

Haselkorn, Avigdor. "Israel: From an Option to a Bomb in the Basement?" In *Nuclear Proliferation: Phase II*, ed. Robert M. Lawrence and Joel Larus, 149–82. Wichita: University Press of Kansas, 1974.

Horowitz, Dan. "Is Israel a Garrison State?" *Jerusalem Quarterly* 4 (1977):58–75.

International Institute for Strategic Studies. *Iran's Strategic Weapons Programmes*. London: IISS, 2008.

———. *Nuclear Programmes in the Middle East: In the Shadow of Iran*. London: IISS, 2008.

Isaacs, John. "A Strategy for Achieving Senate Approval of the CTBT." *Bulletin of the Atomic Scientists*, April 15, 2009. Available at http://www.thebulletin.org/web-edition/features/strategy-achieving-senate-approval of the ctbt/.

Ivry, David. "Nuclear Friction Between Egypt and Israel." Paper no. 21, February 2004, Fisher Brothers Institute for Air and Space Strategic Studies. Available at http://www.fisherinstitute.org.il/Eng/_Articles/Article.asp?ArticleID=60&CategoryID=25&Page=2.

Jentleson, Bruce. "The Middle East Arms Control and Regional Security Talks: Progress, Problems and Prospects." Institute for Global Conflict and Cooperation, 1996.

Johnson, Rebecca. "The NPT in 2004: Testing the Limits." *Disarmament Diplomacy* 76 March/April 2004. Available at http://www.acronym.org.uk/dd/dd76/76npt.htm.

———. "Politics and Protection: Why the 2005 NPT Review Conference Failed." *Disarmament Diplomacy* 80 (autumn 2005):3–32.

Jones, Peter. "Arms Control in the Middle East: Some Reflections on ACRS." *Security Dialogue* 28, no. 1 (1997):57–70.

———. "Negotiating Regional Security and Arms Control in the Middle East: The ACRS Experience and Beyond." *Journal of Strategic Studies* 26, no. 3 (2003):137–54.

Kam, Ephraim. "A Nuclear Iran: What Does It Mean, and What Can Be Done." Memorandum no. 88. Institute for National Strategic Studies, February 2007.

"The Kenneth Waltz–Scott Sagan Debate: The Spread of Nuclear Weapons—Good or Bad?" *Security Studies* 4, no. 4 (1995):149–70.

Laswell, Harold. "The Garrison State." *American Journal of Sociology* 46, no. 4 (1941):455–68.

Levite, Ariel. "Never Say Never Again: Nuclear Reversal Revisited." *International Security* 2, no. 3 (2002/2003):59–88.

Little, Douglas. "The Making of a Special Relationship: The United States and Israel, 1957–68." *International Journal of Middle East Studies* 25, no. 4 (1993):563–85.

Lodgaard, Sverre. "Making the Non-Proliferation Regime Universal: Asking Non-Parties to Behave "As If" They Were Members." WMDC Paper no. 7, 2004.

Margolis, Joseph. "The Peculiarities of Nuclear Thinking." In *Nuclear Weapons and the Future of Humanity*, ed. Avner Cohen and Steven Lee, 153–68. Totowa, N.J.: Rowman & Allanheld, 1986.

McNamara, Robert. "The Military Role of Nuclear Weapons: Perceptions and Misperceptions." *Foreign Affairs* 62 (1983):58–80.

Memorandum of Discussion at the 165th NSC Meeting, October 7, 1953. In *Foreign Relations of the United States, 1952–54*, vol. 2, 532–33. Washington, D.C.: U.S. Government Printing Office, 1953.

Mian, Zia, and Alexander Glaser, "A Frightening Nuclear Legacy." *Bulletin of the Atomic Scientists* 64, no. 4 (2008):42–47.

Michael, George. "Deciphering Ahmadinejad's Holocaust Revisionism." *Middle East Quarterly* 14, no. 3 (2007):11–18.

Miller, Marvin. "Israel and Nuclear Weapons." Unpublished trip report, August 28, 1990.

———. "Trip to Egypt in June 1990." Unpublished trip report, August 15, 1990.

Miller, Marvin, and Lawrence Scheinman. "Israel and a Nuclear Weapons Free Zone in the Middle East." In *Nuclear Proliferation and International Security*, ed. Morton Bremer Maerli and Sverre Lodgaard, 143. New York: Routledge, 2007.

Müller, Harald. "The Future of Nuclear Weapons in an Interdependent World." *Washington Quarterly* 31, no. 2 (2008):63–75.

Nielson, Jenny. "Engaging India, Israel, and Pakistan in Non-Proliferation." *Disarmament Diplomacy* 86, August 2007. Available at http://www.acronym.org.uk/dd/dd86/86jn.htm.

Nosek, Hillel, and Yechiel Limor. "Military Censorship in Israel: Temporary Compromise Between Conflicting Values." In *Democracy and National Security in Israel*, ed. Binyamin Noyberger and Ilan Ben Ami (in Hebrew), 362–90. Tel Aviv: Open University Press, 1996.

Organization for Economic Co-operation and Development. "Nuclear Legislation in OECD Countries." Available at http://www.nea.fr/html/law/legislation/welcome.html (accessed September 29, 2008).

Paul, T. V. "Nuclear Taboo and War Initiation: Nuclear Weapons in Regional Conflicts." *Journal of Conflict Resolution* 39, no. 4 (1995):696–717.

Perkovich, George. "The Samson Option." *Washington Post Book World*, February 19, 2006. Available at http://www.washingtonpost.com/wp-dyn/content/article/2006/02/16/AR2006021601897.html.

———. "Strengthening Non-Proliferation Rules and Norms: The Three-State Problem." 2005 NPT Review Conference, United Nations Institute for Disarmament Research. Available at http://www.unidir.org/pdf/articles/pdf-art2187.pdf.

Perkovich, George, and James M. Acton. "Abolishing Nuclear Weapons." Adelphi Paper no. 396, International Institute for Strategic Studies, 2008.

Rosenfeld, Shalom. "The Press Between Basel and Schenkin" (in Hebrew). Available at http://www.amalnet.k12.il/sites/commun/library/newspaper/comi2713.htm.

Schelling, Thomas. "An Astonishing Sixty Years: The Legacy of Hiroshima." Prize lecture. Beijersalen, Royal Swedish Academy of Sciences, Stockholm, December 8, 2005.

Schiff, Ze'ev. "Comments on the Balance of National Strength and Security." In *The Balance of National Strength and Security* (in Hebrew), ed. Uzi Arad. Tel Aviv: Yediot Achronot Press, 2001.

"South Africa Profile." *Nuclear Threat Initiative*, May 2007. Available at http://www.nti.org/e_research/profiles/SAfrica/Nuclear/index.html.

Spector, Leonard, and Avner Cohen. "Israel's Airstrike on Syria's Reactor: Implications for the Nonproliferation Regime." *Arms Control Today* 38, no. 6 (2008). Available at http://www.armscontrol.org/act/2008_07-08/SpectorCohen.

Squassoni, Sarah. "Missed Opportunity: Nuclear Suppliers Group." Carnegie Endowment for International Peace, September 10, 2008. Available at http://www.carnegieendowment.org/publications/index.cfm?fa=view&id=20448.

Squassoni, Sharon. "Risks and Realities: The 'New Nuclear Energy Revival.'" *Arms Control Today* 37, no. 4 (2007). Available at http://www.armscontrol.org/act/2007_05/squassoni.

Tellis, Ashley. "American Giver." *Forbes*, September 29, 1983. Available at http://www.forbes.com/2008/09/29/bush-singh-nuclear-oped-cx_at_0929tellis.html.

"The U.S.-India Nuclear Deal." Council on Foreign Relations, October 2, 2008. Available at http://www.cfr.org/publication/9663/.

Van Dijk, Ruud. "Defense Condition (DEFCON) Alert System." In *Encyclopedia of the Cold War*, 237–39. London: Taylor and Francis, 2008.

"Why Go Nuclear?" *Bulletin of the Atomic Scientists* 64, no. 4 (2008):14–19.

Zack, Moshe. "The Censora and the Press in Five Wars" (in Hebrew). *Kesher* 13 (1993):5–20. Available at http://www.amalnet.k12.il/sites/commun/law/comi0157.htm.

Newspapers and Magazines

"A Flash of Light." *Newsweek*, November 5, 1979.

"Ahmadinejad at Holocaust Conference: Israel Will 'Soon Be Wiped Out'" (in Hebrew). *Ha'aretz*, December 13, 2006. Available at http://www.haaretz.com/hasen/spages/800098.html.

Alon, Gideon. "The Foreign Affairs and Defense Committee Is Pushing for an Overhaul of Knesset Confidentiality Measures" (in Hebrew). *Ha'aretz*, December 28, 2004.

———. "The GSS Law Was Approved in the Knesset by Great Majority" (in Hebrew). *Ha'aretz*, February 12, 2002.

———. "Justice Committee: The Espionage Law Is Too Sweeping" (in Hebrew). *Ha'aretz*, May 14, 2001.

———. "The Mossad the Next in Line" (in Hebrew). *Ha'aretz*, December 20, 2001.

———. "Panel: Monitoring the Defense System Is Flawed" (in Hebrew). *Ha'aretz*, December 26, 2004.

"Arab League Vows to Drop Out of NPT If Israel Admits It Has Nuclear Weapons." *Ha'aretz*, May 3, 2008. Available at http://www.haaretz.com/hasen/spages/961275.html.

"Arab League Will Call for Leaving Nuclear Treaty If Israel Admits to Atomic Weapons." Associated Press, March 5, 2008.

"Atom Secrets Man Held by Israelis." *The Guardian*, November 10, 1986. Available at http://www.guardian.co.uk/world/1986/nov/10/israel.

Azoulay, Yuval. "Censor: IDF Revealed Classified Data During the Lebanon War" (in Hebrew). *Ha'aretz*, December 10, 2007.

Barnea, Nachum, and Shimon Shipper. "The Button and the Finger" (in Hebrew). *Yediot Achronot*, February 27, 1998.

Barzilai, Amnon, and Yossi Melman. "The Strong Man of the Defense Establishment Decided to Start an Investigation" (in Hebrew), *Ha'aretz*, April 23, 2000.

Ben-Moshe, Yehuda. "25 Years Before Vanunu" (in Hebrew). *Koteret Rashit*, November 26, 1986.

Benn, Aluf. "The Big Projects" (in Hebrew). *Ha'aretz*, November 15, 1991.

———. "Clinton Committed to Netanyahu: Israel's Nuclear Capability Will Be Preserved" (in Hebrew). *Ha'aretz*, March 14, 2000.

———. "Israel Asks Bush to Explain Its 'Special Relationship' with U.S. to Obama." *Ha'aretz*, November 26, 2008.

———. "Lifting the Nuclear Veil, but Cautiously" (in Hebrew). *Ha'aretz*, June 27, 2000.

———. "The Official" (in Hebrew). *Ha'aretz*, September 17, 2001.

———. "The Price of *Amimut*" (in Hebrew). *Ha'aretz*, May 4, 2001.

———."Seven Stages in a Long Corridor." *Ha'aretz*, February 7, 1995.

———. "The Struggle to Keep Nuclear Capabilities Secret" (in Hebrew). *Ha'aretz*, September 14, 1999.

Bergman, Ronen. "The Censor Does Not Grow Up" (in Hebrew). *Ha'aretz*, June 11, 2000.

———. "Hanging the Scissors" (in Hebrew). *Ha'aretz Friday Magazine*, May 26, 2000.

———. "His Lost Honor." *Yediot Achronot*, April 16, 2003.

———. "Inside They Celebrated, Outside They Watched" (in Hebrew). *Yediot Achronot*, April 23, 2001.

———. "The Last Battle over Opacity" (in Hebrew). *Ha'aretz*, August 4, 2000.

Bergman, Ronen, and Gil Melzer. "The Silencer" (in Hebrew). *Yediot Achronot Weekly Magazine*, August 6, 2004.

Bergman, Ronen, and Tova Zimuki. "The Speech of the Prosecutor" (in Hebrew). *Yediot Achronot*, November 5, 2004.

"Breaking Faith with Israel." *Washington Times*, May 6, 2009. Available at http://www.washingtontimes.com/news/2009/may/06/breaking-faith-with-israel/.

Broad, William, and David E. Sanger. "Obama's Youth Shaped His Nuclear-Free Vision." *New York Times*, July 4, 2009.

Broder, Jonathan. "A Challenge to Israel's Nuclear Blind Spot." *Washington Post*, March 11, 2001.

Bronner, Ethan. "Olmert Says Israel Should Pull Out of the West Bank." *New York Times*, September 29, 2008.

———. "Talking to the Censor." *Boston Globe*, February 23, 1995.

"Calls for Olmert to Resign After Nuclear Gaffe." *The Guardian*, December 13, 2006. Available at http://www.guardian.co.uk/world/2006/dec/13/israel.

Carr, Geoffrey. "Life After Death." *The Economist*, June 21, 2008, 24–25.

"CIA Report on Syrian Nuclear Reactor." *Washington Post*, April 26, 2008.

Cohen, Avner. "Between Natanz and Dimona." *Ha'aretz*, May 17, 2009.

———. "Fictitious Opacity" (in Hebrew). *Ha'aretz*, July 1, 2002.

———. "Interim Nuclear Arrangement" (in Hebrew). *Ha'aretz*, July 6, 1990.

———. "The Last Nuclear Moment." *New York Times*, October 6, 2008.

———. "The Nuclear Opacity Route" (in Hebrew). *Ha'aretz*, February 12, 2007.

———. "Point of No Return?" (in Hebrew). *Ha'aretz*, May 17, 2005.

———. "Why India Yes and Israel No?" (in Hebrew). *Ha'aretz*, September 12, 2008.

Cohen, Avner, and Benjamin Frankel. "Gulf War Saved Iraq from Nuclear Attack." *Los Angeles Times*, February 22, 1991.

———. "Why the Israeli 'Spy' Was Imprisoned." *New York Times*, April 15, 1988.

Cohen, Avner, and Marvin Miller. "Diffusing the Nuclear Mideast." *New York Times*, May 30, 1991.

———. "The Nuclear Specter." *Washington Post*, August 3, 1990.

Darom, Naomi. "What Would You Do If Ahmadinejad Drops a Bomb Here Within Two Months?" (in Hebrew). *Ha'aretz Friday Magazine*, October 27, 2006. Available at http://www.haaretz.co.il/hasite/spages/779307.html.

"Dassault Lifts the Lid on the Jericho Missile Story" (Dassault lève le voile sur le missile Jericho). *Air & Cosmos/Aviation International*, December 6, 1996.

"Delivery of Dolphin Sub Expected Today." *Jerusalem Post*, March 29, 1999.

Dickey, Christopher, and Daniel Klaidman. "How Will Israel Survive?" *Newsweek*, April 1, 2002.

Edelist, Ran. "The Man Who Rides the Tamnun" (in Hebrew). *Ma'ariv*, February 25, 2000.

ElBaradei, Mohamed. "Rethinking Nuclear Safeguards." *Washington Post*, June 14, 2006.

"Ex-General Convicted of Passing Secrets." United Press International, May 14, 2002.

Fathi, Nazila. "Iran's Leader Warns West on Support for Israel." *New York Times*, October 21, 2006.

———. "Wipe Israel 'Off the Map' Iranian Says." *New York Times*, October 27, 2005.

Finney, John W. "Israelis Reported to Be Reluctant at This Time to Sign Treaty Barring Spread of Nuclear Arms." *New York Times*, November 20, 1968.

Frankel, Glenn. "Israel's Security Service Has Found New Enemy: Itself." *Washington Post*, July 2, 1987.

Frantz, Douglas. "Israel's Arsenal Is Point of Contention: Officials Confirm That the Nation Can Now Launch Atomic Weapons from Land, Sea and Air." *Los Angeles Times*, October 12, 2003.

Gage, Nicholas. "Shah Said to Plan to Leave Iran Today for Egypt and U.S." *New York Times*, January 16, 1979.

Gali, Elkana. "How Israel Would Respond to Nasser's Missiles" (in Hebrew). *Yediot Achronot*, August 10, 1962.

Gonen, Eyal. "Without Censora" (in Hebrew). *Yediot Achronot Weekly Magazine*, November 3, 2005.

———. "Without Censorship" (in Hebrew). *Yediot Achronot Weekly Magazine*, March 11, 2005.

Gordon, Michael R. "Norway Questions Israeli Use of Nuclear Material." *New York Times*, February 17, 1987.

Gross, Shlomo. "Defense Outlook in the Missile Age" (in Hebrew). *Ha'aretz*, September 28, 1962.

Handverker, Haim. "Let's Talk About It" (in Hebrew). *Ha'aretz Friday Magazine*, September 4, 1998.

Harel, Amos. "Barak: Iranian Nuclear Weapons Would Be an Existential Threat on Israel," *Ha'aretz*, February 17, 2009.

Harel, Zvi. "Yaakov Charged with 'Revealing State Secrets'" (in Hebrew). *Ha'aretz*, May 9, 2001.

Harel, Zvi, and Amnon Barzilai. "Gag Order Partially Lifted in Ya'akov Espionage Case" (in Hebrew). *Ha'aretz*, April 23, 2001.

Hashemi-Rafsanjani, Akbar. "Qods Day Speech (Jerusalem Day)." December 14, 2001. Voice of the Islamic Republic of Iran, in Persian, Trans. BBC Worldwide Monitoring. Available at http://www.globalsecurity.org/wmd/library/news/iran/2001/011214-text.html.

Hasson, Nir. "Vanunu to Return to Prison for Violating the Terms of His Parole" (in Hebrew). *Ha'aretz*, July 2, 2007.

————. "Vanunu to Return to Prison for Violating the Terms of His Parole" (in Hebrew). *Ha'aretz*, March 1, 2008.

Heller, Or. "Nuclear Historian Dr. Avner Cohen Is Expected to Arrive Today and Will Be Arrested" (in Hebrew). *Ma'ariv*, March 12, 2001.

Hess, Pamela. "Hayden: Syrian Site Could Have Produced Fuel for 2 Weapons." *Washington Post*, April 28, 2008. Available at http://www.washingtonpost.com/wp-dyn/content/article/2008/04/28/AR2008042802122.html.

Hirschberg, Peter. "Iran's President Clarifies His Stand on Holocaust." *New York Times*, December 15, 2005.

Hoffman, Ariela Ringle. "Without Secrets" (in Hebrew). *Yediot Achronot*, May 2000.

"How Osirak Was Bombed." *BBC News*, June 5, 2006. Available at http://news.bbc.co.uk/2/hi/middle_east/5020778.stm.

"In the Appropriate Caution." *Ha'aretz*, February 4, 2000.

"Iranian Leader: Holocaust a 'Myth.'" CNN, December 14, 2005. Available at http://www.cnn.com/2005/WORLD/meast/12/14/iran.israel/.

"Israel Allows Vanunu Out of Solitary Confinement." *BBC News*, March 13, 1998.

"Israel Has '150 Nuclear Weapons.'" *BBC News*, May 26, 2008. Available at http://news.bbc.co.uk/2/hi/middle_east/7420573.stm?Aaaah.

"Israeli Given 18 Years in Atomic Secrets Case." *New York Times*, March 28, 1988.

Ivri-Darel, Yael. "Soreq Nuclear Research Center's Reactor to Shut Down in 8 Years." *Ynet News*, March 4, 2008. Available at http://www.ynet.co.il/english/articles/0,7340,L-3514334,00.html.

Joffre, Lawrence. "Ze'ev Schiff: Israeli Author, Military Analyst and Journalist Who Said Things Others Did Not Dare." *The Guardian*, July 23, 2007. Available at http://www.guardian.co.uk:80/israel/comment/0,,2132490,00.html.

Kershner, Isabel. "Support for 2-State Plan Erodes." *New York Times*, September 4, 2008.

Kessler, Glenn. "Israel Submits Nuclear Trade Plan." *Washington Post*, September 30, 2007.

Klein, Yossi. "Six Bands Stretched Across the Scalp Hair" (in Hebrew). *Ha'aretz*, May 2, 2006.

"Knowledge and Discussion on the Nuclear Issue" (in Hebrew). *Ha'aretz*, September 6, 1998.

Krauthammer, Charles. "Never Again?" *Washington Post*, May 5, 2006.

Lake, Eli. "Secret U.S.-Israel Nuclear Accord in Jeopardy," *Washington Times*, May 6, 2009. Available at http://www.washingtontimes.com/news/2009/may/06/us-weighs-forcing-israel-to-disclose-nukes/.

Lavi, Aviv. "Disinformation" (in Hebrew). *Ha'aretz*, April 27, 2001.

Lefkovits, Etgar. "Work on Jerusalem Bunker, Escape Route Predates Iranian Nuclear Threat." *Jerusalem Post*, November 2, 2006.

Livneh, Eliezer. "Nuclear Interim Review" (in Hebrew). *Ha'aretz*, October 12, 1962.

———. "Warning in the Last Moment" (in Hebrew). *Ha'aretz*, January 12, 1962.

Marcus, Yoel. "Don't Stick Your Neck Out" (in Hebrew). *Ha'aretz*, July 6, 2008.

Margalit, Dan. "Ambiguity Is Preferable" (in Hebrew). *Ha'aretz*, September 10, 1998.

Marmari, Hanoch. "Life After the Censora" (in Hebrew). *Ha'aretz*, November 2, 1993.

———. "A Practical Proposal to Abolish the Censora" (in Hebrew). *Ha'aretz*, October 31, 1993.

Melman, Yossi. "The Chief: 2000 Edition" (in Hebrew). *Ha'aretz*, February 18, 2000.

———. "Defense Ministry Security Chief Yehiel Horev Set to Retire This Summer" (in Hebrew). *Ha'aretz*, April 30, 2007.

———. "Discrete" (in Hebrew). *Ha'aretz Friday Magazine*, April 23, 2005.

———. "The First MALMAB" (in Hebrew). *Ha'aretz*, March 16, 2004.

———. "He Wanted to Leave a Legacy" (in Hebrew). *Ha'aretz*, May 4, 2001.

———. "It Is Time to Free Vanunu" (in Hebrew). *Ha'aretz*, April 16, 2008.

———. "MALMAB Will Not Be Israel's Fourth Intelligence Organization." *Ha'aretz*, June 30, 2000.

———. "MKs Want to Change the Scope of Severe Espionage" (in Hebrew). *Ha'aretz*, May 21, 2001.

———. "Peres: Israel Has No Intention of Attacking Iran" (in Hebrew). *Ha'aretz*, October 21, 2006. Available at http://www.haaretz.com/hasen/spages/777440 .html.

———. "The Secret Chief Does Not Want a Minister" (in Hebrew). *Ha'aretz*, June 29, 2000.

———. "Who Is Afraid of Mordechai Vanunu?" (in Hebrew). *Ha'aretz*, April 25, 2004.

———. "Who Is Afraid of Vanunu?" (in Hebrew). *Ha'aretz*, March 16, 2004.

———. "Why Are They Afraid of Yechiel Horev?" (in Hebrew). *Ha'aretz*, April 30, 2001.

Melman, Yossi, and Dalia Shori. "The Case Against Avner Cohen Closed" (in Hebrew). *Ha'aretz*, December 1, 1999.

———. "Why Are They Afraid of Yechiel Horev?" *Ha'aretz*, April 30, 2001.

Meranda, Amnon. "IDF Intelligence: Syria Strengthening Ties with Radical Axis." *Yediot Achronot*, September 15, 2008.

Mikkelsen, Randall. "Syrian Reactor Capacity Was 1–2 Weapons/Year: CIA." *Reuters*, April 29, 2008. Available at http://www.washingtonpost.com/wp-dyn/ content/article/2008/04/28/AR2008042802145.html.

Miller, Judith. "Veteran: Israel's New President on Iran's Nuclear Program, and His Own." Weekend Interview, *Wall Street Journal*, July 21, 2007.

Mills, Tony Allen. "Israel Holds Bomb Scientist in Spy Scare." *Sunday Times*, April 22, 2001.

"Mofaz Criticised over Iran Threat." *BBC News*, June 8, 2008.

"Mordechai Vanunu: The Sunday Times Archives." *Sunday Times*, Available at http://www.timesonline.co.uk/tol/news/article830147.ece.

"Mossad: Iran Will Have Nuclear Bomb by 2014." *Ha'aretz*, June 16, 2009.

Mostaghim, Ramin, and Borzou Daraghi. "Ayatollah Ali Khamanei Says Iran, Israel on 'Collision Course.'" *Los Angeles Times*, September 20, 2008.

Nakdimon, Shlomo. "'Don't Compare Me to Mordechai Vanunu'" (in Hebrew). *Yediot Achronot*, June 12, 2000.

"Netanyahu: It's 1938 and Iran Is Germany." *Ha'aretz*, November 14, 2006.

"Nuclear NPT Extended Indefinitely." *Jerusalem Post*, May 12, 1995.

Oren, Amir. "American Palmachnik Looks for Some Recognition" (in Hebrew). *Ha'aretz*, April 27, 2001.

———. "An Old General's Manhattan Project" (in Hebrew). *Ha'aretz*, May 4, 2001.

———. "A Secret Guard for Nuclear Ambiguity" (in Hebrew). *Ha'aretz*, August 8, 2007.

———. "Nuclear Deterrence with a Grain of Salt" (in Hebrew). *Ha'aretz*, June 10, 2008.

———. "They Still Haven't Learned a Thing." *Ha'aretz*, April 27, 2001

———. "Tsunami in a Test Tube." *Ha'aretz*, May 11, 2009.

———. "Where Did the 300 Million Go?" (in Hebrew). *Ha'aretz*, March 27, 2006.

"Peculiar Decision" (in Hebrew). *Ha'aretz*, April 5, 1962.

Pedatzur, Reuven. "A Brave Judge Stands Up to Security Bullies" (in Hebrew). *Ha'aretz*, November 28, 2001.

———. "The Establishment Against Citizen Cohen" (in Hebrew). *Ha'aretz*, August 8, 2000.

Pedatzur, Reuven, and Yatza Yaacov. "250,000 Deaths and Half a Million Wounded." *Ha'aretz*, May 23, 2008.

Porter, Gareth. "Iran Nuke Laptop Data Came from Terror Group." *IPS News*, February 29, 2008. Available at http://ipsnews.net/news.asp?idnews=41416.

"The Prime Minister: Ten Minutes Against Four Years" (in Hebrew). *Ha'olam Hazeh*, July 17, 1963.

"Professors Against Nuclear Armament in the Middle East" (in Hebrew). *Ha'aretz*, March 13, 1962.

Rafsanjani, Akbar Hashemi. Jerusalem Day Speech, "Voice of the Islamic Republic of Iran" (in Persian). Trans. BBC Worldwide Monitoring, December 14, 2001. GlobalSecurity.Org, available at http://www.globalsecurity.org/wmd/library/news/iran/2001/011214-text.html (accessed April 29, 2008).

"The Reactor: Open Secret in Beer Sheba" (in Hebrew). *Ha'aretz*, December 22, 1960.

Reinfeld, Moshe. "State Wants Ya'akov in Jail, Not in Hotel" (in Hebrew). *Ha'aretz*, May 23, 2001.

Richter, Paul. "International Approves U.S.-India Nuclear Deal." *Los Angeles Times*, September 7, 2008.

Rozen, Imanuel. "Israeli Nukes: All Talk" (in Hebrew). *Ma'ariv*, February 10, 1993.

Sadeh, Sharon. "Israel Said Holding Nuclear Scientist" (in Hebrew). *Ha'aretz*, April 22, 2001.

Salpeter, Elyahu. "The Nuclear Treaty Vis-à-Vis Israel's Security: Conventional and Nuclear Guarantees Are Needed Prior to Signature" (in Hebrew). *Ha'aretz*, November 24, 1968.

Sarid, Yosi. "Divide and Save" (in Hebrew). *Ha'aretz*, September 12, 2008.

Schiff, Ze'ev. "A Fortified Nuclear Wall" (in Hebrew). *Ha'aretz*, January 27, 1995

———. "The Law of the Red Button" (in Hebrew). *Ha'aretz*, March 13, 1998.

———. "The Meridor's Report." *Ha'aretz*, April 24, 2006.

———. "No Change in Nuclear Policy" (in Hebrew). *Ha'aretz*, September 11, 1998.

———. "Nuclear Opacity for How Long?" (in Hebrew). *Ha'aretz*, August 24, 2000.

———. "Preferring Political Ambiguity" (in Hebrew). *Ha'aretz*, January 23, 1992.

———. "Six Difficult Nuclear Questions" (in Hebrew). *Ha'aretz*, February 24, 1995.

———. "Why Nobody Debates the Nuclear Issue?" (in Hebrew). *Ha'aretz*, March 29, 2000.

Schwarz, Benjamin. "Will Israel Live to 100?" *Atlantic Monthly*, May 2005.

"Scientists Call for Regional Denuclearization" (in Hebrew). *Ha'aretz*, July 25, 1962.

Segal, Ze'ev. "The Courts Should Not Be the Censor" (in Hebrew). *Ha'aretz*, April 24, 2001.

Shachar, Ilan. "Knesset Approves Expanding Powers of National Security Chief" (in Hebrew). *Ha'aretz*, July 29, 2008.

Shalev, Meir. "Brain *Amimut*" (in Hebrew). *Yediot Achronoth*, August 23, 2002.

Shavit, Ari. "Dimona" (in Hebrew). *Ha'aretz Friday Magazine*, December 12, 1999.

———. "Dimona: Thought at the End of the Zionist Century" (in Hebrew). *Ha'aretz*, December 31, 1999.

———. "Unity Before Calamity." *Ha'aretz*, February 26, 2009.

Shibi, Haim. "Don't Commit *Censora* Offense" (in Hebrew). *Yediot Achronot*, March 6, 1993.

"Shimon Peres Criticizes Public Figures and Scientists Who Demanded Denuclearization" (in Hebrew). *Kol Ha'am*, September 17, 1962.

Shori, Dalia. "The Knesset Discussed Israel's Nuclear Policy for the First Time." *Ha'aretz*, February 3, 2000.

Simpson, Cam. "Israeli Citizens Struggle Amid Iran's Nuclear Vow." *Wall Street Journal*, December 22, 2006.

Smalley, David. "Kerry Rebuffed, Frustrated in Attempt to See Nuclear Targets Plan." *Inside the Air Force*, December 22, 2000. Available at http://www.fas.org/sgp/news/2000/12/iaf122200.html.

"Sneh: If Iran Gets the Bomb, Many Will Leave" (in Hebrew). *Ha'aretz*, November 12, 2006.

Sobelman, Daniel. "Avner Cohen Was Interrogated" (in Hebrew). *Ha'aretz*, March 14, 2001.

———. "Israeli Researcher Avner Cohen Will Return to Israel" (in Hebrew). *Ha'aretz*, March 11, 2001.

Sommer, Allison Kaplan. "Revealed: The Secrets of Israel's Nuclear Arsenals." *Sunday Times*, October 5, 1986.

———. "Ya'akov: I Did Not Believe I Was Revealing Secrets" (in Hebrew). *Jerusalem Post*, December 20, 2001.

Sontag, Deborah. "Israel Arrests Ex-General as Spy for Spilling Old Secrets." *New York Times*, May 2, 2001.

Steinberg, Gerald. "The Arab Double Standard." *Jerusalem Post*, February 27, 1998.

"They Still Haven't Learned a Thing" (in Hebrew). *Ha'aretz*, April 27, 2001.

"TV Report of an Israeli A-bomb Draws a Denial in Washington." *New York Times*, January 9, 1969.

"Unacceptable Intervention" (in Hebrew). *Ha'aretz*, March 27, 1962.

"The United States Exerted Heavy Diplomatic Pressure on Israel" (in Hebrew). *Ha'aretz*, August 2, 1963.

Urquhart, Conal. "Speculation Flourishes over Israel's Strike on Syria." *The Guardian*, September 17, 2007.

———. "Vanunu Jailed Again After Talks with Foreigners." *The Guardian*, July 3, 2007.

"U.S. Assumes the Israelis Have A-Bomb or Its Parts," *New York Times*, July 17, 1970.

"U.S. Blocks Israeli's Appointment over China Deal." *World Tribune.Com*, April 3, 2007. Available at http://www.worldtribune.com/worldtribune/07/front2454193.63125.html.

"Vanunu Released After 18 Years." *The Guardian*, April 21, 2004.

Walsh, James. "Bombs Unbuilt: Power, Ideas, and Institutions in International Politics." PhD diss., Massachusetts Institute of Technology, June 2001.

The World's Worst-Kept Secret." Review of *The Samson Option: Israel, America and the Bomb*, by Seymour Hersh. *The Economist*, October 26, 1991.

Worth, Robert F., and Fathi Nazila. "Ahmadinejad Sworn in for 2nd Term as Iran's President." *New York Times*, August 5, 2009.

Wright, Robin. "Syrian Nuclear Plant." *Washington Post*, April 25, 2008. Available at http://www.washingtonpost.com/wp-dyn/content/discussion/2008/04/25/DI2008042501853.html.

Yemini, Galit, and Guy Leshem. "The Private Spies of the Ministry of Defense" (in Hebrew). *Yediot Achronot*, December 19, 1997.

Zachariah, Janine. "'Exiled' Israeli Academic Seeks Knesset Hearing on Book About Nuclear History" (in Hebrew). *Jerusalem Post*, June 13, 2000.

Zarchin, Tomer. "High Court Extends Vanunu's Travel Ban by 6 Months." *Ha'aretz*, July 7, 2009.

Government Documents

Atherton, Alfred, and Myron Kratzer to Joseph Sisco. "Response to Congressional Questions on Israel's Nuclear Capabilities." October 15, 1975. Record Group (hereafter RG) 59. Records of Joseph Sisco, box 40.

Barbour, Walworth, to Joseph Sisco. November 19, 1969. Nixon Presidential Materials Project (hereafter NPMP), National Security Council Files (hereafter NSCF), box 605, Israel vol. 3.

"Conference Report on H.R. 3230, National Defense Authorization Act for Fiscal Year 1997." 1996. *Congressional Record*. Available at http://www.fas.org/irp/congress/1996_cr/h960730r.htm.

"Conference Report on H.R. 3230, National Defense Authorization Act for Fiscal Year 1997: Honorable Robert S. Walker." August 1, 1996. *Congressional Record*. Available at http://www.fas.org/irp/congress/1996_cr/h960801r.htm.

Davies, Rodger, to Mr. Austin et al. "Review Group Consideration of Response to NSSM-40, June 26, 1969." June 30, 1969. RG 59. Top Secret Subject, Numeric Files 1970–73, box 11, Pol Isr.

Davies, Rodger, to Elliot Richardson. "Call on You by Israeli Ambassador Rabin, Thursday, August 28, 1969 at 11 a.m." August 28, 1969. SN 67-69, DEF 12-1 Isr.

Department of Defense. "Findings of the Nuclear Posture Review." January 9, 2002. Available at http://www.defenselink.mil/dodcmsshare/briefingslide/120/020109-D-6570C-001.pdf.

Department of Energy. "Fact Sheet." Available at http://www.fas.org/sgp/othergov/doe/fs_stockpile.html.

———. "Fact Sheet: Proposed Declassification of the Locations of the Former Nuclear Weapons Storage Sites." Available at http://www.fas.org/sgp/othergov/doe/fs_sites.html.

Department of State. "Acheson-Lilienthal and Baruch Plans, 1946." Available at http://www.state.gov/r/pa/ho/time/cwr/88100.htm.

———. Cable no. 127273 to Tel Aviv. July 31, 1969. SN 67–69. Def 12-5 Isr.

———. "Political Statements Concerning the Israeli Reactor." January 17, 1961.3207, National Security Archives, Washington, D.C.

Eliot, Theodore L., to Henry Kissinger. "Briefing Book: Visit of Mrs. Golda Meir." September 19, 1969.

Enclosing "Background: Israel's Nuclear Weapon and Missile Programs." Subject-Numeric Files (hereafter SN) 67–69, Pol 7 Isr.

Goettemoeller, Rose, U.S. Assistant Secretary of State, UN NPT Preparatory Meeting, May 5, 2009. Available at http://www.unmultimedia.org/tv/unifeed/d/12805.html.

Hart, Parker T., to Dean Rusk. "Issues to Be Considered in Connection with Negotiations with Israel for F-4 Phantom Aircraft." Briefing memorandum, October 15, 1968. SN 67–69, Def 12-5 Isr.

Israel Atomic Energy Commission. "About Us." Available at http://www.iaec.gov.il/pages_e/card_e.asp.

Israeli Knesset. Basic Law: The Government, 1968 (original version). Available at http://www.knesset.gov.il/laws/special/eng/basic1_eng.htm.

———. Basic Law: The Government, 2001. Available at http://www.knesset.gov.il/laws/special/eng/basic14_eng.htm.

Israeli Prime Minister's Office. "At the Weekly Cabinet Meeting," May 24, 2009. Available at http://www.pmo.gov.il/PMOEng/Secretarial/Cabinet/2009/05/govmes240509.htm.

Israeli State Comptroller and Ombudsman. "Basic Law: State Comptroller." Available at http://www.mevaker.gov.il/serve/site/english/eyesod.asp.

Israel Security Agency. "Core Values of the Israel Security Agency." Available at http://www.shabak.gov.il/English/about/Pages/valuseEn.aspx.

"The Issues for Decision." n.d. (early July 1969). NPMP, NSCF, box 604, Israel vol. 2.

Kissinger, Henry, to Richard Nixon. "Discussions with the Israelis on Nuclear Matters." October 7, 1969. NPMP, NSCF, box 605, Israel vol. 3.

———. "Israel's Nuclear Program." November 6, 1969. NPMP, NSCF, box 605, Israel vol. 3.

———. "Rabin's Proposed Assurances on Israel Nuclear Policy." October 8, 1969. NPMP, NSCF, box 605, Israel vol. 3.

Kissinger, Henry, and Yitzhak Rabin. Memorandum of conversation. February 23, 1970. NPMP, Henry A. Kissinger Office Files, box 134, Rabin/Kissinger 1969–1970 vol. 1.

Laird, Melvin, to William Rogers et al. "Stopping the Introduction of Nuclear Weapons into the Middle East." March 17, 1969. NPMP, NSCF, box 604, Israel vol. 1.

Letter from Soviet Premier Nikolai Bulganin to Israeli Prime Minister David Ben-Gurion, *Jewish Virtual Library*, November 5, 1956. Available at http://www.jewishvirtuallibrary.org/jsource/History/bulganin.html.

"Meeting of Special NSC Review Group on Israeli Assistance Requests." Minutes. January 26, 1970. NPMP, NSC Institutional Files, box H-111, SRG Minutes Originals 1970 (5 of 5).

Mossad. "About Us." Available at http://www.mossad.gov.il/Eng/AboutUs.aspx.

Munn, Robert, to Joseph Sisco. "Scheduling of Visit to Dimona Reactor." June 12, 1970, RG 59. Records Relating to Israel and Arab-Israeli Affairs, 1951–1976. box 26, NSSM-40.

National Intelligence Council. "Iran: Nuclear Intentions and Capabilities." National Intelligence Estimate. November 2007.

National Intelligence Estimate. "Nuclear Weapons and Delivery Capabilities of Free World Countries Other Than the U.S. and U.K." No. 4-3-61. U.S. Central Intelligence Agency, September 21, 1961. Available at www.gwu.edu/~nsarchiv/NSAEBB/NSAEBB155/index.htm.

———. "Special National Intelligence Estimate: Prospects for Future Proliferation of Nuclear Weapons." 1974. Available at http://www.gwu.edu/~nsarchiv/NSAEBB/NSAEBB240/snie.pdf.

National Nuclear Security Agency. "About NNSA." At http://nnsa.energy.gov/about/index.htm.

National Security Council. "Presidential Decision to Ratify Nuclear Non-Proliferation Treaty." National Security Decision Memorandum no. 6. February 5, 1969.

Owen, Henry, to William Rogers. "Impact on U.S. Policies of an Israeli Nuclear Weapons Capability." February 7, 1969. RG 59, SN 1967–1969, Def 12 Isr.

Pentagon Briefing, April 23, 2009. Available at http://www.defenselink.mil/transcripts/transcript.aspx?transcriptid=4408

"President Eisenhower's "Atoms for Peace" Speech." *Atomic Archive*, December 8, 1953, http://www.atomicarchive.com/Docs/Deterrence/Atomsforpeace.shtml

Richardson, Elliot, and David Packard. "Israel's Nuclear Program." August 28, 1969. SN 67-69. Def 12-1 Isr.

———. July 16, 1969. Elliot Richardson Papers. Library of Congress. box 104. Telcons: July–Aug 1969.

———. "1969 Dimona Visit." Memorandum of conversation. August 13, 1969. SN 67–69, AE 11-2 Isr.

Richardson, Elliot, to Richard Nixon. "Israel's Nuclear Program." Memorandum of conversation attached. August 1, 1969. NPMP. NSCF. box 604. Israel vol. 2.

Rogers, William, to Richard Nixon. "Suggested Position for You to Take with Israeli Prime Minister Meir During Her Forthcoming Visit." September 18, 1969. SN 67–69, Pol 7 Isr.

Rumsfeld, Donald. "Munich Conference on European Security Policy (transcript)." Office of the Secretary of Defense. February 7, 2004. Available at www.defenselink.mil/speeches/speech.aspx?speechid=96.

Saunders, Harold, to Henry Kissinger. April 4, 1969. NPMP, NSCF, box 604, Israel, vol. 1.

———. December 8, 1969. NPMP, NSCF, box 605, Israel, vol. 3.

Sisco, Joseph, to William Rogers. "Israel's Nuclear Policy and Implications for the United States." April 3, 1969. SN 67–69, Def 12 Isr.

"Strategic Nuclear Weapons Policy." June 30, 2000. *Congressional Record*. Available at http://www.fas.org/sgp/congress/2000/kerrey.html.

United Nations General Assembly. 1st Session: Resolution 41, "Principles Governing the General Regulation and Reduction of Armaments," December 13, 1946. Available at http://daccessdds.un.org/doc/RESOLUTION/GEN/NR0/032/92/IMG/NR003292.pdf?OpenElement.

United Nations General Assembly. 48th Session: Resolution 75, "General and Complete Disarmament," December 16, 1993. Available at http://www.un.org/documents/ga/res/48/a48r075.htm.

United Nations General Assembly. President William Jefferson Clinton: "First Address to United Nations," September 23, 1993.

United Nations Office at Geneva. Conference on Disarmament: "Seven States Join Growing Consensus Around Conference on Disarmament Draft Programme of Work." May 28, 2009. Available at http://www.unog.ch/unog/website/news_media.nsf/(httpNewsByYear_en)/C1DAB4F8EECDEB56C12575C40037C344?

White House. "Remarks by President Barack Obama in Prague." April 5, 2009. Available at http://www.whitehouse.gov/the_press_office/Remarks-By-President-Barack-Obama-In-Prague-As-Delivered/.

———. "White House Fact Sheet on the Middle East Arms Control Initiative." May 29, 1991.

———. "White House Fact Sheet on the United States-India Peaceful Atomic Energy Cooperation Act." December 18, 2006. Available at http://www.whitehouse.gov/news/releases/2006/12/20061218–2.html.

Interviews and Correspondence (with Avner Cohen unless otherwise noted)

Abramov, Shneor Zalman. Interview, Jerusalem, August 26, 1992.

Aftergood, Steven. E-mail correspondence, September 14, 2008.

Arad, Uzi. Personal correspondence, July 2008.

Arens, Moshe. Interview, September 7, 1992.

Azaryahu, Arnan. Interviews, Kibbutz Yiron, August 22, 1992, and January 26, 2008.

Benn, Aluf. Personal correspondence, May 2008.

Bundy, McGeorge, to Marvin Miller. March 3, 1992. Private collection.

Burr, William. Telephone conversation with Melvin Laird. January 23, 2006.

Cohen, Avner, to the Secretariat of the Supreme Court. Case 2220/94. January 9, 1995. Personal collection.

Freier, Shalheveth. Interviews, 1991–1994.

Halperin, Morton. Interview, Washington, D.C., January 20, 2006.

Hermony, Avraham. Numerous interviews, July/August 1992.

Kerrey, Hon. Bob. Letter to Hon. William Cohen. October 11, 2000. Available at http://www.fas.org/sgp/congress/2000/kerrey2.html.

Kitner, Edward. Interview, mid-1990s.

Korchin, Amos. Interview, Tel Aviv, August 18, 1992.

Laird, Melvin. Telephone interview, January 23, 2006.

Nimrod, Yoram. Interview, Ein Hahoresh. September 4, 1992. Nimrod was a member of the committee.

Nixon, Richard. "An Evening with Former President Richard Nixon." *Larry King Live*, CNN, January 8, 1992.

Peres, Shimon. Interview with *Davar*, August 24, 1962.

———. Interview with *Ma'ariv*, July 27, 1962.

Rivlin, Chaim. Broadcast on Channel 2, Israel, January 18, 2002.

Sher, Gilead. Letter to the Secretariat of the Supreme Court. Case 2220/94. January 9, 1995.

Vaknin-Gil, Colonel Sima. Testimony at Vinograd Commission, November 2006.

Warnke, Paul. Interview, Washington, D.C., May 21, 1996.

Zadok, Haim. Interview, December 23, 1992.

Ziforni, Gavriel, to Eliezer Livneh. Letter, January 5, 1961, Livneh Archive, box 29, Efal.

Index

accountability, Israeli nuclear policy, 178–181, 315n17

ACDA. *See* Arms Control and Disarmament Agency

Achdut Ha'avodah, 63, 65, 126, 127, 130, 286n29

ACRS. *See* arms control and regional security meetings

Adams, James, 25–26

AEC. *See* Atomic Energy Commission

Agrant State Inquiry Commission, 186, 187

Ahmadinejad, Mahmoud, xxii, xxiv, 220, 221, 259–260, 268n17, 279n7, 323n14

al nakba, xxii

Albright, David, xxvii

Alfvén, Hannes, 217

Allon, Yigal: Dayan and, 67, 80, 177; on disarmament, 41; nonintroduction of nuclear weapons, 38, 40, 41, 59, 131; Nuclear Non-Proliferation Treaty and, 40; nuclear politics and, 63, 64, 67, 75, 127, 177, 286n29, 291n61; Rusk and, 30

Alon, Gideon, 308n47, 320n51

Amam. *See* Meyuchadim, Emtzaim

AMAN (Israeli Military Intelligence), 164

amimut: about, xxxii–xxxiv, 35, 263; accountability and, 178–181, 315n17; advantages of, 47–52; anachronism of, 242–243, 322n8; Arab proliferation and, 50; as bureaucratic asset, 107–108;

Censora and, 88, 109–119, 171, 209; citizenry and, 121–146; conflicts of interest resulting from, 189; conservatism and, 188–189, 190; democracy and, 153–155, 165; democratic cost to Israeli public, 147–170; democratic governance and, 171–202; democratic oversight under, 164, 193–201; deprivation of history and, 160–163; disadvantages of, xxxiv–xxxv, 171–202, 241–258; Fissile Materials Cutoff Treaty (FMCT) and, 234–236, 246, 327–328n55; function of, x, 32, 146, 263; "gang of three" attack on, 243–245, 246; "groupthink" and, 190; heuristics for reform, xiii, 212–213; history of, xi, xii, xxxii–xxxiv, 100; infrastructure of, 88–120; Israeli body politic and, 143–146; Israeli legal system and, 181–183, 185, 207; jurisdictional ambiguity and, 172–178, 185; *kdushat habitachon* and, 52, 102, 109, 110, 111, 113, 116, 122, 125, 130, 132, 141, 165, 193, 194, 200, 201; legal-constitutional confusion, 181–183; liberal democracy and, 153–155; Livneh affair, 122–129, 301n51, 303nn1, 4, 304n14; media and, xxix, 114–118, 140–143, 146; nonacknowledgment and secrecy, 45–47, 48, 56, 91; normative argument against, 245–247; nuclear decision-making process, 186–188, 189,